This book considers the literary and cultural significance of spice, and the spice trade, in Romantic literature, shedding new light on the impact of consumerism and capitalist ideology on writers of the period. Timothy Morton demonstrates how the emerging consumer culture was characterised by an ornate, figuratively rich mode of representation which he describes as 'the poetics of spice'. This is the focal point for a probing analysis that addresses a host of related themes – exoticism, orientalism, colonialism, the slave trade, race and gender issues, and, above all, capitalism. Employing a mixture of Marxist, deconstructive and psychoanalytic theory, Morton explores how capitalist ideology was inscribed in the very materials of consumption. The book takes a wide historical view, surveying a range of literary, political, medical, travel, trade and philosophical texts and includes new readings of Milton, Coleridge, Keats, Landon, Shelley, Leigh Hunt, Helen Maria Williams, Erasmus Darwin, Charlotte Smith and Southey among many others.

TIMOTHY MORTON is Associate Professor of English at the University of Colorado at Boulder. He is author of *Shelley and the Revolution in Taste: The Body and the Natural World* (1995) and, with Nigel Smith, *Radicalism in British Literary Culture, 1650–1830* (forthcoming).

CAMBRIDGE STUDIES IN ROMANTICISM 42

THE POETICS OF SPICE

CAMBRIDGE STUDIES IN ROMANTICISM 42

This series aims to foster the best new work in one of the most challenging fields within English literary studies. From the early 1780s to the early 1830s a formidable array of talented men and women took to literary composition, not just in poetry, which some of them famously transformed, but in many modes of writing. The expansion of publishing created new opportunities for writers, and the political stakes of what they wrote were raised again by what Wordsworth called those 'great national events' that were 'almost daily taking place': the French Revolution, the Napoleonic and American wars, urbanisation, industrialisation, religious revival, an expanded empire abroad and the reform movement at home. This was an enormous ambition, even when it pretended otherwise. The relations between science, philosophy, religion and literature were reworked in texts such as *Frankenstein* and *Biographia Literaria*; gender relations in *A Vindication of the Rights of Woman* and *Don Juan*; journalism by Cobbett and Hazlitt; poetic form, content and style by the Lake School and the Cockney School. Outside Shakespeare studies, probably no body of writing has produced such a wealth of response or done so much to shape the responses of modern criticism. This indeed is the period that saw the emergence of those notions of 'literature' and of literary history, especially national literary history, on which modern scholarship in English has been founded.

The categories produced by Romanticism have also been challenged by recent historicist arguments. The task of the series is to engage both with a challenging corpus of Romantic writings and with the changing field of criticism they have helped to shape. As with other literary series published by Cambridge, this one will represent the work of both younger and more established scholars, on either side of the Atlantic and elsewhere.

For a complete list of titles published see end of book

THE POETICS OF SPICE

Romantic Consumerism and the Exotic

TIMOTHY MORTON

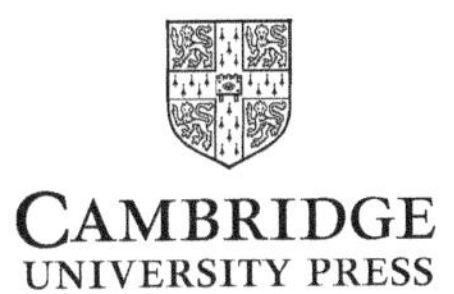

CAMBRIDGE
UNIVERSITY PRESS

CAMBRIDGE UNIVERSITY PRESS
Cambridge, New York, Melbourne, Madrid, Cape Town, Singapore, São Paulo

Cambridge University Press
The Edinburgh Building, Cambridge CB2 2RU, UK

Published in the United States of America by Cambridge University Press, New York

www.cambridge.org
Information on this title: www.cambridge.org/9780521771467

First published 2000
This digitally printed first paperback version 2006

A catalogue record for this publication is available from the British Library

Library of Congress Cataloguing in Publication data

Morton, Timothy, 1968–
The poetics of spice: romantic consumerism and the exotic / Timothy Morton.
p. cm. (Cambridge studies in Romanticism: 42)
Includes bibliographical references and index.
ISBN 0 521 77146 3 (hardback)
1. English literature – History and criticism.
2. Spice trade in literature.
3. Capitalism and literature – Great Britain – History.
4. English literature – Oriental influences.
5. Consumption (Economics) in literature.
6. Romanticism – Great Britain.
7. East and West in literature. 8. Exoticism in literature.
9. Orient – In literature. I. Title. II. Series
PR408.S665 M67 2000
820.9′355 – dc21 99–087472

ISBN-13 978-0-521-77146-7 hardback
ISBN-10 0-521-77146-3 hardback

ISBN-13 978-0-521-02666-6 paperback
ISBN-10 0-521-02666-0 paperback

For Stephen and Charles, my brothers

'Gimme the tea, Guitar. Just the tea. No geography.'
'No geography? Okay, no geography. What about some history in your tea? Or some sociopolitico – No. That's still geography. Goddam, Milk, I do believe my whole life's geography.'

Toni Morrison, *Song of Solomon*, p. 114

we were 'not so much sub-continent as sub-condiment', as my distinguished mother had it. 'From the beginning what the world wanted from bloody mother India was daylight-clear,' she'd say. 'They came for the hot stuff, just like any man calling on a tart.'

Salman Rushdie, *The Moor's Last Sigh*, p. 5.

Flavor most, put it on ya toast
Eat it an taste it an swallow it down
Imperial Flavor gives you da crown
Of the king called Flavor, da king of all flavors
Rolls an rolls an rolls of live savers.

Flavor Flav, 'Cold Lampin with Flavor', on Public Enemy, *It Takes a Nation of Millions to Hold Us Back*

Contents

Illustrations

All illustrations are reproduced by permission of the James Ford Bell Library, University of Minnesota, except for figure 12, which is reproduced by permission of the British Museum.

Acknowledgements

This book was written at New York University and the University of Colorado at Boulder. I received generous support from a New York University Research Challenge Fund Grant in 1995. At the University of Colorado at Boulder I was funded by a Junior Faculty Development Award in 1996, a Graduate Committee for Arts and Humanities Research Award in 1997, a Small Grant in 1998 and an award from the Dean's Advancement Fund in 1999.

Special thanks are due to my research assistants. Daniel Peddie read the second draft and worked painstakingly, and with great insight, on my citations and prose style. Our conversations concerning both form and content were invaluable and I am very grateful for his inspiration. Kathryn Pratt, now at Vanderbilt University, skilfully copy-edited the first draft and researched the writers in the Women Poets of the Romantic Period collection at the University of Colorado. I would also like to thank James Chandler, Alan Richardson and the other, anonymous reader at Cambridge University Press. Josie Dixon at Cambridge University Press provided strong support and intellectual help, as ever, and the book was seen into production by Linda Bree.

I would like to thank the staffs of the following libraries for their assistance: the Bodleian Library, Oxford; the British Library, London; the Butler Library, Columbia University; the Elmer Holmes Bobst Library, New York University; the Firestone Library, Princeton; the James Ford Bell Library, University of Minnesota, Minneapolis; and the Norlin Library, University of Colorado at Boulder (most notably Susan Dean and the staff of the special collections). Carol Urness, Brad Oftelie and Brian Hanson of the James Ford Bell Library helped me in my reading of primary texts about European trade.

For their helpful comments at all stages of the book's production, and for their inspiration and friendship, I would especially like to thank: Sharon Achinstein, Leonard Barkan, Jonathan Bate, Kim Bird, David and Pat Bloxam, Jeremy Braddock, Bridget Brown, Susan Buck-Morss, Marilyn Butler, Roland Cohen, Jeffrey Cox, Jessica Damian, Michael Eberle-Sinatra, Margaret Ferguson, Beatrice Fink, Bruce Holsinger, Kate Flint, Barbara Foley, Kay Fowler, Timothy Fulford, Denise Gigante (especially for her kind and incisive reading of a draft of the second chapter), Ann Goldman, Jeffrey Goldman, Nick Groom, Kim Hall, Hilary Hammond, the Hegel reading group at the University of Colorado at Boulder (Richard Halpern, Karen Jacobs, Daniel Peddie and Sue Zemka), Bruce Holsinger, Carolyn Howitt, Debbie Howitt, Steven Kaplan, Peter Kitson, Nigel Leask, Erin Mackie, Paul Magnuson, Robert Markley, Iain McCalman, Jon Mee, Perry Meisel, Sidney Mintz, Cindy Moran, Gina Nocera, David Norbrook, Blanford Parker, Megan Phelan, Adela Pinch, Strother Purdy, Alan Rabold, Robert Raymo, Elizabeth Robertson, Jeffrey Robinson, the Romantics Colloquium at the University of Colorado at Boulder, Andrew Ross, Richard Sennett, Joel Simon, David Simpson, Nigel Smith, Ruth Sternglantz, Kathleen Sullivan, Charlotte Sussman, Michael Taussig, Karuna Thompson, Jennifer Wicke and Mike Wiley. I discussed and wrote much of the theoretical material in a number of domestic and public scenes of consumption, of which the following were the most overused: Café Reggio, MacDougall Street, New York City; Dunkin Donuts, Lynbrook, New York; the cafeteria at Hofstra University, New York; the Trident Café, Boulder and the Boulder Bookstore Café.

Shorter early versions of the second and fourth chapters have appeared in Kate Flint, ed., *Essays and Studies* (1996) and Timothy Fulford and Peter Kitson, eds., *Romanticism and Colonialism*. Some material from the third chapter has been published in *Eighteenth-Century Life* 25 (May, 1999).

This book is dedicated to my brothers, Steve and Charlie, whose love and friendship mean so much to me, especially now that I am far away from them.

Introduction

A SPECIES OF ANECDOTE

Spice is still very much with us. In the United States, where 'spicy' means anything hot or, often, any kind of seasoning, an 'energy fuel' drink called Hot Sauce interpellates the macho chili consumer, appealing to the image of the human as car. The role of spices in medicine is being revised. Cocaine is commonly referred to as spice. The British pop group Spice Girls, the US hip-hop crew Spice 1, the German techno group Spicelab and Eon's techno track *Spice* are manifestations of spice in popular music culture. Laura Esquivel's *Like Water for Chocolate* and Patrick Suskind's *Das Parfum* exploit the erotic aesthetics of spice. The popular culture of pheromones and the West Coast phenomenon of no-fragrance zones in bars and restaurants demonstrate the power of scent. Parallel with my 1993 apartment in the West Village in New York City, the Spice Shop jostled for attention with the neighbouring crystal shop. The exotic, erotic and esoteric are still being associated.

What is spice? What are spices? How are they represented, and how do they function as units of social discourse about food, capitalism, trade and so forth? These questions were uppermost in my mind as I ventured forth on my first shopping expeditions in the United States: perhaps not quite uppermost, for I recall abject poverty to have been at its peak around the time of my year-long stay at Princeton. How to afford the blasted things in the first place was probably uppermost, as *spice* on this side of the Atlantic appeared to mean something rather different from, and a lot more expensive than, the spice to which I was accustomed at home. Where I had found 'seasoning' on a product's list of ingredients, I now found 'spices', and this generic term could include such items as chiles and peppers. The Americans seemed to have a different sort of love–hate relationship with flavourings from the British, though generalisations such as these quickly ceased to seem valid. While British spice racks in Sainsbury's, Tesco and so on owed much to a post-imperialist celebration of the Raj and its orientalist blessings, America seemed primarily to be looking to Central and South America and the Pacific Rim. Diverse global networks of circulation and flow collected in the aisles of distant supermarkets.

This was a time when commodities seemed to be having a lot more fun than I was, their purchaser, often reduced to choosing between a Nishin noodle soup and a Three Musketeers bar. The fetishism of commodities had never seemed so depressingly, and expensively, real. What were the cultural Imaginaries that broached and sustained their hegemony over mere flesh and blood? A dream of far-off lands of plenty and opportunity had brought me to New Jersey, where I found too late that my wallet was empty. My research into vegetarianism in the early modern period was showing me the extent to which cultural patterns of consumption, and the figuration of consumption, involved the representation of other lands, both as exploitable resources (as in the myth of *Terra Australis incognita*) and as the loci of diverse, exoticised modes of consumption (as in the stories of Indian Brahmins which reached the ears of the European vegetarians).

I wanted to think about the world, about transnational capitalism and orientalist, exoticist ways of consuming and representing. I also wanted to write a book that would be in direct contrast to the themes explored in my doctoral thesis: something, perhaps, which would take me away from the monosodium glutamate and degradation of life on a couple of dollars a day. *Re-Imagining the Body*, which became *Shelley and the Revolution in Taste*, was about purity, abstention, anti-capitalism, guilt and redemption narratives and anxiety about the disfigurative qualities of language. I fantasised about a mirror-image book discussing luxury, eroticism and capitalism and celebrating language's tropological twists.

The 'politics and poetics' of gender and race, as well as the rhetoric of commodities, play a large part in *The Poetics of Spice*. My mother's ex-partner, Maurice, a Jamaican, informed me that Grenada is called 'the spice island', an appellation it shares with the Moluccas or East Indies, as they used to be called. The singularity of the definite article in that phrase, contradicting the cultural map of the world, carries with it a freight of oppression, exploitation, capitalist utopianism and slave labour. What role do spices and such luxuries of the New World as chocolate and sugar play in the construction of oppressive and liberating ideologies? Moving to Wimbledon Park when I was about ten years old, at the height of a media panic about racial unrest in Britain's council estates and inner cities, my mother and I were horrified to find that the underground station had been peppered with graffiti: 'Pakis stink' ('Paki' being racist slang for Pakistani). The racist implication was what the Lacanian post-Marxist philosopher Slavoj Žižek describes as the fantasy of the theft of enjoyment: the fear that the Other has stolen the racist's enjoyment, by appearing to enjoy in a different way. In this case, curry and balti spices were being used to circulate this fantasy: 'Pakis stink' meant 'stink of curry'. In an early demonstration of what I eventually understood to be a form of Debordian *détournement*, some local genius, undoubtedly from the offended party, had written 'GREAT!' after the racist slur. I have always been impressed by the way in which the inclusion of a monosyllable could so disrupt and parody the supposedly rugged, aggressive new fixture on the walls of our train station. Spice, race and language were connected inextricably.

ORGANISATION

The Poetics of Spice is an experiment in the literary and cultural history of the commodity. I am not a trained anthropologist or cultural historian, but interdisciplinarity, if it is to mean anything at all, must let the object of inquiry answer back concerning what sorts of knowledge might be applied to it. I have brought my skills as a literary critic to a more open field. My discussion of the role of spice in literature and culture is not a comprehensive study. Nor is it a recapitulation of literature through spice. *Spice* is a discourse, not an object, naively transparent to itself.

Jacques Derrida has provided some of the more useful terms, such as *pharmakon* (discussed in chapter 2) and 're-mark'. His sense of the empty play of language is appropriate in the light of the transumptive and spectral qualities of spice and *spice*. His terms draw attention to the role of spice as a sign. Derrida is not the last word, however. Because the study of spice demands an engagement with ideology, there has to be some engagement with relationships between language, desire and power. Thus I have turned to the work of Žižek.

This mixture of Derrida and Žižek may sound eclectic, but 'theory' is used quite simply in this book, either as a way of developing an argument or as the subject of discussion itself. Ultimately, as in *Shelley and the Revolution in Taste*, theory is viewed as liquid evidence and evidence as hardened theory. Moreover, evidence can be used to critique theory. My reading of Derrida's omission in his analysis of *Timon of Athens* is a case in point. It is never assumed that evidence is just an excuse for theory. Deconstruction has, however, helped to produce a more subtle interpretation of how spice was represented in culture.

The Poetics of Spice is not a literary history of spice, nor is it a spicy history of literature. It studies how a certain commodity is ideologically conceived in figurative language, and how certain forms of figurative language and theory are ideologically conceived through the commodity. *The Poetics of Spice* is not a meditation on the nature of eating in general, not what D. W. Curtin and L. M. Heldke, in a Heideggerian vein, call 'Cooking, Eating, Thinking'. It is more like Jocelyne Kolb's *The Ambiguity of Taste* (1995), a wide-ranging study of the relationships between poetic and culinary applications of 'taste' in the works of Molière, Fielding, Byron, Heine, Goethe and Hugo.

The Poetics of Spice is *not* an example of New Historicism, with its constrained epistemic contextualism. Nor is it quite cultural studies, with its antitheoretical narratives of authentication. It is historical in a different sense from these, taking a long view and gesturing towards a large, general picture. It is incomplete, not because I do not approve of totalising narratives for fear of their assumed totalitarian implications, but just because it is. I have tried to avoid coy assertions of incompleteness under the banner of post-structuralist anti-totalitarianism.

Why does *The Poetics of Spice* emphasise the late eighteenth and early nineteenth centuries? Aside from professional habits, there are five reasons why I have chosen this period as the focal point:

(1) it was the point at which the spice trade *qua* traffic in cinnamon, pepper, and so forth had declined in importance relative to other trades that had taken over in its stead (tea, coffee, opium), but which shared similar functions with the spice trade
(2) it witnessed the rise of empire, new forms of global hegemony. Orientalism became significant in imperial narratives and the

period witnessed an 'Oriental Renaissance', a flourishing of European texts about Asia and in particular India[1]

(3) it was a period of archaism in culture and literature: intriguing *new* uses of spice were invented due to the development of that novel form of commodity, the antique

(4) the cult of nature militated against and in part created the modern concept of supplementarity with which spice was perceived to be endowed

(5) most significantly, as Colin Campbell has shown, Romantic-period styles of consumption included highly aestheticised modes for which the poetics of spice acted as a template.[2] It became possible to mount a critique of consumerism in a sophisticated way through poetry.

Studies of spice have tended to focus on periods before the eighteenth century. But the above factors show why the Romantic period is so rich a source for *The Poetics of Spice.* It was during the Romantic period, as Campbell points out, citing Joyce Appleby, that the modern consumer was born out of the consumer society of the eighteenth century depicted by Neil McKendrick, John Brewer and J.H. Plumb. Late seventeenth- and early eighteenth-century ideas of the benefits of seeing humans as consuming animals with limitless appetites 'did not gain widespread acceptance for almost a century'.[3] So the Romantic period tells us about quintessentially modern discourses of consumption, and lets see how they may be enjoyed, attacked, parodied or ironically supported.

Immanuel Kant's *Critique of Judgment* demonstrates in the 'Analytic of Aesthetic Judgment' how the consumption of spice is non-purposive and hence aesthetic: 'If a dish stimulates [*erheben*] our tasting by its spices and other condiments, we will not hesitate to call it agreeable while granting at the same time that it is not good; for while the dish is directly *appealing* to our senses, we dislike it indirectly, that is, as considered by reason, which looks ahead to the consequences.'[4] Spice is strangely half-way between the beautiful (a non-purposive delight in the good) and the practical. What Pierre Bourdieu calls a Kantian mode of consumption is in effect here: a sophisticated way of consuming something which does not emphasise the practical benefits, but instead the aesthetic richness, of the experience. This is an aesthetic, self-reflexive interest in spice. Campbell describes the Romantic consumerist style as placing a direct value on pleasure, fetishising the novel and strange. It was a form of bohemianism, mocking the everyday bourgeois, but in doing so, legitimating modern consumption (one might for the sake of a clear image reduce this to the notion of 'window shopping' – aesthetic consumption without 'purpose' or purchase). The middle classes became concerned with aesthetic objects but not with emulating the upper classes. This is where Thorstein Veblen's and Bourdieu's emphases on emulation and conspicuous consumption are inadequate to the task of describing Romantic consumerism. This study has found semiotics, and related modes of reading such as deconstruction, to be more useful than Campbell finds them. For someone trained in the stringencies of literary theory it is hard to distinguish between a style of consumption and a way of representing that style, in that all styles are forms of representation.[5]

The first chapter of *The Poetics of Spice* sketches out some ways in which spice could be mapped historically and theoretically. Chapter 2 examines poetic discourses on trade, showing how spice's role as a mark of tropological instability provided a means of imagining the circulating liquidity of capitalism. Even when ostensibly anti-capitalist poets such as Percy Shelley picked up the pen, they had the poetics of spice available to them in just this way. The book then explores the role of consumption in the poetics of spice in the Romantic period, showing how ekphrastic poetry was linked to discourses of luxury which both troubled the stable subject of the working world and suggested a dangerous surplus of enjoyment. Chapter 4 investigates how the language of surplus associated with sugar could be used in poetry not to promote but to criticise the labour exploitation inherent in capitalist production and most evident in the slave trade. The final chapter reads the poetics of spice as an emblem for poetry, placing a special emphasis on the representation of space. It reveals how the poetics of spice is an 'ambient poetics'.

By taking the long view, by adopting a diachronic approach to the material and by including 'images of spice in' chapters, *The Poetics of Spice* may seem to violate certain current notions of literary-critical decorum. I acknowledge that this book looks at close range like a deconstructive essay, while from far away it appears, like a pointillist painting, to resemble an illustration of social life. Marxist and deconstructive readers may be sharpening their pencils and waiting in ambush either for a lapse into Whiggish history or for a lack of attention to figurative language. But a long view needs to be taken to respect the manifold speeds and spatiotemporal processes that make up literary history and the history of trade. If the thought of talking about everything from the Song of Solomon to *Song of Solomon* seems old-fashioned, I hope it will be tempered with a sense of the unusual but necessary nature of this project. The political is found to be inscribed within the minutest particulars of the poetic.

This is not a book about the changing political contexts of a recurring topos. I do not want to suggest that a 'contextualist' reading is adequate for the texts described here: this would be to concede the validity of a caricature in the recent backlash against historicism. It is not as if political meaning takes place somewhere behind the text, like a moving background of political life behind a coherent figurative stencil, for the political is saturated with figurality. Spice presents us with extraordinarily rich objects of investigation; indeed, the study of spice is of riches and value. It is also necessarily wide-ranging: I have found powerful, contradictory stories about spice from the Roman Empire to Frank Herbert's *Dune*; from medieval recipes to modern aromatherapy and food 'supplements'; from the Bible to Buddhism; from the Koran to Keats.

CHAPTER I

The confection of spice: historical and theoretical considerations

. . . cinnamon, and odours and ointments, and frankincense, and wine, and oil, and fine flour, and wheat, and beasts, and sheep, and horses, and chariots, and slaves, and the souls of men.

(From the description of Babylon ('the merchants of the earth shall weep and mourn over her' . . . , 11), Revelation 18:13

INTRODUCTION

Capitalism arose not only from concrete economic and social relations, but also from desire – it was in itself a kind of poetry. Fantasies about an ideal substance, of extraordinary wealth and beauty and located in distant imaginary realms, percolated into poetic language. This language persisted even after the economic and social relations within which it had emerged passed away. Romantic writers inherited this long literary tradition, and their evocation of the ideal substance encapsulated it. Moreover, they modified the tradition to depict the developing consumer culture of their age. Even when they were reacting against capitalism, their poetic language was shaped by the fantasy substance.

The fantasy substance was spice. Long after the demise of Roman cuisine, Europeans heard about spices from reports brought back from the Crusades. Literary fantasies about spice flourished – legends of the Land of Cockaygne and descriptions of Paradisal gardens as in *Le Roman de la Rose*, fantastic medical discourses, and so forth. The search for the Terrestrial Paradise, a land of inexhaustible plenty, became a realisable objective. The spice race resembled the space race, as John Keay has noted: like the moon, which was visible but could not at first be reached, the spice islands had swum into Western Europeans' ken before they were accessible. Renaissance commemorations of the discovery of 'actual' spice islands in the East Indies celebrated the incarnation of a legend. The East Indies, bent to serve the realisation of desire, became spice monocultures. European consumers of spice grew more sophisticated, refining their tastes for spice, developing non-Christian discourses on luxury and leaving behind the civic humanist distaste for luxurious consumption. Consumer society was born.

The apex of this history – the point at which consumer society began to know itself as such – was the Romantic period. Forms of self-reflexive consumerism developed, producing a bohemian culture that gradually permeated almost all levels of civil society. It even became possible to criticise luxury in new ways. Writers parodied the advertising language of luxury culture, blowing it up hyperbolically rather than simply opposing it. This is where John Keats's poetry achieves its brilliant, camp reworking of a language underpinning capitalist ideology – the language I have chosen to call *the poetics of spice.*

Spice participates in discourses of spectrality, sacred presence, liminality, wealth, exoticism, commerce and imperialism. It is caught up in, but not limited to, forms of capitalist ideology. A literary-critical approach to this topic is apposite principally because spice itself is such a figurative substance. It could even be considered a sign made flesh, a hypostasised signifier. It served as money in the absence of an exchange rate on trade routes to the Far East; and it has become a metaphor about metaphor, as in the case of analogies between the Eucharist and spice. *Spice* is a complex and contradictory marker: of figure and ground, sign and referent, species and genus; of love and death, epithalamium and epitaph, sacred and profane, medicine and poison, Orient and Occident; *and of the traffic between these terms. The Poetics of Spice,* the first long literary critical study of its topic, principally explores the persistence of tropes, figures, emblems and so forth involving spice. Moreover, these readings offer something to cultural historians of capitalism. Literary criticism, aware of the complexities of figurative language, is able to demonstrate aspects of this topic which have not been pursued in cultural anthropology and histories of the commodity. It is able to treat issues of rhetoric, representation, aesthetics and ideology, including notions of race and gender, in ways that make us sensitive to the power and ambiguity of sign systems.

This book investigates how, principally in the English literature and culture of the late eighteenth and early nineteenth centuries, the representation of spice operated within ideologies of consumption, including notions of trade, abstinence and luxury. The Romantic period was the acme of developing, overlapping discourses of spice. This is the point at which a new, reflexive kind of consumerism became possible, following the growth of a consumer society (as investigated by McKendrick, Brewer and Plumb). Campbell has made some useful observations about this kind of consumerism, and the title of this book is partly an echo of his *The Romantic Ethic and the Spirit of Modern Consumerism* (1987). Reflexive consumerism encapsulated ideologies of consumption latent in bourgeois values of efficiency, productivity, work and reified market forces: fantasies of cornucopian consumption. These fantasies had been prepared for by the poetics of spice.

The Romantic period came at the end of a century during which the actual *economic* value of spice had been declining, but also during which its *ideological* value, because of the debate on luxury, had been rising. It was also the period that witnessed the birth of imperialism, the global institutionalisation of those forces that had been inspired by and caught up in the poetics of spice since the later Middle Ages. The haunting trace of spice was left, a perfume that had opened up global space. For Keats and Percy Shelley, to talk about spice was to talk about capitalism, and most notably, consumerism and luxury. These poets mounted a critique of capitalism through a poetics that could register the new kinds of consumerist desire that had gradually deconstructed the civic humanist self throughout the eighteenth century.

This does not mean that the Romantic period is in *all* respects different from the other periods under discussion – a formalist proposition Romantic studies is commonly in danger of making. Our criteria for distinguishing among the medieval, early modern and modern periods in general, and between the Romantic period and the long eighteenth century in particular, need to be reconsidered. The Romantic rhetoric of spice draws on a *long history* of representation, economics and politics, and the period is not hermetically sealed. A diachronic approach to studying the poetics of spice is therefore required. For instance, a study of the long eighteenth century indicates political, economic and poetic reasons for Keats's representation of spice in such poems as *The Eve of St Agnes*. This is why I prefer to use 'the Romantic period' rather than 'Romanticism'. To think of an author who wrote between, roughly, 1776 and 1830, is not necessarily to think of a 'Romantic' author in the old-fashioned sense.

Besides being a way of making my American colleagues pronounce Gaston Bachelard's phenomenological study, *The Poetics of Space*, with a cockney accent, *The Poetics of Spice* is, to use the well-worn phrase, about the 'politics and poetics' of spice. I still believe in the usefulness of 'ideology', despite ubiquitous postmodern Father Christmases bearing gifts for humanities departments in the guise of literary approaches to non-literary disciplines. This book is a study of ideology, broadly conceived to include ideas about poetry and poetics. Unlike some historicist works, however, it does not shun close reading: after all, it analyses a *style* of consuming.

Ideology is externalised in food. As Žižek jokes in *The Plague of Fantasies*, imitating the catchphrase of the TV series *The X-Files*, 'The Truth is Out There'.[1] Consider *Little Derwent's Breakfast* (1839), a collection of poems addressed to Samuel Taylor Coleridge's seven-year-old grandson. Written by Emily Trevenen, an acquaintance of William Wordsworth and friend of Charles and Mary Lamb, it is an educational poem in the sense that education is an externalised form of ideology, embodied in what Louis Althusser called Ideological State Apparatuses. Trevenen does not merely exhort Derwent Coleridge to behave like a little gentleman at the breakfast table, though it is an ideal scene of instruction in manners. She also provides lessons on the commercial origins of sugar, exotically illustrated by the idyllic fantasy realms of the West Indies, China and Arabia. She furnishes a homily on class relations entitled 'The Rivals; or, Sugar and Salt'. The presence at table of both condiments provides an opportunity for a quarrel and reconciliation (by 'Nature') between the bourgeoisie (in the form of sugar) and the working class (in the form of salt). The poem 'Coffee' begins with an indecorously surreal depiction of the coffee blossom petals falling 'Like the flakes of a fresh-fallen shower of snow'.[2] But perhaps this exposition is not indecorous, if it is a celebration of the artificiality of commodities, a tribute to how the world has been turned into an aesthetic object. The last two stanzas depict *Arabia Felix*:

> The land where the choicest of coffee is grown,
> Is a country for costly productions well known;
> For jewels and spices – fruits richest and best –
> And hence they have named it, 'Arabia the blest'.

Again, in our West India islands 'tis found
That coffee plantations now richly abound:
But none can with coffee from *Mocha* compare,
Which the Turks with their hookas luxuriously share.[3]

The close is significantly orientalist. The slippage of 'fruits . . .' indicates either actual fruits, or the jewels and spices in a metaphorical register: the fruits of trade and empire. The naturalising depiction of trade as the plucking of fruit is strongly ideological. *Little Derwent's Breakfast* resembles David Harvey's opening question to his geography students at Johns Hopkins: where did your breakfast come from?[4] To think about this is to uncover global networks of power. The difference is that *Little Derwent's Breakfast* is a didactic work designed to *produce* ideology rather than *unmask* it:

How many different hands 'twill take
A single loaf of bread to make! –
That tea and sugar must be sought
In distant lands, whence they are brought:
In short, what time it will employ
Only to feed one little boy![5]

HISTORICISING SPICE

My principal sources for the history of spice are Wolfgang Schivelbusch's *Tastes of Paradise*, Fernand Braudel's three-volume history of capitalism, and the works of Piero Camporesi (*The Incorruptible Flesh*, *Exotic Brew* and so forth). Also figuring in this study are the many histories of Levantine trade and the European East India Companies, treatises on the relation betweeen sugar and slavery, and material and textual microhistories of spice.

Literature on spice is divided into the history and theory of consumption and the history of commerce. Sidney Mintz's monumental work on sugar, *Sweetness and Power*, and Massimo Montanari's discussion of medieval and early modern diet, *The Culture of Food*, have been strong influences. John Brewer and Roy Porter's *Consumption and the World of Goods* has been invaluable. I have also drawn inspiration from *The Machiavellian Moment* and *Virtue, Commerce, and History*, J. G. A. Pocock's studies of the interaction between civic humanism and capitalist ideology.

Schivelbusch's history is phenomenological. Some may disagree with his idealist, teleological and anthropocentric model of spice bootstrapping the Middle Ages into modernity.[6] He claims that 'With the help of spices the Middle Ages were, so to speak, outwitted. Spices played a sort of catalytic role in the transition from the Middle Ages to modern times.'[7] This catalyst image is reified, omitting a sense of the actual flows of labour and capital. *Tastes of Paradise* lacks the story of spice's changing mediation through history.

In its inclusion of chapters on such items as chocolate and opium, *Tastes of Paradise* belongs to a group of popular studies of the history of food and eating. Henry Hobhouse's *Seeds of Change*, for instance, discusses sugar, quinine, tea, cotton and potatoes. *The Poetics of Spice* is not as inclusive, in that it does not study coffee, chocolate, tobacco and opium *per se*.[8] While it does refer to commodities such as coffee and opium, it would be misguided for it to approach commodities as phenomenologically discrete entities. To write a chapter on spice which concluded with the end of the Middle Ages would be easy, but how would one account for spice's persistence in cookery, poetry and other discourses, and how would one explore attributes such as 'spicy' which apply to substances other than cinnamon, pepper and so forth?

Histories of food often restrict spice to the Middle Ages. References to spices in the literatures and cultures of Britain are not confined to the medieval period, however, but are found in eras beyond the time when the spice trade was a significant factor in the development of long-distance trade. References to trade with the Spice Islands appear in the poetry of Sir Richard Blackmore and mid-eighteenth-century mercantile panegyrics, such as James Thomson's *Summer*, as well as in Romantic period works. Robert Southey, Mary and Percy Shelley, Landon and Keats provide some of the most interesting references, though there are some in Wordsworth, William Blake and Coleridge. The writers of novels and other narratives of the period, such as William Beckford and Jane Austen, also take an interest in spice. Moreover, the significance of items such as sugar, coffee, tea and tobacco cannot be underestimated. The chapter 'Blood Sugar', which considers the relationship between the representation of sugar and anti-slavery poetry, barely broaches the huge number of literary texts waiting to be studied in this light.

In addition to the literary representation of spice and other kinds of products that we now think of as 'food supplements', there is an extensive medical and dietary discourse in the period. The vegetarian literature of the long eighteenth century contains invectives against the adoption of highly seasoned cooking amongst the middle and upper classes, who were often inspired by French culinary fashions. These invectives, far from being merely locally significant, were caught up in emergent ways of talking about the body, economics and the nation that flourished between 1790 and 1820. A new kind of consumer and producer, efficient, hard-working and yet capable of consuming vast surpluses when required, was being created. The role of what Christian discourse called temperance became freshly significant, not as self-abnegation but as what Michel Foucault would have called a technique of the self.

This book is not just a book about history, but it does have certain historicising features. *The Poetics of Spice* takes a non-biographical approach to literature. In contrast with *Shelley and the Revolution in Taste*, it focuses less on individuals and their milieux. With this in mind, we could reflect on two issues of historical analysis and methodology:

(1) what a long narrative can tell us about the history of the representation of trade and capitalism
(2) what such a narrative can tell us about methodological approaches to the study of the commodity.

Braudel has usefully opened the field of speculation on both these points. *Civilization and Capitalism* deals with ways in which the spice trade was crucial to the establishment of capitalism in Europe. A renewed interest emerges in what counts as a 'luxury' commodity. Most sociological approaches to spice, such as that of Arjun Appadurai in the introduction to *The Social Life of Things*, consider it purely as a luxury product, thereby establishing a simple binary distinction between spice and a 'necessity' such as wheat. Braudel reveals how useful and 'necessary' to the development of capitalism spice was as a commodity, and how the Annales School overlooked the spice trade in its eagerness to study what appeared to be ordinary and essential about daily life.

Unlike Schivelbusch's phenomenology, Braudel's approach more thoroughly historicises spice. *Civilization and Capitalism* was written with an eye for labour and capital which might unbalance its sublime project of total history. But perhaps not: the details Braudel relates are significant as local information and as part of the larger history of capital flow. Braudel is appealing for his gathering together of a mass of primary evidence and deploying it in a long narrative that questions distinctions between the medieval and modern periods. His trilogy on capitalism surpasses previous research, both empirical and Marxist. Christopher Berry's *The Idea of Luxury* (1994), an exemplary long history, has also been a significant influence, as it demonstrates how 'luxury' has shifted through the rise and fall of Christian, civic humanist and capitalist discourses. Berry is sensitive to the changes that could take place in the meaning and value of luxury as capitalism developed a culture of surplus.

Shelley and the Revolution in Taste discussed how food played many different roles in literature. It also showed how food itself was an object permeated with ambiguous and shifting figurative meanings and values. I am continuing this approach in *The Poetics of Spice*, trying to move beyond a naive 'economism' that relates all signs and meanings to an economic base. There is no easy economic way of assessing the role of spices in, for example, the poetry of Richard Crashaw and Henry Vaughan, two so-called metaphysical poets of the seventeenth century. They often describe God's providence as a flow of spices from heaven. Concepts such as Marcel Mauss's potlatch and contract sacrifice could be used to illuminate this. Similarly, eighteenth-century panegyrics to trade, which modified this mystical language into a form of economic mysticism, cannot be discussed solely in terms of a one-to-one reference to a 'base', as the spice trade was now less an economic reality than a literary code. Moreover, works such as Lord Tennyson's *Maud*, Frank Herbert's *Dune* novels or Toni Morrison's *Song of Solomon* have more recently developed the literary language of spice in English.

The resistance of figurative language to naive economism is especially true of the Romantic period. It is impossible to do a vulgar Marxist reading, concocting a one-to-one relationship between culture and the economy. In fact, what really becomes necessary is to account for the gap between the economic and poetic value of spice in the Romantic period. For despite Wordsworth's and Coleridge's attempts to write non-ornamented, non-'luxurious' poetry, the value of spice was high, due to the development of self-reflexive consumerism. The culture of surplus had made it possible to reflect on one's acts of consumption. One way in which this was achieved was that the very 'age' of spice, the aura of antiquity surrounding both spice and the rhetoric of spice, made it a valuable aesthetic commodity.

Recent literary study has described relationships between texts and their historical contexts. Even more recently, scholars have read literature closely again, informed by new thinking about contexts. Romantic-period studies has left the intellectually rarefied realm of abstract philosophical speculation to become more devoted to the play of culture and history. Apart from my work, some attention has been directed towards the representation of food, and more particularly spice. Marjorie Levinson's discussion of Keats's *The Eve of St Agnes* in *Keats's Life of Allegory* shows an awareness of the significance of the image of a spiced meal of sweetmeats. In addition, fresh work on the rediscovered women poets of the Romantic period has renewed the significance of close reading. There is no necessary contradiction between 'contextual' and 'close' approaches.

There have also been notable contributions to a growing field of research into relationships between economics, literature and culture, such as in the work of Kurt Heinzelman, Marc Shell and the conference 'New Economic Criticism' at Case Western Reserve University in October 1994. Lisa Jardine's *Worldly Goods* (1996) is a history of the Renaissance which links cultural to economic changes. Studying Florentine ideology in the fifteenth century, Jardine shows how money and an abundance of purchases were related to the metaphorical rebirth of culture. In so doing, however, *Worldly Goods* distinguishes too rigidly between medieval and modern worlds. The study of themes associated with orientalism and colonialism has grown in importance since the publication of Edward Said's *Orientalism*, and any work on the economic figuration of spice must account for Western mappings of the Orient.

In addition, social science disciplines such as anthropology and sociology have benefited from the study of figurative language and a heightened sensitivity to the ways in which meaning is produced, as in the work of Michael Taussig. The historian Sidney Mintz, whose work on sugar is of great significance, has moved into areas of cultural history. *Shelley and the Revolution in Taste* owed much to Keith Thomas, whose *Man and the Natural World* pioneered the study of cultural formations through time and challenged the idealism of the 'history of ideas'. Moreover, there is a growing interest in the history of international trade.

Within the growing critical genre which one could call 'literature and . . .', studies of relationships between food and figurative language have grown in number and scope. Michel Jeanneret's *A Feast of Words* (1991) is a study of eating and rhetoric in the Renaissance, and Emily Gowers's *The Loaded Table* discusses food in

Latin literature. Maggie Kilgour has written about Coleridge's addictive personality in her wide-ranging *From Communion to Cannibalism* (1990). To write about food and literature is to encompass a broad range of approaches, from cultural and literary history to Marxism, psychoanalysis and deconstruction.

The cultural study of scent has been increasing in recent years. Annick Le Guérer's *Les pouvoirs de l'odeur* (1988), which contains a section on spice, was translated into English as *Scent* in 1994. Constance Classen, David Howes and Anthony Synnott published *Aroma: The Cultural History of Smell* in 1994. The recent work of Hans J. Rindisbacher on smell in literature and culture, *The Smell of Books* (1992), has been an inspiration for my study of aromatic spices. Rindisbacher's work, however, reproduces hegemonic literary-historical teleologies. Thus the distinction between ancient and modern depends upon an opposition between the smells of primal sexuality and perfume, which *The Smell of Books* equates with an opposition between nature and technology. Older Europe, he declares, used scent to cover the stench of thanatos; later, perfume was created as a supplement that simultaneously brought out and dissimulated a natural sexuality. The real opposition here is between a ruse with one twist and a ruse with two twists, two layers of disguise. Moreover, it is unclear whether disguise was ever a primary motive in the medieval use of spice.

Furthermore, perfume was used medically in the Middle Ages, as a means towards positive thinking: not smelling or not feeling bad could keep the plague at bay. In William Bullein's *A Dialogue Against the Fever Pestilence* (1564), the doctor, Medicus, tells the protagonist Antonius to avoid all but the most sanguine (hot and moist) foods. Spices and rotten fruit are both out, spice being choleric, but Medicus does recommend saffron, cloves and mace in his medicine: for example, pills of saffron, myrrh and aloes. Medicus prescribes a pomander of storax, calamite, cinnamon, sandalwood, aloes, lilies, violets, mastic, poppy seed, camphor, amber, musk and spikenard to defend against the plague. Bullein's play also prescribes perfume as medicine against corrupt air and urges the avoidance of anger and the cultivation of mirth (Bullein, *Dialogue*, fo. 83ff). Certain features of the AIDS panic are remarkably similar: the avoidance of negative thinking about HIV in counselling and advertising as a precaution against full-blown AIDS. The ruse with one twist is still with us.

The Poetics of Spice is thus informed by historical and cultural approaches to the study of food in literature and culture. It is not preoccupied with empirical distinctions between one kind of substance and another (pepper and coffee, for example). It deals principally with *spice* as a cultural marker rather than as a solid substance. Moreover, *The Poetics of Spice* is interested in the way in which spice as substance is never divorced from notions of language, including the languages of economics and money. This book does not assume a teleological narrative or a rigid division between modern and pre-modern. It tries to be sensitive to questions concerning figurative language while remaining interested in historical context. Finally, it shows why the Romantic period was a formative moment in the development of the poetics of spice.

THEORISING SPICE

Spice is a linguistic and ideological operator rather than an essentialised object. It has only quasi-objective status: almonds and dried fruits in the Middle Ages were classified as spice, along with the expected pepper, cinnamon and nutmeg. The foods listed alongside spice in Bullein's *Bulwarke of Defence* (1562), a medical treatise, include crushed gems and stones and animal flesh, notably oxen, weasel, fox and earthworm, powdered hedgehog (good for baldness), and mandrake, unicorn's horn and medicinal dung.[9] According to Christopher Dyer, the medieval category of spice 'included dried fruits or rice as well as condiments such as pepper and ginger'.[10] Consider the first lines of *Speke Parott* (1521) by John Skelton (1460?–1529), a lampoon of Cardinal Wolsey:

> My name is Parot, a byrd of paradyse,
> By nature deuysed of a wonderous kynde,
> Dyentely dyeted with dyuers delycate spyce,
> Tyl Euphrates, that flode, dryueth me into Inde;
> Where men of that contrey by fortune me fynd,
> And send me to greate ladyes of estate:
> Then Parot must haue an almon or a date.[11]

The almonds and dates are part of the parrot's luxurious diet of spices.

Examining closely poetic representations of spice, we find that one of their strangest aspects is the way in which *spice* is used as a general term. Spices may be separately named: the members of the genus *spice* are occasionally listed. For example, there is Milton's 'flowering odours, cassia, nard, and balm' (*Paradise Lost* v.293), but spice is only occasionally directly named in the particular. More significantly, it is hardly ever given an extensive figurative description. Not a single device is used, whether it be metaphor, metonymy, synecdoche . . . Even if there is a list of spices, as in Milton's line, the generalisation of 'flowering odours' takes priority over its specific instantiations. The use of spice as a term denoting a general quality or kind of object, moreover, occurs outside English literature and outside the early modern period. For instance, there is the *Spice* (and *More Spice*, and *Even More Spice*) show on New York's Time Warner Cable channel 35, the sex channel. And there is the notion that certain kinds of perfume contain 'spice notes'.

This is part of what I have chosen to call 'the spice effect'. In figurative language, spice appears as a species, or appearance, which has the qualities of a genus, or larger set of which the species is a part. The other aspect of the spice effect, however, seems to contradict the apparently blank, empty, generic set-like quality of the use of the word *spice*. Paradoxically, there is a potent concreteness about the empty signifier *spice*. Less an external substance than a cultural coefficient, spice behaves like a computer program, simulating value. To paraphrase Shakespeare, some commodities are born spicy, some achieve spiciness, and some have spiciness thrust upon them.[12] *Spice is a confection.*

Two theoretical issues inform this book. The first derives from the cultural significances of spice, the second from the etymological significance of *spice*. Among the most fascinating attributes of *spice* is its status as a cultural marker, and a strange one at that, halfway between object and sign, goods and money. Spice can become a sign of signs, and in poetry it serves as a figure for poetic language itself, a special kind of figure that Harold Bloom has called 'transumptive'.[13] In this role it approximates one of the economic values of spice in the early modern period, its capacity to be used as a sign of other goods, as a form of money. Moreover, spice in its consumption becomes an index of social value. It is a highly self-reflexive kind of substance-sign: 'about'-ness is what it is 'about'. However much spice is brought into the realm of *intellectus*, it also still remains within the realm of the *res* as a hard kernel of the Real, a flow of desire.[14] The poetics of spice is not only about materiality, however – it is also about poetics. Thus there are two aspects to the poetics of spice, which are in a rather asymmetrical relationship: materiality and transumption.

Lord Byron's poetry shows how transumption is found in the representation of spice. The poetic uses of spice in the Romantic period were partially caught up in orientalism, as is evident in images of spice as a metaphor about poetry itself. The luxurious, highly spiced dinner in Byron's *Don Juan* III (1818–20) includes wall hangings that feature delicate embroidery and 'Soft Persian sentences, in lilac letters, / From poets, or the moralists their betters' (III.lxiv.511–12).[15] The moralisms are ironised in their juxtaposition with the scene of luxury, of which the narrator wittily remarks:

These oriental writings on the wall,
  Quite common in those countries, are a kind
Of monitors adapted to recall,
  Like skulls at Memphian banquets, to the mind
The words which shook Belshazzar in his hall,
  And took his kingdom from him: You will find,
Though sages may pour out their wisdom's treasure,
There is no sterner moralist than Pleasure. (III.lxv.513–20)

Pleasure acts as both poison and cure, a phenomenon closely associated with the representation of spice in Milton. The stern message is inscribed into the fabric of the arabesqued wall, the 'Oriental' writing functioning as in De Quincey both as the promise and as the threat of Otherness, as meaning but also as exquisitely embodied signifiers, 'Embroider'd delicately o'er with blue' (III.lxiv.510). The 'sentences' are 'Soft' and 'Persian', evoking luxury in their literal, tongue-in-cheek materiality. They also evoke the Asiatic, dangerously copious style desired and feared by masculine Renaissance rhetoricians flexing their Arabic-inspired intellectual muscles.

The writing is the culmination of a figurative series in which spice plays a dominant role:

The dinner made about a hundred dishes;
  Lamb and pistachio nuts – in short, all meats,
And saffron soups, and sweetbreads; and the fishes
  Were of the finest that e'er flounced in nets,
Drest to a Sybarite's most pamper'd wishes;
  The beverage was various sherbets
Of raisin, orange, and pomegranate juice,
Squeezed through the rind, which makes it best for use.

These were ranged round, each in its crystal ewer,
  And fruits, and date-bread loaves closed the repast,

> And Mocha's berry, from Arabia pure,
> In small fine China cups, came in at last;
> Gold cups of filigree made to secure
> The hand from burning underneath them placed,
> Cloves, cinnamon, and saffron too were boil'd
> Up with the coffee, which (I think) they spoil'd.
> (III.lxii–lxiii.489–504)

The Middle-Eastern banquet is sensually overwhelming despite the exquisite individual components, marked in the judiciously placed 'I think' in the final line. The writing gluts the eye and ear as much as its content. There is an effeminate tone: 'flounced' (a figure not of death but of erotic display), the figure of the Sybarite, the 'Drest' fish. Don Juan's meal employs figures of the Middle East as self-reflexive emblems of the power of poetic fancy. Figures are explicitly overcoded as writing – arabesqued pleasure becomes its own warning.

The second theoretical issue stems from the etymology of *spice*. *Spice* derives from the Latin *species*, from which we obtain notions of appearance and particularity, and also of money, specie.[16] The most significant detail of the Song of Songs, a work much reproduced by early modern writers, is the use of *double entendre*, a practice recalling Sumerian love songs.[17] The bride is addressed as *šemen tûraq šĕmekā* ('flowing perfume, your name' (line 3)), a phrase playing on the synonymy between 'perfume' and 'name' in Hebrew. Christian commentaries on the Song of Songs often interpreted this to mean Christ, since 'Thy name is an ointment' suggests the Greek for the anointed one.[18] The notion of perfume as name is most significant for the poetics of spice. These two notions of appearance and particularity are features of poetry that employs spice, for two modes are generally in play. One uses *spice* as a sign caught up in connotations of aesthetic detail; another uses *spice* to suggest wealth.

In pursuing the association of spice with money and appearance, *The Poetics of Spice* is informed by Shell's analysis of relationships between money, language and thought, though it also departs from this analysis. If, as Shell observes, coined money is as metaphorical as paper money,[19] how does it appear so? Is this only a feature of money visible to us, retrospectively, in the wake of the move towards paper money? Speculation about coinage was already out of date by the late eighteenth century. The furore over paper money, in which Percy Shelley became involved, was simply a moment when people saw that the historical process of capitalism was 'really happening'. But the bill of exchange, crucial in the spice trade, had already erased the difference between money and sign.

In its derivation from *species*, both in the sense of money and in the sense of sheer appearance, and with value and wealth, *spice* requires us to explore the paradoxes inherent in the dialectics of substance and subject, appearance and reality. Since a naive interpretative mimeticism is untenable, I have avoided solidified dichotomies between poetics and politics, poesis and praxis. If the discourses of spice constitute various ideologies, then it is necessary to develop ways of reading texts which reveal the transformation of prescriptive into descriptive statements. This inevitably involves *not* reading the text as a transparent mimesis of political reality. Unlike Roland Barthes' *Empire of Signs*, which orientalises Japan by reading it like a text, inside out, with the signifiers betraying no depth, *The Poetics of Spice* sees the orientalism inherent in its topic's emphasis on the play of surfaces as part of the ideologies which that topic sustains. In this I have been influenced by Marxist theories of ideology and culture. Since writers such as Georg Lukács, commodity fetishism has been on the agenda for cultural theory. *The Poetics of Spice* is meant to be a study of the cultural forms of commodity fetishism.

A form of Romantic Marxist analysis, often confused with Hegelianism, encourages the thought that ideology is an alienated expression of some original consciousness or labour. The arguments presented here have tried to avoid this by not assuming that there is anything 'behind' or 'beyond' cultural fantasies about spice. Rather, those fantasies contain a kernel of reality in their very form. Historians and theorists of consumption such as Mintz and Campbell have shown that 'dreams of satisfaction' are just as important as satisfaction itself.[20] The engaging fusion of ideas about desire and the study of ideology in Žižek has proved invaluable for sharpening this approach.

I return now to the first theoretical issue, the cultural significance of spice. How has spice been described in previous works on the rhetoric of commodities? Spice is usually denoted as a luxury good. In *The Social Life of Things*, Appadurai defines luxury goods 'not so much in contrast to necessities . . . but as goods whose principal use is *rhetorical* and *social*, goods that are simply *incarnated signs*' rather than simply sustaining life. For example, he lists 'pepper in cuisine, silk in dress, jewels in adornment, and relics in worship'. Acknowledging Campbell, Appadurai declares that these signs exhibit 'a high degree of linkage of their consumption to body, person, and personality', and 'can accrue to any and all commodities to some extent'.[21]

It is made clear that goods other than those Appadurai names can be incarnated signs, although he states this rather cautiously, adding the phrase 'to some extent', which threatens to cancel the previous phrase if read too emphatically. But what happens when a necessity, so called, is used as an incarnated sign? What if asceticism in vegetarian discourse became attached to an image of personality or subjecthood? In other words, is semiotic incarnation, or what Appadurai calls 'semiotic virtuosity', a sufficient condition of 'luxury'?[22]

As Timothy Murphy's work on William Burroughs and the heroin trade suggests, a substance that seems epiphenomenal in a necessity/luxury model may actually turn out to be the Thing in itself.[23] All binary models of consumption, such as necessity/luxury models, if they only attach signification to one term, such as luxury, tend to be metaphysical, however much leeway or 'virtuosity' they allow for the attachment of the signifier of luxury (objective and subjective genitive) to the substance in question.

This argument about binary models resembles Hegel's critique of Kant. Kant failed to find the Thing in itself in the noumenal realm because the noumenal is really the reflection into the phenomenal of the phenomenal itself. The Thing does not lie behind the surface of some veil, but is itself that veil: hence 'the spirit is a bone', 'wealth is the self' and all the other Hegelian paradoxes. Spice, then, is not a special kind of commodity distinguished by its unusual capability for becoming an incarnated sign. *Spice is the very form of the idea of the commodity itself*, a form of what Žižek calls ' "spiritual substance" '.[24] We can see this in the way poetry uses general forms such as 'spicy' instead of particular ones such as 'smelling of saffron'. Figure 1 illustrates the confluence of sign and matter in the foods discovered in the New World.

Spices, then, cannot simply be an example of how 'luxury' is culturally commodified. *Shelley and the Revolution in Taste* proposed that vegetarianism deconstructed Appadurai's implicit opposition between commodities that are invested with the 'incarnated' sign of luxury and those that are not. Not that all products could not hypothetically be designated luxurious, but that 'luxury' was the

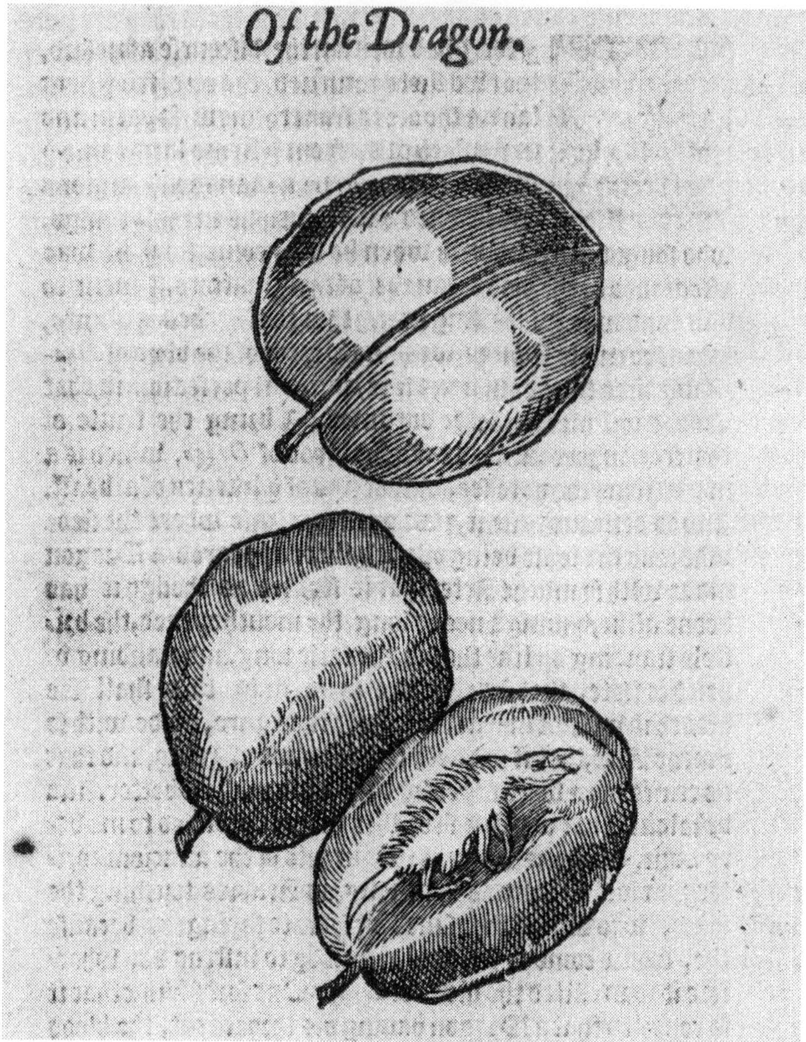

Figure 1 Signs and matter: 'Of the Dragon', from Nicolás Monardes, *Ioyfull Newes out of the New-found Worlde* (tr. 1596), fo. 71. Monardes describes 'Dragon's Blood' as a mythical substance written about by the Greeks, Arabs and Romans. No one really knows what it is but a tiny dragon likeness was found in this West Indian fruit (fos. 70–1). Symbols are found engraved in living matter, like the likeness of a monarch stamped on a coin. Like money, spice resides half-way between sign and matter.

exclusive outcome of such acts of designation. This issue is repeated in discussions of different modes of consumption amongst different social classes. Bourdieu's opposition between bourgeois and proletarian modes of distinction also becomes problematic when we consider the case of vegetarian diet. Braudel rearticulates these patterns when he describes luxury as the only 'culture' there is: the European upper classes amuse themselves with their riches, including spice, while the rest of us are left with the dregs. Yesterday's banquet ingredient becomes today's Dunkin Donuts apple cinnamon item. Campbell and I resist this notion of 'emulation'.

Thought about consumption often sets up too rigid oppositions between structure and superstructure, signifier and signified, material and immaterial culture. The history of the representation of spice, however, shows that the description of the commodity needs to become more complex. For example, the eighteenth century witnessed the growth of the concept of 'comfort': where is the space for comfort in a model that pits 'luxury' against 'necessity'? If the two terms are functional definitions within contemporary ideologies of capitalist trade, then that is all the more reason to analyse them critically.

The problem lies in the notion of incarnation. For Appadurai luxury is the sign of a sign's incarnation in a commodity. The notion of incarnation is mystifying, not really solving the ways in which we 'get from' use value to exchange value, from substance to trans-substance. Modern concepts such as 'comfort' deconstruct the oppositions luxury constructs between surface and essence, between supplement and deep structure. Comfort or *Gemütlichkeit* tends to belong to the discourses of the bourgeoisie rather than the aristocracy, which claims luxury as its own.[25] For that matter, why does Romantic poetry on bourgeois commerce employ potentially aristocratic images of spice?

Moreover, studies of spice need to take the fluidity of time and space into account. Appadurai leaves room for accounts of historicity. Because of its phenomenological tendency, Schivelbusch's *Tastes of Paradise* makes spice seem eternally invariant. For example, he generalises in asking 'Why did the Middle Ages have such a pronounced taste for dishes seasoned with oriental spices, and why did this craving disappear so suddenly in the seventeenth century?'[26] While it is in a limited way possible to draw such lines in the sand, it is not as interesting as considering the *persistence* of spice in literature and culture. What about the spiced confectionery discussed in chapter 3, or the kedgeree and mulligatawny soup popularised in Victorian Britain? One might even suggest that premodernity only *appears* to be different from modernity in terms of the poetics of spice. However, there *are* changes and developments which this book sets out to chart.

The mobility of spice over great distances surely contributed to its premodern status as medicine, a status that is now reappearing in other guises in the cults of homeopathic medicine, herbal remedies, and vitamin and other dietary 'supplements' of all kinds. The notion of spice as medicine tends to collapse the distinction between luxury and necessity, if necessity is viewed as that which is essential to the health of the body. Indeed, this distinction smacks too much of the tendency in Britain and America to regard food as pure nutrition, a kind of 'magic bullet' approach to food which has given us vitamin pills, certain forms of vegetarianism and BSE or 'mad cow disease'. BSE could only arise when eating had become capital-intensive at the level of production and as abstract as Piet Mondrian at the level of consumption. The US Health and Education Act (1993) contained clauses that might have given the FDA far greater control over dietary supplements, and a 'save our supplements' campaign was launched. Modernity is anxious about supplements.

Moreover, spice itself is more a flow than a solid object: as pulverised substance, it has already been liquefied. In the psychoanalytic language of Melanie Klein, it is a partial object. As a sign of wealth, spice is often figured as a flow, as in the poetry of Crashaw and Percy Shelley. Spices themselves are crossroads of spatiotemporal processes. This is obvious, since they have undergone numerous processes in their production which have rendered them hardly objects at all: pulverised, fluid, capable of being substituted for currency at a pinch.

We need to find a way of thinking about commodities which takes process rather than product as its main point of reference. The Kantian notion of absolute space regards space and time as a container unaffected by its contents. The Leibnizian notion of relative space conceives of space and time as processes. When things dominate processes in studies of society, Kantian space predominates. For example, the city is often construed as a container in social theory. But if the spice trade was involved with spatiotemporal processes, then a city such as Venice, one of the most active in the spice trade in the late Middle Ages and early modern period, could not be thought of as a thing but as a fluid mixture of processes. The process-oriented approach requires a longer view of history and a more nuanced sense of the representational strategies involved in that history.[27]

Marx understood that political economy had been trying to understand money in itself without considering *Verhältnisse*, his notion of 'relatedness', similar to the notion of 'process' which I have been suggesting here. 'Things' derive from certain conditions of spatiotemporality, which in turn derive from processes. This is not, however, to claim that poems about spice are on the same ontological plane as toothbrushes. As the anthropologist Marshall Sahlins has recognised, it is important to stress the relative autonomy of cultural symbolism.[28] Nevertheless, the symbols under discussion in *The Poetics of Spice* evoke materiality. It is not so easy to dismiss historical materialism in a book about cultural materialism.

The study of 'imagery' alone is a highly limited way of understanding figurality. It is rather fixed and scopic. The same applies to the cultural history of the commodity. In both cases, attending to flow and circulation is appropriate. The cultural representation of spice as flow is bound up with its representation as supplement or as luxury. For the discourse of the supplement becomes significant in the case of spice when its flow becomes suspect, needing to be controlled. This involves distinctions between centre and border, essence and decoration.

'Luxury' and 'necessity' have suffered from the substantialism with which cultural concepts are frequently imbued. If consumption involves a dialectic of desire, then the difference between luxury and necessity is only the semantic difference between the position of the subject in the following phrases: 'You need two litres of water a day to stay healthy'; 'you need a good spanking.' 'Need' in the latter, if not in the former, is the want of the Other (a form of demand), demonstrating the disjunction between the subject of enunciation and the subject of the enunciated. If there is such a disjunction, then there is certainly no clear way of distinguishing between luxury and necessity. This part of the theoretical framework of *The Poetics of Spice* is informed by Žižek's fusion of psychoanalysis and ideological analysis.

These features of the social symbolic order are what is left out of Berry's *The Idea of Luxury*. While Berry sees objects as capable of shifting their status as luxury items, his empiricist and sometimes nominalist approach to the argument, anxiously disavowing the extreme nominalism of Jean Baudrillard, cannot show how 'luxury' is not exclusively located in the object or in the subject, like the components of a machine on the one hand, or an aspect of the soul on the other. Apprehending luxury as a lived relation to capitalism would show that the category works *between* these two.

If the relationship between subjects and spices were to be annotated using Jacques Lacan's 'mathemes', two formulae would be needed:

(1) '$ ◇ *spice*', showing the subject (barred 'S', because the subject is never fully present to itself) constituted by its relationship to *objet petit a*, that obscure object of desire

(2) but also, '*spice* ◇ $', the formula (or matheme) of need or demand, where the object of desire appears to be giving the orders.

The quality of a spectral voice that hails the subject to far-away horizons, the curious 'in-between' status of spice as object and non-object, is summed up in the difference between these two annotations.

The Idea of Luxury approaches this ambiguity when Berry categorises luxury according to negative criteria: the luxurious is what you do not need, what could be replaced by any other commodity.[29] However, despite this negative categorisation, *The Idea of Luxury* does not realise the paradox of this superposition of negativity and positivity. It posits the luxury object as more *and less* real than other objects, infinitely substitutable and unrequired, an unattainable condition that forms the substrate of advertising language. Max Weber's assumption that Protestant asceticism 'restricted consumption, especially of luxuries' needs to be challenged: the ideological role of luxury is not necessarily coterminous with what is put into one's mouth. The point of advertising language, for example, is not necessarily just to make a consumer purchase a product. Otherwise it might be assumed that Satan's role suits everyone: there is plenty of enjoyment with no enjoyer. The Protestant religions, pushing towards Benjamin Franklin's conception that time is money, had no time for consuming spices, just for pushing them on others.[30] This is where a literary-critical approach has an edge over a sociological one.

SPICE NOTES

There is a passage on money in *Timon of Athens*, of which Marx was fond. In his misanthropic desperation, Timon is digging in the earth for roots in IV.iii.24–5, for 'Who seeks for better of thee [the earth], sauce his palate / With thy most operant poison.' A dialectic is being established around the topoi of poison/cure, and meat/sauce, or spice; a dialectic that suits the vegetarian hermit Timon has become. It is a dialectic familiar elsewhere in Shakespeare, such as in Lady Macbeth's famous lines about all the perfumes of Arabia being incapable of sweetening her guilty little hand (*Macbeth* V.i.49–50). But Timon finds gold in the miasmatic fecundity of the earth, reminding him of the social and symbolic order he has left behind:

> Gold? Yellow, glittering, precious gold? No, gods,
> I am no idle votarist. Roots, you clear heavens!
> Thus much of this will make black white, foul fair,
> Wrong right, base noble, old young, coward valiant.
> Ha, you gods! why this? What, this, you gods? Why, this
> Will lug your priests and servants from your sides,
> Pluck stout men's pillows from below their heads –
> This yellow slave
> Will knit and break religions, bless th' accurs'd,
> Make the hoar leprosy ador'd, place thieves
> And give them title, knee, and approbation,
> With senators on the bench. This is it
> That makes the wappen'd widow wed again –
> *She whom the spital-house and ulcerous sores*
> *Would cast the gorge at this embalms and spices*
> *To th' April day again*. Come, damn'd earth,
> Thou common whore of mankind, that puts odds
> Among the rout of nations, I will make thee
> Do thy right nature. (26–44, my emphasis)[31]

In his search for stability and unitary meaning Timon ignores the reversibility of the tropes employed here: if white can be made black, then surely black could be made white? The picture of gold knitting and breaking religions, or the remarrying of the 'wappen'd widow', exemplify this reversibility. But Timon is also evoking an image of corrupted nature glossed with false artifice. The language of authenticity and alienation must have appealed to Marx. The irreversibility Timon requires of the tropological scheme he has set up is achieved in the lines about embalming and spicing the widow 'To th' April day again'. The association of spice with the woman's body is common. In *The Miller's Tale*, Chaucer has Absolom address Alison:

> 'What do ye, hony-comb, sweete Alisoun,
> My faire bryd, my sweete cynamome?
> Awaketh, leman myn, and speketh to me!' (512–14)[32]

The passage alludes to the Song of Songs, the Western urtext for the poetics of spice.

In his discussion of the passage from *Timon* in *Specters of Marx*, Derrida omits an analysis of the reference to spice. Derrida understands the significance of the metaphorical substitution of prostitute and capital, for later in his study of the ontology of the commodity form he writes: 'It is in thinking of this original prostitution [of the commodity]' that Marx liked to quote Timon.[33] Because the commodity cynically equates everything, it resembles Timon's spicy gold. But in his earlier analysis of *Timon* Derrida misses what he elsewhere calls the *pharmakon*, the tropologically unstable mark here incarnated as spice, despite its relevance to any discussion of the spectrality of money. By not exploring this reference, Derrida cannot show how it encapsulates something highly significant for his reading of the notion of the commodity fetish.

It is the notion of the fetish which is so elegantly captured in the transitive use of 'embalms and spices'. The spicing of the body appears to move it in two directions at once, forward and backward, to resurrection and to youth. 'Embalm' connotes an immersion, bestowing a richness and depth upon the body. Additionally, however, spice is imagined as the *opposite* of what bestows depth: a coat, coating, surface or appearance. An embalmed body has no organic insides. Marx's frustration and fascination with the asymmetry between surface and depth, an asymmetry that is the mark of the fetish, illustrates the power of the agency of spice. There is something uncanny here, for embalming brings a corpse to life, just as Tamburlaine in Christopher Marlowe's play (1590) mourns Zenocrate:

> Though she be dead, yet let me think she lives,
> . . .
> thou shalt stay with me
> Embalm'd with Cassia, Amber Greece and Myrre . . .
> (*II Tamburlaine* II.iv.127–30)[34]

There is also a temporal dialectic here in the asymmetry between fleeting flavour and embalming which endures.

'Spicing'/'embalming' is best understood in terms of 'marking'. The spice-marked body becomes uncanny, suggesting that the Other is self: the spiced corpse is dead but it is vivid – or as Lacan would put it, $\$ \diamond a$, the matheme for fantasy. The uncanny sensation arises that *we* are a corpse, that subjectivity is a kind of embalming. When police searched the kitchen of the late twentieth-century cannibal Jeffrey Dahmer, so the story goes, they found nothing but the refrigerated flesh of his victims and . . . condiments; no fruit, vegetables, cereals or dessert. The spiced corpse remains a potent image, hovering outside the bounds of food-as-nutrition. In the following chapters, ideologies of marked products being consumed by unmarked consumers will be investigated – Europeans eating exoticised Eastern food – as will ideologies of marked food flavouring unmarked food: spice and meat, for example, two signs uniting in the strongly transumptive sign of the Eucharist, as shown in the work of Camporesi and Carolyn Walker Bynum. Thus the still-current fantasy arises that other cultures spice their food to disguise the taste and stink of rotting meat, a logical extension of the notion that a marked commodity can flavour an inert, unmarked substance: a spiced corpse. The idea of a spiced corpse becomes significant in the analysis of Keats and Percy Shelley.

Eighteenth-century dictionaries such as Johnson's and Sheridan's associate spice with small quantities and aroma. Johnson's use of 'production' equates spice with artifice:

'1 A vegetable production, fragrant to the smell, and pungent to the palate; an aromatick substance used in sauces.
2 A small quantity, as of spice to the thing seasoned.'[35]

The *Oxford English Dictionary*'s seventh definition of spice is 'a trace, touch, dash, specimen'.[36] Thus Keats's phrase 'tinct with cinnamon' (*The Eve of St Agnes*, 267) could be paraphrased as 'spiced with spice'.[37] This is the reflexive quality of the poetics of spice, in which *spice* appears to be a species of the set whose name is itself.

Derrida's observations on the spectrality of capital bring into play the notion that marks, traces, touches and dashes are not real or unreal but quasi-real. Quasi-reality opens up a third realm, not of things or of thoughts but of the reality of desire. Derrida punningly refers to the reading of these signs as 'hauntology', since it is a spectral realm. The definition of spice does not simply entail a listing of the positive attributes of the commodity. This is what the sociology of the commodity would do. The luxury commodity is not just an 'incarnated' sign, as Appadurai calls it, but is spectral. The luxury commodity is in the realm of the signifier but also somewhat spookily 'really there': a sign of incarnation. 'Incarnation' then is a more bizarre concept than Appadurai's use of it suggests. Spectrality suggests the supernatural, a different, parallel order of materiality. In horror fiction, ectoplasm is not of this earth, nor does it belong to the realm of the ideal; it is quasi-material, transcendental, a sublime object. (The strongest instance of luxury's incarnation in the twentieth century is surely the spice in Frank Herbert's *Dune* (1965).)

A spectral mark that renders a fleshly, solid-seeming reality brings us to the fetish. Fetishes have at least four properties: materiality, historicity, boundary-marking and affect. The self-moving power of the commodity fetish was praised by pro-capitalists for its role in demystifying the superstitions of the ages. The potentially utopian feature of capitalism, according to Emile Durkheim, was that people were connected through things, not linguistically as Benedict Anderson has recently imagined. This connection through things left their subjectivity relatively free, constituting it as free in fact. This is why the socialist and surrealist collectives were preoccupied with a certain orientation to objects, such as in the work of Rodchenko.[38]

When two cultures are not self-contained but metonymically touch each other, the concept of the fetish marks the degraded status of the gods in the culture that loses in the transaction. (In an age of so-called postmodern 'globalisation', when everywhere is touching everywhere else, the notion of fetishism perhaps becomes more degraded, particular, strategic and liquid.) The conflict thus generated renders relativism impossible in global capitalism. The term *fetish* grew up to circumvent the idea that in the object there was something more than a signifying property. This something more could be named a materiality, that which Theodor Adorno called 'the priority of the object'.[39] The notion of the *fetisso*, coined by the Portuguese in their navigation of the coasts of Africa in their search for the fabled Spice Islands, was designed to legitimate the spectral concept of the incarnated sign. As William Pietz has argued, it was a way of creating an abstract measure that would function as a general equivalent in the realm of the Other.[40] There is thus a strong link between the fetish and the history and discourses of the spice trade.

In Marxist critiques of political economy, the demystifying work of capital is revealed to be structured around another inscrutable mystery, the relationship between capital and labour. The free-floating *mana* of capital invades all objects. *Spice* gestures towards this *mana*, generating the disconnection between surface and essence characterised by Timon's 'spices and embalms'. *Spice* may designate a strange, hybrid subject-substance. In Enlightenment-period texts we witness the fetishism of topoi about trees breathing spice. At that time the riches of the world appeared to be available to the European consumer and capitalist as a substantive subject. In turn, self-empowered substantiality is legible in the phrase *the spice.*

Spice plays between terms such as *sign*, *money*, *matter* and *commodity*. In Shakespeare, this transaction accounts for the sexual and economic humour of *The Winter's Tale* IV.iii. Before he is waylaid by Autolycus, the Clown prepares for the feast, trying to find 'Three pound of sugar, five pound of currants, rice . . . I must have saffron to colour the warden pies; mace; dates – none, that's out of my note; nutmegs, seven; a race or two of ginger, but that I may beg; four pound of prunes, and as many of raisins o' th' sun' (36–46). Autolycus picks his pocket, declaring: 'Your purse is not hot enough to purchase your spice' (113). *Spice* is to be construed here as purse, as spice and as sex. It is also a sign of mobility, part of the language by which the high and low can communicate.

The poetics of spice is rather like an emulsion: the two elements of materiality and figurality are not dissolved into each other but are really a vigorous blending of two distinct principles, a materially dense quality and a fluid, empty quality. The poetics of spice is a Möbius strip upon which an object appears to behave like a subject, until we have followed this behaviour right round to the 'other' side, upon which a subject appears to behave like an object. The distinction, however, between subject and object is not collapsed, and they remain in tension. The ground, the signified, matter, the body of woman, the colonisable territory, the fantasy island, the realm of the Other, remain distinct from the figure, the signifier, money, the spirit of Christ, the medicinal principle, the process of mediation, the fluidity of time and space. They are related, but precisely in their capacity to miss one another. In the mystical Christian poetry of the heavenly potlatch, for example, the soul can never entirely be cleaned of its blemishes by the spicy perfume of divinity, but the language of redemption depends upon the fantasy that this is *exactly* what is happening. Another way of saying this is:

fantasy is fantasy, but nevertheless it is real. This is why the Lacanian notion of the Real of desire is helpful in describing the poetics of spice.

In *The Wealth of Nations* (1776), Adam Smith comments that 'Europe . . . has hitherto derived much less advantage from its commerce with the East Indies, than from that of America', even though there are many more 'advanced' countries in the East to trade with.[41] This is because of the creation of huge monopolies for handling commerce with the East Indies. Thus there has to be a strong element of desire, fantasy, ideology at the core of European commercial capitalist enterprise: if not, then how else could something as ineffective as Smith describes be justified? And where else but in the Romantic period would this theme be realised with such poignancy?

The common use of *spice* enacts what one might call a kind of ekphrasis. Literally, ekphrasis means 'speaking out'. Ekphrasis usually refers to the attempt to describe visual art using verbal art: the attempt of language to thrust itself forth, as it were into three-dimensional space, and appear as paint or stone. For example, the description of Aeneas' shield in Virgil's *The Aeneid* is ekphrastic. Ekphrasis always involves a paradox, for how can words, whose meanings depend upon a temporal flow, describe what is necessarily static? Beyond this, ekphrasis tends to involve self-reflexive language: to try to create an effect of painting in words often throws the reader's attention back on the nature of words themselves. According to Murray Krieger, ekphrasis in Hellenistic rhetoric meant the 'verbal description of something, almost anything, in life or art'.[42] *Spice* functions as a kind of nasal ekphrasis, and if one considers its brilliant colours and powerful tastes, it engages the eyes and the tongue as well. Language is trying to become fragrance and flavour.

Consider the other luxury commodities derived from trade with the Indies: for example cloth and jewellery. Now 'cloth' and 'jewellery' are on the same level of generalisation as *spice*. Silk is not often described as 'clothy' or sapphires as 'jewel-like'. Furthermore, *spice* is as much a generalisation about cinnamon, nutmeg and so on as 'world' is a genus that contains the species 'continent', 'country' and so on. *Spice* is not only an umbrella term for a number of different spices, as if the writer concerned could not be bothered to list all the different types of spice. *Spice* functions as the descriptor for the sensual appearance of the general itself; or, to put it the other way round, *spice* connotes sensual appearance construed through a universal descriptor.

This observation is the inverse of the first one. As a kind of nasal ekphrasis, *spice* is a symbol that has within it more than what it symbolises. It is language trying to touch, or incarnate, the Real. But in the second observation, *spice* is actually the negation of the real *qua* non-linguistic, sensuous and punctual reality. The two observations can also be exemplified through the etymology of *spice*. *Species*, *specious* and *specie* suggest that *spice* belongs to a set of words that denote the non-universal, particular, contingent realm of appearance. But when we look 'behind' spice to find some general or universal category that might substantiate its meaning or fix its place, we find none. We simply re-encounter spice. It is as if the universal were on the side of the particular itself, as if it were an empty mark by means of which the particular was reflected into itself.

This empty mark functions like the 're-mark' as described in Derrida's *Dissemination*, marking the sequence of marks *as* a sequence.[43] The re-mark is that mark that designates a set of marks as such: the mark that differentiates between figure and ground. Žižek explains:

> in any series of marks there is always at least one which functions as 'empty', 'asemic' – that is to say, which re-marks the differential space of the inscription of marks. It is only through the gesture of re-marking that a mark becomes mark, since it is only the re-mark which opens and sustains the place of its inscription[44]

Žižek demonstrates that, as Derrida himself remarks in his work on Mallarmé, the re-mark has precedents in the philosophy of Hegel.[45] This is what *spice* does to cinnamon, pepper, nutmeg and so forth. What Derrida does not note, however, and what is picked up by Žižek in his book on enjoyment as a political factor, is how this 're-mark' maintains the difference between itself and other signifiers while simultaneously pointing to the depthlessness of the signifying chain. In an Escher painting, figure and ground are confused precisely insofar as it is still possible to make a distinction between figure and ground. 'Cinnamon' and *spice* function as figure and ground in the discourse of spice. But poets have used *spice* and 'spicy' as a figure among figures. *Spice* warps the fold of meaning so that there appears to be nothing on the other side. *Spice*, then, is like the twist in a Möbius strip, which flips one 'side' of a two-dimensional shape kinked in three dimensions onto its 'other' side. Derrida observes that *pharmakon*, used in the second chapter to describe the rhetorical register of spice flow, can imply both painting, painters, and 'pictorial color' itself, 'an artificial tint': compare Keats's 'tinct with cinnamon' (*The Eve of St Agnes*, 267).[46] *Spice* similarly implies both genus and species.

In this respect, *spice* is really a sexy word for 'currency', or even 'capital', to a certain extent. Currency is not literally a flow of coins and notes; but this is how it is often imagined. Capital is even less a physical entity; it functions rather as a kind of re-mark of commodities. The first chapter of Marx's *Capital* is quoted by Žižek: 'the "expanded" form [of the commodity] passes into the "general" form when some commodity is excluded, exempted from the collection of commodities, and thus appears as the general equivalent of all commodities, as the immediate embodiment of Commodity as such, as if, by the side of all real animals, "there existed *the* Animal, the individual incarnation of the entire animal kingdom"' – or as if, by the side of all real spices, there existed *the* spice.[47] Spice, on the other hand, really is a flow of brightly coloured, fragrant, delicious powder. It is that 'particular commodity' in which value is constituted according to spice's 'quasi-"*natural*"' properties.[48] But its status as a physical entity is in question. As an item of trade and consumption it has undergone a severe and manifold number of transformative processes, including the growing, drying and pulverisation of the original plant, its substitution for currency or promissory notes in a series of trading manoeuvres, its transportation across huge global distances, its combination in a palette of flavourings or its use in medical preparations and other sorts of treatment. Part of the luxury status of spice, I contend, has nothing to do with the ways in which it is consumed, but with the ways in which it sensualises certain fantasies about the nature of money and capital.

Spice, as a fragrant substance, is ideal for an expressive use in the discourses of fetishism. A fetish, simply described, is a self-moving object, an object that seems to have a will of its own. Money, for example, in Marx's famous critique of capitalism, appears to act 'all by itself' without the mediation of what he considers to be the more fundamental social force of labour. In their trade with western Africa, the Portuguese were the first to coin the concept of the *fetisso* in order to deal with modalities of culturally constructed objects and

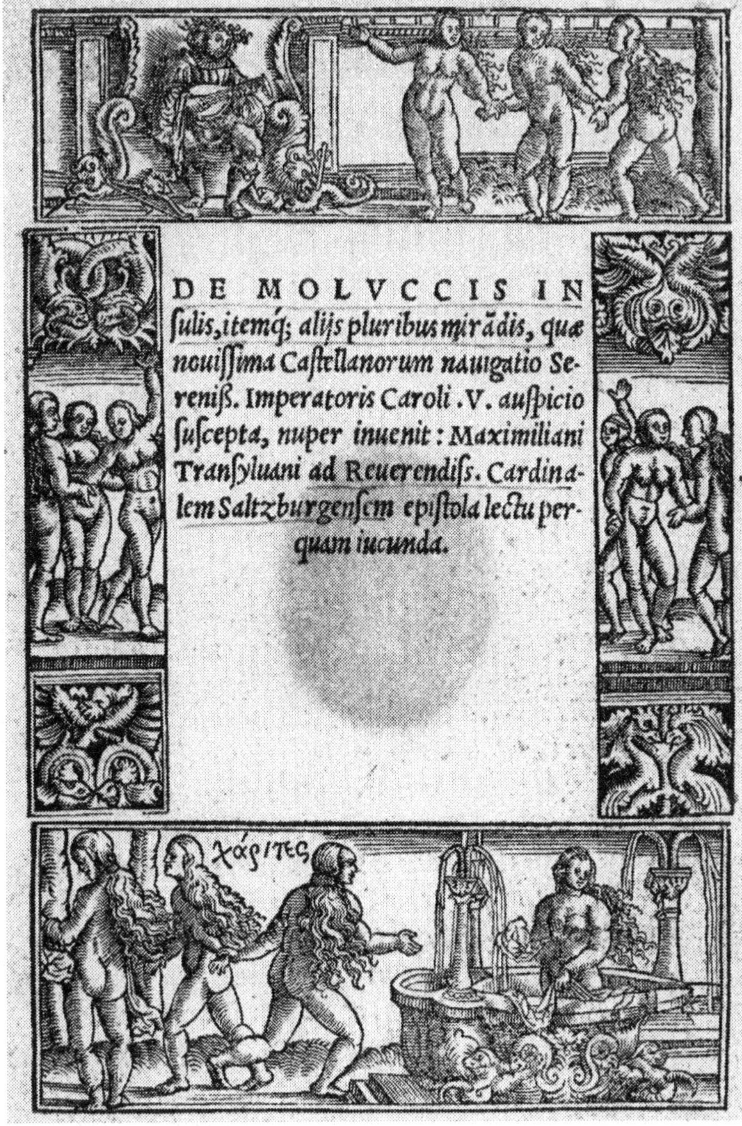
DE MOLVCCIS IN-
ſulis, itemq; alijs pluribus mirãdis, quæ
nouiſſima Caſtellanorum nauigatio Se-
reniſs. Imperatoris Caroli .V. auſpicio
ſuſcepta, nuper inuenit: Maximiliani
Tranſyluani ad Reuerendiſs. Cardinalem Saltzburgenſem epiſtola lectu perquam iucunda.

Figure 2 The spice trade as poetic discourse: Maximilianus Transylvanus, *De Moluccis insulis* (1523), title page. There could be no better illustration that the representation of the spice trade was bound up with thoughts about poetics: note Apollo and the dancing Graces. Maximilian poeticises the voyages of the Portuguese to the Hesperidean Moluccas, and declares that they have out-troped the myth of Jason and the Argonauts (A2v, B7v).

circulation which were seen to differ greatly from theirs.[49] Spice, without doubt, is farmed, produced, subjected to all sorts of labour processes, which down the transnational chain are highly gendered and racialised, as well as falling under the sign of class. Slaves farm spices in the Moluccas and women prepare spicy meals in the kitchen. However, as odoriferous substances, spices appear to owe their power or virtue to nothing but their own sweet or pungent selves. The richness of Blackmore's imagery, for example, depends upon his conception of the spontaneous, odour-emitting properties of spices: just so, he figures, trade itself wafts across the ocean. The production of smell appears to involve no labour. This bestows upon spice both a highly naturalised quality, and a supernatural or spectral one.

CHAPTER 2

Trade winds

I sing of Venus crowned with gold; renowned
For faire: that Cyprus guards, by Neptune bound.
Her in soft some mild-breathing Zephyre bore
On murmuring waues unto that fruitfull shore.

George Sandys, *A Relation of a Iourney Begun An: Dom: 1610* (1615), p. 218

This thy COMMERCE, *Child* of thine *Industrie*,
Joyning both POLES in neere *affinitie*,
Nurse of thy Countries *honor* [*sic*], and by which
Onely, all *Kingdomes* of the *World* grow rich;
And (by the *Currant* of a *mutuall Trade*)
Thou shewst how *happie* all the *Earth* is made.

Dedicatory epistle from Lewes Roberts, *The Merchants Mappe of Commerce* (1638), a3 (lines 7–12)

INTRODUCTION

Towards the end of Joyce's *A Portrait of the Artist as a Young Man* (1916), in a fusion of Thomist and Neoplatonic aesthetics, Stephen Dedalus makes his notorious distinction between kinetic and static art. Only the latter is guaranteed access to the status of the truly aesthetic, for the former is the realm of pornography and horror, exciting either desire or loathing. Static art, moulded by an impersonal, nail-paring artist, is to be contemplated for its internal relations alone, in a sphere removed from the hurly-burly of practical, kinetic life. Stephen's definition of art's true mode is supremely anti-political.[1]

This definition is ironic in a novel, and from a character, whose revelations come alternately on the spice-perfumed winds of figurative patterns derived from the Song of Songs,[2] and in the nauseating stench of the bodily functions from which the narration often turns in disgust – in short, from the beatific and abject poles of the poetics of spice. This novel's *modus operandi* is actually kinetic. It appeals to what should be the lowest of faculties for a Neoplatonist, the all too corporeal sense of smell. Although Ficino, in his revision of Plotinian theories of beauty, would not deny that smell could, through the satisfaction of lower bodily impulses, lead to the higher pleasures of contemplation and so to the One,[3] Stephen's religiose moments are borne on the smoke of incense wafting towards heaven: 'A faded world of fervent love and virginal responses seemed to be evoked for his soul by the reading of its [Saint Alphonsus Liguori's] pages in which the imagery of the canticles was interwoven with the communicant's prayers.'[4] The angel–whore binary that so dominates Stephen's imagination focuses on the woman's body as the site of perfumes of desire and loathing. And there is the young artist's reading from Ecclesiasticus 24:17–20, redolent with the spicy aroma of Mariolatry: 'I was exalted like a cedar in Lebanon . . . I gave forth a sweet smell like cinnamon and aromatic balm.'[5] In general, in the terms established by Gérard Genette, *A Portrait* is about the erasure of narrative by smelly discourse.

The flow of perfume is related both to the eroticised body and to the flow of traded commodities. In *A Portrait*, trade operates as a basic figurative ground whose association with the tropological qualities of language is clarified in a passage in which Stephen plays with the associations of 'ivy'. He ponders the phrase '*India mittit ebur*', literally 'India sends ivory', implying that country's export of a luxury good.[6] This phrase derives from maps which displayed the Orient as a cornucopia. One of these, Sebastian Münster's *Cosmographia* (1544; the 1555 version is referred to here), which taught three generations of laymen about the world, has a border by Holbein, with pepper bushes top right and cannibals bottom left. There is a large central inscription about India, typical of maps of this period: 'fert cynnamomum, piper & calamum aromaticum'. Similarly, a map by Jan Huigen van Linschoten (1563–1611) contains an inscription: 'Insulæ Moluccæ celeberrimæ sunt ob maximum aromatum copiam quam totum terrarum orbem mittunt.'[7]

India, like the Arabia conjured up in Joyce's *Dubliners* story 'Araby', is read as an exotic storehouse of expensive, highly desired items of decoration or food.[8] It is a kind of orientalised shop, a displaced apothecary. Moreover, figurative language itself is presented as a kind of pharmacy. Whether good or bad, attractive or repulsive, the olfactory particles of language waft around the text, as

Stephen in his reveries breaks words down into their sonic and graphic components. The novel is a sustained act of *pharmakopoeia*.

The drift of figurative language has been termed *pharmakon* by Derrida.[9] The word means either poison or cure, and an unstable, destabilising flow.[10] It is impossible to tell whether the smells or signifiers invoked are poisons or antidotes. Moreover, an antidote is often the poison it cures. In Diodorus Siculus, *Arabia Felix* is a land of miraculous spice forests (III.xlvi.4), but it is also infected with poisonous serpents (III.xlvii.1f).[11] In Bullein's medical treatise, coriander cures the King's Evil but in excessive quantities causes dumbness and madness.[12] The pharmacological register of spice is emphasised in a passage in Keats's (1795–1821) *Isabella; or, the Pot of Basil* (1818; published 1820):

> But, for the general award of love,
>   The little sweet doth kill much bitterness;
> Though Dido silent is in under-grove,
>   And Isabella's was a great distress,
> Though young Lorenzo in warm Indian clove
>   Was not embalm'd, this truth is not the less –
> Even bees, the little almsmen of spring-bowers,
> Know there is richest juice in poison-flowers. (stanza xiii)

Keats's reference to embalming reworks a common feature of the poetics of spice: the topos of the spiced corpse or 'mummy'. Mummy is both substance and sign, like money: the term is thought to be derived from the Persian *mūm* (wax) and the Arabic *mūmiyah* (pitch).[13] In the myth of mummy, the corpse is a subject-turned-into-substance; a corpse that has been spiced is then a mystical subject, existing in a sublime state beyond life and death, like the incorruptible bodies of saints.

Keats's superposition of 'dead' and 'alive' is pharmacological. Another frequent *pharmakon* topos is the relation of religion to vice. The second part of Samuel Butler's *Hudibras* (1678) contains the lines: 'So in the *Wicked* there's no *Vice*, / Of which the *Saints* have not a spice' (II.ii.245–6).[14] Arthur Hugh Clough's *Dipsychus* (1850) says much the same thing: 'Religion's self must have a spice of evil' (I.iii.47).[15] In *Isabella* Keats eroticises this spiritual ambiguity. The cockney rhyme of 'love' and 'clove' repeats this ambiguity at the level of the signifier, for in the Romantic and Victorian periods there was a play on a comic derivation of 'cockney' from 'Cockaygne'.

The representation of the trade and consumption of luxury goods played a special topical role in relationships between poetry and political conceptions of the trading status of Britain. The 'trade winds' topos was common in seventeenth-, eighteenth-, and early nineteenth-century panegyrics to trade, in the form of didactic poetry and epic, but the Romantic period provided special conditions for the critique of trade, and hence the revision of the topos.

The topos represents the perfumed winds, scented with spice, blowing from the islands associated with the spice trade, for example the Moluccas, towards the imaginary nose of the reader, although it does not necessarily imply the actual trade winds. It is part of the contested figuration of transnational trade, the language of praise and blame. While it is employed in poems that advertise or criticise Britannia's trading powers, it is also used in the poetry of natural science, religious mystery and theodicy. The politics of these figurative structures is significantly orientalist, exoticising the lands from which the spices flowed and the flows of trade themselves, and spicing up the poetry in which they are placed. Moreover, since it is preoccupied with translation, metaphor, tropology – all forms of trade – its political and poetic functions are virtually inseparable. The rhetoric of advertising or dissuasion classifies the poems as examples of what Stephen would call kinetic art. Moreover, the kinesis represented in the topos itself could not be clearer.

The persistence of the trade winds is remarkable, given the waning of the spice trade's power in the eighteenth century as a motor of capitalism. Indeed, the topos recurs in Virginia Woolf's *Mrs Dalloway* (1925), threatening to destabilise the modernist aesthetic autonomy of the text, its detachment from its conditions in imperialism, when Clarissa Dalloway imagines herself as a diamond, and the outside world of empire threatens to impinge upon the enclosed, interiorised text of consciousness. As Perry Meisel puts it, 'After all, "diamond" resonates with the novel's seemingly unrelated tropology of finance, empire, and material resources of colonialism "where only spice winds blow".'[16]

Like the remarkable persistence into the eighteenth century of Milton, who wrote during the British struggle with the Dutch for supremacy in the spice trade, the topos continued even as it became an archaism. The topos developed during a period in which the spice trade affected many European cultures. Seventeenth-century Dutch culture offered ways of representing, criticising and dealing with the spice trade, from maritime art to the development of the still-life painting, from moral treatises against luxury to recipes for up-market versions of the *hutsepot* or spiced stew.[17]

The novel consumption and figuration of tea, coffee, chocolate and sugar, intoxicants and flavourings of the New World and of expanded trading empires, did not prevent the constant reuse of the trade winds topos. Milton and capital, just as surely as canons and the Bank of England, the National Debt and the anxiety of influence, are all emergent features of a long history of the modern era in British politics and literature. And as Milton has a strong influence on the Romantic period in general, so does his use of the trade winds topos in particular.

Ostensible differences between spices and other luxury commodities break down before the evidence of their consistent representation as aspects of capitalist panegyrics and culinary encomia. Cultural historians of spice have often tried to establish clean temporal and categorical demarcations, yet this often simply leads to cliché by pointing out distinctions between medieval and modern in terms of phenomenological distinctions between spices, coffee and chocolate.[18] Chocolate, tea, tobacco, coffee and sugar, *pace* these historians, are *not* wholly products of the New World, nor are they products of modernity, advancing capitalism, bourgeois consciousness (coffee) or luxurious Catholicism (chocolate), and so on; nor were they prepared, circulated or represented in a realm separate from spices. This is not to deny that distinctions were made between different commodities at different times, and that different cultures employed different kinds of rhetoric, but there is a remarkable consistency over time and space. For example, Giovambatista Roberti praised sugar in 'Le fragole', found in the first volume of *Raccolta di varie operette* (1767):

> From Virginia and from Caracas,
> The Moluccas and far Macao,
> Others wait for cinnamon,
> Vanilla, cocoa and carnations;
> And that which modern noses yearn,
> Like Helen searching for Menelaus,
> Powder from Brazil and Havana,
> Soft, subtle and sweetly scented.[19]

The topos of products of the world wafting towards the sensorium is common. In the sonnet *Il mondo creato diviso nelle sette giornate* (1686), Giuseppe Girolamo Semenzi wrote:

The Indian ship carries to European lips
The sugars of Brazil, the nuts of Banda,
And strong-smelling goods originating from
The Moluccas, Ceylon and other strange shores.

He also warned of the dangers of the '"Indian broth"' of chocolate, which could inflame the blood too much and create a state of appetite in which '"taste turns remedy to poison"'.[20] The pharmacological aspect of this rhetoric is hard to miss, but does not concern spice as such, though chocolate was often prepared with spices and other fragrant substances. Camporesi describes a new Enlightenment taste for delicate rather than powerful flavours, such as chocolate with a light dusting of vanilla and cinnamon, and delicacies prepared with great difficulty, such as jasmine chocolate. It is evident, however, that the 'global' ideologies of long-distance trade tended to provide a long-lasting framework for these cultural highlights. Pocock has discussed the importance of 'Notions of refinement and politeness' in 'the ideology of eighteenth-century commerce'.[21]

Lorenzo Magalotti (1637–1703) worked in didactic and panegyric genres, translating John Philips's *Cyder* and attempting the first Italian translation of *Paradise Lost.* He employed the topos of the spicy Zephyr in a poem about drinking chocolate from *Lettere sopra le terre odorose d' Europa e d' America dette volgarmente buccheri* (1695):

You feel running through your veins
The rush of wind from a fan and bellows,
As if the Zephyr hard was blowing
Fully throated through your lips:
As if its breath was bringing you
All the western drugs from sunrise:
Balsam, bezoar and, melted, drenched,
Several tears of rich quinquina:
Soconosco, Guatemala's source of wealth.
And also, as if it has attracted,
Through the power of its breathing,
Not western fragrances alone
But in an instant each and every
Perfume of the Orient,
The rivers of the mosques and harems
And all is fetched to noble lungs
As to a precious gold alembic,
And in a fresh new style's distilled,
The twinning treasure of East and West.[22]

The 'new style' is expressed through rather old styles, in which aristocratic taste becomes an alchemical vessel for the transformation of the raw materials of orientalism into the pure gold of European cultural capital.

The trade winds topos was deployed from different political positions throughout the seventeenth and eighteenth centuries. Milton used it to suggest the mercenary quality of Satan's journey, and to establish a register of figurative instability in which spice could be either a poison or a cure. John Dryden, in seeking to encourage the expansion of the British monopoly in the East Indies, poetically redirected the flow of commodities away from Amsterdam and towards London. Blackmore employed the topos to justify Britain's place at the centre of the theatre of the globe; trade was figured as the performance of divine providence. Thomson revised Dryden, justifying a later phase of colonial expansion through a paternalism which claimed that the Edenic medicines of the tropics were being wasted without profit. Darwin modified the medical mode of the topos in a panegyric to the British appropriation of a naturalised, global pharmacy. The role of the spice trade in Percy Shelley's vegetarian rhetoric, which is associated with the places in *Queen Mab* where the trade winds topos appears, is negative, supplementary and corrupting, both of the individual body and of the nation. Shelley wished to divide the drug-poison trope mode of the pharmacological register neatly from the providence-islands-medicine mode. The presence, however, of commerce, economy, circulation or flow in both modes contaminated his attempt at division. Similar things happen in the work of Anna Seward and Charlotte Smith.

Percy Shelley and other Romantic period writers do appear to shift the employment of the topos. 'Medicine' is effectively disconnected from *spice*. Nevertheless, books of *materia medica* in the nineteenth century, such as Sir Alfred Baring Garrod's (1819–1907), still described the medical properties of spices. Amidst all the machinery of industrial production, however, the 'spontaneous' fragrances of the spice trade's providence perhaps seemed anachronistic to many.

Despite all these changes, however, the luxurious quality of spice-as-figure remained, and its role as a literary device persisted. More self-reflexive or transumptive than ever before, spice became a figure of pure opulence, the richness of figurative language itself. In this respect the fetishistic representation of spice in Romantic and

Victorian poetry reappropriates the mystical use of spice. It seems that anyone who focuses on spice as a mediator between two worlds, Occident and Orient, mind and matter, spirit and substance, and so forth, as a form of what Hegel would call 'sense-certainty', is never going to be able to do away with spice or its linguistic equivalent.

This chapter begins with a discussion of the tropological qualities of the spice trade. It moves to the literary figuration of the spaces of trade. It then discusses the representation of spice in Milton, paying special attention to *Paradise Lost* (1667).[23] Milton sets the figurative agenda. The second section contains readings of the topos in Dryden's *Annus Mirabilis* (1667), Blackmore's *Creation* (1712), Thomson's *The Seasons* (1726–30), Darwin's *The Botanic Garden* (1789, 1791), William Cowper's *The Task* (1785), Percy Shelley's *Queen Mab* (1813), *A Vindication of Natural Diet*, 'Fragments of an Unfinished Drama' and *The Witch of Atlas* (1820), Mary Shelley's *The Last Man* (1826), Anna Seward's *Colebrook Dale* (1810) and Charlotte Smith's *Beachy Head* (1807). The conclusion discusses the persistence of spice in the capitalist imaginary and compares the poetics of spice with the language of advertising, paving the way for the next chapter.

SPICE AND SUBSTITUTION

'"If God allowed the inhabitants of Paradise to trade, they would deal in fabrics and spices,"' declared Mohammed.[24] Practised by an upper echelon of merchants, long-distance trade, including that of spices, was a powerful motor of early capitalism. Historians such as Jacques Heers and Peter Matthias, according to Braudel, often downplay the importance of the spice trade in the post-medieval economy.[25] In this they share something with the monoeconomic French Physiocrats of the eighteenth century. In the age of Turgot and Quesnay, the remarks of the Abbé Galiani, which challenged the Physiocrats 'with the sacrilegious notion that the grain trade cannot provide the wealth of a country', cannot have been popular.[26] For Braudel, however, the apparently superficial luxuries of life, often marketed as what Igor Kopytoff would call 'enclaved commodities' (circulated only among social élites), are not so easily distinguishable from those necessities that seem to underpin 'everyday life'.[27] For, Braudel says, technological development followed the persistence of desire.[28] Developments in cartography beyond portulan charts, for example, involved new technologies of perspective in order to allow the Portuguese to navigate beyond the equator, around the coast of Africa and towards the Spice Islands in the Indian Ocean. Moreover, long-distance trade helped to create early versions of firms, and mediated between local and global trading concerns, and between pre-capitalist and capitalist economies.[29] Phillips and Phillips declare that international trade supplied new forms of capitalist technology, insurance and law.[30] It is possible to demonstrate that even though the trade in spices was less valuable than other forms of trade, the trade in opium during the Romantic period was extremely large; and opium inherited some of the features of the poetics of spice, as did tea, chocolate and coffee in the previous century.[31]

Samuel Purchas's monumental collection of myth, history and narrative associated with trade commences with allegorical readings of the biblical journey of King Solomon's navy from Eziongeber to Ophir. But Purchas is keen to point out that the difference between then and now is the difference between allegory and literalism: 'Lo here then . . . in open *Theatre* presented a *Shew* of *Discoueries* on an English *Stage*, wherein the *World* is both the *Spectacle* and *Spectator*; the *Actors* are the Authors themselves, each presenting his own actions and passions in that kind, kindly (in generous and genuine History) *acting* their *acts*.'[32] If Purchas can reinterpret Ophir as everything in the Gulf of Bengal as far as Sumatra, then he can justify trade as the Christian redemption of our souls which have been pirated by Satan. As trade helps the cosmopolitan streak of 'uniuersal tenure' in man,[33] it also enables him to master himself in imitation of Christ.[34] This is aided in the macrocosmic world by creaming off the 'superabundance', in the form of luxury goods such as spices, from all parts of the world, making for an image of even, temperate distribution.

A commodity that could be stored and transported with great ease, spice approached the status of specie, yet it was also often used as a form of payment in kind.[35] *Baratto* or barter (for instance of spices for glassware) was central in the Levantine trade, as a way of 'avoiding paying cash'. Alexandro della Purificazione's *Arithmetica practica* (1714) still contained exercises on barter for schoolboys. The rule of three or *la regola di tre* (for example, 'wax against pepper') turned trade into an exercise that was half barter, half money, the barter serving to 'cover up the price of interest, just like the bill of exchange'.[36] Unlike the British East India Company, the Dutch East

India Company used spice as an indirect mode of payment.[37] The spice trade, then, always involved something tropological, aside from its figuration in poetic language. The flow of spices, their troping from East to West, substituted for gold and silver, which flowed east to saturate India and China, so that Europe's balance remained in deficit here, well into the nineteenth century.[38] Spice gradually and sporadically intermingled the roles of food, capital and money. These roles took it beyond its status as an object of aristocratic luxury consumption and popular feast-and-fast economies, at festivals such as Christmas and Easter. Spice itself was not necessarily destined for a particular dinner plate: it was often imported in order to be recirculated, at a greater profit, in an act which the economic writer Thomas Mun (1571–1641) called *Transitio*.[39]

A story in *The Fable of the Bees* (1714, 1723) by the Dutch-born Bernard de Mandeville (1670?–1733) illustrates the tropological deviousness of mercantile activity in the then luxury trade in sugar. The sugar trader, Decio, deceives Alcander through discourse alone.[40] The sugar trade relies on sophisticated mediations that alienate one man from another. Mandeville's prose is a quasi-satire that is *not* all that ironic about human behaviour in mercantile urban society, entailing and extolling disjunctions between private and public.

It is common to bewail the loss of a Garden of Eden where this disconnection did not exist. Mark Poster assumes that 'technically advanced' societies in the late twentieth century are experiencing something

> similar to that of the emergence of an urban, merchant culture in the midst of feudal society in the Middle Ages. At that point practices of the exchange of commodities required individuals to act and speak in new ways, ways drastically different from the aristocratic code of honor with its face-to-face encounters based on trust for one's word and its hierarchical bonds of interdependency. Interacting with total strangers, sometimes at great distances, the merchants acquired written documents guaranteeing spoken promises and an 'arm's length distance' attitude even when face-to-face with one another, so as to afford a 'space' for calculations of self-interest.[41]

(Poster is here referring to Jean-Christophe Agnew's work, *Worlds Apart*.) Whether true or not, and I suspect largely not, this is another instance of myths about the emergence of capitalism in which the spice trade is the crucial factor in the motivation of long-distance trade.

Face-to-face contact in trade was a myth, as in Dryden's emporium model of London. During the rise of capitalism, exchanges usurped the place of fairs. Zones of close human contact shifted towards zones of close commodity contact. The Amsterdam Bourse controlled not only flows of capital, but flows of Asian spices.[42] As early as 1111, money-changers meeting near St Martin's church in Lucca emulated an exchange, needing only the presence of long-distance trade.[43] The East India and South Sea companies were significant forces in the growth of the London Stock Exchange in the early eighteenth century. The tropological uncertainty of the stock market affects Braudel's uncertainties about the nature of tropical trade. It is difficult to tell whether *le commerce d'Inde en Inde* or *inlandse handel*, to use the Dutch term, resembled a 'village market' or an 'outdoor Stock Exchange' powered by the cyclical flows of the monsoon.[44] Besides, long-distance European trade provided ways of synchronising other kinds of trade: the spice trading fairs of Cairo and Alexandria could be intercepted with a working knowledge of the movements of caravans and pilgrims.[45]

Niels Steensgaard concludes that four factors influenced long-distance trade in the period, two of which have a tropological element: 'unpredictability of success', whereby rational 'laws' of consumption appear to have had no effect, for example, in the story of coffee and tea; and 'geographical transfer', whereby the production of popular commodities was moved to more advantageous places, for example in the case of the move of ginger from the East to the West Indies.[46] Coins and glass beads left Venice for Alexandria, to be exchanged for 'pepper, spices, and drugs' and brought back to Venice to be sold at the Fondaco dei Tedeschi.[47] On the Coromandel coast, where the Dutch East India Company bought fabrics, the common currency was copper or spice.[48] The longer the return journey, the higher the profit. Certain goods had their luxury status thrust upon them through transportation. The Javanese, living in the Spice Islands themselves, were observed by Johann Albrecht Mandelslo to be inflating the price of imported *rice* in 1639.[49] From the standpoint of exchange value, there is no inherent distinction between luxury and necessity.

Because of its value, a certain measure of duplicity was a feature of the spice trade. The Grocers Company of London employed 'garblers' by the end of the fourteenth century to detect spice adulteration.[50] By the eighteenth century, the feature of tropological substitution was significant enough for it to be used as a social marker. It was employed in the work of Susanna Centlivre (1667?–1723), whose play *The Busie Body* (1709), performed at the Theatre Royal, is about a lover who disguises himself as a Spanish merchant to win the favour of Sir Jealous Traffick, a merchant who lives in Spain, in order to obtain his daughter Isabinda. Charles and Sir George make it known that they can proffer the money, five thousand pounds 'for a Joynture of [Sir Jealous's] Daughter', v.i.162: 'he has sent it in Merchandize, *Tobacco*, *Sugars*, *Spices*, *Limons*, and so forth, which shall be turn'd into Money with all Expedition: In the mean time, Sir, if you please to accept my Bond for Performance' (63). Eroticism and political economy are figuratively associated throughout. To declare 'she does not value thee a spoonful of Snuff' (II.i.23) is to acknowledge the figurative power of the tobacco trade, which along with the trade in chocolate and coffee was taking over where the spice trade had left off. In *A Bold Stroke for a Wife* (1718), the libidinal power of a Dutch merchant is celebrated: 'How would the ladies sparkle in the Box without a Merchant?'[51]

Spice was associated with rhetoric and tropology in Neoplatonic thought. Unlike sights and sounds, smell and taste belong to an almost entirely gross species of *integumentum*: they are highly corporeal, material veils of mind, soul and God. In both St Augustine and Ficino, seasoning has no inherent 'reasonableness': it acquires this only through serving some purpose, such as health or nourishment. Similarly, rhetoric is desirable only in sustaining dialectics. As Augustine says, 'even though food be seasoned by a cook, we still may say that it is reasonably seasoned. But in accordance with accepted usage, it is not said to taste reasonably whenever without any extrinsic cause it satisfies a momentary craving.'[52] Yet because dialectics requires the arousal of strong emotions to persuade, rhetoric is required as that portion of reason which is 'more replete with lack than with enlightenment, its lap heaped high with charms which it would scatter to the crowd so that the crowd might deign to be influenced for its own good'.[53] Similarly, for Ficino, smell and flavour must serve only an instrumental function. Thus 'Certainly, odors, flavors, temperatures, and the like either harm or help the body a great deal, but they have little effect on the admiration or censure of the soul.'[54] In the Romantic period, by contrast, the ideology of lifestyle had overtaken the ideology of soul, as Campbell has shown, to the extent that correct consumption *was* an indication of a rich inner essence. In the modern period beggars began to be defined as improper consumers. The discourse of internality which *Paradise Lost* developed with other epics in the English revolutionary period, underlies the Romantics' cultivation of the subjectivity of consumerism. Even Romantic anti-consumerism is a form of consumerism.

The tropological instability of spice is symptomatic of the instability of commodities in general. The Romantic period political economist David Ricardo (1772–1823) realised that there was no transcendental economic signifier, and that the gap between what he called riches (or exchange value) and value (or use value) was thus arbitrary. Ricardo deconstructed ideas in Smith about riches as the command of labour power.[55] First, the difference between value and utility ensured that 'Many of the errors in political economy have arisen from errors on this subject, from considering an increase of riches, and an increase of value, as meaning the same thing, and from unfounded notions as to what constituted a standard measure of value.'[56] Secondly, therefore, 'why should gold, or corn, or labour, be the standard measure of value, more than coals or iron? – more than cloth, soap, candles, and the other necessaries of the labourer? – why, in short, should any commodity, or all commodities together, be the standard, when such a standard is itself subject to fluctuations in value?'[57] Ricardo's *On the Principles of Political Economy and Taxation* (1817) contains nothing in particular on spices, but much on corn, perhaps reflecting contemporary agricultural crises.

FIGURES OF TRADE

The conclusion of the Portuguese epic *The Lusiads* (1572) by Luis de Camões (1524?–80) presents a vision of the Moluccas or Spice Islands. Here is Sir Richard Fanshawe's translation (1655):

> Through all these *Orientall* Seas behold,
> Sown infinite of *Isles* that have no name!
> TIDORE see! TERNATE, whence are roll'd
> (Holding black *Night* a Torch) thick *Plumes* of *Fame*!
> See *Trees* of burning *Cloves*, that shall be sold
> For LUSIANS blood, and water'd with the same!
> Heer are those *golden Birds*, which to the ground
> Never descend, and only *dead* are found.
>
> See BANDA's *Isles*, inamled curiously

Figure 3 'Indiae orientalis, insularumque adiacientium typus': Abraham Ortelius, *Theatrum orbis terrarum* (1570), between pp. 48 and 49. The caption in the centre right reads: 'Insulae Moluccae celebres ob maximam aromatum copiam, quam per totum terrarum orbem transferunt' ('The Molucca Islands, famous for their enormous abundance of spices, which are traded throughout the entire world').

With various *Colours* which the *red fruit* paints;
With various *Birds*, from Tree to Tree that fly,
To take their *tribute* of the NUTMEG-PLANTS!
Behold BORNEO likewise, in which dry
Coagulated Liquor never wants
  From a fat Tree which CAMFORA they name,
  For which this *Isle* is in the *Book* of FAME!

There (look you!) is TIMOR, that sends the Wood
Call'd *Saunders*, *Physicall* and *Odorous*.
See SUNDA, painted at half face, so broad
That the *South-side* lies now quite hid from *Us*!
The *Natives* here (and *Those* who from abroad
Travail the *Land*) of a miraculous
  River report; which, where it slides alone,
  The *wood* that falls therein, converts to *Stone*.

In *that* (which Time, I told you, made an *Isle*;
Which likewise trembling flames with smoke expels)
Two wonders see, a *Fountain* that runs *Oyle*;
And *Balsamum* that from *Another* wels,
Sweeter then [*sic*] *that*, ADONIS Mother vile
Weeps in the Blest Arabia where she dwels.[58]

The Lusiads continued in importance into the Romantic period: in 1821 Percy Shelley discussed it. The Spice Islands are celebrated as cornucopian places of miraculous, spontaneous production. The sea has been 'sown infinite' by the islands themselves. The rhetorical register combines heat and liquidity: 'burning Cloves', 'blood', 'Coagulated Liquor', 'a Fountain that runs Oyle'. There is also a register of luxury commodities, presented principally to the gaze: '*golden Birds*', the enamelling of Banda, the 'Tribute' taken from the nutmeg by the colourful birds. Wonder, which Stephen Greenblatt has shown to be a feature of the proto-colonial as well as of the colonial text, appears in the 'miraculous / *River*' that turns wood to stone and the fountain of balm. The allusion to Myrrha, 'Adonis Mother vile' (she was involved incestuously with her father Cinyras), suggests the liminal, half-alive state of the islands and their commodities: the dead golden birds strewn on the ground like coins, the way the magical river Timor 'sends' sandal-wood. The description is an amalgam of heightened detail and fantastic myth. Why does the poetics of spice involve such an amalgam?

The idea of cornucopia also appears in myths of the spontaneous production of spices. One of the most famous of these is the myth of the Nile's overflowing. The Other's realm, that distant land from where spices emanate, appears to produce them without labour. William Bullein asks, 'what shall we say unto the capiter [*sic*] Riuer of al this worlde called *Nilus*, in which Egipt ther is no Rayne, but only the swellyng and ouerflowyng of that fludde, which being falne downe within his bankes, eftesones great plentie of spices, Herbes, Plantes, and fruites do grow, in so muche that the people of the lande doo liue with out any greate trauell, payne, or labour'.[59] Similarly, the best rhubarb comes from the Troglodytes, a 'Barbarous people' from a hot distant African country who dwell in underground caves eating dragons' flesh: 'wheras [*sic*] these precious spices and rootes doe growe, doe rather grin like Dogges, than speake like menne'.[60] William Caxton, translating Gautier de Metz's *L'Image du monde*, writes of a realm full of 'playsances and delices', where the four principal rivers of the world flow from Paradise, near India, full of precious gems and stones but also populated by dragons and griffons, and people who kill their elderly relatives. They have to burn their white pepper black, for 'the Germyne is there to grete': the realm is superabundant.[61] This is a myth about people who do not know what to do with their surplus. Gilles Deleuze and Félix Guattari have speculated that myths of capitalism existed prior to capitalism's social dominance.[62] If so, then this is one of those myths. The transition from the kind of mythologising of the Orient to be found in late medieval writing to the mythologising of the 'actual' Spice Islands simply requires the literalisation of fantasy, 'making it real' by embodying it in actual travel and trade narratives. Thus in the *Lusiads* Da Gama and the sailors are a literalisation of Jason and the Argonauts, whose capture of the golden fleece is also transformed into the historical discovery of spices in Maximilian (1523).[63] Richard Eden's *The History of Trauayle in the West and East Indies* (1577), and Samuel Purchas's *Purchas his Pilgrimes* (1625), the major early mythologisations of the spice trade in English, were keen to play on the idea of literalising fantasy.[64]

Trade, then, is the realisation of Christ's redemptive promise. It is a fitting irony that St Thomas's territory, India, should be the land of the spicy symptoms of early capitalism; or as Lacan would have called it, the 'sinthome'.[65] Both Camões and Purchas discuss St Thomas, the disciple who needed to place his hand in Christ's wound in order to realise that He was truly risen.[66] The discoveries of the West Indies were a further chapter in this realisation of redemption. The East Indies were figured as the earthly Paradise, east of Eden. Paradise in the New World, however, was not simply *found* but *created*: the Europeans could not pull the Spice Islands nearer, so they invented some more. This is a pornographic aesthetics: the fantastic illusion of reality, and the realisation of a fantasy. The assassins described by Marco Polo believe in the material reality of the Terrestrial Paradise, and this helps them be more effective killers.[67] Columbus and Frobisher read Mandeville's *Travels* and the romance-like narratives of Marco Polo.[68] Fantasy was not replaced by realism, but the later voyage narratives, unlike the tales of wonder, employed the fantasy support of scientific nomenclature and local specificity.

By the time commercial capitalism was in full swing, the cornucopian myth was still in place. Daniel Defoe's *A New Voyage Round the World* (1724) presents a fantasy of infinite production which in the late twentieth century grates against capitalist ideologies of scarcity, of our ecological inability to deal with the Real.[69] The Tories in Defoe's time laid a strong emphasis on land-value: Aphra Behn praised the Golden Age in a poetic preface to a work by the Behmenist vegetarian Thomas Tryon. By contrast, expansionists saw value as an imaginary relation: it lay 'over there'. The myth of *Terra Australis incognita* and other fantasies about territory in the poetics of spice had prepared the way for such conceptions. The 'over there' quality of value was what writers in the Romantic period engaged with, either straightforwardly, as with Wordsworth, Charlotte Smith and Percy Shelley, or ironically, as with Keats, Letitia Landon and Byron.

In the late eighteenth century a strain of Romantic literature made the earthly paradise internal to Britain – to literalise through domestication. The 'gentle breeze' which lulls Wordsworth's cheek in the first line of *The Prelude* (1805, 1850) seems a once-removed relation of the bountiful effects of providence praised in the spiritual first-person narration of Henry Vaughan. The Anglicising of Paradise is evident not only in writers such as Wordsworth but also in geographers. Peter Crosthwaite's 'An Accurate Map of the beautiful Lake of Ullswater, situate in Cumberland and Westmorland', surveyed in the 1780s and early 1790s, contains a verse encomium to the Lake District employing Dantesque language:

Figure 4 'The Beast which Yeilds [*sic*] Musk': from Jean Baptiste Tavernier, *The Six Voyages* (1678), II. between 152 and 153. The fetishisation of the exotic is an aspect of the oneiric horizon.

> Salute the noble Trav'ler, as he leaves the Plains.
> In those enchanting Lakes, the finest fish are caught;
> And from our Alpine heights, exquisite Food is brought;
> An *Earthly Paradise*, a feast for every sense
> This Northern Tour affords (and health) at small expence![70]

The Lake District is mapped onto the Orient.

The realm of the Other in medieval fantasies, like the myth of the Terrestrial Paradise, has been named the 'oneiric horizon' by Jacques Le Goff. Montanari elucidates:

> Signs of social distinction and of ostentation, spices also assumed dreamlike qualities, those same qualities that characterized the distant and mysterious Orient . . . According to the maps of the period [the Middle Ages], the Orient lay next to the earthly paradise, and so should be profoundly influenced by this nearness. These were the worlds of abundance and of happiness, and above all of immortality, inhabited by multiple-centenarians, evergreen trees and the ineffable phoenix; and it is there that spices grow.[71]

The concept of the oneiric horizon is an invaluable tool for studying the poetics of spice (see figure 4). Commercial capitalism relied on the literalisation of the oneiric horizon. William and Cara Phillips note that Columbus advertised his discovery of the West Indies in prose that rhapsodised about vast quantities of spices: he was creating an oneiric horizon.[72] This myth was not restricted to the Middle Ages but flourished in the long eighteenth century. As Bryan Waller Procter (1787–1874; otherwise known as 'Barry Cornwall') wrote in 'A Dream' in *Dramatic Scenes and Other Poems* (1819):

And over all rich gardens hung,
Where, amongst silver waterfalls,
Cedars and spice-trees and green bowers,
And sweet winds playing with all the flowers
Of Persia and of Araby,
Walked princely shapes; some with an air
Like warriors, some like ladies fair
Listening, and, amidst all, the king
Nebuchadnezzar rioting
In supreme magnificence. (65)

The 'sweet winds playing' ultimately derives from the Song of Songs, while the final scene presents an image of courtly life, with the warrior-like 'princely shapes' and the 'ladies fair / Listening'; control is implied here. Consumption is viewed 'amidst all', associated with despotism and loss of control ('rioting'). The image is thus quintessentially one of Romantic consumption: a view of loss of control within a culture of control. A hallucinogenic landscape is imagined in which oriental luxury and sensual bliss are associated with spice. This landscape resembles the one in Coleridge's 'Kubla Khan' (a narrative found in *Purchas his Pilgrimes*, which is predominantly concerned with the spice trade).[73] The oneiric horizon is a place where desire, often figured as the unrebuked command of a despot, is realised in the consumption of heaven's bliss on earth. What is curious about modernity is its attempt to incarnate the oneiric horizon, to make the Terrestrial Paradise even more terrestrial, by trading with it.

Trevenen's *Little Derwent's Breakfast* contains a poem called 'West India Islands', that represents the oneiric horizon. Beginning in idyllic fashion, it pictures cocoa, tamarind trees, aloe and flowers. Six stanzas begin with the locative 'There' (distinguishing it, of course, from wherever 'here' is):

There – loveliest flowers are blooming,
  While creepers that gracefully twine,
The air with rich odours perfuming,
  In colours harmonious combine. (stanza 3)

The islands contain brilliant birds, shells, turtles for 'epicures' and other 'sweetmeats' such as orange, shaddock, lime and arrowroot. The narrator then turns to the unseen, unthought-of dangers in the idyll: hurricanes, thunder and hail; nasty-sounding birds (unlike those in England); gnats and mosquitoes. So little Derwent Coleridge must be aware, while 'these wonders they're telling', that the oneiric horizon remains a fantasy support of the organicism of domestic pastoral: 'There's no place like *England* to dwell in, – / There's nothing like England for home.'[74] Moreover, one might ask, who are 'they'? Trevenen herself has just told these wonders, and so banishes her own discourse to the realm of fantasy. The poem closes on an imperial note: Derwent is exhorted not to despise other lands (that would not be very sporting either). They are beautiful in their own way; an Englishman would not mind being banished there.

The 'oneiricisation' of England also happens in Landon's *The History of a Child* (1836; Landon lived 1802–38). The little girl protagonist constructs an idyll out of exotic fantasies such as *Robinson Crusoe* and the *Thousand and One Nights*, reading them amidst the exoticised spaces of her family's park, ornamented with foreign rhododendrons and domestic English roses. Her favourite dog dies (it is named Clio, after the Muse of history) and the 'real' (her word, not Lacan's) abruptly shatters her imaginary idyll. To compensate she befriends a girl named Lucy and together they visit Mrs Selby's cottage on the edge of the family park. Yellow musk roses entwine around the porch in a standard Romantic period image of the domestic bliss of the English village lower class. The rose anticipates the trade winds, in the evening filling 'the whole air with its peculiar and aromatic fragrance'. The girl and Lucy 'read of the gales that bear from the shores of Ceylon the breathings of the cinnamon groves. I have always fancied that the musk rose resembles them.' As the girl says: 'Still the imagination conquers the real.'[75] Such exchanges between domestic and oneiric fantasy-spaces are common in the poetics of spice. A quite different kind of oneiric horizon arose in the Romantic period around the Oceanic islands such as Tahiti, the *Nouvelle Cythère*, marked by free sexuality and the miraculous breadfruit – a more natural space which opposed the values of commercial civilization.[76] But the poetics of spice persisted.

Journeys from 'this' to 'that' and vice versa, the invasion of (or translation into) the world of the self by the realm of the Other, are good reference points for examining the causes of the immense value and richness evoked in the poetics of spice. The simplest way to describe this would be as a form of differential semiosis, in which what is named as 'over there', 'that', 'the Other', increases in value as it is differentiated from, and yet impinges upon, that which is named as 'over here', 'this', 'the self'. Richness is created through disequilibrium, resulting in the flow of over-there (the territory of the marked) to over-here (the territory of the non-marked). This is not only a rhetorical but also an economic point. Spice is not only a metonym for the emptiness and arbitrariness of language. It is also a symptom of uneven development, manifested, for example, in the huge prices created by spice's increased distance from its point of origin, the gap exploited by merchants between one territory and another. Spice is about space: between prices, territories and signs.

Amœnitarum exoticarum politico-physico-medicarum [fasciculi v] (1712) by Engelbert Kæmpfer (1651–1716) contains a magnificent illustration of an important trading post on the inland spice route, Isfahan (figure 5). The Western artist is shaded by a servant at the bottom right, observing and drawing the orientalised scene. A caravan troop snakes in arabesque towards the city, studded with minarets. A caravanserai is seen in the upper left-hand side of the picture, at the base of the mountain. The picture presents a sharp juxtaposition of nomadic and state space, or as Deleuze and Guattari would say, between 'smooth' and 'striated' space.[77] Such juxtapositions became essential in the capitalist economy of transnational trade. Monocultural spaces were produced for farming spice, without diverse social stratification but with rigidly imposed quasi-modern hierarchies of workers and owners. This is what Adam Smith complained of in his critique of the English and Dutch monopolies' handling of the East Indies. The burning of spices by the Dutch prevented the natives from trading with other nations; this 'barbarous policy has now . . . almost totally extirpated' the naturally growing clove and nutmeg trees.[78]

When considered as part of global trade networks, moreover, those colonial spaces look even flatter and more open. They are designed for the increase of commercial speed. The spaces where spices were consumed, on the other hand, were highly striated, hierarchically variegated into varieties of consumption and display, marked by the different uses to which spices were put. In the illustration, the fluidity of the caravan train, cutting a swathe through the picture plane, is an emblem of the smooth 'nomadic'

Figure 5 'Isphahanum': from Engelbert Kæmpfer (1651–1716), *Amœnitarum exoticarum politico-physico-medicarum fasciculi v* (1712), before A2.

space of spice production and trade. The orientalised, jumbled city swimming into view and expanding to fill the horizontal axis, suggests the oneiric horizon, the mirror-image of Western Europe.

Capitalism depends not only on regional and temporal difference but also on flows between those differences. Luxury is a marker that may attach to commodities that flow between relatively large differentials of space and time. Braudel demonstrates the relativity of this marker when he proves the efficacy of long-distance trade in rice and salt in Java. Rice there underwent the same price inflation as spice in Europe, at the height of the importance of the European spice trade. Rice is not a luxury in a phenomenological sense: it is a dietary necessity. Braudel sees luxury and necessity fitting together in a gear-like operation of differing speeds and intensities. The spice trade worked like a large gear, an overdrive of trade.

Spice is employed as a figure about figurative language itself, and as a token of the distant, the exotic, the erotic, and the poetically inspired. Shakespeare exploits these connotations in the opening scene of *The Merchant of Venice*, playing on comparisons between fantasy, a merchant's cargo and winds favourable to the 'ventures' of trade (I.i.21). Milton reimagines the medieval discourse about the Indian Ocean as a space of luxury, exuberance, liberation and cosmic fear, whose inhabitants' cultures were sometimes conceived as at odds with the anti-humanism of medieval Christianity. For instance, in the Alexander cycle, original sin was contrasted with the 'natural' humanism of Indian Brahmins.[79] Milton's Adam and Eve are a collage of these cultural traces, vegetarians who know how to enjoy love-making and spice.

MILTON'S PHARMACY

The range of moods associated with the literary representation of spice is nowhere more powerfully demonstrated than in Milton's representation of long-distance trade. J. Martin Evans has recently discussed the way in which *Paradise Lost* intersects with the discourse of colonialism in the New World, but more work needs to be done on Milton's representation of the East Indies.[80] Because of the narrative of the forbidden fruit, food plays a powerful role in Milton's epic. Food and rhetoric are associated in language that links digestion and interpretation. Space prevents a thorough reading of the role of spice winds in *Elegia quinta* (1629, published 1645), on the coming of spring and the onset of poetic inspiration: 'Cinnamea Zephyrus leve plaudit odorifer ala . . .', the Zephyr being the usual poetic trade wind of choice (69).[81] Nor is there enough room to discuss the use of Arabia and India as exotic, counter-Mediterranean spaces which are juxtaposed with Mediterranean pastoral geography in *Epitaphium Damonis* (1639) and *Naturam non pati senium* (1627).

Through figures of the spice trade in *Paradise Lost*, Satan is gradually established as a merchant, indeed a drug merchant, a pusher who finally seduces Eve with the aromatic and ambrosial food which, in the words of John Carey, became the most unfortunate snack in human history.[82] However, spice is present in Eden before Satan arrives. It is part of the 'wilderness of sweets' (V.294) which Adam and Eve are bidden to maintain in good order. Eden is a displaced figure for the New World, according to Evans, but it also makes sense to consider it as a heightened vision of the Terrestrial Paradise.[83]

Milton takes the Spice Islands in this beatific state and retranslates them into Eden itself – the model for which they became the model. Eden could thus be said to be a 'simulation' in the strict sense of a copy without an original (as Deleuze or Baudrillard would describe it) – the ultimate oneiric horizon.[84] Milton cannot really escape, as later the Romantics could not, the lure of capitalist rhetoric. Like the Phoenix of *Arabia Felix*, the angel Raphael, scintillating with gorgeous colour, emerges through Eden's forest and approaches Adam:

> to all the fowls he seems
> A phoenix, gazed by all, as that sole bird
> When to enshrine his relics in the sun's
> Bright temple, to Aegyptian Thebes he flies. (v.271–4)

It is a queer moment:

> Into the blissful field, through groves of myrrh,
> And flowering odours, cassia, nard, and balm;
> A wilderness of sweets; for nature here
> Wantoned as in her prime, and played at will
> Her virgin fancies, pouring forth more sweet,
> Wild above rule or art; enormous bliss.
> Him through the spicy forest onward come
> Adam discerned . . . (v.292–9)

There is much to explore here about the interminability of consumption; the role of labour in Eden, which seems suddenly to be secondary to the profusion of the garden itself, despite Milton's Puritanism; and the importance of fancy, often granted handmaid's status to the imagination, discursive thought or mind, in gendering and ungendering desire. In short, there is much to explore about the role of *jouissance* or enjoyment. Eden, through the referential and figurative instability of the topoi associated with spice, is more of a process than a thing: a place which flows. *Enargeia* galore pours from 'nature', in an ekphrastic display of wantonness with which its very virginity is simultaneous. Milton's Eden is thus a revision of the *hortus conclusus*, mapping the ambiguous female body onto external space in the Song of Songs, medieval castle design and *Le roman de la rose*. Chaucer's *Romaunt of the Rose* (1366) describes the Paradise garden as a symmetry of spices:

> The gardyn was, by mesuryng,
> Right evene and square in compassing;
> It as long was as it was large.
> Of fruyt hadde every tree his charge
> But it were any hidous tree,
> Of which ther were two or three.
> There were, and that wot I full well,

Of pome-garnettys a full gret doll;
That is a fruyt full well to lyke,
Namely to folk whanne they ben sike.
And trees there were, gret foisoun,
That baren notes in her sesoun,
Such as men notemygges calle,
That swote of savour ben withalle.
And alemandres gret plente,
Fyges, and many a date-tree
There wexen, if men hadde nede,
Thorough the gardyn in length and brede.
Ther was eke wexyng many a spice,
As clowe-gelofre, and lycorice,
Gyngevre, and greyn de parys,
Canell [cinnamon], and setewale
  [zeodary, a form of ginger] of prys,
And many a spice delitable
To eten whan men rise fro table. (1349–72)

The geometry and luxury of the pleasure garden in Coleridge's 'Kubla Khan' is strongly reminiscent of this passage. The iconography of the *hortus conclusus*, ultimately derived from the Song of Songs, suggests a mandala-like space in which all the possibilities of love may be played out:

A garden inclosed is my sister, my spouse; a spring shut up, a fountain sealed. Thy plants are an orchard of pomegranates, with pleasant fruits; camphire, with spikenard, spikenard and saffron; calamus and cinnamon, with all trees of frankincense; myrrh and aloes, with all the chief spices. (Song of Songs, 4:12–14)[85]

Close and far away have been collapsed – all is available here. The enclosed spice garden is an ambiguous space, a space of chastity but also of *luxuria*, lusty eros. In the passage from Chaucer, the final mention of spices to be consumed at the end of the meal refers to the 'void' or 'voidee' course of wine accompanied by spices, comfits and so forth which closed a dinner when the guests withdrew; or it may refer to the 'bedroom spices' described in the *Ordinaziones* of Peter III the Great of Aragon which were used, like twentieth-century breath mints, as something between medicine and dessert; confectionery in general originally had this status.[86] In the voidee, spices are again associated with both nothingness and infinite riches. 'Void' signifies a gap, but it also signifies flow, superfluity or even waste and destruction (and hence consumption).[87] Superfluity, closure, medicine and eros are juxtaposed in the evocation of an imaginary realm where contraries coexist.

Moreover, spice is already present in forms that do not associate it immediately with poison, the Fall or corruption. In *Paradise Lost* III, the Son is established as a cure for the ills of the world *before* those ills have taken precipitous effect. Eden is described in language that echoes *Othello* V.ii.346–7: 'Groves whose rich trees wept odorous gums and balm' (IV.248). Following an observation by Empson in *Some Versions of Pastoral*, Fowler comments: 'Nature's balm precedes the "wound" of Nature in the same way that Election to salvation precedes the Fall.'[88] The language of balm, difficult to separate from the representation of spices, is part of the poem's linguistic register of healing. If the poison and its antidote exist before any poisoning or curing has occurred, then Milton is creating a pharmacy, and spice assumes the role of *pharmakon*, a figurative ground that sets up all the tropological possibilities prior to their varied articulation.

The two modes of spice could respectively be named the topical and the tropical. They are both examples of a transumptive (metaleptic) or self-reflexive sort of discourse. On the one hand there is the Edenic and Filial mode. Spice becomes a delicious feature of Paradise as a place: the topos of a topos. Through the topical application of balm, as in the ceremony of anointing, the wounds of the flesh and spirit are healed: 'Christ' means 'the anointed one'. And through the correct digestion of food or language, the base is converted to the pure, the luxury of spice into the love of God. Here Milton is working within a Neoplatonic framework that prescribes the correct use of drugs. Digested properly, figurative language and spice lead one up the ladder of being and towards the sheer beauty and love of the good. Through the attraction of harmonious relationships, even a substance as sensual as spice raises the soul upward.

This Edenic register owes something to *Othello*, as noted above. A moment of intoxication inaugurates the play's tragic action, which is full of drowsy syrups and medicinable gums; the intoxicated character is Cassio, whose name in the feminine, cassia, denotes a cinnamon-flavoured spice. *Paradise Lost* is about how not to become intoxicated by rhetoric and drugs, but not about how to deny the role of rhetoric and drugs altogether. As Raphael declares, 'The grosser feeds the purer' (V.416). To use Neoplatonic language, if they are interpreted or digested properly, spices and figures are the *integumenta* of higher truths or states of being:

knowledge is as a food, and needs no less
Her temperance over appetite, to know
In measure what the mind may well contain,
Oppresses else with surfeit, and soon turns
Wisdom to folly (VII.126–30)

Raphael's conversation takes place after a meal at which Eve has served a vegetarian banquet of Indian and Middle-Eastern foods, flavoured with 'rose and odours from the shrub' that has been left 'unfumed', in Miltonically correct anti-papist fashion (V.349).[89] Since one referent of 'odours', however, is the fumes of burnt spices used in sacrifice, it is hard to tell how the figurative language differentiates between acceptable and unacceptable surplus consumption. This passage is a preface to Raphael's account of the true role of language as mediating the acts of God, outlining the possibility of a rhetoric that will not disfigure the Real (V.563–76, VII.126–30, 176–9).

Spice in Milton thus retains the polysemy accrued in other practices and discourses. Boundaries between medicine and food, and between confectionery and nutrition within the category of food, were not fixed as Europe moved towards capitalism. And narratives about the value of substances traded over transnational distances were associated with orientalist legends about medicines. Networks of trade established modes of evaluation. Nicolás Monardes' popular treatise on medicinal products from the West Indies (1569), translated from Spanish into English as *Ioyfull Newes out of the New-found Worlde* (1596), contains a treatise on the 'Bezar' stone and the herb 'Escuerconera', categorised with mythical medicines such as unicorns' horns. The stone was taken from a beast like a gigantic hart. The Persian word 'bezoar' literally means 'antidote' and 'is not a stone, but rather a concretion found in the alimentary organs' of certain cloven-footed animals. Reputed to kill venomous animals instantly, it could be worn in a ring or about the neck. Precious and semi-precious stones were also used in the fifteenth century as antidotes against the plague.[90]

The topical use of spice in *Paradise Lost*, however, is placed within a structure of religious meaning that resists the pull of Milton's rhetoric towards its intoxicating, tropological moment. Even in Monardes, the Portuguese pay high prices to the Indians for these stones, which are imported to China: 'and from thence to *Maluco*, and from *Maluco* to *Calicut*, for there is the greatest utterance of them, and they do esteeme so much of them, that one is woorth

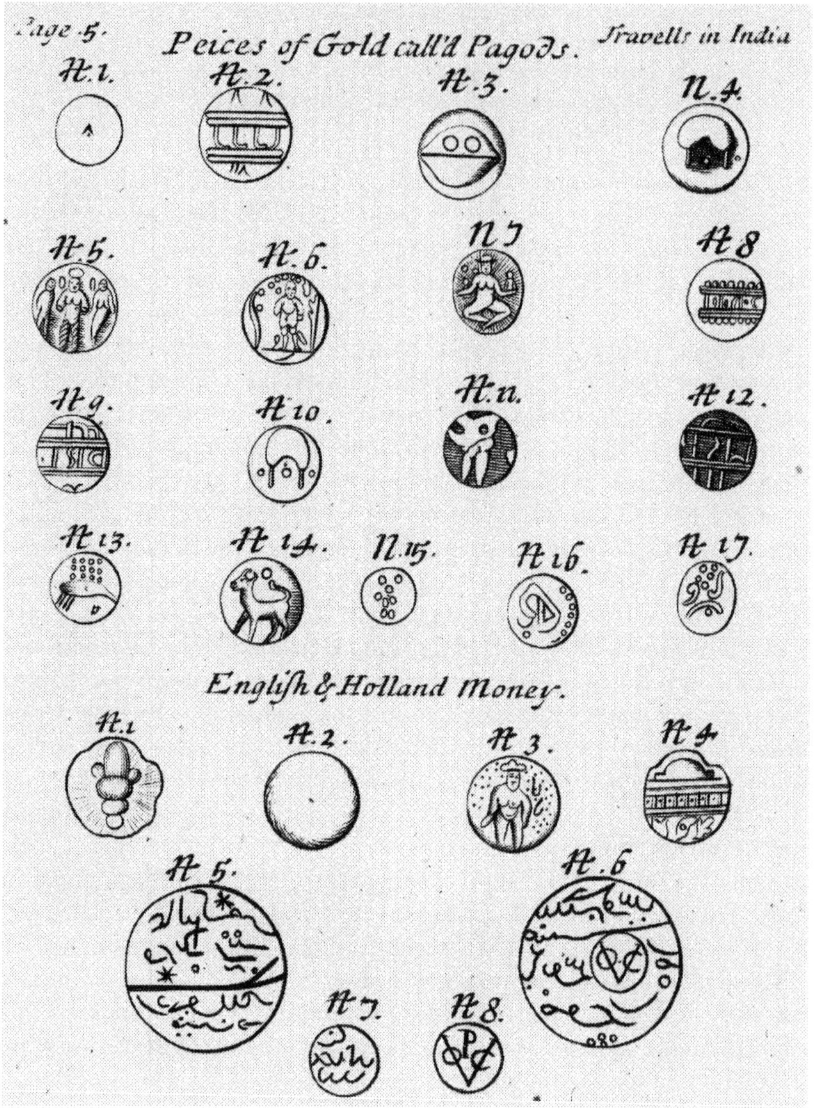

Figure 6 Asian Money 1: from Jean Baptiste Tavernier, *The Six Voyages* (1678), II. between 4 and 5. Asian money including coins by the English in the Fort of St George, Coromandel, called Pagods, like the money of kings and rajas. Notice the tooth and shell, objects used themselves as money, as the next illustration shows.

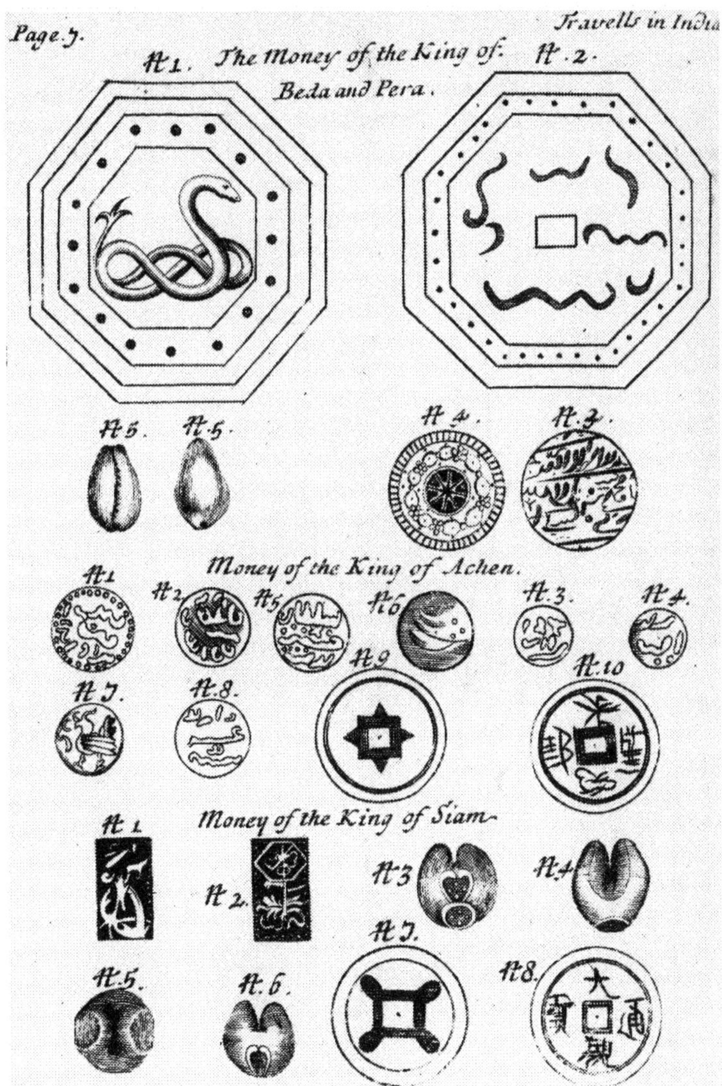

Figure 7 Asian money II: from Jean Baptiste Tavernier, *The Six Voyages* (1678), II. between 6 and 7. Figs. 9 and 10 are 'Copper Money of the King of *Camboya*. The King of *Java*, the King of *Bantam*, and the Kings of the *Molucca* Islands coin no other Money, but pieces of Copper after the same form and manner. As for their Silver Money, they let it pass as it comes out of other Countries, without melting it down. In *Bantam*, in all *Java*, in *Batavia*, and the *Molucca's*, there is little other Money stirring.' A demonstration of the fluidity of objects, oscillating between material and money.

there, beeing [*sic*] fine, fiftie crownes as they are here'.[91] Value is bound up with translation, tropological substitution and trade. From the beginning, Milton's God is described as being worshipped with 'Ambrosial odours and ambrosial flowers' (II.246).

Satan, however, is the exemplar of the tropical use of spice. He is associated with threatening processes of trade, translation, intoxication and metaphor. He traps Eve much as Hamlet traps his uncle – 'Tropically' (III.ii.233). This indicates a larger difficulty in Milton's figuration. Milton's use of epic simile in the context of theodicy suggests that trade and processes of intoxicating fancy have always existed, even in the garden of Paradise. Topos is grounded in *tropos*. Place, indeed the ultimate place of places, exists within a broader context of space and spacing, crossing spaces and reaching other shores, moving towards or away from spaces. Eve can dream and Adam can be carried away on linguistic flights of fancy. Spices are enjoyed and the first humans luxuriate in the sensual. Prehistory is mediated through historical narratives of trade.

Descriptions of the devils at the opening of *Paradise Lost* are often orientalist, but Milton does not let the Occident off the hook. The Orient is the place of meeting between European and Asian traders. It is the place of luxury trade. The devils are likened to merchants flocking to 'Ormus' (II.2–4); a Persian Gulf town, that was important to the jewel trade (figure 8). In book II, Satan leaving Hell for Chaos is described as a trader leaving the Spice Islands, his ship hugging their shores as he sails south-west towards the Cape of Good Hope. Here Milton uses the trade winds topos:

> As when far off at sea a fleet descried
> Hangs in the clouds, by equinoctial winds
> Close sailing from Bengala, or the isles
> Of Ternate and Tidore, whence merchants bring
> Their spicy drugs: they on the trading flood
> Through the wide Ethiopian to the Cape
> Ply stemming nightly toward the pole. (II.636–42)

Some editors explain 'the trading flood' as '"where the trade winds blow"'.[92] 'Bengala' is modern Bengal, while Ternate and Tidore are islands in the Moluccas. The 'spicy drugs' foreshadow the apple. The image also anticipates the moment at which Satan approaches Eden. In a wonderful narrative continuity, book IV describes him as a trader excited to be approaching the exotic

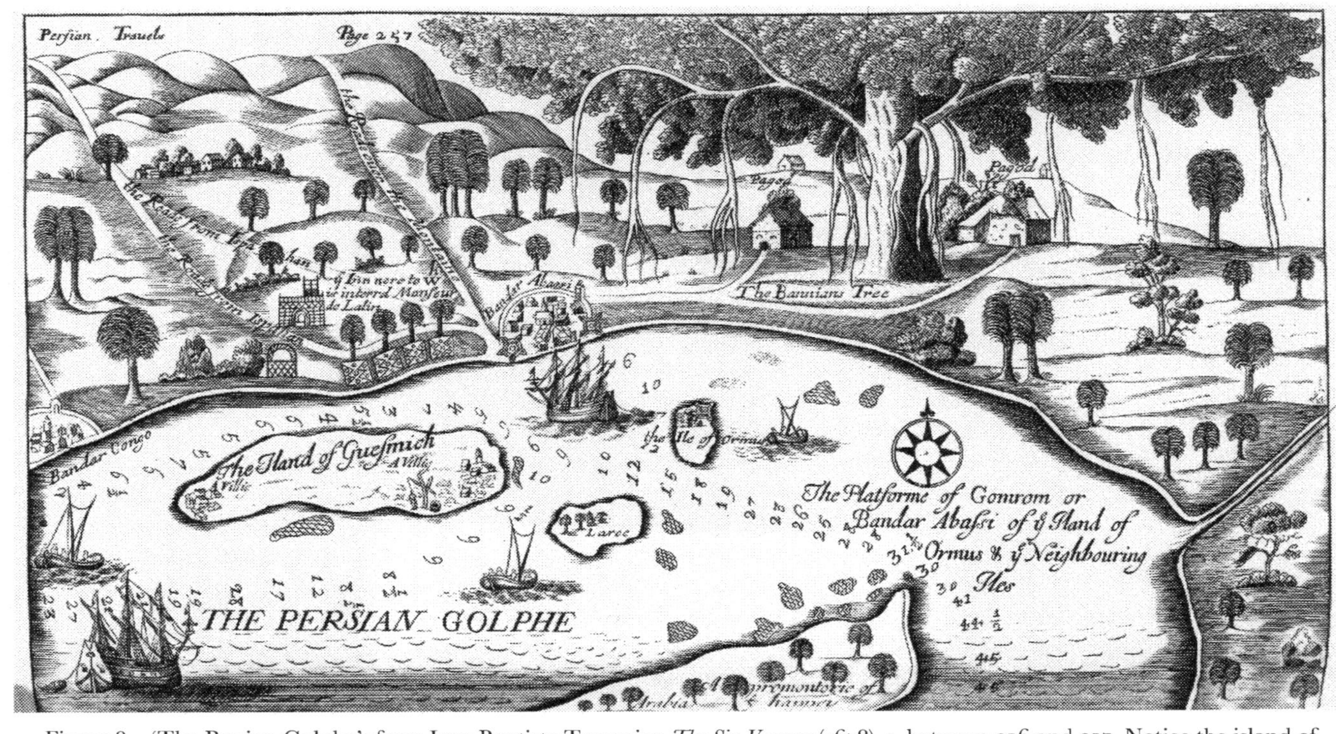

Figure 8 'The Persian Golphe': from Jean Baptiste Tavernier, *The Six Voyages* (1678), I. between 256 and 257. Notice the island of Ormuz, mentioned in Milton: a transitional point in the spice trade. Also notice the roads from Isfahan, another important trading post.

scents of the coast of Mozambique and the island of Madagascar, mediated through archaic topoi about *Arabia felix*. The trade winds topos sounds again:

> and of pure now purer air
> Meets his approach, and to the heart inspires
> Vernal delight and joy, able to drive
> All sadness but despair: now gentle gales
> Fanning their odoriferous wings dispense
> Native perfumes, and whisper whence they stole
> Those balmy spoils. As when to them who sail
> Beyond the Cape of Hope, and now are past
> Mozambic, off at sea north-east winds blow
> Sabean odours from the spicy shore
> Of Arabie the blest, with such delay
> Well pleased they slack their course, and many a league
> Cheered with the grateful smell old Ocean smiles.
> So entertained those odorous sweets the fiend
> Who came their bane. (IV.153–67)

Compare Diodorus Siculus:

> Veris enim tempore uenti ab terra perflantes, ab huiusmodi arboribus odores ad propinqua maris loca perserunt. Non enim remissam aromata, & uetustam, ueluti apud nos accidit, uim habent, sed ingentem recentemque, & quem ad omnes sensus perueniat. Aura quidem ex optimis mixta odoribus ad maritima descendens, multa suauitate nauigantes afficit, & confert ualitudini.[93]

> (For in springtime, as the breezes from right off the land, fragrances from the trees thus permeate to the nearby reaches of the ocean. For aromatic spices have a scent that is not faint and familiar, such as the aromas we smell in our part of the world, but one that is abundant and vigorously fresh, that might permeate all the senses. A kind of mingled cloud of the finest odours, descending to the ocean, seduces sailors with its abundant suggestiveness, and bestows a sense of health and vigour.)

(The rhetorical connotation of 'suavitate' (persuasive, suggestive softness) is hard to miss.) Thus, while seemingly closer to Eden, Satan-as-merchant has now *doubled back* on his course and is travelling in a north-easterly direction around the Cape of Good Hope. Is Satan approaching or leaving a place here? A distance is established between figurative language and what it represents. And by implication, Eden occupies the same place as Hell! As the poetic location of likeness, simile should lead the reader towards a contemplation of the harmonious relationships between what is described and the process of description. Here, figurative language is a kind of trafficking in meaning which does not embody reality, but only remains contiguous with it.

The Portuguese had mastered the particular trade route which the epic similes delineate, around the coast of Africa to the Moluccas. This might suggest a nationalistic impulse behind Milton's choice of imagery as a contribution to the English 'spice race', as Keay calls it.[94] The rise of Portugal in the wake of Vasco da Gama had 'culminated spectacularly in the direct shipment of pepper and spices to Lisbon, a revolution in itself'.[95] Mozambique in particular was a Portuguese province. Madagascar was perceived as strategically important for England in the 1630s, and was invested with fantastic, utopian significance.[96] *The Lusiads* had an enduring interest for English poets: they were commented on by Percy Shelley in 'A Defence of Poetry' (1821); and other works by Camões were translated by Felicia Hemans in 1818. In *The Lusiads*, Mozambique is described suggestively in terms of flow, evoking the circulation of trade and the ocean's currents:

> The *warlike People* the sale *Ocean* plough
> Leaving the *South*, and face the *Orient*,
> 'Twixt MADAGASCAR's Isle, where all things flow,
> And ETHIOPIA's barren Continent. (1.42)

The images of the flow of goods from a wondrous island resemble Milton's representation of the East Indies, and though it is possible to read Camões' poem as less interiorised than Milton's, both are about ennoblement and cupidity, and both attempt to out-trope classical epic.[97] (The Spice Islands, such as Ceylon when it was approached by Constantin Renneville at the turn of the eighteenth century, were often said to smell of cinnamon or other spices.[98]) Some 'specific allusions' to *The Lusiads* have been found in *Paradise Lost*, and Satan's journey has been compared with the Portuguese epic,[99] but the parallels between Satan and Camões' new Argonauts are not clear-cut. In terms of the rhetoric of the spice trade, Satan is acting more like the Dutch as the English might have seen them (as Robert Markley has recently shown,[100]) usurping the wondrous islands, possessing nothing of value himself but only recirculating others' goods, a master of tropological substitution. The Dutch transgressed the old '"treasure" image of wealth': 'No aura of gold and silver, perfumed woods, rare stones, aromatic spices, or luxurious fabrics attended their initial successes.'[101] This equation of Satan with the Dutch is carried out in spite of the sympathy which Milton's circle had for them during the war.[102]

The referential instability of the similes is saying something about the tropological nature of spice, and about Satan as a figure who is himself an embodied trope, a twisting, turning character well suited to a serpentine body. Dalila is imagined in *Samson Agonistes* (1647–53?) as a merchant ship, 'an amber scent of odorous perfume / Her harbinger' (720–1). Dalila is a revision of Desdemona, who is described as both as a precious cargo *and* the vessel in which she travels (a paradox – she is both container and contents, like the Holy Grail).[103] The Moors at Mombassa in *The Lusiads* play a similar role, dissimulating about the riches to which they have access in order to gain control over Vasco da Gama's fleet:

Moreover, if thou seek for *Merchandize*
Produc't by the Auriferous LEVANT;
Cloves, Cinnamon, and other burning *Spyce*;
Or any good or salutiferous *Plant*;
Or, if thou seek bright *Stones* of endless price,
The flaming *Ruby*, and hard *Adamant*:
  Hence thou may'st *All* in such abundance beare,
  That thou may'st bound thy *wish* and *Voyage* Here. (II.4)

The '-ferous' compounds here ('Auriferous', 'salutiferous') are formed as analogues to 'odoriferous', with its denotation of the transmission of scent. There is an etymological connection between trade and translation, seen in the parsing of the Latin root: *fero, ferre, tuli, latum*. The pungency of spice is associated with the brilliance (flaming, bright and hard) of the precious stones and the sheer wealth of gold. Spice is imagined as the incarnation of shining money, and beyond that, as value itself.

Satan's voyage through sheer space, his bridging of Chaos, is described as a figuratively unstable process: is he swimming, sinking, wading, creeping or flying (II.949–50)? By contrast, the animals who walk, swim or fly in the description of creation are precisely differentiated (VII.501–4). Creation provides Chaos with a syntax by cutting into it with 'Silence', spoken by the Son as its inaugurating word. But the syntactical instability of Satan's journey also evokes the radical, or structural, instability of the space of trade, capital and colonialism. Chaos is neither empty nor full – it is a void in many senses, a superfluity as well as a nothingness: a form of ambience. It has a kind of spectral, ectoplasmic existence. So too, trade involves a sense of spatiotemporality as a process that only agglutinates into something as solid as a *place* for particular, strategic reasons, which is then abandoned in favour of another location. If trade was cutting up and rearticulating the world of the seventeenth century, it was doing so in ways that were not always as predictable and providential as the Son's verbal swordplay. The terrestrial space of trade and the extraterrestrial one of Chaos are not so much Judaeo-Christian spatiotemporal constructs as Lucretian ones, seemingly endless fluxes of material in which a single turn, trope or *clinamen* can result in the creation of a universe. If we consider the cultural implications of this, trade and Chaos were equated for Milton because of his reservations about empire-building. Milton's republicanism was 'nostalgic' and Machiavellian, as opposed to the republicanism of expansionism summed up in his portrayal of Satan the colonialist.[104]

In contrast to the uncertainty of capitalism and Chaos, the Edenic representation of spice is concerned with the correct application of tropes. Temperance in eating is the syntax of health and goodness, cutting through and articulating the sensual and material, which are then seen not as epiphenomenal to true experience, but as its divine clothing or *integumentum*. This is why Michael's vision of the lazar-house (*Paradise Lost*, XI.479ff.), which haunted the vegetarian Percy Shelley, is about the consequences of intemperate diet, and why this passage leads directly to a condemnation of the idolatry of icons:

> Why should not man,
> Retaining still divine similitude
> In part, from such deformities be free,
> And for his maker's image sake exempt?
> Their maker's image, answered Michael, then
> Forsook them, when themselves they vilified
> To serve ungoverned appetite, and took
> His image whom they served, a brutish vice,
> Inductive mainly to the sin of Eve.
> Therefore so abject is their punishment,
> Disfiguring not God's likeness, but their own,
> Or if his likeness, by themselves defaced
> While they pervert pure nature's healthful rules
> To loathsome sickness, worthily, since they
> God's image did not reverence in themselves. (XI.511–25).

To be attracted to what is on one's plate *qua* sheer sensuality, pure appearance, is to be unable to ascend the Neoplatonic ladder.[105]

The ekphrastic moment of the purely sensual freezes the consumer in his or her chair, as Comus freezes the Lady. In *Paradise Regained* (1667–70), Christ resists the spicy temptation of Satan's superbly prepared meal, with its ambergris flavouring: 'Thy pompous delicacies I contemn, / And count thy specious gifts no gifts but guiles' (II.390–1). Here Milton plays on the significance of 'specious', which is etymologically linked to *spice* and 'specie', as well as to 'species', from the Latin *species*, signifying appearance. The association of spice with gift was explored in Milton's time in devotional representation, such as Crashaw's (1613?–49) hymn on the name of Jesus and Vaughan's *Silex Scintillans* (1650): the transmission of grace is imagined in 'Mount of Olives' as a redemptive flow of spicy odours, burnt in sacrifice (3–8).[106] The *pharmakon* status of spice, the fact that it could be either gift or guile, provides the energy of Christ's words, drawing on a tradition that included the words of *Piers Plowman*: 'For truthe telleth that loue is a triacle of heuene: / May no synne be on hym seene that vseth that spice' (I.148–9). In both of Milton's epics, the language of standing implies the steadfastness of individual conscience and faith, and a resistance to the tropical, twisting qualities of language which undermine the place on which one stands. But this does not mean negating the role of spice, balms and drugs, or their eroticism. In reward for his steadfastness, Jesus is rewarded with celestial food at the end of *Paradise Regained* (IV.588–94). Dalila's tomb will be 'With odours visited' (*Samson Agonistes*, 987). The Attendant Spirit in *Comus* (1634) leaves for the Hesperides, where 'west winds, with musky wing / About the cedarn alleys fling / Nard, and cassia's balmy smells' (988–90). Nard, found in Milton's Eden, was used to anoint Jesus' head in Mark 14:3, 8. Henry Hawkins's *Partheneia sacra* (1633) described myrrh as a 'prophylactic against devils'.[107] Indeed, it is Satan who comes as 'the bane' of the spicy 'odorous sweets' of Eden (*Paradise Lost*, IV.166–7). He will put an end to sensuality by peddling it.

In the literature of the following century, the rhetoric of spice played between topography and tropology, between the uneasy instability of scent, desire, flavour and drug and the fixed location of righteous consumption, love and medicine, and between the boundaries of national place and the locus of a meal, and the unstable fluctuations of commerce. Balachandra Rajan and Homi Bhabha have recently explored the doubleness of Milton's relationship to imperialism.[108] For all the particularities of his politics, poetics and religion, Milton established the framework for the use of the trade winds topos. His full and ambivalent approach to colonialism and imperial power provided rich poetic resources.

TRADE WINDS FROM DRYDEN TO SHELLEY

Dryden: poet of the emporium

Braudel has noted the decline in the vogue for pepper after 1650, around the time of *Paradise Lost*, and moreover the general decline in tastes for 'spice, the primary object of trade with the Levant'.[109] The war between the Dutch, Portuguese, English, French and Danish over spices was running out of steam. It reached a limit between 1715 and 1732, during which pepper ceased to be preeminent in the spice trade.[110] Even in Milton and Dryden's time, then, spice had begun to take on an archaic quality, redolent of oldfashioned tastes. The medieval desire to flavour foods with perfumes such as musk and amber had disappeared long ago. Since the desire for exotic spices was no longer driving the long-distance trade of Europe in quite the way it had, the poetic representation of spice was in excess of any content. As the eighteenth century continued, *spice* assumed all sorts of registers beyond the merely referential. The trade winds topos continued to figure long-distance trade. But it was used against the background of the diminishing importance of the spice trade.

In the long history encompassing Milton and Percy Shelley, Dryden (1631–1700) stands out as the strongest proponent of such a poetics. Many of his works are paradigmatic of a novel kind of capitalist poetics, relying on the representation of the spice trade. From a Miltonic point of view, he is writing in the Satanic mode. Spice is not a balm but an object of trade, a trope to be carried across boundaries, standing in for money: a metaphor about metaphor. Dryden is on the side of the merchants, the luxury consumers and the protectionists who wish to control the flow of spices for the material benefit of Britain. Dryden's work is saturated with ideas, images and other kinds of figurative language about trade, most notably the spice trade. *Amboyna* (1673) is about the Dutch massacre of the English in the Moluccas in 1623.[111] In *Astraea Redux* (1660) Dryden had written about the threat of Holland's VOC or the Dutch East India Company (306–307; see figure 9). An apologist for mercantilism in *Annus Mirabilis* (1667), he exhorts the country to let the spices flow

Figure 9 The seal of the VOC (Dutch East India Company), from Jean Baptiste Tavernier, *The Six Voyages* (1678), II. 201. The VOC coined silver Reals with their insignia on it for the Chinese, 'who loving silver better than Gold, carri'd away all the Silver that was coin'd at *Batavia*'.

freely from the East Indies to the thriving emporium of London. Commerce is its explicit subject.[112] A war with Holland, the role of the king, the benefits of international trade to London and the presence of the Royal Society are subordinate themes. The poem is a non-Lucanian sea battle which attempts not to narrate historical events too precisely but rather to set up a figurative and ideological register in which the trade winds topos plays a powerful role.

There is little doubt about the Satanic register of Dryden's figurative attempt to out-Dutch the Dutch. Dryden appears to support the naked opportunism that characterises their trade. *Annus Mirabilis* describes the interruption at Bergen of a Dutch spice fleet from India, in which the Dutch, described as 'perfum'd prey' (101), are killed by luxury commodities:

Amidst whole heaps of Spices lights a Ball,
  And now their Odours arm'd against them flie:

Some preciously by shatter'd Porc'lain fall,
And some by Aromatick splinters die. (113–16)

This passage was found somewhat ridiculous by Samuel Johnson, and the entire poem was later criticised by Sir Walter Scott as too full of such conceits.[113] However, an anonymous contemporary pamphlet (1673) praised *Annus Mirabilis* as if poetry were both trade and plunder, and Dryden a merchant adventurer in poetics.[114] The linguistic register is a poetically just echo of the ways in which the Dutch torture the English in *Amboyna* (v.i.145–7, 360–2). There, burning matches placed on the fingernails are associated with hot nutmegs. The Dutch are described as 'Castors' or hunted beavers, whose sacs furnish a perfume.[115] The lines suggest Waller's 'Of a War with Spain, and a Fight at Sea', and perhaps influenced Lady Winchelsea's 'The Spleen', while the description of the dying Dutch echoes the description of the Phoenix in Dryden's *Fables*, 'Of the Pythagorean Philosophy': 'He liv'd on Odours, and in Odours dies' (599).[116] Besides showing the Dutch to be hoisted on their own spicy petard, the lines convey the fetishistic, self-moving power of the commodities over their consumers, rising up as if in revenge against too luxurious an appetite. To play with spice is to play with fire: to risk the object becoming more powerful than the subject who assumes he or she is in control of his or her own desires.

A more benign version of the Phoenix passage is found in the dedicatory epistle to London: 'You are now a *Phœnix* in her ashes' (49). The fetishism of commodities is celebrated more peacefully in the poem addressed to the Duchess of York. The winds hover over the sea battle like Jupiter presiding over the battle between Aeneas and Turnus: 'Those, yet uncertain on whose sails to blow, / These, where the wealth of Nations ought to flow' (proem, 19–20). The prophetic phrase 'the wealth of Nations' is caught up in a phrase about the natural flow of commodities. Dryden is preparing for his use of the trade winds topos. It is precisely in terms of commodity flow that mercantilism, the economic strategy which the poem celebrates, was articulated.

The term *mercantilism* was not strictly in use at the time – Adam Smith, for instance, talks about 'the mercantile system' in *The Wealth of Nations* (1776). Mercantilism was intended to overcome the limitations on economic flow imposed by local trading structures in place since the Middle Ages. It established uniform measures and standards, shoring up the monarch's powerful role in trade. It provided protection in moments of oversupply which might otherwise lead to unemployment. It encouraged the augmentation of gold and silver reserves through foreign trade and challenged the landlord's paternalistic support of the labourer.[117] Mercantilism was preoccupied with fitting aristocratic tastes to international business. Sir William Petty (1623–87), a member of the Royal Society who distinguished between money and capital, wrote: 'There is much more to be gained by Manufacture than Husbandry, and by Merchandise than Manufacture.'[118] On the other side of the debate, domestic manufacturers railed against the importation of foreign luxury goods. The Tory economic writer Nicholas Barbon criticised what he saw as an overly grave position in his defence of luxury, *A Discourse of Trade* (1690). Barbon and John Law contributed to the new thinking about demand which followed upon the reconception of England not as a workhouse but as a market, an emergent modern discourse: 'An economy contained within the limits of supply slowly became attuned to the peculiarities of demand.'[119] A rhetorical register of effeminacy, inherited from Plato and the Stoics, underpinned the critique of luxury: spices, amongst other things, would emasculate the *res publica*. By contrast, the mercantilists were part of a nascent discourse of economics that did not reject but rather revised the language of frugality and industry while neutralising the moral taint of luxury.[120]

Mercantilist discourse was debated in such journals as Defoe's *Mercator* (1713–14), Richard Steele's *Guardian* and the Earl of Halifax, Charles Montague's *British Merchant* (1713–14). The market for luxury goods could be used as a tax resource, such as when Sir Robert Howard levied a special excise duty on spices, linen and other goods in 1670. Mercantilism relied on the emergent discourses of natural law and the balance of trade championed by such writers as Thomas Mun (1571–1641), a director of the East India Company whose *England's Treasure by Foreign Trade* (1622) was not published until 1664. The influence of London grew considerably because of the power of mercantilism. The torch of mercantilism was passed from Cromwell to George Downing after the Restoration; Charles II made very little personal effort towards its success.

Literature that celebrated mercantilism, and the transnational flows that sustained it, differed from that which celebrated domestic production, though the differences can be exaggerated. John Dyer's

The Fleece (1757) is, though domestic, a poem of the remorselessly global and general. Dryden seems to differ from Mun in his poetically expressed concern for goods over bullion. But his representation of the spice trade was also a sensuous representation of the flow of currency into Britannia's arms. The second stanza of *Annus Mirabilis* overcodes the English Channel and the circulation of the blood in an image of the stoppage of free-flowing trade:

> Trade, which like bloud should circularly flow,
> Stop'd in their Channels, found its freedom lost:
> Thither the wealth of all the world did go,
> And seem'd but shipwrack'd on so base a Coast. (5–8)

The obstructions of the Dutch are figured as unhealthy, as Dryden draws upon natural law notions about economics. Hugo Grotius (1583–1645) construed the winds as given by God for human advantage in exploration and trade.[121] Dryden's position in the third and fourth stanzas resembles Grotius'. In the fourth stanza, the sun and tides bring the Dutch home safely:

> The Sun but seem'd the Lab'rer of their Year;
> Each wexing Moon suppli'd her watry store,
> To swell those Tides, which from the Line did bear
> Their brim-full Vessels to the *Belg'an* shore. (13–16)

Stanza three makes the environment curiously active in its being-for Holland:

> For them [the Dutch] alone the Heav'ns had kindly heat,
> In Eastern Quarries ripening precious Dew:
> For them the *Idumæan* Balm did sweat,
> And in hot *Ceilon* Spicy Forrests grew. (9–12)

At the time the poem was published, the merchants and rural gentry were confident that defeating the Dutch navy would 'open trade routes and return lucrative trade to England'.[122] Capitalism is described as the ambient effect of a beneficent world.

The commodities circulated in trade are figured as fixed raw material, vulnerable to plunder as simple as the plucking of Eden's forbidden fruit. The East Indies are a zone 'Where wealth, like fruit on precipices, grew, / Not to be gather'd but by Birds of Prey' (43–4). The dialectic between restriction and flow is here expressed in combative terms that bring to mind Montaigne's maxim about one man's profit being another man's damage: a zero sum game. The large structure of the poem gradually accumulates, hardens and fixes spice in place within the processes of imperialism. The early contemplation of trade's fluidity, mediated through natural law theory, was only a gambit to get the figurative movement started. Flow is justifiable only if it is in a certain direction, towards a certain territory. London becomes the territory into which the flows of spice, perfume and porcelain are concentrated: an emporium of luxury.[123] It is imagined as the final resting-place of 'The vent'rous Merchant' (1197), a happy play on words which suggests both adventure, the 'venting' of trade, and the Merchant Adventurers' Company. Stanza 298 celebrates the 'silver Thames' (1189), a revision of Spenser which was in turn revised by Blake, in 'London', whose early draft contemplated the 'dirty Thames' and later the 'charter'd Thames' (2).[124] (Later still it was revised by T. S. Eliot in *The Waste Land*, the third part of which deals with trade.) Dryden's Thames is a veritable 'domestick Floud' of prosperity (1189). The final stanza proclaims 'Thus to the Eastern wealth through storms we go' (1213), figuring trade as better for profit than sheer piracy. The free trade of Grotius's *Mare liberum* has become the imperial *pax Britannica* of a 'British Ocean':

> And, while this fam'd Emporium we prepare,
> The *British* Ocean shall such triumphs boast,
> That those who now disdain our Trade to share,
> Shall rob like Pyrats on our wealthy Coast. (1205–8)

The final two lines again echo the providentialism of Grotius:[125] 'A constant Trade-wind will securely blow, / And gently lay us on the Spicy shore' (1215–16).

Dryden employed the market as a metaphor for the relatively free contact of enfranchised subjects.[126] The poem can be construed as a market bringing together, in Edmund Burke's words, 'consumer' and 'producer'. In terms of the poetics of spice, the 'producer' is more a conjurer, an entrepreneur: there is no sense of the labourer. The market was an emerging public institution. For Jürgen Habermas this public sphere, emerging from the coffee house/stock exchange culture of Dryden's era, becomes part of a myth of an ideal meeting place for ideas about trade and for trading ideas. In Centlivre's *A Bold Stroke for a Wife*, a scene takes place in Jonathan's Coffee House involving trading in the South Sea Company. A coffee boy offers fresh coffee and tea all the while (IV.i). In such a sphere, panegyrics might play the role of anchor.

The notion of trade as a civilising process was refigured in the Romantic period. Trevenen celebrates commerce in her poem on tea in *Little Derwent's Breakfast*:

> And this is the *commerce* of which you will read,
> For which we must wish our merchants 'good speed',
> Whereby different lands an exchange may fulfill,
> And all may be gainers – in peace and good-will.[127]

The 'exchange' of goods is made to imply an exchange of cultures. The model is mercantile: an exact and equal exchange takes place, as if culture were a marketplace of ideas. This is not a zero-sum game: 'all may be gainers', despite the specific instance of tea being traded for opium to the detriment of the Chinese. The idea of turning a profit is erased. The sly 'of which you will read' anticipates the child's insertion into capitalist ideology: little Derwent will grow up to read Adam Smith and Ricardo (or just the newspapers). It also anticipates and patronisingly deflates any possible objections to that ideology: 'this is the real meaning of that funny word you will encounter in our society'. 'We must wish our merchants "good speed"' in their task because no alternative is thinkable. The finality of Trevenen's rhetoric is a symptom of the poem's existence at the height of British imperialism.

Blackmore and Thomson

The emerging market culture gave rise, after Dryden's death, to numerous experiments in the literary figuration of trade, providence and nation. Queen Anne's physician Sir Richard Blackmore (d. 1729) published *Creation* in 1712; it was later praised by Dr Johnson. It employs the trade winds topos to augment the power of the Creator and the providential place of the consumer. The world is imagined as a theatre, developing a figure employed in early modern cartography: the *theatrum orbis terrarum*. Contemporary theatres employed devices that sprayed the audience with fragrance.

Blackmore's didactic poem declares itself as of the highest genre, with the Holy Ghost as its muse.[128] While accepting recent scientific paradigms such as those of Gabriel Harvey, the poem is anti-Lucretian and anti-Epicurean, and specifically criticises Hobbes and Spinoza.[129] It thus falls into the filial mode of the representation of spice. The sensuality of spice is a demonstration of God's providence, that the world is not just a random concatenation of atoms. Blackmore seeks to imagine the full body of the earth, God's theatre, unfolding according to a divine dynamics. There is no room for the unstable trope or Lucretian *clinamen* that brings a merchant, or Satan, round the Cape of Good Hope. Nevertheless, tropology is here, magnificently folded into the poem's baroque design. There is no inherent contradiction between socioeconomic realities and figurative language, as a post-Enlightenment reader may misperceive. Hegel remarks that the Enlightenment exuded a perfume that could not help being absorbed by the most theological of noses.[130] In a similar fashion, capitalism and the growth of secular science do not merely warp the poem out of its true shape. They are its very armature: a dynamic, evolving and revolving structure.

The evolutionary figures suggest that God is unnecessary, so attractive is Blackmore's representation of self-determining flows. To forestall this reading, the poem presents a counter-Lucretian flux, using recent scientific observations about the digestive system and the growth of the embryo for the purposes of theodicy. It trickles with winds, waters, seasons, blood and magnetism, all for God's greater glory. The spontaneous flow of the winds and the trade which they bear indicates the workings of providence. The flows unfurl in a vivid spectacle and smell, as in a theatre of wonders, comes from some divine source. It is a masque of commerce, a baroque panegyric to trade. Blackmore oscillates between the terrestrial and the cosmic, between commerce and crown. Just as the Royalist court cook William Rabisha had opened up the animal body for Royalist display in *The Whole Body of Cookery Dissected* (1675), so Blackmore opens up the earth, as well as the human stomach and embryo.

'We ask you whence these constant motions flow':[131] in throwing Lucretian atomism into doubt, Blackmore describes a series of flows that should be comprised of atoms that move more slowly than he allows. If it were not for God, water would engulf the world.[132] The *ne plus ultra* of the rapid flows which Blackmore observes is found in the odoriferous plants:

> Light exhalations, that from earth arise
> Attracted by the Sun-Beams thro' the Skies,
> Which the mysterious Seeds of Thunder bear,
> Of Winds, and all the Meteors of the Air,
> Tho' they around us take their constant Flight,

Their little Size escapes the sharpest Sight.
The fragrant Vapours breath'd from rich Perfumes,
From *Indian* Spice, and *Arabian* Gums,
Tho' many Years they flow, will scarce abate
The Odoriferous Body's Bulk of Weight.[133]

Chance troping or *clinamen* of particles is overruled in favour of a mysterious divine flow. This naturalises trade, making it as easy and providential as the breeze bringing the merchant ships to Britain:

Ye *Britons*, who the Fruit of Commerce find,
How is your Isle like a Debtor to the Wind,
Which thither wafts *Arabia*'s fragrant Spoils,
Gemms [*sic*], Pearls and Spices from the *Indian* Isles,
From *Persia* Silks, Wines from *Iberia*'s Shore,
Peruvian Drugs, and *Guinea*'s Golden Oar?
Delights and Wealth to fair *Augusta* flow
From ev'ry Region whence the Winds can blow.[134]

Blatantly colonial luxury is celebrated, with a touch of ostentatious violence in 'spoils'.[135] The acquisitive narrator roves rapidly over a global chart. The merchant is proclaimed in tune with the 'Rise' and 'Fall' of the day, the tides and the winds, exploiting nature 'to mutual Gain'.[136] The section on the seasons describes winter and spring as respectively stopping and starting the flows of life; autumn is the season in which nature is transformed into culture through the harvest or the vintage. Summer, meanwhile, is the season for the consumption of natural riches – much sweat, but no labour:

Th' austere and ponderous Juices they sublime,
Make them ascend the porous Soil, and climb
The Orange-Tree, the Citron, and the Lime:
Which drunk in Plenty by the thirsty Root,
Break forth in painted Flow'rs, and golden Fruit.
They explicate the Leaves, and ripen Food
For the Silk-Labourers of the Mulberry Wood:
And the sweet Liquor on the Cane bestow,
From which prepar'd the luscious Sugars flow;
With generous Juice enrich the spreading Vine,
And in the Grape digest the sprightly Wine.
The fragrant Trees, which grow by *Indian* Floods,
And in *Arabia*'s aromatic Woods,
Owe all their Spices to the Summer's Heat,
Their gummy Tears, and odoriferous Sweat.
Now the bright Sun compacts the precious Stone,
Imparting radiant Lustre, like his own:

He tinctures Rubies with their Rosie Hue,
And on the Saphire [*sic*] spreads a heav'nly Blue;
For the proud Monarch's dazling [*sic*] Crown prepares
Rich orient Pearl, and Adamantine Stars.[137]

The tears of gum and sweating spice recall Milton's Terrestrial Paradise, and the aromatic woods are reminiscent of Diodorus Siculus. The heat of summer works like the *fors formativa* which Aristotle describes as directing the development of the embryo, a masculine force that unfolds matter into form. The luxury of endless, sultry consumption is terminated and territorialised by the hardening of the imagery from liquids to gums to gems on a crown. The rainbow hues of the Middle Eastern fruits and wine, and the lustre of the sugar and spices, modulate into the red, white and blue of monarchist representation in the rubies, sapphires and pearls. That which flows in space is turned into a place, a topos. Tropological trade hardens into a decoration for an enthroned monarchy.

The very flows are architectonic, evidence of God as the divine architect, a metaphor Blackmore might have enjoyed sharing with Harvey. The power of God prevents the spread of a 'licentious . . . Tide' over the land:

Their Bands, tho' slack, no Dissolution fear,
Th' unsever'd Parts the greatest Pressure bear,
Tho' loose, and fit to flow, they still cohere.
This apt, this wise Contexture of the Sea,
Makes it the Ships driv'n by the Winds obey;
Whence hardy Merchants Sail from Shoar to Shoar,
Bring *India*'s Spices Home, and *Guinea*'s Oar.[138]

The sea itself enjoys the benefits of condiments: God has 'Season'd all the Sea' with salt to stop its 'Stores' from stagnating.[139] In an atheistic Commonwealth, the law would be challenged and the 'correct' channels undermined. Society is imagined as a complex process of consumption in which the 'Exorbitant Thirst' of princes must be checked, lest they strive too eagerly for power.[140] The channels that direct the flow of consumer goods aright are not hard enough to be despotic, but are not entirely soft either.

In the seventh book Blackmore sees fit ironically to order a spicy Epicurean feast to make the reader feel guilty about luxury consumption.[141] Commerce, however, is consistently praised. Blackmore justifies a providential mercantilism to a restored monarchy: he must thus lay luxury on thickly, but not too thickly. Otherwise the

Lucretian argument would hold: 'The Glebe untill'd might plenteous Groves have born, / And brought forth spicy Groves instead of Thorn.'[142] 'Industry' has its rewards over 'Luxury'.[143] The conclusion exhorts the whole of nature to praise God. Fish, lions, thunder, sea monsters, hail, rain, meteors, the cedar and the pine are called upon, and finally, before man, Blackmore asks: 'Let every spicy odoriferous Tree / Present its Incense, and its Balm to Thee.'[144] God stands in the place of the monarch: He is the ultimate consumer. A consumer society is being legitimised in verse.

James Thomson (1700–48) distinguishes the poetic muse from the process of commerce and 'the purple tyranny of Rome' in *Summer* (747–83), which formed part of his cycle *The Seasons* (1726–30).[145] The Old World and the New World are described as aggressive wildernesses (898–938). The muse returns again, however, in the description of gold, flowing 'virgin' from a 'disembowelled earth' (769). The parallel with Caesarean birth is significant here given Thomson's criticism of the 'purple tyranny of Rome'. Africans and Indians, states Thomson, are incapable of enjoying, or putting to good use, the fruits of their luxurious lands, and so the British may have to do that in their place:

> But what avails this wondrous Waste of Wealth?
> This gay Profusion of luxurious Bliss?
> This Pomp of Nature? what their balmy Meads,
> Their powerful herbs, and *Ceres* void of Pain?
>
> By vagrant Birds dispers'd, and wafting Winds,
> What their unplanted Fruits? What the cool Draughts,
> Th' ambrosial Food, rich Gums, and spicy Health
> Their Forests yield?
> . . .
> what avail their fatal Treasures, hid
> Deep in the Bowels of the pitying Earth
> . . .
> Ill-fated Race! (860–75)

Winds are present here, but not those of trade. They scatter the products of an unspoilt Paradise before they can be put to profitable use. The 'wondrous waste of wealth' signifies our continued presence in the Miltonic space of Eden. But the wilderness of sweets has been modified. It is not a place where healthy toil will tame the profusion, but an untapped wellspring of instant economic benefit. Spice becomes both food and medicine, but the adjectives 'ambrosial . . .

rich . . . spicy' suggest a superior level of luxurious consumption. This unexploited *pharmakon* is left alone because the inhabitants of the regions in question have no knowledge of peace, piety, temperance, logic, science or equality. These terms derive poetically from the sober temperance of Milton's representations of the ideal eater and/or thinker. In a line that seems to justify the human intervention of the slave trade, the 'Parent-Sun himself' is depicted as a tyrant 'o'er this world of slaves' (884–5), which exists without 'Love' (890) or 'sweet Humanity' (893). A qualified imperialism is justified. Commerce and the muse mine for economic and aesthetic profit what are construed as natural resources. In *Eighteen Hundred and Eleven*, Anna Letitia Barbauld (1743–1825) records the history of progress in Thomsonian fashion, describing the benefits of commerce: 'commerce spreads her sail / And wealth is wafted in each shifting gale' (273–4).

The naturalising of imperial expansion is chilling. Britain's designs on the world become descriptions of things as they are – 'Ill-fated Race!' The twentieth-century search for drugs among the shamans of remote indigenous peoples continues this cornucopian rhetoric. In a sadistic mode, the oneiric horizon is viewed as *needing* to be violated. It is against this rhetoric that Romanticism evolved its proto-ecological discourse of the wilderness. Romanticism revealed a wilderness within, a revision of Milton's internalising of Paradise. However, this wilderness itself relied on some notion of surplus consumption, free time, even when this was heavily naturalised in Rousseau, Charlotte Smith and Wordsworth, or by Percy Shelley's vegetarian rhetoric. Thus colonialism could become a subjective mode – a way of consuming oneself. In an ironic twist, then, there is a continuity between Thomson and Keats.

Darwin

As the eighteenth century continued, natural history became one of the corollary discourses through which trade was figured. The botanist Erasmus Darwin (1731–1802), the grandfather of Charles, was a liberal and an early theorist of evolution. A spoof attributed to him in the form of a letter to Thomas Beddoes, entitled *The Golden Age*, included the image of plants providing butter, an idea no longer ridiculous in the wake of margarine. Darwin's didactic *The Loves of the Plants* (first published 1789), the second part of *The Botanic Garden* (the complete poem was published 1790–1), was parodied in the *Anti-Jacobin* as 'Loves of the Triangles' by Canning and Frere. It was a treatise on natural philosophy, history and botany, its second part developing an erotic conceit of plant reproduction. *The Economy of Vegetation*, the poem's first part, had at its first printing at least five plates engraved by Blake.

In the spirit of abolitionism, *The Botanic Garden* contains a passage on anti-slavery in *The Economy of Vegetation* (I.ii.421–30). Trade, however, is not unequivocally criticised, but mediated through the language of natural history and philosophy. The fourth canto includes a long address to the trade winds by the goddess of nature:

> I. SYLPHS! your light troop the tropic Winds confine,
> And guide their streaming arrows to the Line;
> While in warm flood ecliptic breezes rise,
> And sink with wings benumb'd in colder skies.
> YOU bid Monsoons on Indian seas reside,
> And veer, as moves the sun, their airy tide;
> While southern gales o'er western oceans roll,
> And Eurus steals his ice-winds from the Pole.
> YOUR playful trains, on sultry islands born,
> Turn on fantastic toe at eve and morn;
> With soft susurrant voice alternate sweep
> Earth's green pavilions and encircling deep,
> OR in itinerant cohorts, borne sublime
> On tides of ether, float from clime to clime;
> O'er waving Autumn bend your airy ring,
> Or waft the fragrant bosom of the Spring. (I.iv.9–24)

Many phrases evoke tropological play, embodied in the sylphs: the 'streaming arrows', the way the sylphs 'veer' the tide (a trope is literally a veering), their 'playful trains' and 'fantastic toe' and the 'bending' of the 'airy ring'. The fragrance of spring, if not of spice, is represented. Islands and breezes appear, while trade ships are conspicuous by their absence. The eroticism of the islands and India is strongly achieved through the alliterative 'soft susurrant . . . sweep' and the connotations of 'playful' and 'sultry'. The susurration associates ambient sound with spice. The mystificatory mechanics of the sylphs, figures derived from Pope's *The Rape of the Lock* (1714), further eroticises the passage. They perform actions comparable to their assistance at the toilet of Pope's protagonist, Belinda: the earth, in fact, becomes a sort of Belinda writ large. Drugs and spices are displayed in a glamorous profusion of identities. *The Loves of the Plants* describes balm as 'adored' by knights and squires at her 'fragrant altar' (II.i.59–60); turmeric is cold, shy and virginal (II.i.65–8); the poppy is predictably heavy-lidded, enjoying the luxury of a silken sofa (II.ii.267–76), and 'fair CANNABIS' walks lazily up a beach, trailing a dishevelled distaff (II.iv.111–12).

Following a frequent topical juxtaposition, the Occident is praised over the Orient towards the end of the canto. From Milton to Charlotte Smith and Percy Shelley, pastoral England appears right next to the exotic East. This suggests an increasing poetic sensitivity to global trade as we approach the Romantic period. 'Britain's happier clime' (I.iv.582) is admired for its roses and oaks. The beneficent flow of spices towards Britannia's coffers and plates, and its apothecaries, ends in the ambient tinting of terrestrial space:

> XV. SYLPHS! who, round earth on purple pinions borne,
> Attend the radiant chariot of the morn;
> Lend the gay hours along the ethereal hight [*sic*],
> And on each dun meridian shower the light;
> SYLPHS! who from realms of equatorial day
> To climes, that shudder in the polar ray,
> From zone to zone pursue on shifting wing,
> The bright perennial journey of the spring;
> Bring my rich Balms from Mecca's hallow'd glades,
> Sweet flowers, that glitter in Arabia's shades;
> Fruits, whose fair forms in bright succession glow
> Gilding the Banks of Arno, or of Po;
> Each leaf, whose fragrant steam with ruby lip
> Gay China's nymphs from pictur'd vases sip;
> Each spicy rind, which sultry India boasts,
> Scenting the night-air round her breezy coasts;
> Roots whose bold stems in bleak Siberia blow,
> And gem with many a tint the eternal snow;
> Barks, whose broad umbrage high in ether waves
> O'er Ande's [*sic*] steeps, and hides his golden caves;
> – And, where yon oak extends his dusky shoots
> Wide o'er the rill, that bubbles from his roots;
> Beneath whose arms, protected from the storm
> A turf-built altar rears it's [*sic*] rustic form;
> SYLPHS! with religious hands fresh garlands twine,
> And deck with lavish pomp HYGEIA's shrine. (I.iv.587–612)

The ease with which the heroic couplets carry their phrases to the reader, an ease which was criticised by Leigh Hunt for its dullness in *The Feast of the Poets* (1815), is an analogy for the goods and benefits of earth flowing easily towards Britain. Hygeia, the goddess of health, then blesses 'BRITANNIA's throne' (623) with the caduceus, the serpent wand of medicine. Spice is part of a figurative sequence of medical products, but they are described through the language of luxury trade – another *pharmakon*. Expensive china is used for sipping tea, Arabia's flowers glow like the jewels of Ormuz in *Paradise Lost*, and the roots tint the Siberian snow like gems; the tea is drunk not from cups but from decorative 'vases'. Beth Kowaleski-Wallace has explored the '"china fever"' spreading at this time throughout England, in which 'China came to figure . . . in the British popular imagination as an exotic, luxurious landscape'.[146] It is hard to tell whether we are looking at sipping nymphs or a picture of nymphs sipping. Luxury consumption is associated with the power of signs. India, like the islands earlier in the canto, is 'sultry'. The international sweep of the writing is curtailed by the em dash, which relocates readers in Britain while they watch a primitive sacrifice.

The oak and the rill are Britain's version of the tree that weeps medicinable gum in *Othello*. Yet even in their bubbling enjoyment they represent an English paternalism that affords protection rather than the despotism of the cedar, commonly used to figure oriental power. The oak frequently stands for Englishness, national unity and the values of 1688. In the Romantic period, the reinvention of nature heightened the political significance of trees. Wordsworth's 'The Haunted Tree' establishes the possibility of comparing the Prince Regent with an oriental despot, through the iconography of oaks in Cowper, Burke, Price, Payne Knight and Southey. The poem makes two subtle references to matters associated with luxury trade. The oak, beautiful as anything fashioned by art, is an 'eastern Sultan, amid flowers enwrought / On silken tissue' (12–13). And though the wind might have revealed a trapped, feminised suffering pent like a Hamadryad within the safety of the tree, now 'Not even a Zephyr stirs' (32).[147] The trees come to represent the aristocracy's consumption of luxury goods.[148]

Darwin's oak and its rill are the first natural objects in thirty lines which have not been cut, packaged, produced, distributed or traded: in short, they are the first whole natural objects. The 'spicy rind' is a double metonymy: it is literally part of a fruit, and stands in for the Indian spice trade. The fragmentation and serialisation of tradable objects significantly locates and then dislocates them from their places of origin: trade is *différance*. The fruits whose 'fair forms in bright succession grow' are in a series of substitutable commodities such as the leaves sipped from the china 'vases'. The suppressed term in the last metonymy is, perhaps surprisingly, the drink of tea itself: it is as if the very leaves are becoming steam. Spice as pulverised dust is at the zero degree of materiality; it is about to turn into pure money. It represents not just gem-like colour and erotic perfume, but flow and liquidity as well. It is a form of sexy money.

Anti-capitalism

The later eighteenth century also witnessed an expansion of discourses against long-distance capitalism. In the middle of the third canto of *The Loves of the Plants*, Darwin comments on the environmental devastation caused by the Javan Upas or Poison Tree:

> Where seas of glass with gay reflections smile
> Round the green coasts of Java's palmy isle;
> A spacious plain extends its upland scene,
> Rocks rise on rocks, and fountains gush between;
> Soft zephyrs blow, eternal summers reign,
> And showers prolific bless the soil, – in vain!
> – No spicy nutmeg scents the vernal gales,
> Nor towering plaintain [*sic*] shades the mid-day vales;
> No grassy mantle hides the sable hills,
> No flowery chaplet crowns the trickling rills
> . . .
> Fierce in dread silence on the blasted heath
> Fell UPAS sits, the HYDRA-TREE of death. (II.iii.219–38)

Despite its decline in status as a luxury commodity, nutmeg is still imaged as a delicious aspect of a Terrestrial Paradise, an eternal season where zephyrs, the harbingers of spring, blow, and the spice makes the gales fragrant in their 'vernal' beauty; 'eternal summers' may simply be an unfortunate debt to correct scansion. But the 'blasted heath', an allusion to *Macbeth*, reconfigures the Edenic island as a space of death, in a grotesque juxtaposition of Shakespeare's Scottish landscape with the East Indies. The spice trade features as the Other of *Macbeth*'s bleakness in the play itself, when in I.iii one of the Witches declares: 'Her husband's to Aleppo gone, master o' th' Tiger' (I.iii.7; Aleppo is also mentioned in *Othello* (V.ii.355); and in Hakluyt's roughly contemporary *Voyages and Discoveries*, Ralph Fitch described his voyage in the *Tiger* to the significant trading posts of

Aleppo and Pegu).[149] A similar moment of inversion, juxtaposing the overwhelming spice of the Orient with Scotland, occurs in *A Vision* by the Chartist poet Ebeneezer Elliott (1781–1849):

> Ah, then, in burning climes afar,
> ('Mid stinks of spices, fruits, and tea,
> That turn my nasal soul to thee,)
> Eden of odours! what will be
> The fragrance of thy memory? (23–7)[150]

Thoughts on Scottish nationality are traumatically disrupted by the space of the Other. Scotland becomes Paradise, rather than the Spice Islands.

Just as there is a sliver of the spice trade in the Scottish play, so there is a wedge of *Macbeth* in Darwin's Java. Each one operates as a bizarre anamorphic image, like the elongated, compressed skull in Holbein's painting *The Ambassadors*. The blasted heath in the Spice Island is, like the skull, a *memento mori*. But the spice trade in *Macbeth* is a *memento emporii*, a disruptive shift in the relationship between figure and ground which betrays the anachronism of the play's feudal setting. The blasted heath and tree of death in Darwin, however, points to a weird kind of *reverse anachronism*, hinting at the persistence of a feudal mode of cultural logic, with overtones of original sin and a stark anti-humanism. The spice trade is not always about the fixed present or a fixed place, but about differential relationships between one place and another, one topos and another.

It is strange, then, that in his sophisticated radical allegory *Queen Mab* (1813) Percy Shelley (1792–1822), self-styled poet of anti-capitalism and anti-feudalism, would figure commercial activity as the Upas tree, deriving his image from this section of Darwin's poem. Given that the tree devastates the trade in nutmeg which, along with Java's coffee trade, made the island famous, the irony also has a historical reference point:

> Commerce! beneath whose poison-breathing shade
> No solitary virtue dares to spring,
> But Poverty and Wealth with equal hand
> Scatter their withering curses, and unfold
> The doors of premature and violent death,
> To pining famine and full-fed disease,
> To all that shares the lot of human life,
> Which poisoned, body and soul, scarce drags the chain,
> That lengthens as it goes and clanks behind. (v.44–52)

The images of the poison tree's scattered leaves and the lengthening chain express the sense of evil circulation. Not only all humans but 'all that shares the lot of human life' will be 'poisoned'. Shelley's vegetarian writings, and other sections of *Queen Mab*, also employ the poison tree image.[151] For example, there is the radicalism of another reference to the Upas tree, echoed in *A Vindication of Natural Diet*: 'Let the axe / Strike at the root, the poison-tree will fall,' Shelley declares, finding the cause of war in aggression (*Queen Mab*, IV.82–3).[152] Commerce is a *pharmakon*: it is part of both nature and culture, representing for Shelley a faulty circulation in the social body which is a corruption of its true nature.

Shelley's re-employment of Darwin's topos, however, is further complicated by his featuring of the Spice Islands, with the spice trade removed, within the reimagined Terrestrial Paradise in the utopian eighth section of *Queen Mab*. The logic of poison and cure is figured through the spice trade. Yet it is underpinned by a flow of circulating processes: the wide circle described by the land which the Upas tree poisons, or the circulation of spicy air in the reinvigorated sensorium of the new age.

The Upas tree also appears in Blake's *Songs of Experience* (1794), in 'A Poison Tree', where it symbolises the unfortunate results of repressed anger. Refusing to tell his 'wrath' to his foe, the narrator nurtures his rage, until it becomes objectified and alienated in the world outside his soul. It parodies the tree in the Garden of Eden, as his friend steals towards it in the depths of night, eats its deadly fruit and perishes beneath its shade. The oppressive architecture suggested by the overhanging branches of the tree in Blake's illumination is also hinted at in Shelley's condemnation of commerce's 'poison-breathing shade' (V.44). (The figure of the Upas tree is also found in Eliza Acton's 'Lines': 'Ne'er did the withering Upas shed / More poisonous blights on all' (6–7).[153])

Commerce has been strangely naturalised as poison, a kind of unnatural nature – a *pharmakon*. Nevertheless, to refute the capitalist economy, its discourses had to be partially employed. Shelley's sceptical dialogue, *A Refutation of Deism* (1814), contains a passage about poison. A remarkable piece of devil's advocacy, it imparts the idea that the Christian God could have done things much better. In order to refute the speaker Theosophus' anthropocentric criticism of the injustice of Christianity, and ironically to play into the hands of the atheist reformer, Eusebes says:

> Poisons, earthquakes, disease, war, famine and venemous serpents; slavery and persecution are the consequences of certain causes, which according to human judgment might have been dispensed with an [*sic*; 'in'?] arranging the economy of the globe.[154]

Eusebes means this ironically but Shelley himself cleaved to the idea. The notion of an 'economy of the globe', a homeostatic system of regulated flows, has overwhelmed any final, arbitrating signifier to which it could be referred. The 'economy of nature' was an element of the discourse of natural religion which was developed further in Haeckel's notion of ecology in the nineteenth century. It is no surprise, then, that *A Refutation* uses vegetarian language to clinch its atheist argument about design: organic form does not need a divine author.

The ideal social system would be a 'restricted economy', where what was circulated always returned to its source. The luxurious squandering of energy would be impossible. Shelley paints this economic system as if it were a secular form of Christianity's narratives of Fall and Redemption. Indeed, in his utopia, the lion frolics with the lamb, much as they do in Isaiah 11 and in Milton's Eden (IV.343–4). The redeemed economy is found towards the beginning of *Queen Mab* VIII:

> The habitable earth is full of bliss;
> Those wastes of frozen billows that were hurled
> By everlasting snow-storms round the poles,
> Where matter dared not vegetate or live,
> But ceaseless frost round the vast solitude
> Bounds its broad zone of stillness, are unloosed;
> And fragrant zephyrs there from spicy isles
> Ruffle the placid ocean-deep, that rolls
> Its broad, bright surge to the sloping sand,
> Whose roar is wakened into echoings sweet
> To murmur through the Heaven-breathing groves
> And melodize with man's blest nature there. (VIII.58–69)

The 'echoings sweet' are a further example of the way in which the poetics of spice involves a sense of ambience, here registered as echoes whose sweetness, reciprocally, is almost gustatory. The Miltonic inverted syntax of the first long clause unleashes the very energies of the planet for the service of a utopian, reformed humanity. Shelley characteristically prefers flow over fixity. The metaphors of 'fragrant zephyrs . . . from spicy isles' and the

'Heaven-breathing groves' recall eighteenth-century mercantile panegyrics ('fragrant zephyrs' is an echo of *The Loves of the Plants*, II.313 (II.309 in the 1789 edition)). The earth has literally tilted back on its axis and therefore the flux of the seasons no longer operates, so that the globe is bathed in the warmth of an eternal spring – a radical scientific as well as millenarian hypothesis. The scent of spicy islands and groves is a sign of the providential quality of the subject-position required to smell it. This is a consumerist utopia. For Blackmore, this subject-position is an expensive seat in the theatre that is English global trade; for Shelley, it is the outlook of a reformist citizen. Shelley was aware of a tradition of epics about trade, as a remark in 'A Defence of Poetry' (1821) makes clear: he does not make much of *The Lusiads*' epic status, for like Virgil's work it is too imitative.[155] However, the passage from *Queen Mab* alludes to *The Task* VI by William Cowper, which gives a biblical colour to its vision of 'Scenes of accomplished bliss' (760):

> Thy rams are there,
> Nebaioth, and the flocks of Kedar there;
> The looms of Ormus, and the mines of Ind,
> And Saba's spicy groves, pay tribute there.
> . . .
> Eastern Java there
> Kneels with the native of the farthest west. (VI.804–11)[156]

The mine reappears in the Shelley passage. Science and poetry will sweat in the dark mine and wrest from it the gem of truth with which to decorate a human 'Paradise of peace' (*Queen Mab* VIII.238). In other words, despite his critiques of imperialism, and imperialist poetry, Shelley is indebted to it.

The image of the dark mine and its decoration could be interpreted according to Derrida's work on Kant's notion of the 'parergon' or frame in *The Truth in Painting*. An 'outside' can become an aspect of an 'inside'. Clothing, decorative columns and so forth are examples of the *parergon*. Shelley's image consists of an inside (the mine), an outside (Paradise), and the parergon (the gem). The gem is taken from the inside to decorate the outside, supplementing it in two senses: bringing out something inherent, and ornamenting something on the surface. It is thus a non-Kantian *parergon*, a utopia of work and leisure superimposed, a self-sufficient interiority. This also applies to the spicy sensorium earlier in section VIII. Spice is the ideal unlocatable frame, better than picture frames because spice is also paint, taint, and tincture – the *pharmakon*. It is spectral, paramaterial, both inside and outside the meal which it flavours.

In general, the *parergon* is a useful concept for understanding the ways in which the poetics of spice invokes ideas of flow. This flow is meant to flatter the nostrils from the margins of trade. And the longer the distance the better: as in long-distance trade, the oneiric horizon is poetically more powerful the more it calls to mind imagined lands far from home. It is not just a matter of exoticism but of framing. The exotic appears as an aspect of the domestic, just as Holbein's pictures of exotic trade and consumption frame Sebastian Münster's *Cosmographia*.

However, Shelley was very critical of the spice trade. In his first vegetarian pamphlet, *A Vindication of Natural Diet* (1813), which is adapted from the notes to the very poem I am discussing, Shelley is highly derogatory about spice. The stimulated taste for the exoticised is, for Shelley, just what is wrong with a transnational economy. All that supplementarity is harmful to the moral fibre of the body or the nation. Alan Bewell has recently shown how *The Triumph of Life* depicts the international flow of disease, a topic of great interest in a period marked by epidemics of yellow fever brought about through colonialism.[157] For Shelley, commerce was global poison.

The idea that spice was a dangerously exotic supplement had roots in Plutarch. At the close of the vegetarian note to *Queen Mab*, Shelley shortens a story told in Plutarch's vegetarian prose about a Spartan who brings fish to an inn and asks the innkeeper to prepare it. The innkeeper asks for cheese, vinegar and oil, and the Spartan replies that if he had those, he would not have brought a fish. Plutarch criticises the use of spice as a trophē, a deviation from nature:

> But we are so refined in our blood-letting that we term flesh a supplementary food and then we need 'supplements' for the flesh itself, mixing oil, wine, honey, fish paste, vinegar, with Syrian and Arabian spices, as though we were really embalming a corpse for burial.[158]

Meat-eating is represented as supplementary to a vegetable diet and thus as unnecessary for nutrition. Meat, moreover, is associated with dietary supplements that both disguise death and prepare for it: in using exotic embalming substances, the consumer is embalming the stomach for an early grave. In addition, spice here would be the supplement of a supplement, in a transumptive role that underlines its demoted status as sheer trope without referential stability. Vegetarianism's logic of double supplementarity posits both that meat undermines its centrality by requiring supplements, and that meat itself is an unnecessary supplement. This had both personal and national implications. The discourse of the supplement affected the orientalised flow of spices across the Roman imperial boundary. In *A Vindication*, 'sanguinary national disputes' are created through wars over 'those multitudinous articles of luxury' such as 'spices from India' or wines, dangerously supplemental commodities.[159] The quotation from Plutarch's second essay sketches the progress from slaughtering 'wild' animals to slaughtering 'domestic' ones, like 'the well-behaved sheep', to 'wars' and 'murder' amongst humans themselves, following Plato's reasoning.[160] Although the European 'nation' was constituted in a dialectical relationship with long-distance trade, Shelley insists on nationalism in *A Vindication* despite his figurative support of internationalism in *Queen Mab*.

Shelley here contradicts the founding justifications of long-distance trade. Elizabeth I, Samuel Purchas (1575?–1626) and Thomas Mun all advocated spending England's surplus money abroad on goods such as spices, drugs, silks and calico from the East Indies. For Mun, international trade is 'the very Touchstone of a kingdomes prosperitie'.[161] Mun links individual and national prudence in this matter, employing the same somatic, moral and economic register as Shelley, but to the opposite end. Mun deals with the objection that spices are unnecessary:

> Who is so ignorant in any famous commonwealth, which will not consent to the moderate use of wholsome Drugges and comfortable Spices? Which haue been so much desired in all times, and by so many Nations, not thereby to surfeit, or to please a lickorish taste . . . but rather as things most necessary to preserue their health, and to cure their diseases . . . But if peraduenture it be yet further urged, that diuers Nations liue without the use of Druggs and Spices: the answere is, That either such people know not their vertue, and therefore suffer much by the want of wares so healthfull, or else they are most miserable, being without meanes to obtaine the things which they so much want.[162]

Like Saddam Hussein's biological agents, spices are a dual-use commodity: they may be used for harm or health. It is impossible to imagine an argument more diametrically opposed to Shelley's vegetarian prose. However, there is a contradiction between *Queen Mab*'s spicy isles and Shelley's condemnation of the spice trade elsewhere. What Shelley criticises at the level of content, he emulates on the plane of expression. Indeed, it is precisely in the context of a healthy, reinvigorated earth that spices are rather archaically represented. But Shelley was also part of a tradition that criticised the use of spices as a form of degrading luxury that undermined the individual and national body. In the sixteenth century, the revolutionary Ulrich von Hütten had attacked spices in a similar vein.[163]

In Britain, this tradition was directed against French cooking and the long-distance spice trade in the eighteenth century – in the medical work of George Cheyne and John Arbuthnot, in Joseph Addison's writing on gluttony, and in Steele's and Robert Campbell's praise of simplicity against Continental tastes amongst wealthy town-dwellers.[164] But Shelley still uses language associated with mercantilist defences of long-distance trade, specifically the spice trade. Nor is it the case that he entirely rejected transumptive or self-reflexive rhetoric. In 'Fragments of an Unfinished Drama', set in 'the Indian archipelago' (the Spice Islands?), the Lady, in conversation with the Indian, depicts a strange plant given to her by a spirit in a dream:

> Its shape was such as summer melody
> Of the south wind in spicy vales might give
> To some light cloud bound from the golden dawn
> To fairy isles of evening. (215–18)

Shelley here demonstrates his skill in hyperreal images that invert conventional similes. Instead of an anticipated concretisation of the abstract, his vehicle is something even more evanescent or figural. (Compare the fragment 'Zephyrus the Awakener', 1821: 'Come, thou awakener of the spirit's ocean' (1).) He exploits the utopian register of the oneiric horizon: the lands of spice as the land of dreams and desires, the Hesperides or evening isles (recall the 'Indian isle' in 'The Triumph of Life' (1822; 486)). But he also uses spice in a figure about figurality, and in a positive way. The synaesthesia of sound and light creates an ambience in the figures of vales, dawn and isles, and the content of the simile (the plant) becomes a frame. The image continues by describing how the plant, mirror-like, reflects everything around it. This positive valuation of dizzying tropology might seem unexpected given other aspects of his culinary rhetoric.

Shelley's employment of tropology in this manner indicates that he was aware of the long literary history of spice. Because of his fascination with incestuous love, he urged Mary Shelley to translate

Myrrha by Vittorio Alfieri (1749–1803), the story of Myrrha's incestuous relationship with her father Cinyras, discussed by Ovid in his depiction of the origin of myrrh in *Metamorphoses*. Mary began the translation in September 1818. The story of Myrrha is crucial in the poetics of spice. To embalm a corpse requires myrrh. Ovid's retelling of the myth of Myrrha (*Metamorphoses* x) also concerns the body's persistence in an uncanny state between deaths. The tale of Cinyras and Myrrha is about the legitimation of the woman's body, with its acceptably feminised *jouissance*, a medicinal weeping. Told by Orpheus, famous for bizarre love stories such as the tale of Pygmalion, it evokes, in Dryden's translation (1700), the far-off, orientalised shores of '*Araby*', boasting of 'Cinnamon, and sweet *Amomum* . . . / Her fragrant Flow'rs, her Trees with precious Tears' (15–17). Orpheus describes the incestuous love of Myrrha for her father Cinyras despite offers of marriage from Oriental princes (28–31). Myrrha can neither live nor die without being cursed or damned: thus she prays, 'Nor let me wholly die, nor wholly live' (335). She is therefore rooted into materiality, with thick heavy bark and branches, permanently exuding gum: 'With bitter tears she wept her last Offence; / And still she weeps, nor sheds her Tears in vain' (351–2). She is not quite natural, not quite artificial – not exactly living and not exactly dead. She is like a mummy, the spiced corpse. As a tree she gives birth to Adonis, the hapless lover of Venus whose corpse's blood nourishes the spring.

The contradiction inherent in Shelley's response to spice is symptomatic of his contradictory feelings about capitalism. These feelings are moreover embedded in his vegetarian philosophy. Shelley's vegetarian response to the expenses, expenditures and waste of nascent consumerism is twofold. Vegetarianism is anti-hierarchical: against the kings, priests and monopolies that block the even circulation of (nervous) energy and food in the body and the kingdom. It thus promotes free, unfettered exchange, trade and circulation. The limbs and mind feel lighter and more poor people are fed. On the other hand, vegetarianism is anti-capitalist: it despises the false appearance of paper specie, and the false supplementarity of spices that degrade the body and the boundaries of the nation. Overall, it proposes a modification of capitalism. The still-popular economic argument for vegetarianism was advocated by Shelley: by switching to vegetables 'The monopolizing eater of animal flesh would no longer destroy his constitution [is there a deliberate play on words here?] by devouring an acre at a meal'; 'vegetable matter' would 'if gathered immediately from the bosom of the earth' provide 'ten times the sustenance' than the same food 'consumed in fattening the carcase of an ox'.[165]

Shelley's ambivalence about spice is also seen in the figure of the Witch of Atlas (from the poem of 1820), who is to some extent a cipher for the decoding, deterritorialising power of commercial capitalism, raised to the idealism of what Jerrold Hogle calls 'radical transference', the ability to cross and transmute codes. The Witch's name suggests a book of maps. She travels about the world on a magical boat, ironising the fixed *logoi* of political power and religion. Like Prospero, another idealised colonialist, she controls the elements. She keeps perfumes much as Prospero conjured spirits. Her cave is filled with incense and other scents: 'And odours in a kind of aviary / Of ever-blooming Eden-trees she kept' (169–70) while a Phoenix-like fire burns with 'many a piece / Of sandal wood, rare gums, and cinnamon' (257–8), an image of fluid wealth in which 'Each flame of it is as a precious stone / Dissolved in ever-moving light' (260–1). Her journey down the Nile, a source of spices, is through a scented ambience:

> And down the streams which clove those mountains vast,
> Around their inland islets, and amid
> The panther-peopled forests, whose shade cast
> Darkness and odours (345–8)

On the 'Austral Lake' (428) she sees the star Canopus, in the constellation Argo, which as Frederic Colwell notes is another allusion to the Argonauts.[166] The panther figured in Leigh Hunt's work the year before *The Witch of Atlas* was written.

Percy Shelley was not the only Romantic period anti-capitalist to employ the poetics of spice. Anna Seward's *Colebrook Dale* (written *c.* 1785–90; published 1810) is an elegy for the countryside undergoing industrialisation. It mourns the rupturing of an ecological and literary fantasy realm, even before it assumed its role as a screen against capitalism in Wordsworth's Romantic ecology. The same spirit appears in Seward's sonnet 'To Colebrooke Dale' (written *c.* 1787; published 1799) and Maria Logan's 'Verses on Hearing that an Airy and Pleasant Situation, near a Populous and Commercial Town, was Surrounded with New Buildings' (1793). Seward's *genius loci* must 'Blush, ah, blush' (104) at its 'outraged groves' (105), specifically at the sight of its metal being turned into money. 'Thy metallic veins' are depicted gleaming around the world as if in a macabre dissection:

> [they] are changed in either Ind
> For all they boast, hot Ceylon's breathing spice;
> Peruvian gums; Brazilia's golden ore;
> And odorous gums, which Persia's white-robed seer,
> With warbled orisons, on Ganges' brink
> Kindles, when first his Mithra's living ray
> Purples the orient. (37–43)

This 'traffic rich' (43) is also a matter of exotic spirituality ('warbled orisons, on Ganges' brink'), to be contrasted with the 'good' femininity of the chaste Sabrina (the saviouress in Milton's chaste *Comus*) and the wood-nymphs and Naiads of Colebrook Dale (9, 10, 20). The warbling of the orientalised 'seer' (an amalgam of Hinduism, Islam and Mithraism) is a poetics of spice: a pure flow of signifiers. The disruption of the *genius loci* is metamorphic, the changes wrought by mining compared both with currency exchange and with scientific alchemy:

> So, with intent transmutant, Chemists bruise
> The shrinking leaves and flowers, whose streams saline,
> Congealing swift on the recipient's sides,
> Shoot into crystals. (77–80)

Seward (1742–90), who lived in the Midlands and was familiar with many members of the Lunar Society, was fascinated by the processes she is describing here. The reader's senses are bombarded with precise observation of industrial, scientific and mercantile activity, in contrast with the natural lucidity of the original 'woodwild glens' (5), discreet scenes 'to vulgar eye / Invisible' (13–14). The pungency and flavour of the spice and gums are juxtaposed with the 'thick sulphureous smoke' emitted by the 'ponderous engines' (23–7). The poetics of spice is part of a global circulation of poison corrupting the purity of local places and poetry. This is not true wealth but a supplement, just as the 'warbled orisons' of the exoticised 'seer' are a dangerous supplement to Seward's sentimental poetics, which like Warton's anxiously strives to police feminine, ornamental language by orientalising it.

In Charlotte Smith's *Beachy Head* (1807), the luxuries of the spice trade are denigrated as a metonym for English luxury at large

(36–99).[167] Here Smith appears to be in ideological cahoots with Wordsworth and Percy Shelley in their opposition to luxury. However, Smith re-employs the language of luxury to decorate the celestial phenomena which, she writes, everyone can afford to consume:

> There, transparent gold
> Mingles with ruby tints, and sapphire gleams,
> And colours, such as Nature through her works
> Shews only in the ethereal canopy,
> Thither aspiring Fancy fondly soars. (81–5)

The 'tints' are part of the pharmacological register of the poetics of spice. This re-employment resembles Percy Shelley's adornment of anti-capitalist utopia in *Queen Mab*. The fundamental trope of *Beachy Head* is 'repose' (re-pose): the grafting of one code on to another.[168] The poetics of spice is ideally suited to this, for spice can become a metaphor about metaphor, a trope of translation and trade. In *Imperial Eyes*, Mary Louise Pratt calls this kind of device a 'density of meaning' specific to the discourses of imperialist expansion, in which 'The landscape is represented as extremely rich in material and semantic substance.'[169] It would, however, be better to call it a luxury topos: topically applying a sign for a luxury commodity on to the location, better to invoke the space of flows.

Beachy Head cannot do without a notion of fantasy as a necessary supplement to the Real, as in the thoughts of the agricultural labourer who dreams of the redeemed luxury consumption of bread-fruit in the South Sea Islands (655–71). This is also true of the shifting narrative point of view itself, which hovers above, stands alongside and penetrates into the world it describes, evidently separate from it but also metonymically attached to it. Similarly, the poem cannot give up its addiction to the poetics of spice, which also supplies an evocation of ambient atmosphere. The narrator observes a merchant ship as she gazes towards Portsmouth, metonymically connecting Beachy Head to the realms of spice:

> The ship of commerce richly freighted, makes
> Her slower progress, on her distant voyage,
> Bound to the Orient climates, where the sun
> Matures the spice within its odorous shell,
> And, rivalling the gray worm's filmy toil,
> Bursts from its pod the vegetable down. (42–7)

These remarkable images of shells and wreaths prepare for the folded forms such as the 'bivalves, and inwreathed volutes' the narrator finds on the seashore (380). *Beachy Head* is a Leibnizian, baroque poem of curving, folded space, putting into question relationships between inside and outside, microscopic and macroscopic. The middle voice ('matures', 'bursts') questions the boundary between active and passive. And is the *spice* its shell or its contents? A similar phenomeon is found in the discussion of the transumptive emblem of the Grail in Marc Shell's *Money, Language, and Thought.*[170]

In Mary Shelley's *The Last Man* (1826), the global plague is imagined as a deadly wind, a 'sister of the tornado . . . and the simoom'. Ryland's hypocritically compassionate, Eurocentric view of the plague that eventually engulfs Europe itself, thus deconstructing the relationship between the clean centre and the diseased margins, plays upon the pharmacological status of the Orient:

> Countrymen, fear not! In the still uncultivated wilds of America, what wonder that among its other giant destroyers, Plague should be numbered! It is of old a native of the East . . . Child of the sun, and nursling of the tropics, it would expire in these [northern] climes. It drinks the dark blood of the inhabitant of the south, but it never feasts on the pale-faced Celt. If perchance some stricken Asiatic come among us, plague dies with him, uncommunicated and innoxious. Let us weep for our brethren, though we can never experience their reverse. Let us lament over and assist the children of the garden of the earth. Late we envied their abodes, their spicy groves, fertile plains, and abundant loveliness. But in this mortal life extremes are always matched; the thorn grows with the rose, the poison tree and the cinnamon mingle their boughs. Persia, with its cloth of gold, marble halls, and infinite wealth, is now a tomb . . . The voice of lamentation fills the valley of Cashmere; its dells and woods, its cool fountains, and gardens of roses, are polluted by the dead; in Circassia and Georgia the spirit of beauty weeps over the ruin of its favourite temple – the form of woman.[171]

The Jeremiac disembodied 'voice of lamentation' evokes an ambience – the East is being haunted by itself, by its pharmacological nature. The note implied by 'envied' here is just right: the sexualised body of the East is desired as the space of capitalist fantasy; but the plague has ironically drained this realm of the Other of its significance, thus undermining the phantasmic support of capitalism. In short it has become *too* pharmacological. The mingling boughs threaten to urinate poison all the way back from the capitalist

Imaginary to the Eurocentric Symbolic Order. One is tempted to coin the term *extrapellation*, an inversion of Althusser's notion of 'interpellation' (the way in which we are 'hailed' by ideology), as a definition of what Mary Shelley is doing here, and this is a strategy we will find in Keats and Leigh Hunt, in the following chapter and in the final one.

'Extrapellation', however, is a more subtle strategy than that used by Anna Seward, Percy Shelley and Charlotte Smith. In Percy Shelley and other Romantic period anti-capitalists, spice is refigured as a subjectless substance, the type or species of the alienated human subject: if only we could disalienate ourselves to find what was repressed 'behind' the veil for which spice can be made to stand, as if the parergon were only an epiphenomenal and not a structural feature. The veil here is of appearance, rhetoric, dissembling luxuries of the sign, the aristocracy – or for Percy Shelley the second, fake(r) aristocracy of bankers and other capitalists. Shelley's alternative model of trade in *Queen Mab* depends upon a version of the Christian narrative of redemption. Here the body of the nation is both cancelled, as a hierarchical and despotic configuration of corrupted emblems and practices, and preserved, as a free-floating flux of capitalist providence that knows no proper name (God, king, monopoly) and no boundaries. What has happened, in Shelley's utopian imagination, is the disenclaving of commodities. The sociologists Kopytoff and Gluckman have designated as 'enclaved' those commodities that undergo a 'monopolistic restriction on [their] flow', exemplified by 'Royal monopolies'.[172] The code for this utopian flux is spice, because historically spice has been so strongly attached to monopolistic trading and naming. Despite Shelley's condemnation, spice *can* stand for a benign flux in *Queen Mab* VIII because the fetishised body of the nation, always already undermined by capitalist flows, is no longer at stake in the beneficent future, the 'happy earth' that is the 'reality of heaven' (IX.I). Royalty or realty has simply been replaced by an unlocatable, impersonal version of itself, 'reality'. Utopia is king. Spice in both cases is the Real of Shelley's capitalist Imaginary, while simultaneously standing on the one hand for corrupt 'reality', the false luxury of pseudo-aristocratic consumers and the disfigurations of rhetoric, and on the other hand for a fantasy, an anti-capitalist dream-world. Thus the economy of the gift can be found both in the spontaneous gift of the earth, the scent of the spicy isles, and in the shared meal between child and basilisk which Shelley adapts from Isaiah. The economics of Christianity, with its spontaneous gift of redemption, can be found at the soft heart of Shelley's transformed panegyric to capitalist trade.

Shelley's apparent anti-capitalism is *none other than the capitalist Imaginary itself* in one of its guises. The myth of spontaneous production flowing from an earthly Paradise 'over there' to the grateful mouths and pockets 'over here', the myth of a divine, though fully realised, potlatch (the ritual destruction of wealth) or cornucopia, is embedded in capitalist ideology. It is not just a case of bottom lines, utilitarian 'efficiency', and so forth. Indeed, Shelley's vegetarianism supplies the embodiment of that aspect of capitalist ideology, with its insistence on turning the body into a light, empty, flexible shell of rationality, responsive to the fluid conditions of modernity.

Queen Mab VIII invokes the spectrality and archaism of spice. There is a sense of contrary moments of production united. In the final lines, the work of fabricating, mining and decorating the gems for the Paradise of peace appears to be performed by one person. There is a mythical unity of labour. Shelley here betrays a nostalgia despite his ostensible futurism. His ideological preference is for capitalism without capital, universalism without a general equivalent, ideology without the Real. Žižek has noted these dynamics in the myth of markets without money.[173] Spice, a species of its own genus, is ideal: the spicy smell, far from being a way of particularising the general utopian scene, is a stain of the universal on the landscape of the particular. As in Blackmore, it is part of a capitalist sensorium. Shelley's utopia feels like heaven and smells like money.

CONCLUSION

It is futile to draw a line in the sand to mark the commencement of the modern period or of capitalism through the use of spice in literature. It is possible, however, to delineate shifting emphases in these different registers and processes. The ideologies of popular vegetarianism in the eighteenth century denigrated spice as a non-nutritious and enervating supplement, and as a transnational commodity enervating to the body of the nation. The commonly held assumption that Romantic period writers augment Milton's representation of Satan can be supported, but not just because of Satan's language of interiority ('my self am hell', IV.75; c.f. I.254–5, IV.18–23). It is also because of the language associating him with mercantile activity. However, the poetics of spice in the eighteenth century newly legitimated luxury. Moreover, the Romantic period witnessed the birth of self-reflexive consumer subjectivity. Thus Shelley's utopian world is able to smell itself. Milton's Satan was a template for this self-reflexive consciousness.

The trade winds topos naturalised trade by showing how the earth was providentially available for the pursuit of trade. Related topoi construed a planet upon which the scattered limbs of humanity could be knitted together by trade. In the preface to the 1598 edition of *Voyages and Discoveries*, Hakluyt declared his intention to 'incorporate into one body the torn and scattered limbs' of English trading narratives.[174] This process of knitting resembles Queen Elizabeth's proclamation about trade in her letter to the king of Sumatra (1600), the document that marked the foundation of the East India Company:

> The eternall God, of his diuine knowledge and prouidence, hath so disposed his blessings, and good things of his Creation, for the use and nourishment of Mankind . . . that notwithstanding they growe in diuers Kingdomes, and Regions of the World: yet, by the industrie of Man . . . they are dispersed into the most remote places of the universall World. To the end, that euen therein may appeare unto all Nations his maruelous workes, hee hauing so ordained, that the one land may haue need of the other. And thereby, not only breed intercourse and exchange of their Merchandise and Fruits, which doe superabound in some Countries, and want in others: but also ingender loue, and friendship betwixt all men, a thing naturally diuine.[175]

Queen Elizabeth invokes a common monotheism shared by Christianity and Islam. The dispersal of riches after the Fall necessitates global trade to repair lapsarian damage; all countries are defective and displaced. Purchas rewrites this justification of trade very early in *Purchas his Pilgrimes* (1625), aiming for the intermixing of states as bodies, so that 'the Superfluitie of one Countrey, should supply the necessaries of another . . . that thus the whole World might bee as one Body of mankind, the Nations as so many members, the superabundance in each, concocted, distributed, retained or expelled by merchandising (as by the Naturall bodily Offices and Faculties in nourishment)'.[176] England, naturally, appears to be rather better for the Sumatrans in this matter than Spain or Portugal. This troping of trade continued in the eighteenth century. In *The London Merchant* (1731), George Lillo remarked that trade 'has promoted humanity . . . diffusing mutual love from pole to pole'.[177] Lillo's diction is strikingly similar to Percy Shelley's, writing eighty years later. Despite local political differences, a rhetorical register concerning free trade persisted, which could be named *antisparagmos*: a drive against the fragmentation of the global body of mankind. In this context the floating islands could be viewed as partial objects which *antisparagmos* attempts to knit together, fragmented body parts which the anxious European tries to master. Fledgling capitalism draws on royal and religious discourses to describe itself.

The role of a rhetoric about nature increased as mercantilism declined and *laissez-faire* capitalism grew in influence, coupled with the rise of imperialism. What seemed free to the spectators of the globe's theatre was highly coercive for its actors in the Spice Islands. While Darwin and Shelley wrote, books appeared on the natural history of the islands, and of the West Indies. They smoothed over 200 years of environmental and social alteration and control with exquisite illustrations of flora and fauna. The genre of the natural history of the East and West Indies could be used subversively, such as in John Stedman's magisterial narrative about the slave uprisings in Surinam. Charles Lockyer's *An Account of the Trade in India* (1711) is not just a book about how to trade but an ideological statement that, in defence of the East India Company, situates trade in nature. Darwin and Shelley employed these new figures. Yet, however natural the islands now begin to seem, they are ultimately the source of the same commodities, and are described as such, just as in the work of Tavernier, who names '*Bantam*, whence comes our Musk'.[178]

Outlines of the Globe (1798–1800) by the naturalist and traveller Thomas Pennant (1726–98) contains botanical and proto-anthropological information about the East Indies, with literary quotations from *The Lusiads*. Pennant, a fellow of the Royal Society (1767), had a high standing in natural history. In the fourth volume, entitled 'The View of the Malayan Isles, New Holland [New Guinea], and the Spicy Islands', Pennant provides a natural explanation of the myth of the Phoenix, whose life and death is intertwined with spice, in the Bird of Paradise, a native of the Molucca islands.[179] He also pays respect to George Everard Rumphius (born 1627), who left the University of Hanover to become the botanist of Amboyna.[180]

The travel narratives of merchants such as Jean Baptiste Tavernier (acknowledged by Pennant[181]) which in their turn had supplanted tales of wonder, had given way to natural-historical accounts, which made less of the perceived superstitions of the Islamic cultures of the islands. These phenomena should alert us to the impossibility of accounting for the persistence of the spice trade in English literature as the effect of a superstructural lag. What was really going on was a development of the poetics of spice in new contexts such as the growth of commercial capitalism and the rise of a consumer society.

The trade winds topos is a form of advertising language. It encourages the pleasurable consumption not only of images of delicious food, but also of images of commercial activity itself. This is one sense in which its poetics is related to various political agenda associated with capitalism. The aesthetics of spice is not static, to use the terminology of Stephen Dedalus in Joyce's *A Portrait of the Artist*, but kinetic: it uses turns of phrase to advert our gaze. Dryden's rhetoric of spice is most clearly designed to fulfil this mission. Percy Shelley's vegetarian rhetoric is ostensibly opposed to this capitalist poetics: it is aversive, rather than advertising, designed to turn the head away.

As Jennifer Wicke says, however: 'advertising does not serve as a simple messenger-boy of ideology, if only because ideology does not exist in some place apart before it is channelled through advertisement. The richness of advertisement as a cultural structure . . . ensures that [it] will not, and cannot, wither away.'[182] The poetics of spice resembles the rhetoric of advertising in its use of the commodity form to talk about erotic taboos. Both are interested in phantasmatic rather than calculative processes. Ravishing tints let the genie of desire loose from its bottle.[183] The trade winds topos, like advertising, is 'self-referential and excessive', for it 'relates . . . the ongoing surplus, the extra that must be deployed in aesthetic form to reveal itself within the social world as a surplus'.[184] And like advertising, the topos is associated with the discourse of the free gift. Trade is construed not as a circle but as a gift. It is spontaneous, not produced: a gift from the Other.

The Romantic period was populated with writers who employed the idea of the gift. It is no accident that the myth of the gift was still available to the opium addict Thomas De Quincey (1785–1859). Charles Rzepka has argued that De Quincey used its power to sublimate history into an interiorised narrative of intoxication in which the drug is the true hero.[185] Indeed, this kind of myth of a gift economy was a style of the Romantic period commodity economy itself, otherwise known as the bohemian style as elucidated by Campbell in *The Romantic Ethic and the Spirit of Modern Consumerism*: a form of self-reflexive consumption where the existential 'feel' of the act of consuming is hypostasised, hence the significance of drug taking as the model for this consumer style. Since the poetics of spice was a precedent for this kind of style, it should not be surprising that it is reworked in the bohemian poetics of Romanticism.

Derrida remarks in *Given Time* that the qualities of the gift are annulled by its supplements as soon as it enters into any kind of system of symbolic or economic exchange.[186] Nevertheless, the fantasy of the gift is very powerful. Writers such as Harry Pearson have asserted the impossibility of describing social systems where material and social 'aspects of existence' are not related in a linear way.[187] However, what if the ideology of the free gift *was* significantly involved in commercial capitalism? The cornucopian fantasy of spice, like the idea that there *is* such a thing as a free lunch, is the remark of capitalism.

There is much to do before we can explore further this curious notion of a core of inert, spontaneous enjoyment at the heart of an ideology ostensibly based upon what Blake called 'ratio', or what Weber called the Protestant work ethic: Georges Bataille's notion of 'restricted economy'. It is what Deleuze and Guattari call 'antiproduction', which they name as the core of capitalism, surrounded by the shell of rationalistic, utilitarian notions of production.[188] Cultural historians often call postmodernity a decisive shift away from what they see as rationalistic modernity. But it appears that the world of useless enjoyment has been with us at least since the age that produced the Land of Cockaygne. It is better to say that fully fledged capitalist society heightens and synchronises the ideological tendencies of trade and consumption. There needs to be an examination of how spice is consumed before we can appreciate the antiproductive heart of capitalist ideology, and this is the focus of the following chapter.

CHAPTER 3

Place settings

And still she slept an azure-lidded sleep,
In blanchèd linen, smooth, and lavendered,
While he from forth the closet brought a heap
Of candied apple, quince, and plum, and gourd,
With jellies soother than the creamy curd,
And lucent syrups tinct with cinnamon;
Manna and dates, in argosy transferred
From Fez; and spicèd dainties, every one,
From silken Samarcand to cedared Lebanon.

John Keats, *The Eve of St Agnes* (1819), 262–70

India's spicy strand
Where fancy's queen has wav'd her magic wand,
And dire oppression lifts his iron hand.

Eliza Tonge, 'Written on the Anniversary of William's Preservation from Shipwreck in the Cabalva, July 1819', 13–15

The fundamental Principle of all
Is what ingenious Cooks the Relish call.
. . .
'Poets and Pastry Cooks will be the same,
Since both of them their Images must frame.'

William King, *The Art of Cookery* (1708), pp. 105, 131

INTRODUCTION

Spice 'slowly began to disappear from culinary use' through the eighteenth century at the point at which it became more abundant. Northern European countries such as Germany and Holland continued to use spices: they were a comparatively '"new" luxury'.[1] European consumption overall, however, was not as it was in the Middle Ages, when in the words of Norbert Elias, 'Spices play a major, vegetables a relatively minor role'.[2] The refined consumption of spice was in vogue, not the ostentation that gave rise to the saffron soups mentioned in some medieval cookbooks.[3] Some authors speculate that aristocratic eating habits had filtered down the social scale, resulting in a new fashion for niceties and a disdain of ostentation at the top. Bruno Lauriaux comments on 'the downward diffusion of an aristocratic model of cookery. Starting with pepper, it spread gradually to the use of the other spices among the lower classes until, in the centuries that followed, the French aristocracy would come to abandon spices almost entirely.'[4] Lauriaux's thesis relies too heavily on a notion of emulation: that the lower classes are simply aspiring to the condition of the upper classes in their habits of consumption. This view is opposed by the idea of Romantic consumerism: though similar ingredients were involved, the ways in which they were consumed were different. Moreover, the aristocracy did not so much abandon spices and flavourings as modify their consumption. In Italy, the aristocracy delighted in such confections as jasmine chocolate, whose delicacy matched the ardour of its preparation. Changing patterns of consumption were emerging, rather than the 'downward diffusion' of a single pattern.

We have been looking at the figuration of the spice trade. What happens when the spices end up on a plate, in a poem, in the mouth of the eater or reader? This chapter is about the poetics and politics of consumption. There were two opposing culinary approaches to luxury in the long eighteenth century. The first berated it, condemning it as a feminising vice. The second celebrated the art of culinary display as a form of aesthetics.

The first section, 'Queer tastes', investigates the feminisation of luxury. Running parallel with discourses about trade were discourses of gendering, which played a role in the representation of consumption. Gendering took place against a background of struggle over what to do with an economy of surplus. William Godwin (1756–1836), here a strong influence on Percy Shelley, attacked the idea of surplus in *Political Justice* (1793), declaring that it was undermining liberty: 'If superfluity were banished, the necessity for the greater part of the manual industry of mankind would be superseded . . . Every man would have a frugal yet wholsome diet . . . none would be made torpid with fatigue.'[5] A vegetarian diet, or at least one opposed to luxury, appears to be advocated. The Regent's high living and infamous banquets intensified awareness of the culture of luxury.[6]

The second section, 'Old spice', discusses the notion of the antique, a modern luxury commodity. The third section, 'Apicius and abstinence', investigates two different responses to the culture of luxury: revisions of the work of the Roman cook Apicius and the discourse of vegetarianism. For the long eighteenth century is the age of popular vegetarianism, revolting not only against cruelty to animals but also against the perceived excesses of a commercial capitalist economy, as evidenced in the medical vegetarianism of Antonio Cocchi (translated 1745).[7] Popular vegetarianism was born in a consumer society. But so were other ways of styling one's consumption, as the reading of Keats will show.

The fourth section, 'The *spice* effect', revisits the view of the poetics of spice as ekphrastic. The fifth section, 'Getting stoned, or petrified enjoyment', examines the relationship between the rhetorical effects of *spice* and the rhetorical construction of the body and enjoyment. We have seen how the poetics of spice involves flow. Now we will examine the ways in which the poetics of spice and of luxury consumption often invoke imagery of heaviness and petrifaction. The final section, 'Keats's blancmange, or having your cake and eating it', discusses the culminating and most important text in this chapter. It is a close reading of the thirtieth stanza of Keats's *The Eve of St Agnes* (1819), in which the amorous Porphyro presents an (ultimately unconsumed) dish of spicy desserts to his sleeping beloved, the cloistered Madeline. I demonstrate how Keats was involved in the discourse of luxury: at the core of supposedly sober ideologies of the market lay fantasies of the Land of Cockaygne, a place with which he himself was associated.

QUEER TASTES

Fantasy was significant in the interaction between Tory and Old Whig ideology and the emergent ideologies of the capitalist marketplace in the eighteenth century. Pocock suggests that the 'reality' of a sober marketplace was constructed to conceal the kernel of irrational enjoyment at the heart of commercial capitalist ideology.[8] Markley has observed: 'At the heart of the middle-class myth of managerial expertise lie fantasies of abundance, of the elasticity of use-value, of recasting the aristocratic assumption that the value of labor is less than the wealth it generates.'[9] The poetics of spice played a part in the formation of capitalist ideology, and the *luxuria* with which it was associated was feminised (hence the 'sexist implications' that

Pocock mentions in the 'epistemological foundation' of the market in 'fantasy'). Even as its monetary value declined, the symbolic value of spice and its cognates was used again and the poetics of spice exerted its ghostly power.

The poetics of spice is connected with the sensualisation of the commodity, and conversely with the commodification of sensuality. These issues are related to the construction of gender. Concepts of masculinity, femininity and effeminacy emerged in relation to the commodity form. Discourses of masculinity and femininity have gone through many historical inflections. But Erin Mackie has recently shown how in the early eighteenth century the discourses of fashion tended to construct gender along binary lines not so rigid in the previous century: effeminate dressiness was nonetheless fashionable (*pace* Jonson's remarks in *Timber*) in male attire until the eighteenth century. The evolution of the fop into the man of sentiment is an indication of such feminisation at work. Characters in Restoration drama such as Sir Courtly Nice of the world of *Mundis Fopensis* and the *Fop's Dictionary* (1697) indicate that before the second decade of the eighteenth century, dressiness was not equated with femininity.[10] But in the eighteenth century, new subjective modes of authenticity and internality – Foucault's 'analytic of finitude' – emerged so that by the time of the Romantics, dressing, including the dressing of food, was coded in a gendered way.[11]

The *Tatler* and *Spectator* began to criticise the superficialities of the fashion 'world', including the transnational fashion for flavourings. They denigrated and gendered exotic and luxurious tastes. Steele and Campbell promoted simplicity against the continental tastes enjoyed by wealthy town-dwellers, while Addison and William Cullen fulminated against gluttony.[12] The medieval upper-class mistrust of fruit and vegetables and love of spice had been reversed by the eighteenth century, but this served only to intensify and render more complex the culture of luxury and protestations of simplicity.

In the *Tatler* for 21 March 1710, Steele recites the ideological lineage of beef as a symbol of aristocratic Englishness: 'The Renown'd King *Arthur* is generally looked upon as the first who ever sat down to a whole roasted Ox . . .' and so on. The urban taste for 'Fricacies and Ragousts [*sic*]' has led to the emasculation of 'many great Families', and the models of health are now to be found among 'the meaner Sort of People, or in the wild Gentry, who have been educated among the Woods or Mountains'. The phrase 'wild

Gentry' indicates the growing distance between country and city, nature and artifice. Associated with this distance was an emerging fascination with 'natural' diet. Peter the Wild Boy became a media phenomenon of 1726, a vegetarian brought from the forests of Hanover to the court and lionised as a noble savage. Another preoccupation was the establishment of imaginary national boundaries through discourses of diet. England was the home of natural food, France of artificial.

Steele imagines the highly seasoned food of fashionable France, 'instigations of high Soups, seasoned Sauces, and forced Meats'. These 'false Delicates' oppose 'Nature', excite the appetite and reject 'natural Form' in favour of 'Disguise'. Steele's description of a French meal culminates in a depiction of dessert, a Rabisha-style concoction of ekphrastic brilliance, cold rainbow tints:

> several Pyramids of Candy'd Sweetmeats, that hung like Icicles, with Fruits scattered up and down, and hid in an artificial kind of Frost . . . with a Multitude of Congelations in Jellies of various Colours . . . I could not but smile to see several of [the guests] cooling their Mouths with Lumps of Ice which they had just before been burning with Salts and Peppers.[13]

The language of origins in Steele's encomium to beef should alert us to the ideological bent of this passage, which strives to redefine the nation by positing a threat to its boundary. In culinary terms, this had long been breached, not only during the time of the early seventeenth-century city comedies when the East India Company started, but in those very medieval feasts here hailed as monuments to noble simplicity. What is distinctively *new* is the structure of feeling based on the notion of the *supplement* of nature.

'Nature' has been confected by exorcising what it is not: effeminising urban sophistication and dissimulation, ignoring the healthy rhythms of the gut for the Petrarchan pleasures of ice and fire. The 'unnatural' consumption of too much spice by the wrong people was the leitmotif of eighteenth-century discourses against sauces, ketchup, foreign food, and in the case of vegetarianism, meat itself. Meat for writers such as George Cheyne (1673–1743) and Percy Shelley was a matter not only of barbarous cruelty disguised as refined civilisation, but also of the *over*-refinements of luxury in a society hyperbolically civilised in its excesses. Vegetarianism became more widespread, as evidenced by the publication of recipe books such as *Adam's Luxury, and Eve's Cookery* (1744), which is intended for 'all who would live Cheap, and preserve their Health to old Age; particularly for Farmers and Tradesmen in the Country, who have but small Pieces of Garden Ground, and are willing to make the most of it'.[14] Its employment of spice is sparing.[15]

Leaner, meaner kinds of body-image were being styled to cope with the advances of capitalism. The extreme example of this would surely be the categorisation and experience of anorexia. Cheyne, the vegetarian doctor who frequented literary circles, was one of the first to recommend treatments for this quintessential dis-ease of modernity. Vegetarianism and dieting were suggested for excessive consumers: 'thumb vomits' were supposed to be healthy self-denial. Shelley's *Alastor* (1816), *Prometheus Unbound* (1820) and 'A Defence of Poetry' contain examples of his pervasive figuration of art as hunger and the artist as anorexic. In *Alastor*, the etiolated Poet declares that, as the punishment and fulfilment of his failed quest for the object of desire (a woman visualised in a dream), his 'bloodless limbs shall waste / I' the passing wind' (513–14). Anorexia is here a hypermodern form of final, fatal control over appetite. The new attenuated body images were concerned with sexuality insofar as they restricted the possibilities of *jouissance*.

Tea was also part of the gendering of luxury. In the Romantic period, it was beginning to slip down the social scale. 'Doctors rail at' it in the words of Shelley's verse epistle to Maria Gisborne (1820):

– a china cup that was
What it will never be again, I think, –
A thing from which sweet lips were wont to drink
The liquor doctors rail at – and which I
Will quaff in spite of them – and when we die
We'll toss up who died first of drinking tea,
And cry out, – 'Heads or tails?' where'er we be. (85–91)

Doctor Thomas Trotter (1760–1832), the author of a treatise identifying the disease of alcoholism, criticised tea consumption. Tea was viewed as effeminising a literary middle class: it put them in danger of becoming quasi-aristocratic. Aristocrats are irresponsible about their tastes, said the fantasy. This notion of irresponsibility was intimately connected with feminisation. The injunction to be individual but not too individual closely resembles the injunction to be feminine but not too feminine (otherwise one is hysterical).

The middle class had to suppress the feminine aspects of consumption. For Trotter, the healthy savage is the true aristocrat: he can eat spices, such as pepper in his soup, in a healthy way. Unlike Matthew Arnold's marauding barbarians, this kind of savage is organically connected to his community and environment. Trotter saw modern life, especially for the literate urban middle classes, as enervating. In an economy of surplus, the consumption of luxury goods to sustain flows of capital needs to be policed. With a growing urban sophisticated public enjoying the fruits of colony and empire, luxury was stripped of its negative connotations in Christianity by writers such as Mandeville and Barbon, and given new, equally gendered ones by writers such as Trotter. For luxury had always been *luxuria*, feminised lust.

Myths of a primitive, natural consumer helped to generate the modern notion of supplementarity that is used to define substances such as spice. Evidence that this was not always the case can be found in Bullein's *Bulwarke of Defence.* In the mid-sixteenth century, Bullein declared that shellfish was good only if cooked with sugar, ginger, pepper, butter, onions and wine; otherwise it was windy and phlegmatic; and the same went for unscaled fish, which he saw as positively dangerous unless seasoned.[16] Seasoning here is construed as an integral rather than an epiphenomenal aspect of cookery. Spice had not been captured by concepts of supplementarity: consider the way in which Bullein uses the verb *temper* in describing the action of fenugreek and honey on barley meal, or his stipulation that apples are not good unless baked or roasted with pepper, saffron or mithradatum in milk.[17] This combination is deemed more important than the merely topical effect of apples on smallpox.

There do exist continuities between older and more recent views of luxury, however. This was in part simply because luxury was a feature of the aristocracy's modes of consumption, and the aristocracy had persisted. Pope Innocent III's *De contemptu mundi*, written in the early thirteenth century, condemned not just wine, beer and cider, but also spices and essences, the 'art of cooks' and wealthy European cuisine.[18] The opposition of luxury and necessity implies morally policing the poor's pleasures (luxury being defined as 'stuff you don't need'). Luxury is a kind of contract sacrifice, a potlatch from the gods or the aristocracy, putting the recipients of its meagre traces in a debt relation to those above. The non-religious homily against luxury common in the early modern period contrasts domestic and exotic consumption. Writing on the exemplary habits of the Madagascans in 1640, Walter Hamond declared:

they eat not, but for Necessity, knowing no other sauce than the Lacedemonian sauce, Hunger . . . whilst we in our Diet are so voluptuous, that we even dig our graves with our teeth . . . the whole world being scarse sufficient to make a Bacchanalian sacrifice for that Deity, the Belly: *France, Spain, Italy,* the *Indies,* yea and the *Molluques* must be ransackt, to make sauce for our meat; whilst we impoverish the land, air and water, to inrich a privat Table.[19]

The rhetorical slide from France to the Moluccas is a precedent for Steele's attack on French over-refinement. These arguments resemble the ones used in Percy Shelley's *Vindication* of vegetarianism over 170 years later (and, as in Shelley, their proto-ecological resonance is clear). While 'they' are temperate, 'we' are gluttonous, and our international travels have brought a host of international vices: 'our voluptuous luxury from the Persians and Indians', our ships loaded with '*fomenta luxuriosa,* stirrers up of Pride, luxury and wantonnese'.[20] In the first book of description of his voyages in the East Indies (1598), Linschoten describes how Portuguese women have learnt from the Indians to chew betel with 'whole handfuls of Cloues, Pepper, Ginger, and a baked kind of meat called *Chachunde,* which is mixed and made of all kinds of Spices and hearbes, and such like meates, all to increase their leachery'.[21]

Spice as transumptive metaphor emerged Phoenix-like from the ashes of the medieval and early modern spice trade, as shown in 'Trade Winds'. Against this, writers such as Rousseau and Warton posited a Spartan machismo. As David Simpson has shown, Tobias Smollett's *Humphrey Clinker* was written in opposition to these ideological and semiological effects, Matthew Bramble lamenting the new '"spirit of licentiousness, insolence and faction, that keeps the community in continual ferment, and in time destroys all the distinctions of civil society, so that universal anarchy and uproar must ensue"'.[22]

Remark L in Mandeville's *The Fable of the Bees,* however, had set the tone for a more playful approach to luxury. Mandeville asserts that he is not as concerned as he used to be about the 'effeminating' effects of luxury. After all, Eastern despots resemble ordinary city tradesmen and sailors:

Those that have such dismal Apprehensions of Luxury's enervating and effeminating People, might in *Flanders* and *Spain,* have seen embroider'd Beaux with fine lac'd Shirts and powder'd Wigs, stand as much Fire, and lead up to the Mouth of a Cannon, with as little Concern as it was possible for the most stinking Slovens to have done in their own Hair, tho' it had not been comb'd in a Month.[23]

The lack of concern about death contrasts with the concern for style in Mandeville's witty inversion of stereotypes. The effect is to elevate consumerism to a giddier height, above the realm of 'necessary' consumption to what Bourdieu would call a 'Kantian' form of consumer identity, loftily aloof from such mundane concerns as having a mortal body.

In Centlivre's *The Busie Body*, matrimony is compared with a set meal not spoilt by 'a Dish of Chocolate in the Morning'; 'And how will it sound in a *Chocolate-House*, that Sir *George* rudely pass'd off a Ladies Mask' (I.i.11ff.). The merchant Sir Jealous Traffick argues with his daughter Isabinda about passion: 'Is your Constitution so hot, Mistriss, that it wants cooling, ha? Apply the Virtuous *Spanish* Rules, banish your Tast, and Thoughts of Flesh, feed upon Roots, and quench your Thirst with Water,' to which she replies, 'That, and a close Room, wou'd certainly make me die of the Vapours' (II.ii.24ff.). Sir Jealous counters: 'No, Mistriss, 'tis your High-fed, Lusty, Rambling, Rampant Ladies – that are troubl'd with the Vapours; 'tis your Ratisa, Persio, Cynamon, Citron, and Spirit of Clary, cause such Swi-m-ing in the Brain, that carries many a Guinea full-tide to the Doctor' (25ff.). Luxury had become a contested term: is it as harmless as a dish of chocolate, or a serious moral failing? In *A Bold Stroke for a Wife* (1718), the inclusion of the Quaker Obadiah Prim, who objects that merchants are proud and luxurious (implying lust), ridicules the old-fashioned religious censure of luxury coded through the cultural politics of the Restoration.

The debate on luxury was being conducted over the bodies and desires of women. According to *The Discovery and Conquest of the Molucco and Philippine Islands* (translated 1708) by Bartolomé Juan Leonardo y Argensola (1562–1631), in return for access to the spice trade the king of the Spice Islands was presented with luxury gifts: handkerchiefs, towels, combs, looking glasses, glass beads, cloth and scissors, commodities for the bedroom and women's bodies.[24] But it is this book's engagement with melancholy that makes it relevant in a century in which that emotion was implicated in the luxury debate.

Leonardo y Argensola associates the Orient with eros and melancholy. When not narrating attacks by giants on the Spaniards, he includes historical and topographical details, but it is significant that a book of fantastic tales, the comic-book version of the spice myth, returns to provide light reading in the history of trade. The book was sold unbound, perhaps to a popular audience who would also lap up a book advertised in the volume about travels through Italy. Leonardo y Argensola tells the tale of the Melancholy Tree. Tristan de Atayde, governor of Ternate, had sought out a bastard brother called Aerio, who had a Javanese mother. Aerio was ten years old, bred

> at a Pleasure-House encompass'd with perpetual Greens, the natural Disposition being improv'd by Art, which so far prevail'd that the Flower so wonderful for its Fragrancy and manner of growing call'd *Triste*, or melancholy; found only in *Malabar* and *Malaca* [*sic*], abounded in this Ladies Gardens. She ador'd the Sun, and brought up her Child in that Folly, that he might forget the Rudiments he learnt at *Goa*, when in the Colledge of the *Jesuits*. The Idolaters believe, or feign, that a most beautiful Daughter or *Parizataco*, a *Satrapa*, or Nobleman, fell in love with the Sun, and that he . . . setled [*sic*] his Affections on another, and the first . . . killed her self. From her Ashes . . . sprung that *Melancholy Tree*, they say, whose Blossoms or Flowers still preserving the Memory of their Original, have such a Hatred for the Sun, that they cannot bear his Light.

The tree exudes perfume only at night. It has become a text, a memorial. The poetics of spice renders nature semiotic. Argensola adds that 'The *Asiaticks* are excessively fond of Perfumes, which is an Argument of their Lasciviousness. Great Taxes are laid in several Provinces, on all sweet Scents.'[25]

Landon could write in lavishly produced gift books in a cockney style similar to Keats. Her narrator in *Erinna* (1827), however, complains of orientalising texts, implying that women's reading grows sterile through surplus enjoyment, just as the Eastern women are fettered to male sexuality:

> O! the mind,
> Too vivid in its lighted energies,
> May read its fate in sunny Araby.
> How lives its beauty in each Eastern tale,
> Its growth of spices, and its groves of balm!
> They are exhausted; and what is it now?
> A wild and burning wilderness. Alas!
> For such similitude. Too much this is
> The fate of this world's loveliest and best. (286–94)[26]

This version of an *ubi sunt* is nostalgic in a melancholy way for the oneiric horizon. It is unclear whether it is the women or the spices and groves that are 'exhausted'. 'Exhausted' implies the unprofitableness both of the spice trade and of *jouissance*. 'Alas for such similitude' is a double-edged phrase: it could suggest the comparison between women's enslavement to the *jouissance* of reading and their subordination to Eastern men; but it could also warn the literary consumer against 'Satanic' figurative language, the language of 'similitude'.

Thomas Warton's elegiac eclogue *The Pleasures of Melancholy* (1747) is an apology for the culture of sensibility which makes intriguing claims about masculinity and consumption. The narrator allows himself the private, non-commodified luxury of tears – an appropriation of feminised sensibilities beyond what Richardson and Sterne allow, with their notes on unmanly tears – in lines negotiating between phallic, ejaculatory masculinity and the feminine. They depict the narrator's homosocial bond with a newly conceived canon, a liberal lineage of male poets, Shakespeare, Spenser and Milton:

> By soft degrees the manly torrent steals
> From my swollen eyes; and at a brother's woe
> My big heart melts in sympathizing tears. (223–5)

However, the luxury of quasi-Mannerist delay, represented as an etiolation of Neoplatonic moral and aesthetic space and time, the indulgence in melancholy and desire unsatisfied, is distinguished in the next verse paragraph from the orientalised 'luxury' of the Muscovian 'satrap' (241; an orientalist elision of Russia and Persia). The satrap is a cultural construct partly created in travel narratives by writers such as Jean Chardin, whose travels portray homosexuality and immoderate luxury. Orientals seem intellectually more highly developed than Northerners, but lacking in courage and willpower.

In Warton, the satrap is left 'to drown / In ease and luxury' (242–3) while the object of the narrator's fantasy, the 'banish'd lord' (238), roughs it out in the manly desolation of the Siberian wilderness, with only a phallic castle of domed battlements and spires for company, and the 'slow clock' (237), which like the 'due clock swinging slow' (209) in his own world (two verse paragraphs before) times the dilation of his sensibility.

The dilated time of luxurious consumption is thus distinguished from the Mandevillian economics of Pope's *The Rape of the Lock*, present in the deftly placed 'ease' that marks 'Augustan' aesthetic ideology, and the 'luxury' enjoyed in the 'laughing hours' both of long-distance, mercantilist enjoyment and of Milton's *L' Allegro*. In a significant anticipation of the hearth-and-home economics and poetics dear to Wordsworth and Coleridge, Warton stakes out a space of macho sensibility, a zone in which men can consume erotically their *jouissance* while distancing themselves from unmanly, exoticised imperialism. Warton here resembles De Quincey, who in *Confessions of an English Opium-Eater* (1821, 1822) seeks, according to his racist desires, to distance himself from the fantasy of despotic imperialism enjoyed by the Chinese, while simultaneously enjoying the orientalised luxury of opium.[27] This privatised, subjective imperialism of the nude masculine soul is precisely what Keats rejects. Indeed, his narrators emulate the satrap.

A literary language of Oriental consumption was thus established, often in contrast with travellers' observations. What did those constructed as Oriental despots actually eat? According to John Ogilby (1600–76), their diet of pilau rice and sherbet was parsimonious, though spicy. His description of '*Peluda*' is intriguingly suggestive of the more refined *Western* tastes in spice which were emerging in Europe during the Restoration and eighteenth century:

> They have likewise a dainty Dish, call'd *Peluda*; made up of *Ameldonk* of *Amelcores*, in the manner of a Tart; either made white like Snow, or else they colour them with Saffron. The Tart cut in pieces, is put into a *China*-Dish, and Rose-water and Sugar pour'd over it, and a great piece of Ice laid by it; which melting in the Rose-water with the Sugar, makes a delicious and cool Liquor; into which are put Almonds, and the Herb Purslan cut into small pieces; which give it a very pleasing Rellish: This Liquor put into the same Dish with the pieces of Tart, is both Meat and Drink, and a choice Delicate in the midst of Summer.[28]

Jean Baptiste Tavernier adds: 'The *Persians* are nothing eager after delicacies or dainties; both the nobler and the meaner sort being very temperate in dyet.'[29] Ogilby was a Scottish miscellaneous writer, a Royalist who lost everything in the Civil War, presented himself to Charles II and the court at the Restoration and was entrusted in 1661 with the 'poetical part' of the coronation. He spent the last years of his life producing lavish books on the geography and topography of the East.[30] We might assume, from his political and literary background, that Ogilby's representation of the Orient was in the service both of colonial expansion and of the courtly culture of the Restoration. In culinary terms, then, Ogilby is keen to present the Oriental ruling classes as participating in a version of the refined luxury of a modern court. He is part of the emergent discourse of refinement in consumption.

OLD SPICE

Simpson's argument about the modern feminisation of literature, the subject, and luxury consumption establishes relationships between commerce and desire. This feminisation depended on 'the debates . . . about divided labour and surplus production and about the domestic and colonialist economies'. Lycurgus banned commerce in the Spartan constitution in order to preserve 'civic virtue'. This kind of thinking gained a new emphasis in the eighteenth century and is one reason why the study of eighteenth-century, including Romantic, representations of spice is so important. More efficient cultivation at home and increasing wealth from the colonies and the stock market pushed 'the defenders of a ruralist (and masculinist) political ideal' into a corner. The 'economy of need' was transmuted into an 'economy of desire' through the greater 'concentration of surplus wealth in the hands of an aristocracy and a burgeoning middle class'.[31] In older models of desire, such as the Renaissance Neoplatonist Ficino's, Narcissus loves his reflection because he is not in tune with true beauty, a body-lover only; but the literature of the Romantic period is about the introduction of desire into the dialectic of the beautiful and the good.

Simpson reads William Paley as articulating this in *Principles of Moral and Political Philosophy* (1785). Adam Smith vaunted the socially cohesive and stimulating effects of 'the luxury cycle (and all non-necessities were defined as luxuries)', while 'Opponents predicted only the collapse of society itself.' Simpson continues: 'Luxury and desire together were the feminized components of social-economic life: unstable, unpredictable, superfluous, and experienced as constant process rather than as finished product'.[32] Spice represents all these features, and its ideologically useful archaism could only serve within this framework to boost a sense of its superfluity. Eve Sedgwick writes:

In *The German Ideology*, Marx suggests that the function of ideology is to conceal contradictions in the status quo by, for instance, recasting them into a diachronic narrative of origins . . . one important structure of ideology is an idealizing appeal to the outdated values of an earlier system, in defense of a later system that in practice undermines the material basis of those values . . .

The phrase 'A man's home is his castle' . . . reaches *back* to an emptied-out image of mastery and integration under feudalism in order to propel the male wage-worker *forward* to further feats of alienated labor, in the service of a now atomized and embattled, but all the more intensively idealized home.[33]

Medievalism was born. The antique, and antiquarianism, are products of this moment of modernity, and spice is an antique marker of capitalist expansion, luxury and desire. Spice *per se* (cinnamon, pepper and so forth) becomes ideologically useful precisely at the point at which it is less materially useful, even for fuelling the capitalist economy. Warton's *History of English Poetry* (1774–81) describes poems about scholastic banquets in its attempt to canonise English literature. In his later works, Marx declares that commodities come with ideology already inscribed in them; and while this appears obvious for the products of later capitalism, it is true too in early capitalism, explaining why food was such a potent ideological tool.[34] It also explains why *spice* as ideology was capable of evoking a whole fantastic age of magical consumption.

A new kind of commodity, the domestic antique, was consumed in and outside literature. A national literary tradition was inaugurated by entrepreneurial supporters of Whiggish liberty at a time of colonial expansion, in the mid eighteenth century. John Guillory has observed how Gray's *Elegy* – a poem categorised by Susan Stewart as a 'new antique' – was ready-made for a nascent liberal Whig entrepreneurial canon.[35] The achieved archaism of commodities, which a late twentieth-century 'luxury' goods catalogue might call 'antiquing' (as in 'antiqued gold'), fits Jan Mukařovský's notions of aesthetic function. The aesthetic has the 'ability to supplant some other function that the item (object or act) has lost in the course of its development'.[36] The very notion of the aesthetic was also a mid-eighteenth-century ideological response to the encroaching ravages of capitalism.[37] The aesthetic, the feminised, the antique and the literary appear to be linked to one another and to the poetics of spice.

Following Guillory's reading of Gray's *Elegy*, Coleridge's *The Rime of the Ancient Mariner* (1798, 1817) is an 'antiqued' text, always already prepared for the literary tradition that it itself helps to instigate. Coleridge's poem is an exquisite instance of the antiquing phenomenon. This quality of antiquing ironically bestows what is most *universal* about *The Ancient Mariner* – the logic of the 'timeless' commodity form, hypostasised and authenticated. Jerome McGann's interpretation of the revision as an attempt to provide a quasi-Christian codex would thus be both off the mark *and* right: there is a patina of codification, in the marginal glosses, which only serves further to antique *The Ancient Mariner.*[38] Trade panegyrics performed precisely this role: ceasing to function as a motor of capitalism, spice was available to poetry. Thus *The Ancient Mariner* is not so very different from Enlightenment period celebrations of imperialism, trade and so forth, just as the Ancient Mariner is himself a queerly familiar Enlightenment subject, the consistent origin of a certain voice, a technology of authentic speech.

The Ancient Mariner presents the metaphysics of the commodity not from the traders' point of view, but from the consumer's, in a sort of phenomenological reduction of the *very same* logic. This might account for its readiness for anthologisation in codices of cultural capital such as the *Norton Anthology*, as against Wordsworth's lyrical ballads, which fare less well. It comes ready-made as a timelessly valuable antique. *The Ancient Mariner*'s superlative Kantian jumps from particular to general without any of the necessary mediating steps in between (an instance of what Hegel would have called 'bad infinity'), with all its hair-raising Gothicism and trauma, is a symptom of a feminised consumer culture. The glittering, glossy sheen of objects in *The Ancient Mariner* is a reflex of the commodity fetish that is the poem itself. Its lack of historical determinants is what is most historical about it.

The Ancient Mariner displays a metaphysical materiality, a lack of historical determinants. Everything seems archetypal; matter itself exerts a supernatural power. But even though it lacks a clear presentation of its historical determinants, it is a historical document. How can one account for *The Ancient Mariner* as a cultural commodity? It is a commodified medievalist text *that retains the form* of a medieval text; a fantasy that becomes reality while retaining the form of a fantasy. The notion of an asymmetrical relationship between fantasy and reality in which both are related and yet retain their identity, in a kind of emulsion, is a feature of the poetics of spice. The poem does not contain spice *per se* – but its rhetoric, even in resisting ornamentation, is related to the poetics of spice. Keats exploits antiquing even more.

The work of the divine and antiquarian Richard Warner (1763–1857) provides further evidence of the distinctive cultural construction of 'antiqued', spiced meals in the Romantic period. Warner became the best-known literary figure in Bath, familiar with all the writers who frequented it and recording details of his encounters in *Literary Recollections*. In 1801 the *Anti-Jacobin* attacked his history of the city. He praised Fox and attacked Pitt in sermons.[39] *Antiquitates Culinariæ* (1791) begins with a rumination on the significance of tracing 'the history of the *Ars coquinaria*'. It concludes with editions of the medieval classic *The Forme of Cury* (1390?), *Ancient Cookery* (dated 1381) and 'Ancient Receipts to Preserve Fruits'. It details the enthronement banquets of George Nevill, archbishop of York in the reign of Edward IV and William Warham, archbishop of Canterbury in the reign of Henry VII. It contains extensive notes on relationships between luxury and necessity, feasting in Judaeo-Christian cultures other than England, the role of minstrels, the history of the fork and, last but not least, 'subtleties': complex, ekphrastic and emblematic sculptures in sugar, jelly, marzipan or pastry.[40]

APICIUS AND ABSTINENCE

Against the cult of luxury, eighteenth-century vegetarians were not only opposed to cruelty, they were opposed to flavour. Cheyne emphasised that the blander food was, the better. Blander food more closely resembled the chyle into which it was broken down in the stomach. This is a fantasy of the essence of food, as departicularised, negated, pure nutrition. Vegetables, according to the theory, were more quickly broken down than meat and thus formed chyle more easily; we now believe the reverse to be true. Eighteenth-century vegetarianism in Britain could be called a form of 'aversive generic' consumption and rhetoric. It is 'aversive' because it is a reaction against luxury, for it was thought to underpin hunting; it is 'generic' because its ideal food is seen not in the particular but in the general, as nutrition. Cheyne's ideas about spice contradicted Francis Bacon's, who in his natural history *Sylva Sylvarum* (1626) had declared that spices send nourishment into the body parts by strengthening the stomach.[41]

Cheyne believed that the emission of constant scent from '*odoriferous* Bodies' was comparable with fixed starlight, a belief that sets up a dichotomy between substance and accidence, just as his vegetarian discourse set up a dichotomy between nutrition in general and foods in particular.[42] He associated strong liquors with foods high in '*Aromaticks, eastern Gums* and *Juices; Opiats*, the *volatile cepacious Roots, Fruits* and *Seeds*, of the *poisonous, soporiferous* or *stimulating* kind', causing '*inflammatory* Distempers, and unnatural and dissolveing [*sic*] Lust'. He continues: 'Most People that enter on a *low Diet* for Health and Spirits, intirely *counteract* and *defeat* its beneficial Effects. I have known some *Men* of *Quality*, and *Gentlemen* of *Fortune*, who have been advis'd a *low Diet*, have their *Vegetables* of the *highest* and *rankest Flavour*, dress'd high with *burnt Butter*, *hot spices*, *Aromatics*, *Onions*, *Eggs* and *Salt*.'[43] Cheyne compares the effects of animal and vegetable food, and concludes that there are at least some vegetable foods, flavoured with spice, which could be just as bad as animal food:

> I must however own, that I think some *vegetable* Food, of much *Salt*, *Oil*, or luscious Juice and *Poignancy*, as much or more deleterious, inflaming, and incrassating, than some mild animal Substances: For Example, *Onions*, *Shallots*, *Mustard*, *Horse-radish*, all the *Nut-kinds*, *Eastern Gums*, *Balsams*, *Raisins*, *Pickles*, *Spices*, *Aromatics*, strong fermented *Sours*, rich and fat late Fruits, as dry yet *plump Grapes*, much *Sugar*, and the like.[44]

White, young meat is better than all these. The orientalised, exotic '*Eastern* and *Southern* Nations' who eat from this list risk '*unnatural Lust* and *Leachery*'.[45] Notice the medieval list-within-a-list: '*Nut-kinds*, *Eastern Gums*, *Balsams*, *Raisins*'. Cheyne partly castigates an *archaic* attitude towards diet, further strengthening the view that the early eighteenth century witnessed a crisis in ideologies of consumption focused on the issue of luxury. A century later Keats was to reverse this rhetoric, celebrating and parodying such antiquarianism.

Generic eating suggests the possibility of *eating nutrition* itself, as if there were no accidence, no species. It is a fetishism of the word: longing for a *res* not killed by *verbum*, symbolised by the act of killing an animal. The consumption of pure thought was a vegetarian philosophical tradition going back to Pythagoras with recent adherents in the Interregnum and Restoration such as Thomas Tryon and Roger Crab. Vegetarianism, a reaction against luxury, was a fantasy about the consumption of pure *value*. The long march towards Marmite had begun. Curiously, it is this modernist attitude towards food *qua* pure nutrition which also gave Britain mad cow disease or BSE, for the lack of scrutiny of industrialised farming and the drive to use the entire animal in the human food chain has its origins in the industrialising and capitalist agricultural moment of the eighteenth century, of which enclosure was a part. When Des Esseintes in Joris-Karl Huysmans' Keatsian *A Rebours* (1884) describes a prose poem as the 'dry juice' or 'osmazome' of literature or as 'essential oil', he was not far from Cheyne's notion of chyle.[46] Osmazome is part of the aqueous extract of meat which is soluble in alcohol and contains those constituents of the flesh that determine its taste and smell – and the chapter in which Des Esseintes makes this comparison begins with a description of its preparation. Elsewhere Des Esseintes praises medieval texts with 'verbs of refined sweetness, substantives smelling of incense', and a chapter on perfume equates different periods' styles of perfumery with different kinds of aesthetics.[47] But this is the opposite of eating nutrition: it is self-reflexively *consuming consumption.*

Keats consumed consumption, Shelley ate nutrition. The painter Benjamin Robert Haydon (1786–1846) reported in his diary on 21 April 1821 that 'For six weeks [Keats] was scarcely sober, and – to show what a man does to gratify his appetites when once they get the better of him – once covered his tongue and throat as far as he could reach with cayenne pepper in order to appreciate the "delicious coldness of claret in all its glory" – his own expression.'[48] The account of the cayenne episode has been disputed,[49] but even if – perhaps especially if – it is only figurative play, it is significantly opposed to Haydon's description of Shelley: 'I did not know what hectic, spare, weakly yet intellectual-looking creature it was, carving a bit of broccoli or cabbage on his plate, as if it had been the substantial wing of a chicken.'[50] Shelley is depicted as interested in food as substance: he sees the difference between broccoli and chicken as merely accidental. (Thomas Love Peacock delighted in describing the heavily peppered mutton chops he served to the apparently sickly vegetarian Shelley on a boat trip.[51]) Keats, however, plays luxuriously with food's excessive and significatory properties. (He signed 'La Belle Dame sans Merci' with the pseudonym 'Caviare' in the *Indicator* for 10 May 1820, and Leigh Hunt's nickname for him was 'Junkets'.[52])

The contestation around spice was concerned not only with gender but also with the exigencies of nation and empire. The debate on luxury took place against a background of anxiety about commercial capitalism, as pamphlets such as *Angliae Tutamen* and replies to it (1696), Defoe's *Mercator* and the *British Merchant* (1713–14) demonstrated. The *British Merchant* 66, for example, expresses the fear that France is going to overwhelm Britain with its toys, preserves and pickles, silks, brandies and wines. Pamphlets warred over foreign trade: was it ruining the domestic trade in wool?[53]

This perhaps accounts for the revival of interest in the Roman chef Apicius. The success of the culinary poet William King (1663–1712) was an aspect of the reappropriation of Apicius in the late seventeenth century. Marcus Gavius Apicius lived during the reigns of Augustus and Tiberius. According to Seneca he poisoned himself rather than eat less after spending a fortune; his work was known to St Jerome and Odo of Cluny. It combined Greek agriculture, Greek dietetic cookery and domestic science derived from Apuleius and others, and contained plenty of spices.[54] William King, a Tory whose Horatian *The Art of Cookery* (1708) is inscribed to the Beef Steak Club, praised the Epicurean 'Apician art' of John Evelyn's *Acetaria* (1699), and *The Art of Cookery* was inspired by Martin Lister's recent edition of Apicius, *De condimentis et upsoniis* [sic] *veterum* ('concerning the sauces and soups of the ancients'; the actual title is *Apicii cœlii de opsoniis et condimentis*, 1705).[55]

The introductory letter expresses patriotism and nostalgia for feudal days, when the family house ruled 'and the Beef and Brown Bread were carried every Day to the Poor' (Austen is still mourning its passing by the end of the century). *The Art of Cookery* is ostensibly founded upon *noblesse oblige*, a Rabisha-like aristocratic generosity. King muses upon Apicius: 'Under what Emperor was it wrote? Might it not have been in the Reign of *Heliogabalus*, who, tho' vicious, and in some things fantastical, yet was not incurious in the grand Affair of *Eating*?' He hopes that 'it will . . . remove the Barbarity of our present Education: For what hopes can there be of any Progress in Learning, whilst our Gentlemen suffer their Sons at *Westminster*, *Eaton*, and *Winchester* to eat nothing but *Salt* with their *Mutton* . . . ?' Every family now needs a '*French* Tutor'. King's parody of Horace plays upon epic openings: '*Muse, sing the Man that did to* Paris *go, / That he might taste their Soups, and Mushrooms know*'. Later, King comments: 'The *French* our Relish help, and well supply / The want of things too gross by Decency'. He means that the older taste for sugared meat is giving way to garlic. French standards have become the map for navigating the tropological uncertainties of 'the various Maze of Taste'.[56]

Continental refinements required an education in the civilising process. The next letter alerts us to this necessity with a spoof cultural history of the toothpick (it was considered a luxury item at the time).[57] King refers tellingly to Homeric ekphrasis: 'he might have been more polite in setting out the *Tooth-pick-case* or painted *Snuff-Box* of *Achilles*, if that Age had not been so barbarous as to want them'. These are the new commodities that for King distinguish eighteenth-century Britain from other empires such as Egypt or Abyssinia. In a passage whose comic effect is remarkably similar to that of *The Rape of the Lock* (1714), King proposes a 'Treatise of *Forks and Napkins*' featuring a study of Chinese chopsticks. The very capacity to treat the imperial theme with delicacy and mock-heroic humour is a token of the civilising process which Elias has traced in the development of cutlery. King notes the importance of having a silver knife on one's sideboard for mixing salads.[58]

Classical sources for the poetics of spice were construed as having established the rhetorical framework. Horace's *Ars poetica* is about poetry, or is it food? In *Odes* v.24, his invitation of Torquatus to dinner results in a culinary discussion of poetry, imitated by King. Indeed, 'a good Dinner is Brother to a good Poem'. The rules of decorum and episodic structure are discussed: hen turkeys are required for tragedies, capons for comedies; the sophisticated differentiation of the meal allows for many episodes, including 'slicing of Cumbers, dressing of Sallads, seasoning the inside of a Surloyn of Beef, breaking Lobsters Claws'.[59] 'Nice Variety' is important:

> Crabs, Salmon, Lobsters are with Fennel spread,
> Who never touch'd that Herb till they were dead;
> Yet no Man lards Salt Pork with Orange Peel,
> Or garnishes his Lamb with spitchcocht Eel.[60]

Rhetorical *inventio* and *dispositio* apply to the choice and seasoning of food, and so King introduces the poetics of spice. This poetics, and the imperial culture of luxury that sustains it, is to be distinguished from the medieval culture of feast and fast. This is why King counsels: 'At Christmas time be careful of your Fame', advising the host to consider the boar's head with 'Sauce like himself, offensive to its Foes, / The Roguish Mustard, dang'rous to the Nose' and spiced wine or '*Hippocras*'. There is a sense of roughness and risk associated with such festivals, which encapsulate archaic modes of spicing; compare Easter and its simnel-cake. The needs of empire are for a more refined luxury, a modesty hinted at by Horace in 'Parturient Montes: nascitur ridiculus mus', which King translates as: 'The Author raises Mountains seeming full, / But all the Cry produces little Wool'.[61] Nevertheless, King allows the use of spice, in opposition to those contemporary vegetarians who were against flavouring. King attacks the vegetarian apologist Plutarch for his attack on spice, lauding 'promiscuous' flavour:

> *Plutarch* says the Antients us'd no Pepper, whereas all, or at least five or six hundred of *Apicius*'s Delicates were season'd with it. For we may as well admire that some *West Indians* should abstain from Salt, as that we should be able to bear the Bitterness of Hops in our common Drink; and therefore we shou'd not be averse to Rue, Cummin, Parsley Seed, Marsh-mallows, or Nettles with our common Meat, or to have Pepper, Honey, Salt, Vinegar, Raisons, Mustard, and Oyl, Rue, Mastick, and Cardamums strown promiscuously over our Dinner when it comes to Table.[62]

THE *SPICE* EFFECT

We may now examine more closely the phenomenological process of the literary consumption of spice. The poetics of spice moves between two poles, which I call *ekphrasis* and *fantasia*. The ekphrastic pole concerns the vivid effect of a substance jumping out, as it were, of its textual frame, appearing to break the tissue of the text and stand forth at somewhat of a distance 'in front of' it. The vivid springing-forth of spice in ekphrasis can be described using the concept of *enargeia*. Revising Plato, Krieger describes *enargeia* (from *argos*, 'bright' or 'shining') as 'The capacity of words to describe with a vividness that, in effect, reproduces an object before our very eyes'; it is closely related to Aristotle's notion of *energeia*.[63] *Enargeia* is also close to the notion of *ekphanestaton* in the discourse of the sublime, that which shines forth as the truth of sheer appearance.[64]

Since classical rhetoric made no rigid distinction between what could and what could not function ekphrastically, the ekphrastic mode does not need to be limited to the purely visual, as in the ekphrastic phenomena of talking statues or inset emblems. The ekphrastic mode of spice can be found in the 1970s UK advertisement for gravy browning: 'Ahhh! Bisto!' The little heads on the trail of gravy scent are figureheads, overcodings of the flow of aroma, or the flow of trade: the exotic captured in the domestic nose. We might call the ekphrastic mode of the poetics of spice the mode of the Real of spice, assuming for a moment a Lacanian model of psychic reality divided into the three realms of the Real, the Symbolic, and the Imaginary. In this model, the Symbolic cannot express the Real, not through any superficial fault but through a structural inability to do so. This incapacity is idealistically resolved in the realm of fantasy, the Imaginary realm, in which words and things are harmoniously related. Ekphrastic *spice* tears a hole in the symbolic tissue of the text. Because of this hole, the unspeakable substantiality that grounds the text and yet from which the text departs is rendered obvious. *Spice* and *spicy* seem *both of and not of* the Symbolic realm. The veil of *spice* is thrust under our noses, imparting both a direct sense impression and a notion of the groundlessness of such impressions, since *spice* is named as genus and not its species, cinnamon and so forth.

The signs *spice*, *spicy* and so forth spice a line of verse without being marked or particularised, say as 'cinnamon' or 'pepper'. The role of *spice* as a re-mark, a mark that marks other marks as such, is ekphrastic in the precise sense that it appears to be at once a textual and an extratextual effect. *Spice* in its ekphrastic mode appears to free the reader from the text only by subduing her or him even more strongly to the grasping of the text *as* a text, *especially* insofar as its vagueness and generality has the magical blend of specificity and ineffable sensuousness.

The other pole is the Imaginary mode of fantasia. Here *spice* evokes an oneiric horizon beyond the capacity of the text to represent it. The relationship between the textual tissue and the spice fantasia is one in which the text appears to be folded into itself, or into a potentially infinite supply of other texts: travellers' tales, mystical stories, narratives of a 'beyond' not in the present here-and-now. The fantastic mode is found in Diodorus Siculus III.xlvi.4, which says that it is impossible to describe the powerful spicy fragrance of Arabia Felix. This is an arresting *occupatio* or *apophasis* – saying something without quite saying it. While spice as ekphrasis roots us in an ineffable here-and-now that, of course, may be grasped and savoured at any moment, spice as fantasia carries us away into a dreamlike state of endless figuration. Fantasia engages with limits and boundaries. When domestic subcultures in eighteenth-century Britain need to control what flows across limits, they rail against the superficialities of spice.

The relationship between the Imaginary and Real poles in Lacan's model of the mind has been defined as the location of ideology by Althusser and Žižek. The varied relationships between ekphrasis and fantasia in the representation of spice map out the realm of ideologies about spice, the spice trade and all that is associated with it. To take a simple example, the imperial representation of spice in Blackmore tends to locate the fantasy substance, poetic *spice*, in the nasal imagination of the reader/consumer of the products of empire. The highly wrought emblems in which spice is manifested in *Creation* also serve as pointers towards a beyond with which the text never quite catches up, but with which it dreams of catching up in its celebration of expanding imperial space. The voyage out to the colonies and into the nose and on to the dinner plate appear to be synchronised in a contrary motion not unlike a fugue.

How similar, then, was Shelley's ideological construal of spice as a fantasy substance to Blackmore's construction, despite its ostensible anti-imperialism. For even in those texts that deplore imperialism in matters of consumption, such as *A Vindication of Natural Diet*, there appears to be a contrary movement out into fantasy space, deeper into the text's Imaginary, and into real space, thrusting out of the text, albeit with revolting consequences. The plate of corpses flavoured with spice (roast meat) stinks of the sickness of the imperial body.

The same cannot be said of Milton or Keats. Both poets in their different ways enact delay effects between ekphrasis and fantasia. The spicy meal in *Paradise Regained* can be resisted by the reader/Christ insofar as there is a specious directness about its presentation, as if it has appeared *ex nihilo*. It is clearly a conjuring trick. Conversely, the line 'whence merchants bring / Their spicy drugs' in *Paradise Lost* (II.639–40) alerts us in its context to the gap between a space of fantasia, the Spice Islands, and the ways in which the fantasy substance is consumed. We are being made to watch Satan, the pusher, at work. Milton operates according to a Neoplatonic hermeneutics of salvation, in which the reader is gradually taught to distinguish between true and specious images of the same thing. The echo and delay effects employed are very helpful here: the fantasy islands from which the merchants import drugs are comparable to the true Eden, the home of safely consumed pleasures.

GETTING STONED, OR PETRIFIED ENJOYMENT

Milton's *Epitaphium Damonis* (1639), an elegy for Charles Diodati, ekphrastically describes two cups donated by Giambattista Manso. They contain an engraving of Olympus. Cupid aims his bow not down but up, in a Neoplatonic allegory of kindly holy minds and forms of the gods.[65] The engraving also represents spicy Arabia, the land of the Phoenix. The cups are symbols of books, the *Erocallia*, twelve Platonic dialogues about love and beauty, and *Poesie Nomiche*, a collection including an Italian translation of Claudian's *Phoenix*. The Red Sea is described, a symbol of 'divine protection'.[66] The fragrant spring promises renewal. The image on each cup is a cornucopia, bestowing a rich gift upon the reader who consumes it with the eyes. Cowper's translation of Milton's epitaph, *On the Death of Damon* (1791–2; revised 1798), describes

> Two cups, that radiant as their giver shone,
> Adorn'd by sculpture with a double zone.
> The spring was graven there; here slowly wind
> The Red-sea shores with groves of spices lined;
> Her plumes of various hues amid the boughs
> The sacred, solitary Phoenix shows,
> And watchful of the dawn, reverts her head,
> To see Aurora leave her watery bed. –
> In other part, the expansive vault above,
> And there too, even there, the god of love;
> With quiver arm'd he mounts, his torch displays
> A vivid light, his gem-tipt arrows blaze,
> Around his bright and fiery eyes he rolls. (260–72)

The vividness of the cup is not only its sheen but its imaginary aroma of sweating gums and its presentation of an oneiric horizon far from the sheep and strawberry plants of the topos of mourning (repeated by Shelley in *Marenghi*). The ekphrastic orientalist scene offers an oasis in the midst of the mourning scene of English Theocritan pastoral that frames it. In Shelley's *Queen Mab* VIII, this relationship between pastoral and oriental geography is inverted.

Spice plays between indiscriminate richness and exquisite detail or discriminating awareness: between imperial wealth and erotic touch. And these effects are often played off against domestic pastoral. This play was crystallised in the Romantic period cult of nature. Domestic nature could be consumed as a luxury in its own right – a sophisticated luxury of simplicity and 'leisure time'. Thus imperial fantasy could be reflected ironically against this new form of luxury. The Italian 'Sonnet: To the Torrid Zone' (1795) by the radical Helen Maria Williams (1761–1827) addresses the indiscriminate aspect of the poetics of spice. Poetic inspiration, here associated with 'musing memory' (13), cannot be awakened by the unsubtle riches of the tropics but instead prefers the 'mild gradations' (10) and melancholy 'fading pleasures' (14) of a flickering world. The tropics are too straightforward, almost binary, in their on–off light:

> Pathway of light! o'er thy empurpled zone
> With lavish charms perennial summer strays;
> Soft 'midst thy spicy groves the zephyr plays,
> While far around the rich perfumes are thrown;
> The amadavid-bird for thee alone
> Spreads his gay plumes that catch thy vivid rays;
> For the gems with liquid lustre blaze,
> And nature's various wealth is all thy own.
> But ah! not thine is twilight's doubtful gloom,
> Those mild gradations, mingling day with night;
> Here, instant darkness shrouds thy genial bloom,
> Nor leaves my pensive soul that lingering light,
> When musing memory would each trace resume
> Of fading pleasures in successive flight.

Williams's use of 'thrown' (4) is another example of cornucopian language. It is the wrong environment for the poetry of sensibility, declares the speaker. Williams's 'Sonnet: To Twilight' also praises the play between manifestation and non-manifestation implicit in the liminal hours of the day. The oneiric horizon is not enough to satisfy this Romantic consumer of light.

Williams's 'Sonnet: To Love' (1795) makes use of a figure of too-bright tropical light without the darkness necessary for a truly sentimental spirit. In so doing, it employs the zephyr and the odour of a tamarind tree:

> Ah Love! 'ere yet I knew thy fatal power,
> Bright glowed the colour of my youthful days,
> As, on the sultry zone, the torrid rays
> That paint the broad leaved plantain's glossy bower:
> Calm was my bosom as this silent hour,
> When o'er the deep, scarce heard, the zephyr strays,
> 'Midst the cool tamarinds innocently plays,
> Nor from the orange shakes its odorous flower:

But ah! since Love has all my heart possest,
That desolated heart what sorrows tear?
Disturbed, and wild as ocean's troubled breast,
When the hoarse tempest of the night is there!
Yet my complaining spirit asks no rest –
This bleeding bosom cherishes despair.

The play between spicy and non-spicy geography here evokes a play between rich 'sultry' potential (3) and a troubled but inspiring fulfilment. The 'Sonnet: To the Strawberry' (1795) also plays with a poetics of spice and non-spice, this time drawing a contrast between the exotic and the domestic. This contrast is again used to distinguish between poetic inspiration and its lack, conceived, as in 'Sonnet: To the Torrid Zone', as the variegation of memory. A third term, however, is introduced here, which suggests that the present may be too full of pain truly to recall the 'modest' beauty of the strawberries (12):

The Strawberry blooms upon its lowly bed,
Plant of my native soil! – the lime may fling
More potent fragrance on the zephyr's wing;
The milky cocoa richer juices shed;
The white Guava lovelier blossoms spread –
But not like thee to fond remembrance bring
The vanished hours of life's enchanting spring,
Short calendar of joys for ever fled! –
Thou bidst the scenes of childhood rise to view,
The wild-wood path which fancy loves to trace;
Where veiled in leaves, thy fruit of rosy hue
Lurked on the pliant stem with modest grace –
But ah! when thought would later years renew,
Alas, successive sorrows crowd the space!

Exotic food is associated with overpowering and unpoetic richness. Part of the *spice* effect, then, is to reflect on the nature of poetic language. The literary consumption of *spice* becomes a way of calibrating the role of fancy and ornamentation. Butler's *Hudibras* comments on the futility of ornamental poetry:

She that with *Poetry* is won,
Is but a *Desk* to write upon;
And what men say of her, they mean,
No more than that on which they *lean*.
Some with *Arabian Spices* strive
To embalm her cruelly alive;

Or *season* her, as *French* Cooks use
Their *Haut-gusts*, *Buollies*, or *Ragusts*. (II.i.591–8)[67]

In Williams, the strawberry provides its own fantastic pathways to the dream-world of an imagined childhood. The domestic pastoral scene is declared not to be different from, but to be *more potent than*, the colonial and imperial oneiric horizon. Romantic period poetry again adapts the poetics of spice to make sophisticated statements about consumption – here, the self-reflexive consumption of one's life. Butler's poem, by contrast, relegates spice and women's consumption of poetry to the status of a degraded writing.

As Enobarbus' description of the wedding barge in *Antony and Cleopatra* shows, the sense of smell can become involved in a repertoire of overwhelming ekphrastic effects that superimpose the massive and overpowering on the flowing and erotic:

The barge she sat in, like a burnish'd throne,
Burn'd on the water. The poop was beaten gold;
Purple the sails, and so perfumed that
The winds were love-sick with them; the oars were silver,
Which to the tune of flutes kept stroke, and made
The water which they beat to follow faster,
As amorous of their strokes. For her own person,
It beggar'd all description. She did lie
In her pavilion, cloth-of-gold, of tissue,
O'erpicturing that Venus where we see
The fancy out-work nature. On each side her
Stood pretty dimpled boys, like smiling Cupids,
With divers-colour'd fans, whose wind did seem
To glow the delicate cheeks which they did cool,
And what they undid did. (II.ii.195–209)

The crasis induced by the tension between erotic cooling and heating at the end has been prefigured by the doublespeak that juxtaposes *occupatio* and ekphrasis in the picture of things that 'o'erpicture' nature. The hypnotic brilliance of this crasis has been established through the vivid quality of the opening lines, which rub our noses in perfume and our eyes in colour until there is not much to do except marvel.

Spice in culinary ekphrasis poses the same problem as pigment in visual ekphrasis: the issue of evoking the immediacy of smell in the temporality of language. However, the reader's appreciation of culinary ekphrasis seems to run counter to this: the perfume of spice appears to flow, while the reader (or subject of focalisation in the literary text) is still. Frozen ekphrastic time, as at the end of Shakespeare's *Cymbeline*, petrifies the onlooker. It is appropriate that the play's conclusion describes a trail of incense rising towards the nose of God. There is something in the symbol which exceeds what it symbolises: the phenomenality of sheer appearance, or what Longinian theory calls the *ekphanestaton* of the sublime. *Ekphanestaton* literally means 'that which shines forth the most', 'the most phenomenal'. The sheer sparkling appearance of the phenomenal world is that very excess that *is* the Real, beyond its symbolic content. Spice, in culinary art and representations of culinary art, is the *ekphanestaton* of food.

Emblematic ekphrases on the subject of trade were often affixed to geographical descriptions and maps in the early modern period. For example, there is the frontispiece to the Dutch Ortelius' *Theatrum orbis terrarum* (1570; figure 10):

> Adspicis à dextris *ASIAM*, quæ splendida Eoïs
> Tota nitet gemmis, tota est ornata lapillis.
> Ostentat, myrrham redolens, stactenque suavem,
> Et gummi croceum, pigmenta, & aromata, & omnes
> Assyrios fucos, Arabum prædita dona.[68]

(Behold Asia on the right, who glitters all over with brilliant Eastern gems, decorated entirely with precious stones. She gives out a scent of sweet myrrh oil, and saffron gum, colours and aromatic spices, and all the Assyrian dyes, endowed with gifts of Arabia.)

Setting the stage for the dramatisation of Eurocentric trade, Asia and Africa are depicted on the left and the right holding symbolic objects, a burning censer and a balsam branch. Such allegorical figures are illustrated as if carved in stone. The ekphrastic register petrifies its addressee.

What enjoyments are presented to the reader in the dialectic between ekphrasis (the language of stasis) and fantasia (the language of flow)? A swing between stasis and flow is often articulated through the image of the weeping tree. Let us return to the lines about the oak and the rill in Erasmus Darwin, discussed in the previous chapter. The verse sweeps internationally from the balms of Mecca and the spices of India to the scene of domestic consumption:

> – And, where yon oak extends his dusky shoots
> Wide o'er the rill, that bubbles from his roots;
> Beneath whose arms, protected from the storm
> A turf-built altar rears it's [*sic*] rustic form;

Figure 10 Ekphrasis: Abraham Ortelius, *Theatrum orbis terrarum* (1570), frontispiece. Asia and Africa stand on the left and right holding symbolic objects, a burning censer and a balsam branch.

SYLPHS! with religious hands fresh garlands twine,
And deck with lavish pomp HYGEIA's shrine.

(*The Economy of Vegetation*, I.iv.607–612)

The language of trade in the preceding lines is mediated by the feminine machinery of nymphs and sylphs, and the territories of trade are feminised. The oak is an emblem of masculinised enjoyment, as the transnational flows of goods modulate into the contained ejaculation of the rill. The weeping tree, as in Ovid's recounting of the myth of Myrrha, or Othello's lines about medicinable gum, is a feature of the poetics of spice. Here enjoyment is being domesticated through the image of the rill and the oak.

The tree that weeps gum is a wounded tree, a tree in trauma. The image hardly differs from that of the gum-weeping tree. The equation between the flow of water and the flow of spice, the flow of trade and the flow of the consumer's enjoyment, suggests two principles: a body that absorbs and exudes the flows; and the proliferating flows themselves. This kind of consumer enjoyment is connected with petrifaction: the solidifying or hardening of a flow indicating its arrival at its proper destination. The ecstasy described by Luce Irigaray and St Theresa places the soul or self in a static relationship to an outer source of enjoyment (ek-stasis), an umbilical cord or nipple through which the flows of spice or eros run. Deleuze and Guattari's image of the Body without Organs, a cosmic egg running with plural flows of desire, captures the way in which the poetics of spice imagines enjoyment. The realm of enjoyment becomes like the Land of Cockaygne.

In St Teresa's *Meditations on the Song of Songs*, a mystical union with God is described, a form of living in the aesthetic, a realm of pure fragrance. This entails a liquefaction of the self, in which the subject 'becomes' spice/Christ, the anointed/anointing. When the soul is 'absorbed' in God, but not in full union, it smells a sweet fragrance arising as if from within. Her description is ambient: 'if we were suddenly to enter a place where this fragrance was strong and not from one thing but from many, and we did not know what it was or where it came from except that it permeated everything, we would have some idea of this most sweet love of our God'.[69]

For St Teresa one smells sweet fragrances in the second and third degrees of prayer before rapture leading to absolute union with the divine, while the corporeal senses are still working.[70] St Bernard's commentary on the Canticles also remarks that when one is closer to

God one smells a sweeter and fresher fragrance. The spiritual connotations of spice dovetail with its connotations in capitalist society. The development of a consumer aesthetic was spearheaded by sensualists such as Lorezno Magalotti. *Lettere sopra i buccheri* contains a passage in which ecstatic communion is experienced not in the presence of God but in a Neoplatonic unity, construed as a negative space, an 'abyss of odorous light' achieved through 'immersion, absorption . . . inebriation of the fancy . . . in a continuous and ideal bath in abundant aromatic spices'. The crasis of light and smell, often kept apart in Neoplatonic theory, is striking. In a chapter in *The Incorruptible Flesh* on the power of aromatics and other perfumes in the early modern period, Camporesi glosses the passage by this 'mystical odorist' as 'the language of mysticism translated into fragrant emanations', a discourse that mixes mind, matter and space.[71]

Thus a relation of the ego to its fantasy is played out. The fantasy-Thing is found to be none other than the outer protruberance of what psychoanalysis calls the ego. This Thing, this embodied enjoyment, is actually the very aspect of the ego unavailable to consciousness. Identification with the non-self is naturally a paradox that evokes a realm of fantasy, consisting not of solid things or solid thoughts, but of 'real illusion'. The smell of spice thus invokes *jouissance*, specifically the enjoyment of illusion. This enjoyment of self from the Other's fantastic 'point of view' is also significant in orientalist ideologies about spice. Beings 'over there' (morally or spatially) smell of spice. Eighteenth-century consumer society takes the spiritual discourse of the experience of the Other as its paradigm for consumerist fantasies of luxury enjoyment. This form of enjoyment in the Other is self-reflexive: enjoying the Other as oneself and vice versa. The Romantic aesthetic of self-reflexive consumption grew from this.

The fantasy enjoyment-of-the-Other is strongly gendered, and here it is worth recalling the long-standing association of spice with the feminine. *Ancrene Wisse* is a Christian appropriation of the biblical poetics of spice in the context of monastic modes of distinction. Spice is imagined as gift, expenditure, mobility, trade and transference, the mark of the Other's territory, whether the Other is the ultimate good or the ultimate evil. The chapter on protecting the heart through the senses contains the following gloss of Isaiah 30:15, 'In silence and hope shall your strength be':

hope is a sweet spice within his heart, which sweetens everything bitter that the body drinks. But whoever chews spice must keep her mouth shut, so that the sweet scent and the strength of it stays within. But she who opens her mouth with much jabber and breaks silence, she spits hope right out, and the sweetness of it, with worldly words and loses spiritual strength against the fiend.[72]

The image of spice in the mouth is the image of an unreciprocable gift: the body does not naturally smell of spice, far from it. The abjection implied here is a prologue to the work of humiliation described later. The mouth is imagined as a container of excrement that can only be made to smell sweetly with 'that', the Other, some token of God's bounty:

In your body there is filth and weakness. Does there not come out of a vessel the sort of thing that is in it? Does the smell of spices or of sweet balsam come from your flesh's vessel? What! Do dry twigs bear grapes? Briars rose-blooms? What fruit does your flesh bear at all its openings? In the middle of the glory of your face, which is your most beautiful part, between the mouth's taste and the nose's smell, do you not bear two toilet holes, as it were? Are you not come of foul slime, are you not a vat of filth, will you not be worm's food?[73]

Backbiters are figured as opening the latrines of the devil and making the other nuns smell them. As in the Buddhist Vinaya, the precepts for monks and nuns, the woman's body is figured as a conduit of excremental flows. The huge expenditure of anointing Christ (the anointed one) with precious oils and spices is thus easy to turn into a central figure of penance, an anointment of 'bitter spices' such as myrrh and aloes preceding the sweetness. The theme of the spiced corpse re-emerges here. The author continues: 'If you are hungry for the sweet, you must first assuredly bite on the bitter.'[74] The woman's body maintained a connection with spice in the medieval Christian Imaginary. Stories about the Assumption are preoccupied with spice, for example the liturgy of Virgin as the seat of wisdom, deriving from Ecclesiasticus 24:15.[75]

The abject body and the beatified body are both boundless; the only difference between them is that one smells of spice, the other of dirt. In Herodotus, laudanum is obtained from the filthy beards of billy goats, in a magical Arabian realm of flying snakes and frankincense: it is Saba, the land whence the Queen of Sheba, the possible addressee of the Song of Songs, may have come.[76] Julia Kristeva's theory of the abject, expounded in *Powers of Horror*, describes how a person becomes a subject by rejecting a boundless interconnection with the mother's body, represented as the abject. St Teresa's and the nun's liminality are the same. Similarly, in the Romantic period, feminised forms of consumption were feared as breaking down rigid, gendered boundaries between subject and object. Medievalism provided a fantasy space in which these anxieties could be played out, and the work of Keats demonstrates how medievalism could serve the interests of self-reflexive, Romantic consumerism. Keats was infamously vilified by John Gibson Lockhart and John Wilson ('Z') as a queer man who did not know how to consume properly, that is, in a masculine way: he had no knowledge of the proper classical discourses that support civic humanism, he could not read poetry correctly . . . Keats's images of non-utility are sexually and economically provocative: his pictures of wealth in superabundant 'heaps' recalls the fantasy of the potlatch that undermines the acceptable middle-class fantasy of hard-working wealth.

In *The Fall of Hyperion: A Fragment* (1819), Moneta's altar is described:

> I looked thereon,
> And on the paved floor, where nigh were piled
> Faggots of cinnamon, and many heaps
> Of other crisped spice-wood . . . (238)

Through the logic of ekphrasis, a tension arises between the liquid flow of enjoyment and the solid body of enjoyment. Marjorie Levinson senses this tension in *The Eve of St Agnes*, which she sees as 'capably alienated and aggressively material', a sort of negativised virtuosity, 'a deep frieze[/freeze]'.[77] The body of enjoyment is that unravished bride of quietness described in Keats's ode *On a Grecian Urn*, or the suffocated body of Desdemona, wept over by Othello with his fantasia about Arabia Felix. Desdemona is figured as a commodity, an inestimable luxury fraught with the trauma of trade, a form of cargo attacked by Turks. The economics of *Othello* is of absolute loss and gain. The jewelled heaviness of the Moor's language and Iago's 'drowsy syrups', the contrary medicine of thyme and hyssop (I.iii.319–31), and the handkerchief scented with mummy, indicate how the poetics of spice sets up a petrified body of enjoyment. The language of the precious object and dangerous Other is present in the description of the handkerchief in *Othello* III.iv. The handkerchief has been seasoned with mummy:

> There's magic in the web of it.
> A sibyl that had numb'red in the world
> The sun to course two hundred compasses
> In her prophetic fury sew'd the work;
> The worms were hallowed that did breed the silk;
> And it was dy'd in mummy which the skilful
> Conserv'd of maidens' hearts. (III.iv.69–75)

The material itself is a poetic text (*tego*, I weave), and its mummy seasoning is charged with eroticism. The 'spicing' of something pure with powerful seasoning is what Keats works with in stanza 30 of *The Eve of St Agnes*. It also calls to mind the topos of the spiced corpse and the Eucharist – a crasis of spiciness and neutrality (the unmarked quality of the bread).[78] Camporesi has discussed how the preservation of corpses was part of a culture that sought to maintain memory in the form of this ghostly in-between state. In this way mummy resembles the literary text, whether it is orally or textually transmitted.[79] Though Camporesi states that it belongs only to a culture of oral transmission, the image of the printed text as mummy appears in the works of Alexander Pope and Joyce.[80]

Othello is preoccupied with olfactory attraction and revulsion. Cowper revised Shakespeare's representation of Desdemona in his tribute to his dead mother, comparing the receipt of her picture and her death to the safe arrival of a ship in a spice port:

> Thou, as a gallant bark from Albion's coast
> (The storms all weather'd and the ocean cross'd)
> Shoots into port at some well-haven'd isle,
> Where spices breathe and brighter seasons smile.
> (*On the Receipt of my Mother's Picture out of Norfolk*, 88–91)

The slippage between the dead mother's body and her picture is significant, as is the association of this slippage with the Spice Islands. The stasis of the picture contains, like a fetish, some living quality.

The petrified body is asleep, dreaming but still, like the overstuffed denizens of Breughel's depiction of the Land of Cockaygne (1567). This recalls the oneiric horizon. This time, however, that horizon is not only an externalised land of riches but is mingled with the interior Other-world of sleep. This internal world was colonised in the name of Romantic subjectivity. Outer and inner worlds mix in Felicia Hemans's 'The Festal Hour'.[81] Every time the mighty feast they fall:

> Such things have been of yore,
> In the gay regions where the citrons blow,

> And purple summers all their sleepy glow
> On the grape-clusters pour;
> And where the palms to spicy winds are waving,
> Along clear seas of melted sapphire, laving,
> As with a flow of light, their southern shore. (64–70)

The language of flow – 'pour', 'waving', 'melted', 'laving', 'flow' – synaesthetically bonds light and colour with the wetness of the sea and the scent of spices. The ambient poetics (in which a 'sleepy glow' is poured, for example) ensures that no rigid distinction is drawn between inside and outside. Something similar happens in Mary Ann Brown's *Ada* (1828).[82] Ada is taken from her father by pirates, whose ship founders; she is saved by a pirate who turns out to be a woman in drag called 'Lama', who comes from an Eastern isle where

> The deep coral blushes through
> The waves that catch its crimson hue,
> . . .
> And where the very zephyr comes
> O'erladen with such rich perfumes,
> It sighs and droops its airy wings,
> And sleeps amidst the sweets it brings. (55–6)

There is a continuum of topoi associating spice, luxury and sleep. The body is sympathetically evoked in the way the coral 'blushes through', a strong image of the ambient diffusion of colour. Another complex corporeal environment is achieved in the image of the 'drooping' zephyr – as the wind dies the scent of spices grows, as if the wind had expired in their delivery, in an exhausting orgasm.

In Keats's *Sleep and Poetry* (1816; published 1817) the narrator wishes to be immersed in Otherness, 'a death / Of luxury' (58–9). This Otherness is imagined as an erotic enticement through an ambient space marked not by Cartesian co-ordinates but by intensities of spice:

> Another [nymph] will entice me on, and on
> Through almond blossoms and rich cinnamon;
> Till in the bosom of a leafy world
> We rest in silence, like two gems upcurled
> In the recesses of a pearly shell. (117–21)

That 'will' is nicely poised between a wish and a demand, indicating the imperiousness of the consumer's desire. The narrator becomes a luxury object (a gem), in a strong enactment of Romantic self-reflexive consumerism. The ambiguous effect of 'upcurled', suggesting 'curled up', a twirling motion and 'the recesses of a pearly shell' evokes ambience, which is associated with the notion of figurative language as perfume. In 'Z' 's vindictive fourth article on the Cockney School in *Blackwood's*, this passage is called 'very pretty raving'.[83] 'Z' instructs Keats to go 'back to the [apothecary's] shop', for 'It is a better and a wise thing to be a starved apothecary than a starved poet', without realising the irony that Keats is a true poet of the *pharmakon*.[84] Alan Bewell has demonstrated in his work on the language of flowers in Keats that the spice in *Sleep and Poetry* creates a world that is 'not natural, but textual, its floral elements, like the "spiced dainties" . . . that Porphyro offers Madeline . . . , are sights, drawn from exotic bookish regions, to be seen more than eaten'.[85] Bewell's use of 'sights', which he links to Keats's commodification of nature, illustrates the ekphrastic quality of Keats's poetics of spice.

In 'The Veiled Prophet of Khorassan', in the orientalist romance *Lalla Rookh* (1817) by Thomas Moore (1779–1852), Phoenix-like creatures are described in a similarly eroticised landscape of intoxication:

> Those golden birds that, in the spice-time, drop
> About the gardens, drunk with that sweet food
> Whose scent hath lur'd them o'er the summer flood;
> And those that under Araby's soft sun
> Build their high nests of budding cinnamon. (881–5)

The birds do not fly but 'drop', with quasi-inanimate languor. Creatures have become things. Intoxication entails a form of reification.[86]

De Quincey's *Confessions* is full of Hegelian jokes, playing with the paradoxical notions of substance as subject and subject as substance in a realm of petrified enjoyment. The real hero of the tale, we are told, is opium. De Quincey fantasises that his body is turning into a piece of furniture, and that pieces of furniture are sprouting legs and heads to terrorise him, an uncanny mythologisation of the actuality of tables and chairs with animal heads and feet. Opium has the magical power both to revive and to put De Quincey to sleep, as if he were a zombie. Ann of Oxford Street revives him with spiced port, which he anticipates as a stimulant ('stimulus') rather than a narcotic, and therefore like opium (borrowing Brown's and Cullen's rather than Trotter's theories).[87] Like the alien in John Carpenter's remake of *The Thing* (1982), De Quincey's body, including his objectified, hallucinating mind, is undead, a threatening simulation of normal life. It is an instance of what Deleuze and Guattari call the Body without Organs, a body reduced to sheer surface. In this the other De Quincey, the one who gives himself the opium, treats himself the way he believes the British should treat China, with vigorous and stimulating violence.

The association of the Chinese with artificial objects also appears in the poem on tea in Trevenen's *Little Derwent's Breakfast*.[88] The second stanza declares that the Chinese are 'A people who deem themselves wondrous wise, / Whose industry nobody need despise', an incredibly casual assertion of the English gaze over the Chinese, though oddly different from the standard contemporary racist depiction of the Chinese as lazy and in need of stimulation, as Nigel Leask has argued.[89] Naturally, there is no mention of the opium trade in exchange for tea. The third stanza celebrates Chinese artifice:

> Their ivory carvings, their fans, and their toys,
> Where whimsical fancy their genius employs, –
> Their drawings, their colours, their rare Indian ink,
> Their beautiful tea-cups from which we may drink,
>
> Are brilliant to look at, and pleasant to use;
> How few would such elegant presents refuse!
> Besides which, of many more things you may read
> Of this land that supplies us with much that we need.[90]

The language of artifice and gift exchange ('elegant presents') belies the violence of imperialism.

The body in narcosis is present in *Antony and Cleopatra* and Eliot's adaptation of it in 'A Game of Chess', the second section of *The Waste Land* (1922):

> The Chair she sat in, like a burnished throne,
> Glowed on the marble, where the glass
> Held up by standards wrought with fruited vines
> From which a golden Cupidon peeped out
> (Another hid his eyes behind his wing)
> Doubled the flames of sevenbranched candelabra
> Reflecting light upon the table as
> The glitter of her jewels rose to meet it,
> From satin cases poured in rich profusion.
> In vials of ivory and coloured glass

Unstoppered, lurked her strange synthetic perfumes,
Unguent, powdered, or liquid – troubled, confused
And drowned the sense in odours; stirred by the air
That freshened from the window, these ascended
In fattening the prolonged candle-flames,
Flung their smoke into the laquearia,
Stirring the pattern on the coffered ceiling.
Huge sea-wood fed with copper
Burned green and orange, framed by the coloured stone,
In which sad light a carvèd dolphin swam.
Above the antique mantel was displayed
As though a window gave upon the sylvan scene
The change of Philomel, by the barbarous king
So rudely forced; yet there the nightingale
Filled all the desert with inviolable voice
And still she cried, and still the world pursues,
'Jug Jug' to dirty ears.
And other withered stumps of time
Were told upon the walls; staring forms
Leaned out, leaning, hushing the room enclosed.
Footsteps shuffled on the stair.
Under the firelight, under the brush, her hair
Spread out in fiery points
Glowed into words, then would be savagely still. (II.1–34; 77–110)[91]

Eliot's figuration is strongly Keatsian, for instance in the presence of Philomela and the 'antique mantel'. The reader becomes a passive spectator of active art, though art itself is revealed as stasis in the kinetic flow of poetry. The figure of glowing, found at the beginning of the passage and modulating through the flowing perfumes to the image at the end of the glowing words, creates a sense of artificial radiation. The radiation of words is their *ekphanestaton*, that which in their symbolic properties goes beyond what they symbolise. It is a figure of richness, of overwhelming treasure ('rich profusion'), a potlatch. All these connotations are consonant with the poetics of spice, most notably the ambience which the passage evokes, a thickened, heightened atmosphere. The details of the room, meanwhile, are fetishistically fascinating: consider the Popean 'vials of ivory and coloured glass' reminiscent of *The Rape of the Lock* and Shelley's *The Witch of Atlas*. The detail, and more basic than that, the shine (*schein*) of the room as emanation of the woman, flow ekphrastically towards the reader and narrator.

Ekphrasis gets the reading subject stoned. The reader of Eliot

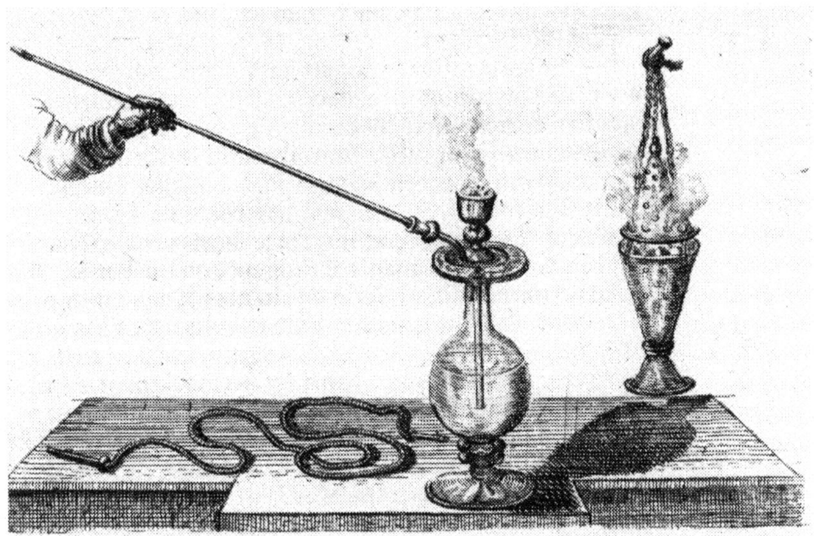

Figure 11 Pipe and censer: from Engelbert Kæmpfer, (1651–1716), *Amœnitarum exoticarum politico-physico-medicarum fasciculi* v (1712), p. 641.

focalises through the narrator, who is ordered to 'think' by the woman speaker. Eliot emphasises the physicality of the words, glowing from the hair (compare the vatic poet in the orientalist 'Kubla Khan'.[92]) Perfume is construed as word (compare the Hebrew pun in the Song of Songs), intoxicating, drowning the senses. Eliot uncannily links a scene of rape with a scene of high artifice, stasis and threat, in a gesture typical of his phobic poetics, hovering between fascination and repulsion. Eliot's use of the poetics of spice creates a frozen hell, while Keats creates a frozen heaven. Keats's version of the domestic scene, like Shelley's in *Queen Mab* VIII, is utopian: a frozen photograph of an offered meal, never consumed. Pierre et Gilles' photographic presentation of artificial worlds of impossible fulfilment follows exactly the same scheme (Pierre et Gilles are French photographers of the late twentieth century whose parodies of Catholic icons luxuriate in an artificial version of nature). Both Eliot's and Keats's (and Pierre et Gilles') approaches, however, are predicated on an infantilisation of the consumer/reader. It is just that Pierre et Gilles and Keats are playing queerly with this infantilisation: a sophisticated form of child's play.

Eliot's and Keats's narrator resembles Milton's Comus, who

infantilises the Lady and tries to force her to drink a perfumed drug:

> And first behold this cordial julep here
> That flames, and dances in his crystal bounds
> With spirits of balm, and fragrant syrups mixed. (671–3)

Whether or not it can be shown, as Debora Shuger has recently tried to do, that the 'gums of glutinous heat' (917) that affix the Lady to Comus' chair of temptation are associated with wet dreams, they are associated both with the representation of exotic foods and with their transfixing powers, and these carry an undeniable erotic charge.[93] The Lady easily resists:

> If every just man that now pines with want
> Had but a moderate and beseeming share
> Of that which lewdly-pampered Luxury
> Now heaps upon some few with vast excess,
> Nature's full blessings would be well-dispensed
> In unsuperfluous even proportion. (767–72)

The Lady does not propose the abolition of those items distributed by luxury, only their just distribution and temperate consumption. Milton thus associates intoxication and infantilisation with the power structure within which the consumption of luxury goods takes place. In *Lamia*, Keats describes 'God Bacchus . . . / Stretched out, at ease, beneath a glutinous pine' (I.209–10). In *The Eve of St Agnes*, he plays again with the glutinous power of luxury. As Leigh Hunt wrote, 'Milton would have relished the supper [in stanza 30], which his young successor, like a page for him, has set forth.'[94]

KEATS'S BLANCMANGE, OR HAVING YOUR CAKE AND EATING IT

It is no surprise that Keats's consummate passage on spice as display would mount a critique of luxury in the guise of *double entendre*, and the latter in the mode of ekphrasis. In classical rhetoric, ekphrasis is not necessarily limited to the visual, but here it usefully bridges the space between writing, soiling (*Hamlet* III.iv.91: the 'tinct' of spots of black connotes a taint), painting, drugs and spice, conjured up in the brilliant *pharmakon*, 'tinct'.

Nicholas Roe has made a strong case for regarding Keats seriously as a 'pharmacopolitical' poet, as William Maginn claimed, with humour, in a letter to William Blackwood (10 April 1821).[95] In its presentation of a parodic view of capitalism through the poetics of spice, *The Eve of St Agnes* supplements this case. 'Z' attacked Keats by declaring that he should go back to his apothecary's shop (Keats was an apothecary and trained as a physician). But what if this shop was figuratively present in his poetry?

Unlike Milton, Keats confuses the true and specious, and in that confusion he gently takes apart the substantiality of illusion that is an effect of the poetics of spice. Moreover, the apparently reverse effect also takes place. By letting the reader notice the dreamlike qualities of reality, Keats shows them the reality of dreaming. It is thus not enough to agree with Walter Jackson Bate, for whom the sensual world of the meal contradicts the metaphysical realm.

In the thirtieth stanza of *The Eve of St Agnes*, the reader is both here and there, in the Real and in the Imaginary, experiencing ekphrasis and fantasia. There is, however, no easy conduit between here and there, and our sense of remaining exclusively in either domain is attenuated. The poetics of spice is about holding on to or letting go of reality grasped as a substantial illusion of great value and promise. Stanza 30 sums up the problematic of the entire poem, which turns around the tension between reality and ideality, as Tilottama Rajan has shown.[96]

Every relationship in stanza 30 – between spice and its 'argosy', between spice and the food it spices, between Porphyro and Madeline, between Porphyro's presentation of the unconsumed meal and the reader or between Madeline and the reader – has an asymmetrical, 'off' quality. This was perhaps noted in Bloom's reading of the meal as a belated revision of the Song of Songs (he also reads the meal in *The Fall of Hyperion* as belated). Levinson, revising Lionel Trilling, moves towards it in her view of the meal's onanistic or infantilising regression.[97] This 'off' quality points out a contemporary asymmetry between fact and value, substance and sign, even capital and labour. The poem's medievalism is in an odd relationship with the capitalism that engendered it as a fantasy, and whose fantasy is of an archetypal form of capitalism, the spice trade.

The Eve of St Agnes lays bare the capitalist device, to use Russian Formalist language: the device of fantasies about trade and its linguistic equivalent, metaphor, as unproblematic equalising superpositions of one sign, one commodity, one civilisation, one gender, upon another. Keats alerts us to the jump between tenor and vehicle, subject and object, fact and value. The 'jumpy' quality of Keats's stanza betrays the jumpy quality of the capitalist Imaginary, itself a product of Hegelian bad infinity, leaping from particular to general in sudden, unmediated ways.

I call this jumping 'the blancmange effect'. Here we should recall the argument about the increasing tension between bland and spiced food in the eighteenth century. Before its modern reincarnation as an instant food, blancmange was a luxury and/or medicinal medieval and early modern food that skilfully combined utter blandness or transparency with delicate spicing. Montanari observes that blancmange was 'an expression of the gastronomic *koine* which European culture developed in the thirteenth and fourteenth centuries'.[98] *The Forme of Cury* contains recipes for 'Blank-mang' with capons, rice, sugar and blanched almonds (one recalls the 'blanchèd linen' in Keats); the even more sophisticated 'blank desire' contained ground capons, almond milk, rice flour, lard ('white grece'), 'blanche powder' (ginger ground with sugar) and 'mawmenye' (made of cheese, capons, almond milk, rice, egg yolks and saffron, clove sauce and galingale).[99] This significant redoubling of ingredients interlaces different subtle *flavours of whiteness*, a culinary paradox. Mintz has observed:

> the famous Spanish dish traditionally employed as a remedy for illness, the *manjar blanco* . . . is composed of breast of chicken, rice flour, milk and sugar – all of which ingredients are white. The *blanc mangier* or *blanc manger*, which turns up in the cookbook of Philip the Fair (1268–1314), was also made of breast of chicken, to which was added almond milk, white bread and ginger. This dish was cooked and flavored with a brew of rosewater . . . These curative combinations . . . strongly suggest that whiteness itself may have been thought to be inherently curative.[100]

The eater eats both solid substance and appearance, flavour. Because of this paradox, the Eucharistic blancmange suggests the spiced but bland or transparent foods served by Porphyro.

The curds and syrups of stanza 30 were menu items in sophisticated medieval and early modern food, and Keats's use of them is sophisticated. Fruit syrups and quince entered the European diet from Isfahan in the Persian Gulf, as recorded in a ninth-century Arab manuscript on trade. They belonged to a range of expensive Middle-Eastern confectionery and other exotic goods including sugar candy, saffron, rosewater, water-lily, jasmine ointment and candied capers.[101] Can stanza 30 really be said to be about infantilism? Unless one's only source were the nursery rhyme about Miss Muffett, the spider and the curds and whey, it seems inappropriate to concur with Levinson that 'Porphyro prepares a banquet consisting entirely of children's foods.'[102]

Levinson discusses the significance of Milton in stanza 30. Keats, she asserts, uses un-'digested' sources as a metaphoric 'substitute for the missing authority', a phenomenon she associates with relationships between sign, money and reference.[103] In *Paradise Lost*, as opposed to *The Eve of St Agnes*, 'Adam and Raphael *eat* their supper'; in Keats 'the food is used on the dramatic plane for its secondary characteristics (color, form, aroma, texture), on the narrative plane for its enhancement of sexual tension (foreplay), on the discursive plane for its verbal qualities (forepleasure), and on the conceptual plane for the abstention it signifies'. Levinson summarises her reading of non-consumption: 'A luxurious banquet not eaten is a lot more luxurious. The passage produces the supplemental virtues of the food' in contrast with the 'frank and mutual orality' of the meal in *Tom Jones*.[104] The anti-banquet, a manifestation of regal power over the means of production, consumption and representation, is figuratively present in stanza 30. Keats's deletion of an earlier stanza about the 'viands' described here only heightens the insubstantiality of the meal.[105]

Levinson associates Keats's disconnection between sign and thing with a Miltonic, utopian vegetarianism, a regressive realm of fantasy enjoyment: 'While we would gag on these foods if we actually had to eat them . . . we can enjoy reading them.' She adds, however, that the point of the meal is to convince the reader of the sheen of the Real through its vivid punctuality.[106] *Keats's Life of Allegory*, however, overextends a distinction between perversion in pornography and perversion in food magazine orality. The poetics of spice appears to be pornographic. In both the poetics of spice and pornography, the supplement is taken for the incarnation of the Real. Similarly, Levinson asserts that Keats converts 'substitutive' food (referring to 'primary objects: here, mother's milk, Edenic food, Milton') into 'a *supplemental* character'.[107] Milton becomes Milkton. But does that conversion take place? Surely we are presented with two radically different kinds of food, existing together in an emulsion? Milky food and spice, Miltonic and Keatsian embellishment coexist without collapsing into each other. That is the awkwardness of Keats's relationship with Milton. This emulsive tension precisely mirrors the larger figurative patterns of *The Eve of St Agnes* – a witty staging of the impossible sexual relationship.

To return to the assertion that Milton is the absent logocentric signifier for Keats, it is significant that Milton's linguistic register actually deconstructs the opposition between signifier and signified, rhetoric and logic, spice and blandness. 'Bland' occurs twice in Book IX of *Paradise Lost* in a sense that means not the opposite of *spicy* but *sensuous*, surely connoting rhetorical pharmacological 'blandishments'. Eve speaks in 'bland words' (IX.855) after she eats the fruit that 'ambrosial smell diffused' (852), and later Milton speaks of

> the force of that fallacious fruit,
> That with exhilarating vapour bland
> About their spirits had played. (1046–8)

If the word does mean *bland* in its modern sense in contrast to the 'fragrant smell diffused' of Satan's banquet in *Paradise Regained*, where the narrator scoffs at 'that crude apple that diverted Eve!' (II.349), then what is 'exhilarating' doing?[108]

Levinson is correct to analyse the stanza in terms of the fetish, complaining that 'no critic touches this stuff until it is refined into sensuousness'.[109] In order fully to understand the ways in which the poetics of spice operate here, the notion of the fetish itself needs to be supplemented with an understanding of relationships between (queer) desire and colonial desire. In doing this, the food on offer in stanza 30 becomes far from regressive.

Leigh Hunt described *The Eve of St Agnes* as 'rather a picture than a story'.[110] The elegance of its food, its exquisitely ekphrastic *enargeia*, has a precedent in King's *The Art of Cookery*:

> You that from pliant Paste wou'd Fabricks raise,
> Expecting thence to gain immortal Praise,
> Your Knuckles try, and let your Sinews know
> Their Power to knead, and give the Form to Dough,
> Chuse your Materials right, your seas'ning fix,
> And with your Fruit resplendent sugar mix:
> From thence of course the Figure will arise,
> And Elegance adorn the Surface of your Pies.[111]

Mintz has discussed how in the fifteenth century and after, subtleties were concocted as emblems bearing complex political messages; Warner's *Antiquitates Culinariæ* traces them back even further to lewd ecclesiastical sculpted hosts in the thirteenth century.

Subtleties survived in a more refined form during Warner's time and, with their combination of food and writing, they have echoes in such Western phenomena as the birthday cake and fortune cookies (an American invention). The seventeenth-century cook, Robert May, produced 'a [sugar] stag that "bleeds" claret wine when an arrow is removed from its flank'.[112] *Antiquitates Culinariæ* explores subtleties, linking them to the culinary decorations of the Georgian period.[113] Warton, cited extensively by Warner, records how early sixteenth-century poet Henry Bradshaw's life of St Werburgh describes a feast staged by King Wulser. The description includes a long ekphrastic account of the biblical and Arthurian legends on the tapestry in the hall, the songs sung by the minstrels, and the food itself:

> To this noble feest / there was suche ordynaunce
> That nothynge wanted / that gotten myght be
> On see and on lande / but there was habundaunce
> Of all maner pleasures / to be had for monye
> The bordes all charged / full of meet plente
> And dyuers subtyltes / prepared sothly were
> With cordyall spyces / theyr ghestes for to chere.[114]

Warton describes the 'subtleties' as 'dishes of curious cookery, so called'; Warner, like Warton, also calls them 'curious decorations of the Old English table'.[115] Food could be construed as a text containing emblems, aspects where the figurative element was more highly differentiated.[116] Warner calls subtleties 'devices in sugar and paste': a device is a physical construction, or a rhetorical trope.[117] In Rabisha's *The Whole Body of Cookery Dissected*, spiced confectionery lends itself to self-reflexive, emblematic food: goblets of jelly are decorated with goblets of jelly.[118] Stanza 30 of *The Eve of St Agnes* is a profound meditation on food as emblem.

Warton's 'curious' is well placed, as it could describe both a subjective quality of persons (attentive; particular, especially about details; ingenious; desirous to see or know; minute in inquiry; interested in occult art; a connoisseur in any branch of art); and an objective quality of things (made with care; of food, exquisitely prepared, dainty, delicate; carefully worked out; accurate, minute; intricate; occult, recondite; fine, delicate; calling forth feelings of interest; deserving attention on account of novelty or peculiarity; interesting the curioso or connoisseur). In the nineteenth century *curious* came to be used as a euphemism for pornography.[119] We could be gazing with desire at the delicious food; or it could be gazing at us. Ekphrasis permits both possibilities. The pungency of spice, moreover, constitutes a nasal form of the gaze, in a strictly Lacanian sense: an overpowering, penetrating quality.

Warner's work provides further evidence for the distinctive cultural construction of 'antiqued', spiced meals in the Romantic period. Subtleties 'had some allusion to the circumstances of the entertainments, and *closed* the service of the dishes', like birthday cake, while similar dishes called '*warners* were ornaments of the same nature, which *preceded* them'. *The Forme of Cury* mentioned subtleties, compiled as it was by the master-cooks of Richard II (whose interest in aesthetic form is legendary, for example in Gray's construction of English antiquity).[120] Warner speculates that 'It seems probable, that the splendid desert [dessert] frames of our days, ornamented with the quaint, and heterogeneous combinations of Chinese architecture, Arcadian swains, fowl, fish, beasts, and fanciful representations drawn from Heathen mythology, are only the *remains of*, or, if more agreeable to the modern ear, *refinements on*, the Old English Sotiltees'. This would concur with current arguments that the taste for food as decoration and display became more refined in the eighteenth century: 'the quantity of hot spices, that were mixed in almost all [medieval dishes] . . . would now be relished only by those accustomed to the high-seasoned dishes of the East and West-Indies'.[121] But it also demonstrates continuity with the Middle Ages and an interest in food as sign.

Warner discusses what for him are the grotesque sexual puns of some medieval subtleties, strengthening a link I have made between sexuality, the gaze and ornamental food: food sculptures shaped like penises and vaginas or Eucharistic wafers made to look like testicles. These sexual motifs are associated with the obscene textuality of earlier times in mystery plays, Chaucer, Skelton and Shakespeare and contrasted with the refinements of what Warner calls 'literature', which must mean the new, entrepreneurial canon. Warner lamely compares these obscene subtleties (a redundancy?) with the way in which 'we at present use the little devices of paste, containing mottoes within them, to the same end' of encouraging jokes and conversation.[122] As in Keats, food is associated with the antique, the textual, the ornamental, the exotic and the erotic – a distinctively Romantic attitude towards consumption.

The element of hard work in King's allusion to sculpture is not present in Keats's stanza, where Porphyro simply fetches ready-made food, found sculpture as it were, from the cupboard. Indeed, Porphyro more closely resembles the Abbot in Ann Radcliffe's *St Alban's Abbey*, who fetches spicy desserts from a cupboard (I.xxiv.474).[123] This is a symptom of the heightened role of the consumer in Romantic period culture. As well as never being consumed (at least not with the mouth), the food is never produced (at least not in the poem).

King continues, rewriting Horace's 'Actoris partes chorus, officiumque virile / Defendat':

> 'Tis the Desert [*sic*] that graces all the Feast,
> For an ill end disparages the rest:
> A thousand things well done, and one forgot,
> Defaces Obligation by that Blot.
> Make your transparent Sweet-meats truly nice,
> With *Indian* Sugar and *Arabian* Spice:
> And let your various Creams incircl'd be
> With swelling Fruit just ravish'd from the Tree.
> Let Plates and Dishes be from *China* brought,
> With lively Paint and Earth transparent wrought.
> The Feast now done Discourses are renew'd,
> And witty Arguments with Mirth pursu'd:
> The cheerful Master midst his jovial Friends,
> His Glass to their best Wishes recommends.
> The Grace Cup follows to his Sovereign's Health,
> And to his Country Plenty, Peace and Wealth.[124]

Just as in Horace the chorus offsets, enhances and supplements the action, so in King a spicy dessert is the supplement of the main dish. Luxurious foods are presented on luxurious china, which makes this meal doubly ekphrastic.[125] The chiasmic presence of transparency both in desserts and on dishes is striking. The East supplements the 'nice' West, just as spice appears to flavour the unmarked or transparent: the blancmange effect. The Grace and the toasts follow the spicy dessert, as tokens of sacrificial generosity. Similarly, Keats's stanza is concerned with the fantasy of a pure gift without return. King describes the *noblesse oblige* of showering the poor with food at the gate.[126]

There are other precedents for Keats's overcoding of poetry as spiced food, such as Byron's *Don Juan*. *Address to Poesy* (1797) by Anna Maria Porter (1780–1832) is an extended *occupatio* on the difficulties of writing love poetry. Orpheus and Petrarch are evoked as harbingers of a sentimental tradition whose flights of fancy conjure scenes of 'bleeding sympathy' (6).[127] The poet-narrator wakes up from the dream of fancy and proceeds to 'wake my simple reed' (97), but only after an *occupatio* that rivals Milton's *Lycidas* in its length and daring. Among the many picturesque scenes called forth by fancy, the imagery of spice is used as a figure for the power of fancy's poetics, in a transumptive manner:

> Fancy can bid the softest zephyr's blow,
> Fancy can load them with ten thousand scents,
> More sweet than all the spicy breath of Inde;
> *Her* word can make a new creation rise,
> And mid deep glooms, and sullen-roaring waves,
> (When o'er the scene her magic robe is flung)
> She can on sight, on smell, and on the ear
> Pour beauty, balm, and liquid-lulling sounds. (86–93)

As I have shown elsewhere, an equation is made between the scent of spice and the flow of sound, the middle term being the flinging of the 'magic robe' over the darkness and the waves (where does it land?). This equation is a pharmacological overworking of Genesis. Fancy stands in for the Spirit of God, creating not a three-dimensional world but a dimensionless apparition of sensual phenomena. The world is seduced into existence. The passage concludes the depiction of just such a fantasy new world (66–85). The insubstantial, yet poignant, quality of this world, given and yet taken away in the rhetoric of *occupatio*, is similar to the (non-)gesture of Porphyro's banquet. Porter's evocation of synaesthetic consumption and her stress on the power of fantasy typifies Romantic period self-referential consumerism.

The Eve of St Agnes creates tensions between flow and stasis, for instance in the first stanza's description of breath and of incense. The study of the commodity distinguishes between flow and stasis in terms of *meuble* and *immeuble* (the movable and the immovable or inalienable). Like the body in sacrifice, the inalienable is only of value insofar as it could be alienated *in extremis*: Abraham's sacrifice of Isaac. In a sublation, inalienability becomes a function of the very alienability that logically 'succeeded' it. Thus precisely insofar as it is the ultimate *meuble* commodity can incense be used to adorn the inalienable, the dead. The commodity form of incense is thus reterritorialised on the form of the ultimate 'antiproduction', death. This adornment of the dead manifests something perverse at the heart of the commodity itself. The body is rendered sacred, taboo, by smearing it with an excremental pungency.

The flow of incense and breath also captures the flow of spice in general, as a partial object. By *partial*, I mean to suggest that it is radically undecidable whether it belongs to an inside or an outside. It mediates food and is thus not the same as the bland, smelly objects of babyhood. Keats heightens *both* objectivity *and* subjectivity. The spicy meal is only infantile if one regards partial objects in a Winnicottian way as transitional, part of a phase of development which could be passed through.[128] Could social reality itself be a transitional object, a good-enough illusion? Is the difference between partial and 'whole' qualitative or quantitative? People need enough illusion to soothe them, and one function of ideology is surely to create a partial, liminal zone between social actors and the territory they inhabit. Spice is a transitional object that copes with the absence of God and the exigencies of long-distance trade: the pleasures and anxieties of capitalist power. Twentieth-century couples describe sadomasochism as a way of 'spicing' up their sex lives. A heightened sense of reality here accompanies a heightened sense of loss – the realm of the fetish.

Keats's use of 'argosy' and 'Samarkand' plays in a sophisticated way upon the routes of the early modern spice trade. This is a form of culinary medievalism. The line actually names two quite different spice routes. Although the etymology of 'argosy' has been argued to be closer to the large Venetian Ragusan merchant ships than to the Argo, the association with Camões' portrayal of Da Gama's men as literalising the myth of the Argonauts is clear.[129] The connotation of sea routes taken by the Venetians and others, as opposed to land routes, is there all the same. Barabas in Marlowe's *The Jew of Malta* (1592) hails 'Mine Argosie from *Alexandria*, / Loaden with Spice and Silkes, now under saile' (I.i.44–5), and Shakespeare's *The Merchant of Venice* links the trade winds with argosy: 'the ocean; / There where your argosies, with portly sail . . . / Do overpeer the petty traffickers' (I.i.8–12). 'Samarkand' connotes the earlier land-based route that exploited caravans. Tamburlaine came from Samarkand. Here is an example of the kind of despotic consumption against which Warton feigned rebellion, also imagined in Hemans's 'Belshazzar's Feast':

> But prouder mirth was in the kingly hall,
> Where, midst adoring slaves, a gorgeous band!

High at the stately midnight-festival,
Belshazzar sat enthroned. – There Luxury's hand
Had shower'd around all treasures that expand
Beneath the burning East; – all gems that pour
The sunbeams back; – all sweets of many a land,
Whose gales waft incense from their spicy shore;
– But mortal Pride look'd on, and still demanded more. (10–18)[130]

Belshazzar was a focus for the aesthetics of counter-luxury in the Romantic period. In Hannah More's *Belshazzar: A Sacred Drama*, Belshazzar proclaims the *carpe diem* philosophy of Epicureanism, echoing the secular, eudaemonist view of luxury propagated by supporters of long-distance trade in the eighteenth century:

To-night, my friends, your monarch shall be blest
With every various joy; to-night is ours;
Nor shall the envious gods, who view our bliss
And sicken as they view, to-night disturb us.
Bring all the richest spices of the East;
The od'rous cassia and the drooping myrrh,
The liquid amber and the fragrant gums;
Rob Gilead of its balms, Belshazzar bids,
And leave the Arabian groves without an odour.
Bring freshest flow'res, exhaust the blooming spring,
Twine the green myrtle with the short-liv'd rose;
And ever, as the blushing garland fades,
We'll learn to snatch the fugitive delight,
And grasp the flying joy ere it escape us.[131]

The feast imagery, though strong in More ('leave the Arabian groves without an odour'), is in both More and Hemans one-dimensional in comparison with Keats. Keats's hallucinatory, transumptive over-stocking of the image repertoire plays on illusions that offer two choices simultaneously. This ironic strategy does not neatly progress from early to modern, but instead plays with an ideology by twisting it upon itself, collapsing medieval and modern into each other.

Keats presents the logos and the *pharmakon* simultaneously: unmarked and tainted food. In the sonnet to sleep, 'O soothest sleep', the narrator wishes that the object would talk, but it is not a wish for the object to become a subject. It is more like wishing objectivity would talk to the narrator, or wanting to experience what it might be 'like' as an object. We experience the notion of a fantasy that becomes reality while retaining the form of a fantasy: the poetics of spice. It is manifested, for instance, in Peter Martyr's *Decades of the*

Newe Worlde. To discover the 'Ilandes of spices', 'owre men' had to travel around the world, 'The which nauigation . . . being the most marueylous thynge that euer was doone by man uppon the earth sence the fyrst creation of the worlde.'[132] We inhabit a world that is simultaneously marvel and reality, a legendary out-troping of legend.

In order to achieve this, Keats must preserve a hierarchical distinction between fantasy and reality. The consistent *double entendre* on the word 'pure' in *The Eve of St Agnes* depends upon the irreversibility of figure and ground, substance and accidence, the set and its members, while simultaneously playing with these categories. The 'azure-lidded' sleep and 'lavendered' sheets, the 'candied' apple, 'silken Samarcand' and 'cedared Lebanon', turning nouns into adjectives, play between substance and accidence. The accidence, what 'spices' the noun, is more vivid and 'substantial' than what it is qualifying – a form of *hysteron proteron* – while the distinction between an object and its accidental qualities are preserved. (Something similar happens with the ambient 'beechen green' in 'Ode to a Nightingale', 9.) On a moral level, a potentially threatening and acquisitive situation involving commodification, voyeurism and the threat of rape is placed in suspense, but not abolished. After all, at the end the boy takes the helpless girl into the outer realm of dragons and heterosexist ideology is restored. But Porphyro is no Comus and Madeline is no Lady. The poem is about having your cake and eating it (a maxim which forms the epigraph to Keats's sonnet on fame.[133]) It uses the language of the oppressor in a hyperbolic but self-defeating way.

The twenty-fifth stanza describes the wintry moon (217), evoking the empty, unmarked body. The frozen light erotically colours Madeline, reversing the habitual tropology of the poem where eros is frozen like the 'sculptured dead' (stanza 1). Falling on Madeline through the stained-glass window, the heraldic gules (red), rose and amethyst light, whose last term resembles the 'blanchèd' and 'lavendered' sheets of stanza 30 line 263 in colour if not in scent, connotes a rainbow's diffraction. This is despite Keats's condemnation of Newton at Haydon's famous dinner party, recorded in 'The Immortal Dinner' (28 December 1817). The tinting of blankness and smoothness in stanza 30, the blancmange effect, also applies to the 'azure-lidded sleep' and the 'blanchèd linen, smooth and lavendered', echoing the registers of stained glass and friezes. Stillness and motion, frozenness and liquidity oscillate.

Whose language is this? Porphyro's or Madeline's? It is like the optical illusion of the duck/rabbit: is this passage for her or him? This is especially urgent given the last line of stanza 26, where Madeline looks with an anamorphic (or sidelong) gaze to see her own desire (the desire of desire), just like Porphyro who also sings *La belle dame sans mercy* (234; see XXXIII.292). Keats's poem 'La Belle Dame Sans Mercy' also contains a sidelong gaze. The last line of stanza 25, 'She knelt, so pure a thing, so free from mortal taint', recalls the use of 'tinct' in the spice stanza (XXX.267). Madeline could not be closer to mortal taint with the erotic stain of purple light. 'Tinct' also brings to mind *Hamlet* III.iv.91, describing the 'tinct' of black spots, suggesting the taint of sin. Madeline is to light as syrup is to spice. 'Half-hidden, like a mermaid in sea-weed' (XXVI.231) suggests that her legs are hidden. The part of her that enables us to tell that she is a mermaid is not there; what then is the point of the image? If it had been Coleridge, the light entering the windows would have been a ghastly green, making Madeline look like death warmed up or life cooled down. A reading of the mermaid as Medusa comes closest to Coleridge's poetry of abjection. The phallic woman of *The Rime of the Ancient Mariner*'s Life-in-Death demonstrates the difference between phobic cosmetics and the queer cosmetics of Madeline and Porphyro. Keats is certainly allusive here, however, with the 'panes of quaint device' (XXIV.211) echoing the 'miracle of rare device' that is the 'sunny pleasure dome with caves of ice' in 'Kubla Khan' (35–6). Recall Steele's icy, tinted dessert (p. 113).

Readers can have their fantasy cake and eat it too, in a superposition of reality and fantasy like light on Madeline's body. We witness the form of an image belying its content, supplementing it, spicing it – so can one tell it is there? This does not mean that it is not there, that all is form or all is language, or that all is masculine voyeurism. There is something there though it is unnameable. Andrew Bennett has discussed how *The Eve of St Agnes* approaches the theme of reading as disfiguration in terms of voyeurism and the gaze.[134] A 'quaint device' is etymologically a vaginal trope.

Madeline's name evokes Mary Magdalen, the archetypal fallen woman and saint. There is a sense of having already fallen before one is beatified, though for the poem's eroticism to work it has not to look like that. If the poem endorses a patriarchal view, then this is about how purity has to be established for a good price to be set in the patriarchal marketplace. But in fact the poem chases the pink dollar of *double entendre*. Bewell has shown how the discourse of flowers available to Keats had both heterosexual and homosexual registers through the ruse of *double entendre*.[135] The poetics of spice also presented a similar range of erotic registers, because of the gendering of luxury in the long eighteenth century.

Porphyro's voyeurism is hardly conventionally masculinised, given the details he is noting. 'Smooth and lavendered' achieves the same effect as the spiced syrups in a hendiadys. Hendiadys is an appropriate trope for a poem that keeps creating the impression of the fantasy reversal of real irreversible tropological processes, for example the image of the rose regressing (XXVII.243). This is not necessarily an infantile image. The view of Madeline that hovers over this passage recalls the Phoenix-like angel Raphael in *Paradise Lost*, viewed by Adam, tinted with the sky:

> to his proper shape returns
> A seraph winged; six wings he wore, to shade
> His lineaments divine; the pair that clad
> Each shoulder broad, came mantling o'er his breast
> With regal ornament; the middle pair
> Girt like a starry zone his waist, and round
> Skirted his loins and thighs with downy gold
> And colours dipped in heaven; the third his feet
> Shadowed from either heel with feathered mail
> Sky-tinctured grain. Like Maia's son he stood,
> And shook his plumes, that heavenly fragrance filled
> The circuit wide. Straight knew him all the bands
> Of Angels under watch; and to his state,
> And to his message high in honour rise;
> For on some message high they guessed him bound.
> Their glittering tents he passed, and now is come
> Into the blissful field, through groves of myrrh,
> And flowering odours, cassia, nard, and balm;
> A wilderness of sweets. (V. 276–94)

(Beth Lau notes that Keats marked up his copy of *Paradise Lost* at precisely this passage.[136]) Colour and scent move through a field of colour and scent: figure and ground have been confused in ambience. Subject and object are of the same gender. The male gaze of Adam looking upon Raphael is eroticised. This may have been in the mind of Catherine Grace Garnett (later Godwin, 1798–1845) when in 'Indian Scenery' she described exotic birds moving through the forest:

There the flamingo's scarlet plume is seen,
Flaunting beneath th' arika's verdant screen;
And sweeping stately through the tamarind glade,
With jewell'd crest triumphantly display'd,
The peacock to the sunset doth unfold
His proud array of purple and of gold.
Cloth'd in the rainbow's bright and blending dyes,
The loxia in the changeful sunbeam flies;
Or in the branches' quivering maze entwined,
Pierces the wild acacia's spicy rind. (215–26)[137]

There is a sense in Garnett as in Milton of colour and scent diffusing through a world of colour and scent: an ambient poetics. The description dazzles and intoxicates with its jewels, purple, rich textiles, spice; and the ekphrastic, erotic register of unfolding and display. The Miltonic original, depicting Raphael as a Phoenix landing in Eden (*Paradise Lost*, v.271–99), is tropologically unstable. Eden is worked, but is here a chaos 'wild above rule or art' (v.297). Just as topos depends on tropology, place depends on flowing space. The unstable space of the *hortus conclusus*, reimagined in Milton's Eden, is also figured in the enclosed feminine space of Madeline's chambers, the closet from which Porphyro brings the erotic feast emblem, and the feast itself. Furthermore, gender identity depends on the liquidity of performance. For a second Milton appears capable of being used by the Keats who wrote the sonnet on the sonnet, and the poem 'Fancy'. Milton is not the facile 'Milkton' imagined in *Keats's Life of Allegory*.

Keats's remarks on negative capability (to Richard Woodhouse, 27 October 1818) are well known.[138] Keats emphasises the idea of the fecund chameleon poet, who can personify Iago as much as Imogen. The slip from an unnamed Desdemona to Imogen suggests the voyeuristic Iachimo in the closet beholding her chilling ekphrastic beauty. Criticism that emphasised fecundity would revise *Ode to Psyche*, which is usually read as being concerned with internalisation. But the world invades, for example in the last stanza, which is effectively a manifesto for the ornamental poetics of spice:

And there by zephyrs, streams, and birds, and bees,
  The moss-lain Dryads shall be lulled to sleep;
And in the midst of this wide quietness
  A rosy sanctuary will I dress
With the wreathed trellis of a working brain,
  With buds, and bells, and stars without a name,

With all the gardener Fancy e'er could feign,
Who breeding flowers, will never breed the same:
And there shall be for thee all soft delight
That shadowy thought can win,
A bright torch, and a casement ope at night,
To let the warm Love in. (56–67)

The *occupatio* 'no incense sweet' (32) heightens the tropological self-reflexivity of the poetics of spice. With that and the 'lucent fans' (41), it is in the same linguistic register as *The Eve of St Agnes*. The narrator is not in the position of Porphyro, but of Madeline, letting love in through the 'casement', intoxicated by flows of sound without a signified. In stanza 23 of *The Eve of St Agnes*, Madeline prays like 'a tongueless nightingale' (206), a reference to Philomela, the mythical mistress of ekphrastic tapestry (as in Eliot).

Let us return to the notion that *The Eve of St Agnes* presents the realisation of a fantasy that retains the appearance of fantasy. The line 'Into her dream he melted' (320) echoes and reverses Keats's reading of Adam's dream as an analogy for the imagination: 'he awoke and found it truth' (from the letter to Benjamin Bailey, 22 November 1817). For Keats, melting into the other has a culinary connotation: it is to be done with indiscriminate 'gusto' (from the letter about the 'camelion poet', to Richard Woodhouse, 27 October 1818) – a most un-Miltonic sentiment. In *Paradise Lost*, Adam dreams of Eden:

Each tree
Loaden with fairest fruit that hung to the eye
Tempting, stirred in me sudden appetite
To pluck and eat; whereat I waked, and found
Before mine eyes all real, as the dream
Had lively shadowed. (VIII.306–11)

Adam is ironically giving away more than just what he sees to be 'real': he is speaking the truth of desire that will eventually precipitate the Fall. In *The Eve of St Agnes* on the other hand, there is no sense of waking up but of falling asleep into reality, the realisation of a fantasy. This is the inverse of Adam's dream. 'Argosy' (268) suggests that the Argonauts have been realised while retaining their figurative qualities. The notion of falling asleep into reality evokes the fundamental image of petrified enjoyment, of a life-in-death, or life-in-art. At the end, Porphyro and Madeline disappear into art like the protagonists in Salvador Dali's film *Un Chien Andalou*, who end up as cardboard cut-outs. This is the ideological structure determining the role of consumption in the poem.

Porphyro's spiced blandishments over-identify with the play with boundaries between fantasy and reality. This parody of consumption resembles Hegel's condemnation of people who imagine a neutral substance on to which accidents just seem to stick like pieces of paper. The transumptive food is to be consumed by the reader only: the consumption of consumption. Curiously, it seems as if the logic of vegetarian discourse and the poetics of spice agree at points. As discussed in the section 'Apicius and abstinence', vegetarian food is meant to connote pure health, sublimely unmarked food. The path of delight is imaged as a path of health, just as the Lucretian model of poetry is a sweetened medicine. And this is also a path of non-touching, the non-marking of the sensual animal body. Porphyro's meal is, however, not one on which one would expect a return of investment. It is a form of pure generosity.

Porphyro's meal is a privatised version of the medieval banquet, in which no performance would be staged without the sleeping female/matter/substance as a foil to accidence; Porphyro here functions as spice; the scene reflects upon itself without the waking complicity of its addressee. It is a ritual offering, accidence bowing to substance, that is, bowing to its own emptiness. A relationship is established between perpetuity, under the sign of masculinity, and materiality, under the sign of femininity.[139]

Stanza 30 is a fantasy of pure excess in which the accidents are more vivid than the substances. Keats's noun-heavy prosody suits this. The phrase 'tinct with cinnamon' suggests touching, medicine (tincture), painting and tainting: in short, the *pharmakon*, the graphic substance that is both poison and cure. We are offered both Logos and *pharmakon*: bland food and spice – blancmange. ('White meat' in the Middle Ages included curds and was considered peasant food: Keats also plays with class.)

At the beginning of *Endymion* (1817; published 1818) Keats declares that 'A thing of beauty is a joy forever' (I.1). Marx was puzzled about the eternal charm of Greek statues: how did this square with a historicising imagination? The persistence of the poetics of spice raises similar questions. What this passage is meditating upon, however, is not so much the relationship between history and the imagination as that between enjoyment and the 'thing'. What is the 'bower quiet for us'? Sleep, health, 'quiet breathing' (5) imply something medicinal, a utopian immersion in the body, as does 'A flowery band to bind us to the earth' (7) – Adam and Eve's prelapsarian state, without Miltonic labour. Again, 'An endless fountain of immortal drink' (23) is a potlatch image, a cornucopia. Leigh Hunt, reviewing Keats's *Poems* (1817), declared that 'Poetry, like Plenty, should be represented with a cornucopia'.[140]

The emblems in the middle sequence of this passage are transumptive, not neatly encoded within an ecosystemic feedback. The yellow of the daffodils and the scent of the musk rose in the clearing punctuate the symbiotic relationship between figure and ground. It is suggested that writing also possesses this punctual quality and that this is what perpetuates the materiality of human, natural, poetic life. The emblem stands out ekphrastically, denoting entities that themselves stand out against an undifferentiated ground. Forever wishing to articulate the object from the impossible viewpoint of the object itself, Keats creates a bootstrapping emblem that knots up language and then disappears, revealing the punctual Real of desire. The significant relationship is between enjoyment and the Thing, or as Lacan would say, the Imaginary–Real axis; and as Keats would put it, the central significance of negative capability. This is a fantasy about the Real, for the emblem can only *seek* to bootstrap. If the tropes fall into place correctly, Keats hopes, a jackpot or potlatch of the Real will tumble forth. The tumbling-forth of the Real is what Christopher Ricks finds embarrassing about Keats.

The sleeping/consuming subject-(non-)position resembles the sleeping/tinted Madeline in *The Eve of St Agnes*. The sleeping Madeline resembles Hegel's empty set, the subject without content. In Hegelian set theory, a set can contain itself as a member: hence the possibility of a set with no positive contents, of a ground without figures, or food without spice. The *spice* stanza is a transumptive emblem, like 'A thing of beauty is a joy forever'. 'He brought' is a figure about metaphor, trade, translation: Porphyro is displayed as a figure for poetic language, idealised in the fantasy of traffic from silken Samarkand to cedared Lebanon. Here is another noun-like use of a figure punctuating its ground. Keats plays on the notion of epithet (*epi-tithēmi*, 'I place on'): the spicing of the food is epithetic. Given the relationship between 'transferred' and 'translated', the 'argosy' could be an argot sea. This is a material process, not simply lurking behind the text but also in it. So Keats figures a fantastic economy without reserve, an economy of the gift.

The role of spice in Keats's time was filled by products such as opium and tea. But the dialectic of opium and the body, and the opium trade and China, captured so shockingly in the imperialist paranoia of De Quincey's brilliantly traumatic *Confessions of an English Opium-Eater*, also resembles the infantilisation of the consumer and the dialectic between destabilising flow and petrified enjoyment which I have been examining.

The very anachronism, however, of spice *qua* cinnamon and so forth, its true uselessness, makes it even more effective as an index of meaningless enjoyment. The poetics of spice 'antiques' the modern literary product, the Romantic poem. Keats would have liked the use of a noun as a verb here. For *whom* is the fantasy of the blancmange being staged? For a dreaming sleeper, a non-position? The language is trying simply, fantastically, to stage *itself*, to stage staging. Keats's brilliantly transumptive erotic medievalist fantasy enacts the ideological secret of capitalism, whose advertisements seem also to subvert the viewer and directly 'touch' the unconscious desires. Eliot also claimed this subliminal aesthetics, in a more phobic mode. For capitalist ideologies of consumption tend also to stage staging, simulating the spontaneous, providential power of the commodity to reach the right consumer. The commodity's apparent pursuit of those who 'demand' it is uncannily reminiscent of the Freudian concept of the superego, and it is perhaps no accident that the ultimate slogan of the most powerful capitalist nation on earth in the late twentieth century is 'Enjoy!', especially as in 'Enjoy Coke!' The poetics of spice is encapsulated in this simple prescription, infantilising the consumer. A 1950s advertisement displayed a giant Coke-symbol sun bottle-feeding a baby world.

Keats's 'negative capability' is a fantasy of absorption into the punctual Real of pure gift, pure consumption, the reverse side of the hermit-like and workaday, restricted-economy capitalist ego. The fantasy-Real is a place where despotic objects hold sway, as in Pope's Cave of Spleen. The Real for Keats is a kind of potlatch, an outrageous, excessive inflow of consumable stuff. The demand of and for the Real is reminiscent of a recent US advertising campaign for Eagle Chips, in which a demanding face-without-a-body flies, lamella-like, as if it were a frisbee made of flesh, through domestic environments, consuming chips wherever it sticks and chortling about its overconsumption. This image evokes a world in which the reader or consumer is attached, as if by a drip feed, to the overflowing bottle of reality.

Not quite a cry of the heart in a heartless world, this fantasy is a structural Mandevillian inutility at the heart of capitalist consumption, where private vices breed public virtues. The gloriously useless, surplus enjoyment is a structural place reserved in the Romantic period and after for literature, the feminine and the academy: Cardinal Newman's nineteenth-century model university claims ontological priority over utilitarian institutions precisely in its uselessness. The 'antiqued' consumption of spice evokes a kernel of 'antiproduction' at the heart of fantasies about the regime of the commodity. All these potential fillers of the space carved out by surplus enjoyment, confound the opposition of decoration and heart, epiphenomenon and deep structure. They present a vision of what Lacan called 'the extimate', rather than the intimate: that which is uncannily close and yet threateningly other: sprouts of enjoyment on a smoothly functioning, utilitarian masculinised body.

The dessert, then, is an image of antiqued, useless excess, of stoned, petrified consumption: the last oozings of the gum-weeping tree in *Othello* or the cider press in 'To Autumn', the incarnation of the fantasies parodied in *The Land of Cockaygne*. *Tait's Magazine* associated Keats with this cornucopian medieval realm: 'That unfortunate cockaigner Johnny Keats'.[141] There is even a humorous etymological association between 'Cockaigner' and 'Cockney'.[142] 'Z' described Leigh Hunt as 'the Idol of Cockaigne'; *Blackwood's* magazine used similar language from the late 1810s and early 1820s.[143] Breughel's painting of the Land of Cockaygne depicts fattened, stoned bodies immobilised on an impossible hillside, running with animals whose extra limbs are the knives that prepare them to be eaten. Fast food, infantilised diet, creates a Body without Organs, the spherical, bloated bodies of Cockaygne's inhabitants, swarming with titbits, like the world fed by the Coke/sun. There is redundancy at the core of the work ethic, a superficial, meaningless sprout of enjoyment. The utopian dimension of the Cockaygne myth was analysed by Ernst Bloch, whose study of fairytales showed how such stories undermine aristocratic epic.[144] Benjamin Franklin (1706–90) was keen to distance America from the Cockaygne myth: 'In short, America is the land of labour, and by no means what the English call *Lubberland*, and the French *Pays de Cocagne*, where the streets are said to be paved with half-peck loaves, the houses tiled with pancakes, and where the fowls cry about ready roasted, crying *Come eat me*!'[145] But Franklin's protestation demonstrates, in its denial, how *Cockaygne is also a feature of capitalist ideology*. So does Keats's poem undermine capitalist ideology?

The notion of a functional body with a non-utilitarian heart also applies to modern conceptions of human identity. In a sense, commodities and their ideologies were Romantic poets before Romanticism. They resembled them in all ways, as incarnations of desire, voyaging to the exotic and back again, spontaneously self-existing, in process, always catching up with themselves, rising Phoenix-like again and again, in their sublime state between life and death. As Hegel remarked, wealth is the self. Or as Keats declares, in a language that (without meaning to denigrate him) is so evocative of advertising, 'A thing of beauty is a joy forever.' The permanent, objectified enjoyment expressed in these words is also the petrified 'I' of modernity.

Keats's 'I' without doubt overidentifies with these norms, as 'Z' notoriously declares. Keats is queer because he is too poetic by half. If Keats's poetry does not suggest full complicity with the poetics of spice, it is because he overdoes it. Keats's overidentification with a certain capitalist symptom can be interpreted either through Jean-François Lyotard or Žižek. In *The Postmodern Condition*, Lyotard suggests a mode of subversion in hypercapitalist modernity requiring nothing more than going exactly by the ideological book.[146] This quietism is supposed to introduce entropy into a system that constantly requires something to grate against. In *The Metastases of Enjoyment*, however, Žižek analyses the rock band Laibach's overidentification with fascist iconography, showing how it manipulates transference. The same could be said for Keats, whose spicy bedroom scene begs the question, 'for whom is this being staged?' By identifying too much, rather than being ironic about, 'the obscene superego underside of the system, overidentification suspends its efficiency':

> [The public asks Keats] a question and expect[s] an answer from [him], failing to notice that [Keats himself] *function[s] not as an answer but as a question*. By means of the elusive character of [his] desire, of the undecidability as to 'where [he] actually stand[s]', [Keats] compel[s] us to take up our position and decide upon *our* desire.[147]

This is the opposite of quietism. Furthermore, Keats's play with the sensualisation of the commodity and the commodification of sensuality is subversive in its use of images of petrified enjoyment. The coagulation of enjoyment in the ekphrastic scene suspends the Master-Signifier of binary sexuality. The spiced creams, jellies and syrups are the opposite of phallic monuments, and thus this particular ekphrasis does not commemorate very well the royal power which its medievalism implies. It resembles what Žižek observes in the monument at the Mexico City university campus:

> Monuments are usually 'phallic': towers, spires, something that protrudes and 'stands out' . . . [but on the Mexico City campus] a large jagged ring of concrete encircles the formless black undulating surface of lava. What we have here is a true monument to the Thing, to coagulated *jouissance*, substance of enjoyment.[148]

Keats subverts expectation through hyperbole, by *overdoing* a topos, a quasi-Mannerist device that could be described as dioptric, as Ricks explores in *Keats and Embarrassment*, and as Bewell has demonstrated.[149] Keats is indeed a 'pharmacopolitical' poet as Maginn remarked: this is the politics of the *pharmakon*.

One could say that Keats aesthetically limns the commodity form as it is sensuously grasped in the particular. Percy Shelley, on the other hand, describes its general form. Shelley's use of fractal imagery, where similes appear to map onto themselves with a ratio of slightly more than one, as in *Adonais* (XIII.116–17 and elsewhere), suggests that the concept has become more real than the thing: the play of the concept is emphasised over the play of the thing.[150] In contrast, Keats's use of transumptive emblems suggests that *the thing has become more real than the concept.* Since spice is already the *ekphanestaton* of food and hence indicates a sublime drawing upon *occupatio* to achieve a reality more real than the concept, the thirtieth stanza of *The Eve of St Agnes* is a sophisticated instance of the coagulation of the Thing.

Keats wants to make words dissolve and things emerge; his art is ekphrastic to the core. As Krieger says of the use of ekphrasis: 'It is the romantic quest to realize the nostalgic dream of an original, prefallen language of corporeal presence, though our only means to reach it is the fallen language around us.'[151] As Levinson declares, Keats is a poet of the thing, endowing his work with 'a conceptual physis', giving 'no things but in Ideas, and no ideas but in the script-things that render them absolute'.[152] But Keats is also the poet of yearning for the embodiment of a realm of fantasy that can only appear *as* fantasy for a world that constitutively lacks it. Pierre et Gilles' Keatsian fantasy images parody kitsch religious iconography to create a humorous and erotically charged realm of yearning parallel to the real world, a Land of Oz. Levinson grasps the similar quality of Keats when she writes: 'What we want to explain here is the *badness*, and thus the greatness of these poems.'[153] Thus modernity has its own versions of Paradise, which Camporesi calls 'a mirror image of the real and historic worlds . . . in which . . . the quality of life reached absolute perfection . . . [It is] the world turned upside down'.[154]

A common attitude to the spice stanza in *The Eve of St Agnes* is that it reflects Keats's narcissism, voyeurism, infantile or onanistic tendencies. However, a study of the long eighteenth century clearly indicates political, economic and poetic reasons for Keats's presentation. The foods are not in themselves infantile, nor are they simplistically presented: they are 'antiqued', becoming the most valuable kind of modern circulating commodity. In a *faux-naif* gesture typical of camp, the archetypal parodic form of consumer fetishism, Keats parodies the rhetoric of the commodity by redoubling it, in a traversal of the fantasy. This traversal is 'extrapellation', the very opposite of what Althusser means by 'interpellation' – the way in which ideology incorporates us by advertising a possible identity.

The Eve of St Agnes inhabits the inconvenient space between Madeline and Porphyro, substance and accidence, dialectics and deconstruction, pre-Socratic and post-Socratic philosophy, history and textuality, content and form. Between love and madness, as they say, lies Obsession. As the TV advertisement used to say: 'Oh, the smell of it.'[155]

CHAPTER 4

Blood sugar

Transmitted miseries, and successive chains.

Hannah More, *Slavery* (1788), 103

Each thought it was the way freedom smelled, or justice, or luxury, or vengeance.

Toni Morrison, *Song of Solomon*, p. 185

INTRODUCTION

What happens to poetry when it articulates resistance to the narcosis of consumption? In the late eighteenth century new forms of poetry emerged that addressed the question of abstinence from luxury. Furthermore, new forms of spectacular politics emerged, based on boycotting and abstinence: the Boston Tea Party was a particularly flamboyant instance. Boycotting was a feature of Romantic consumerism, a mode of consumption that could reflect on itself. In both poetics and politics, what was being played with was the symbolism of non-consumption. The forces of negation, aversion and revulsion were invoked. Seward's *Verses Inviting Stella to Tea on the Public Fast-Day [During the American War], February, MDCCLXXXI* (written 1781, published 1791) is a witty play on the significance of abstinence for British relations with America. Seward draws a comparison between the chaos of the Boston Tea Party and the banquet of Thyestes, in which Thyestes' sons were served to the gods. The Americans, like the abolitionists during the 1780s, 'Saw poison in the perfumed draught' (38). Até, the Greek goddess of madness, 'mingled with th' envenomed flood / Brothers', parents', children's blood' (43–4). Tea is imagined as a *pharmakon*, an 'Indian shrub' whose 'fragrant flowers / To England's weal has deadly powers' (29–30). The medicine became poison when 'Tyranny' employed it to gain power.

Excessive consumption became the target of different kinds of invective, from vegetarianism to anti-slavery writing. Those who promulgated abstention from luxury invoked notions of supplementarity closely associated with the poetics of spice. These notions had ambivalent political implications that emerged poignantly in the anti-slavery debates at the end of the century.

In *Sweetness and Power*, Mintz has studied how sugar changed from an 'exotic luxury' to a 'proletarian necessity' during the Industrial Revolution. Sugar reduced the cost of 'reproducing' the masses by 'sating' and 'drugging' them.[1] Sugar was considered a spice in the Middle Ages. By the fifteenth century, tonnes of sugar were being brought into Britain. Sugar candy was imported from Italy, along with candied lemon, orange peel and preserved fruit. In addition, treacle, violet and rose sugars were consumed.[2] The Duke of Buckingham's records for 1452–63 mention 'blaunchpoudre' (ginger ground with sugar) and 'powdour marchant' (a ready-made mixture of sugar and cinnamon).[3] The transfer of sugar production from the East to the West Indies, and a corresponding culture of slavery and politics of anti-slavery, gave rise to new inflections of the poetics of spice.

The Sorrows of Yamba (*c.*1795), often attributed to Hannah More (1745–1833), is a slave's monologue that talks about the 'mercy sweet' of God (99). Given that sugar was the commodity, farmed by the slaves, the sweetness is here not without its portion of power. The author delineates a missionary transcendental moralism, affecting slave and 'massa' alike. But her sense of the 'transmitted miseries' of slavery, quoted in the epigraph, registers the ways in which transnational trade traces networks.

What were the ways in which the representation of sugar interacted with discourses on trade and slavery? Produced by slaves, consumed and discussed in diverse ways by the British, sugar is the locus of connections between colonialism and representation. The rhetoric of abstinence from sugar and rum, in which East Indian sugar or honey was substituted for the former, played a role in the discourse of the Anti-Slavery Society and reached its peak in the late 1780s and early 1790s. The texts under discussion here are belated in relation to this tradition of abstinence, and in relation to the slave uprisings in the West Indies with which they are preoccupied. Anti-slavery had become a political football, used by different factions, and often in opportunistic ways.

The rhetoric of abstinence involved a particularly aversive topos, often directed towards the female consumer, as Charlotte Sussman has extensively demonstrated.[4] I call this the 'blood sugar' topos. The sweetened drinks of tea, coffee and chocolate are rendered suddenly nauseating by the notion that they are full of the blood of slaves. As a poem in the *Scots Magazine* for 1788 put it, 'Are drops of blood the horrible manure / That fills with luscious juice the teeming cane?' Franklin articulated the repugnance well:

> A celebrated French moralist said, that, when he considered the wars which we foment in Africa to get negroes, the great number who of course perish in these wars; the multitude of those wretches who die in their passage, by disease, and bad air, and bad provisions; and lastly, how many perish by the cruel treatment they meet with in a state of slavery; when he saw a bit of sugar, he could not help imagining it to be covered with spots of human blood. But, had he added to these considerations the wars which we carry on against one another, to take and retake the islands that produce this commodity, he would not have seen the sugar simply *spotted* with blood, he would have beheld it entirely tinged with it.[5]

Despite his ambivalence towards the slave trade, Franklin sees that the commodity of sugar is permeated, 'entirely tinged', with blood, playing differently on the word from which Keats derives the more pharmakological 'tinct'.

'Epigram' by William Cowper (1731–1800) contains the lines, 'No nostrum, planters say, is half so good / To make fine sugar, as a Negro's blood.'[6] Cowper played on this topos with 'Sweet Meat has Sour Sauce, or, the Slave Trader in the Dumps' (1788, a potent year for anti-slavery poetry):

> Here's padlocks and bolts, and screws for the thumbs
> That squeeze them so lovingly till the blood comes;
> They sweeten the temper like comfits or plums,
> Which nobody can deny.
>
> When a Negro his head from his victuals withdraws
> And clenches his teeth and thrusts out his paws,
> Here's a notable engine to open his jaws,
> Which nobody can deny. (18–25)

The well-placed medieval comfits and plums, not sugar, indicate the medieval quality of the slave-traders' tortures. An antique mode of violence, which inscribes the law directly on the body, is seen to be practised at the margins of society, in a period during which violence against criminals became increasingly internal and psychological, as Foucault has shown in *Discipline and Punish*. Just as the poetics of spice shows the inert heart of enjoyment within the discourse of utility, so it also demonstrates the perverse enjoyment in the commercial coercion of the Other. (Michael Rogin has recently asked whether the cartoonist Richard Newton's illustrations of the flogging of slaves were intended for abolitionists or for collectors of flagellation prints.[7]) The song is deceptively simple. 'Which nobody can deny' has a triple meaning, for the singer, for the slaves, and for advocates of anti-slavery. There is a transition of 'Which nobody can deny' from boisterous sadism to spontaneous compassion.

Shock, not fantasy, jolts the reader out of symbolic identification with the text, displaying a perverse enjoyment of pain in the service of commerce. For example, Stedman's ambiguous work of anti-slavery, *Narrative of a Five Years' Expedition, Against the Revolted Negroes of Surinam* (1796), describes the dangers of producing sugar:

> So very dangerous is the work of those negroes who attend the rollers [through which the cane passes twice to extract the liquefied pith], that should one of their fingers be caught between them, which frequently happens through inadvertency, the whole arm is instantly shattered to pieces, if not part of the body. A hatchet is generally ready to chop off the limb, before the working of the mill can be stopped. Another danger is, that should a poor slave dare to taste that sugar which he produces by the sweat of his brow, he runs the risk of receiving some hundred lashes, or having all his teeth knocked out by the overseer. – Such are the hardships and dangers to which the sugar-making negroes are exposed.[8]

The book masquerades as a natural-historical and social guide book, a late eighteenth-century coffee-table book, with its beautiful illustrations by Blake and Bartolozzi. But this sweetness is undermined by a shocking anti-slavery aesthetic in which Blake played a part, his famous illustration of execution by breaking on the rack forming the model for his own mythological revolutionary hero, Orc.

This chapter analyses the function of the 'blood sugar' topos in Coleridge's 1795 lecture on the slave trade, and in Southey's sonnets on the slave trade (1797). In Southey's sonnets, the metonymic chains that relate colony to colonial power, Hannah More's 'successive chains' quoted in the epigraph are condensed into a powerful and ambiguous metaphor in which sugar stands for the blood of the slaves. I shall also analyse metonymy in *Humanity* (1788), a long poem about anti-slavery by the sentimental Della Cruscan poet Samuel Jackson Pratt (1749–1814), who exerted an influence on the work of Percy Shelley. The commodity as metonymised body is treated powerfully in *Humanity*, but in a much more sophisticated, polyphonic and surprising way by Southey. The title 'Blood Sugar' indicates an anxious play between power and sweetness, *hypsilatos* and *gluchotēs*, terms familiar in Renaissance poetics which informed the discourses of pleasure and sublimity.

THE GUILT TROPE

Paul Gilroy has remarked that 'A sense of the body's place in the natural world can provide . . . a social ecology and an alternative rationality that articulate a cultural and moral challenge to the exploitation and domination of "the nature within us and without us".'[9] The radical millenarianism of the 1790s, problematic for Coleridge and Southey,[10] provided just such an emergent 'sense of the body's place', and so did contemporary arguments about human and animal rights. Within anti-slavery literature, Coleridge's 1795 address on the subject uses the categories of 'natural' and 'unnatural', and under the latter category come the critical notions of luxury, barbarity and social injustice.[11]

The 'blood sugar' topos highlights the artificiality of certain wants, underscoring how acts of consumption can be complicit with the forces of colonialism and exploitation. It is likely that Coleridge was not trying to induce guilt in the specific audience that the speech addresses, an audience which was made up of middle-class Bristol dissenters and reformers including the Unitarian minister John Prior Estlin, the publisher Joseph Cottle and his brothers Robert and Amos. John Thelwall (1764–1834), who associated with the then-radical Coleridge and who came from a background similar to that of the Bristol audience, wrote a poem about sugar in the *Peripatetic* (1793). Coleridge may have been preaching to the converted, in which case the blood sugar topos is designed to produce a sense of self-righteousness, or even complacency: most of the audience may be assumed to be abstainers already.

The blood sugar topos reverses consumption into production, figurality into literality, and supplementarity into essence. The topos is straightforward in its moral shock: imagine, gently bred citizens, as you sit quaffing your sweet tea (or coffee, rum or chocolate), how its sweetness is derived from suffering, how sugar is derived from the blood of slaves. But the topos is remarkable in its underlying assumptions about figurative language, and complex in its ideological effects. It is not just that the topos reveals a 'Real' of slavery underlying the figure of sugar; the materiality of the figure itself is at stake. It is an apocalyptic rhetoric that decodes the slave trade, but its unveiling process draws attention to the materiality of the very veil that has been torn away. Abstinence is found to be an inadequate means of resistance to the slave trade. It is not enough of a disillusionment, and indeed the blood sugar topos questions whether abandoning 'false consciousness' subverts ideology.

Coleridge spoke on the slave trade on 16 June 1795 at Bristol, before his quarrel with Southey and abandonment of Pantisocracy. The lecture was part of a series intended to raise money for the project. It was later reprinted in condensed and revised form in the fourth number of the *Watchman*.[12] Bristol in the mid-1790s was the centre for a burgeoning cultural group that included Coleridge. It was also a centre for the English slave trade. The city was not just the starting-point for the trade but part of the triangle that included Jamaica and Africa, balancing the trade in timber against the trade in human beings. The *Observer* noted that Coleridge '"has delivered many lectures here, one of which (on the Slave-trade) is a proof of the detestation in which he holds that infamous traffic"'.[13]

The lecture is directed at the consumer and at the abstainer. The first paragraph resonates directly with other discourses on luxury and artificiality in the period (for example, Shelley's 1813 pamphlet on vegetarianism): 'Miseries' and 'Vices' arise 'From Artificial Wants'; in contrast, 'What Nature demands Nature everywhere supplies.' The purpose of humans is 'To develope the powers of the Creator', to finish the job that He started: to supplement nature safely.[14] A rhetorical pattern is established that distinguishes this 'good' mode of supplementarity from the 'bad' one of artificial wants in excess of a naturalised norm. Coleridge then focuses on his subject:

> We receive from the West Indies Sugar, Rum, Cotton, log-wood, cocoa, coffee, pimento [allspice], ginger, indigo, mahogany, and conserves – not one of these are necessary – indeed with the exceptions of cotton and mahogany we cannot with truth call them even useful, and not one is at present attainable by the poor and labouring part of Society . . . If the Trade had never existed, no one human being would have been less comfortably cloathd, housed, or nourished – Such is its value.[15]

Contained in this list are luxury commodities: spices, coffee and, to a certain extent, sugar. Various eighteenth-century writers conducted a rich debate about luxury. The protectionism of English-based companies was often in opposition to the protectionism of colonial ones. Early mercantilist debates about consumption focused on the problem of 'necessary' luxuries.[16] Adam Smith later began to develop ways of thinking about modes of individual overconsumption that would be providential for society at large, deploying the rhetoric of the invisible hand. During the American and French Revolutions, the anti-luxury discourse found a place in the evangelical opposition of writers such as Cowper and More.

Sugar was being proletarianised: the working-class break of a milky cup of sugary tea was imminent.[17] Through sugar consumption the European working classes were linked with African slaves and migrant workers on the plantations.[18] However, it is fair to say that Coleridge's remark is aimed towards a middle-class and largely dissenting audience (in particular, it was Unitarian and also probably Quaker). A contribution by Southey then contrasts the Europeans, who dabble with dangerous supplements, with the holistic culture of the Africans: 'The Africans, who are situated beyond the contagion of European vice – are innocent and happy – the peaceful inhabitants of a fertile soil, they cultivate their fields in common and reap the crop as the common property of all.'[19] This image of primitive communism, close to the ideal of Pantisocracy, was designed explicitly to counteract the effect of work that categorised the Africans as savage and hence in need of Christian improvement (a rationalisation for slavery). The image conflicts with the more realistic account of African involvement in the slave trade later in the essay. Africa was a site of contested figuration in the period. Blake may have represented black literary traditions in 'The Little Black Boy', which is derived from first-hand accounts of slavery by figures such as Equiano and Cugoano (and, incidentally, from the Song of Songs, with its invocation of blackness (1:5–6)), and works such as Phyllis Wheatley's 'Hymn to Morning' in *Poems on Various Subjects* (1773). Blake thus pays respect to West African philosophy.[20]

Coleridge starts using the topos of bloody sugar by criticising consumers for what is primarily the fault of capitalists and speculators: another form of Romantic self-reflexive consumerism. He castigates the politics of protest with the discourse of abstinence:

Had all the people who petitioned for the abolition of this execrable Commerce instead of bustling about and showing off with all the vanity of pretended sensibility, simply left off the use of Sugar and Rum, it is demonstrable that the Slave-merchants and Planters must either have applied to Parliament for the abolition of the Slave Trade or have suffered the West India Trade altogether to perish – a consummation most devoutly to be wished – .[21]

Quoting *Hamlet* III.i.63–4, Coleridge begins to tighten the rhetorical screw. He plays on the blood sugar topos, which had already become popular in the discourse of abstinence. Twenty-six editions of William Fox's *An Address to the People of Great Britain, on the Propriety of Abstaining from West India Sugar and Rum* had been published by 1793; the discourse of radical abstinence was already in place. Indeed, the blood sugar topos was itself somewhat outmoded: *A Second Address* had expressed a more anti-sentimental, literalist form of paranoia about the actual contamination of sugar by the sweat of slaves.[22] Coleridge taps this vein by citing the 'cause' of the slave trade as the 'consumption of its Products! and does not then Guilt rest on the Consumers? and is it not an allowed axiom in Morality that Wickedness may be multiplied but cannot be divided and that the Guilt of all attaches to each one who is knowingly an accomplice?'[23] The language of complicity powerfully registers the faults of the capitalists on the blushing cheeks of the consumer.[24] Coleridge's rhetoric speaks through the already-fetishised language of the commodity form, as if all one had to do to change the situation was to resist by desisting from consumption. On the other hand, inasmuch as civil society is shown to be playing a part in mercantile life, the rhetoric empowers the consumer's aggravated sense of choice. Like any other discourse of the fetish, the rhetoric works in more than one way, establishing a bizarre and contradictory reciprocity between the consumed and the consumer.

Coleridge's largely rhetorical address to the Christians in the audience – rhetorical because of the special and radical meanings of such an appellation, connoting Unitarianism – portrays Jesus as a figure who brushes history against the grain. If he were alive today, Jesus would not turn water into wine but sugar back into blood, luxury back into barbarism:

at your meals you rise up and pressing your hands to your bosom ye lift up your eyes to God and say O Lord bless the Food which thou hast given us! A part of that Food amongst most of you is sweetened with the Blood of the Murdered. Bless the Good which thou hast given us! O Blasphemy! Did God give Food mingled with Brothers blood! Will the Father of all men bless the Food of Cannibals – the food which is polluted with the blood of his own innocent Children? Surely if the inspired Philanthropist of Galilee were to revisit earth and be among the feasters as at Cana he would not change Water into Wine but haply convert the produce into the things producing, the occasioned into the things occasioning! Then with our fleshly eye should we behold what even now truth-painting Imagination should exhibit to us – instead of sweetmeats Tears and Blood, and Anguish – and instead of Music groaning and the loud Peals of the Lash.[25]

'Imagination' paints 'truth', not the *pharmakon*. A 'Pause' is added a line below the final sentence: this is persuasive, prescriptive language. Coleridge exploits the long-held Christian fascination and anxiety over what used to be called *metabolē* in the Middle Ages,[26] and from which we obtain the notion of 'metabolism': the transubstantial changes involved in the sacrament of the Eucharist (or thanksgiving: 'Bless the Food'), which is predicated on ways in which potentially cannibalistic food is transmuted into the food of grace.

The rhetoric of metabolism raises the question of metaphorical language itself. Indeed, it is possible to interpret Coleridge's effort to find a suitable linguistic philosophy for his radical politics as an attempt to construct a notion of 'natural signification'.[27] Is it possible to read a metaphor in reverse, to read a figure 'back into' literality? Jesus here acts as the good, inspired man of Unitarian belief: rather than miraculously transforming substances into emblems of divine power, he radically defetishises the object, turning the product into the process of production, in the marvellous pair of phrases towards the end of the passage. Needless to say, it is the metaphorical power of language which enables the retroactive construction of 'literality', a point that separates Coleridge's rich and ambivalent engagements with language in his early writing from other modes of Unitarian discourse.[28]

Disgust is invoked, as the sweet supplement turns clotted and sour in the mouth. This reversal is prevalent in the contemporary literature of abolition. Thomas Somerville's *A Discourse on Our Obligation to Thanksgiving, for the Prospect of the Abolition of the African Slave-Trade* (1792) used prayers that exploited their capacity for shock: 'May the penal effects of vice more and more contribute to over-awe the spirit of violence, and to diminish the number of crimes. – From the established connection between guilt and misery, and the tendency of human laws to avenge more open and atrocious iniquity, may we learn to apprehend thy moral government'; 'Were men, whose hands were *full of blood*, the fit instruments to promulgate the gospel of peace?'[29] Benjamin Flower also achieved such an effect in *The French Constitution*: '"let [the Ladies], if they can . . . continue morning and evening, to sweeten their tea, and the tea of their families and visitors, with the blood of their fellow creatures"'.[30]

The blood sugar topos was an effective ploy. Coleridge continues by relating what is happening in the colonies of the West Indies with the oppression of the peasantry at home:

> But I have heard another argument in favour of the Slave Trade, namely, that the slaves are as well off as the Peasantry in England! . . . I appeal to common sense whether to affirm [this] . . . be not the same as to assert that our Peasantry are as bad off as Negro Slaves – and whether if the Peasantry believed it there is a man amongst them who [would] not rebel? and be justified in Rebellion?[31]

This is a point that Marx made: capitalism imposes forms of slavery, if not economically in the form of wage-slavery in the metropolis, then in actuality in the colony. Just as Coleridge wants to strip trade to its bare essentials (an impossibility?), cutting out the intensive labour of slaves in plantations, so, too, he wishes to reverse language's tropology towards some essential, necessary, causally logical phrase that sums up the Real. The lecture on the slave trade is a pattern of supplements and reversals: between luxury and necessity, sugar and blood, Jamaica and England, slave and peasant. Coleridge is looking for a radical, miraculous language that might reverse a metonymic chain of commodity flow by undoing a metaphorical substitution of blood for sugar, power for sweetness, *hypsilatos* for *gluchotēs*. This jump is exploited in *A Poem on the Inhumanity of the Slave Trade* (1788) by Ann Yearsley (1756–1806), where Luco, 'destined to plant / The sweet luxuriant cane' (215) is punished by being burnt to death. For the virtuous, temperate radical, sweetness is a mode of enjoyment predicated on the repression of production. A lifting of repressed memory tips the sweet into the sour. Romantic poetics is supremely concerned with repression and expression – here that theme becomes external and material. The idea that Romantic culture is about the mind to the exclusion of the body and history needs to be complicated by the observation that it also deals with the realm of fetishism – treating subjects like objects, and objects like subjects.

Deirdre Coleman has discussed the links between cannibalism and the Eucharist in Coleridge's rhetoric, drawing attention to a

Figure 12 James Gillray, 'Barbarities in the West Indias' (London: H. Humphrey, 1791).

cartoon by James Gillray, 'Barbarities in the West Indias' (1791) which depicts a slave being forced into a 'cauldron of boiling sugar juice' like one of the figures in Hieronymous Bosch's depiction of Hell (figure 12).[32] The slave cannot work, and for this reason is put in the cauldron, in an ironic perversion of the myths of cannibalism concerning the indigenous inhabitants of the Caribbean. The grotesque humour is that if the slave is not going to perform as an objectified tool, he or she will be used as another kind of commodity. The slave-driver is saying: 'I'll give you a warm bath to cure your Ague, & a Curry-combing afterwards to put Spunk into you.' Curry-combing is a way of grooming a horse, using 'curry' in the sense of preparation or making ready, and thus producing a macabre culinary pun on 'cure'. Despite the fact that the slave will be removed, according to the caption, the image also allows the viewer to visualise the slave becoming one of the ingredients in sugar production. The puns on curing/currying in the speech contribute to this. The humour is thus dependent upon the discourse of the fetish. The slave remains in an undecidable, abject position between subject and object.

TROPICS AND TOPICS

According to Braudel, the colonial project was often extraordinarily problematic. The West Indies needed the support of England: in 1783, 16,526 tons of salted meat had to be imported.[33] Planters were 'not usually' rich, and Jamaica performed the function of 'a wealth-creating machine' for England, whose net benefit in 1773 was about 1.5 million pounds.[34] Conversely, Europe was shown by Blake to be too feeble to rely on its own strength, supported as it was by Africa and America in one of his illustrations for Stedman's *Narrative* of an expedition to Surinam (figure 13).

Before sugar was proletarianised, it was 'raced' through the discourses associated with slavery and colonialism. The blood sugar topos was a perfect figure for the anxious and ambiguous moment of colonialism, an unstable, dialectical image, both cosy and uncanny in the best traditions of the *Unheimlich*, with its connotations of the 'self-moving' power of the fetish, and the by-turns goulish and smug quaffers.

The notion of 'place' is important, especially considering the topical and tropical qualities of the colonies. Capitalism liquidates the local meanings and values that make a certain territory into a 'place'; it functions better between more abstractly conceived 'spaces', what Manuel Castells calls the 'space of flows'.[35] There were early modern precedents for the space of flows. The early commercial spice trading city, often a port, functioned as just such a space. In *Flesh and Stone*, the sociologist Richard Sennett discusses Venice, *The Merchant of Venice* and *Othello*. The geography of Venice was a product of the spice trade and Jewish persecution, creating a city porous to transnational flows of people and goods but internally rigid in its demarcation and segregation of them, set against the threat of the Turks to disrupt trade via the Black Sea (see figure 14). A tension between space and place created a dialectic of luxury and restraint, a component of the emergence of modernity: thus *The Merchant of Venice* celebrates the redemptive pleasures of calculation.[36]

It is no surprise, then, to find literature on the sugar plantations oscillating between a sense of place and a sense of space. Jamaica (figure 15) is never as solidly 'there' as the Hellenic or English pastoral *loci amoeni* with which, through figurative language, the literature strives to bestow the local colour of 'place'. It threatens to

Figure 13 William Blake, 'Europe Supported by Africa & America': from J. G. Stedman, *Narrative* (1796), between pp. 394 and 395. This is a tropologically dense twisting of topos, a mousetrap designed to catch the conscience of a slave-trading nation. The assertive stances of Africa and America belie the weak contraposta and downcast look of Europe. The sinuous cord connects the three continents in a metonymic bond of sisterhood which subverts the slave bands worn by Africa and America. See Erdman, *Blake*, pp. 231–2.

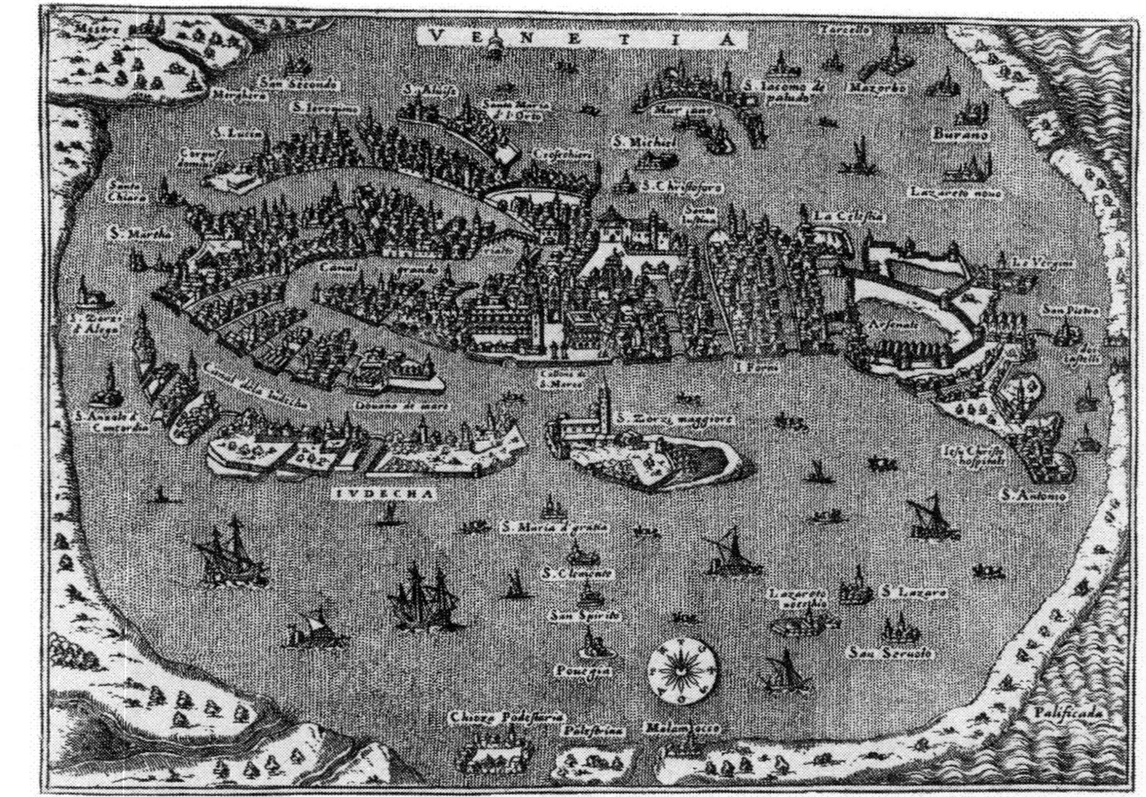

Figure 14 Venice: from Thomaso Porcacchi, *L'isole piu famose del mondo* (1576), p. 65. Venice's openness to the flows of trade is clearly shown in this exquisite map. The island appears like a net, fretted with nodes to catch the incoming currents of commodities.

dissolve and decode all 'placedness' into the pure space of the sugar plantation: a supplementary island growing an imported, supplementary crop.

This was not necessarily a disappointing fact for the radical writer. The very instability of Jamaica would threaten to destabilise the metropolitan culture that it so dangerously supplemented. Certain reactionary writers tried to 'reterritorialise' Jamaica, to present it as another Europe, another belated subject for Shakespeare or Milton (figure 16). But this very belatedness, the need to rely on figures such as *occupatio* ('would that those writers were present to describe the island'),[37] threatened their project, let alone the newer, more capital-happy modes of representation in their writings that celebrate the instability of 'space' through the language of the fetish. Sugar became willy-nilly the hero of the story, and all other voices (Shakespeare *and* the Africans) had to compete with it.

The history of Jamaica reveals relationships with food that are more complex than the reductionist language of the fetish. Seized in 1494 from the Arawaks by Columbus, Jamaica was then taken from the Spanish by the English in 1655. From 1666, African slaves were transported to the island, until the trade was abolished in 1807; emancipation was proclaimed in 1834, and the 'apprenticeship' period in 1838. The relationship between indigenous cultures in Jamaica and their representation by non-indigenous writers and artists has frequently been fraught with contradiction.[38] In terms of food, Jamaica's culture was rich and diverse (figure 17). From the Arawaks, Jamaicans had inherited cassava, corn, sweet potato, yampie, beans, callaloo, hot peppers, pimento, fish, conies, iguanas, crabs, guavas, pineapples, prickly pear, paw-paw and cocoa. The Spaniards had brought the banana, plantain, sugar cane, lemon, lime, orange, coconut, tamarind, ginger, date palm, pomegranate, grape and fig, while the guinep and naseberry were introduced from other New World tropics. Along with beef, cakes and tarts, the English took to Jamaica breadfruit (via Captain Bligh and the Oceanic islands), the otaheite apple, ackee, mango, rose apple, mandarin orange, cheirmoyer, turmeric, black pepper and coffee. Jewish settlers may be credited with egg plant and sesame. The Africans used a wide variety of foods, including yam, pigeon peas, okra, callaloo, corn, cocoa, coffee, oranges, shaddock, hot peppers, pimento, pumpkin and ackee.[39]

It is not surprising, then, that the folk culture of the Jamaican

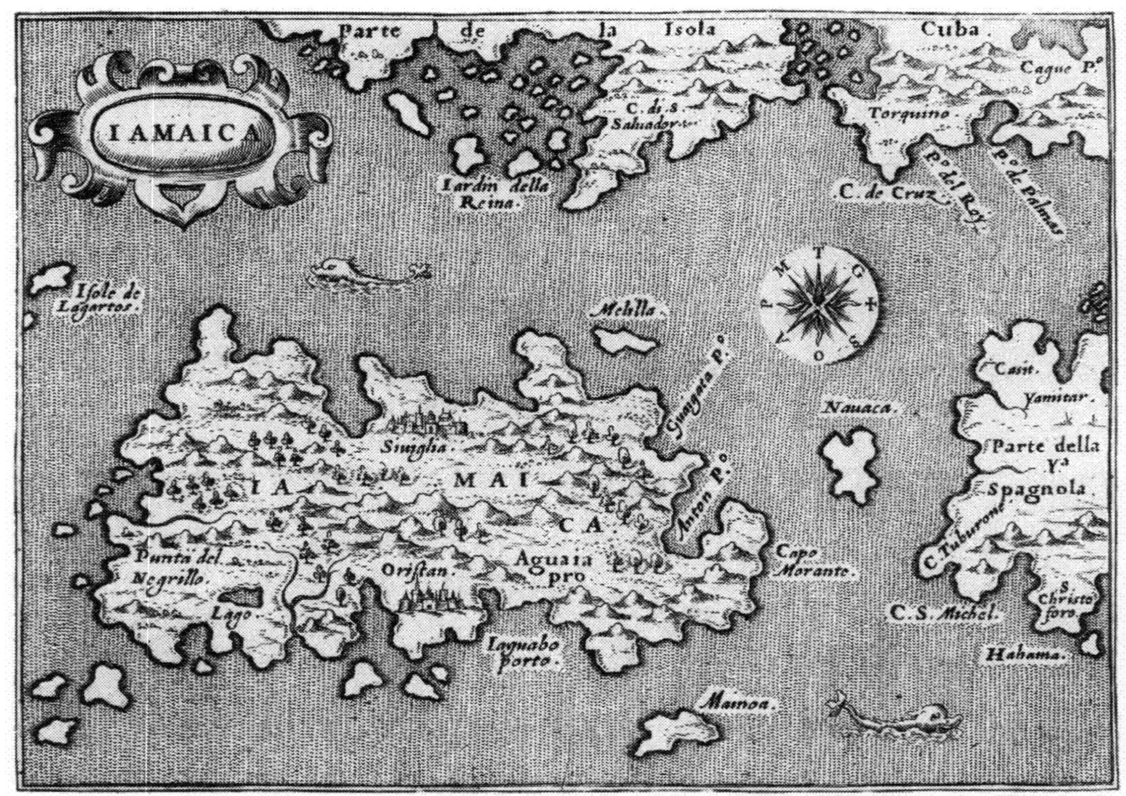

Figure 15 Jamaica: from Thomaso Porcacchi, *L'isole piu famose del mondo* (1576), p. 175.

Figure 16 William Blake, 'The Skinning of the Aboma Snake, Shot by Cap. Stedman': from J.G. Stedman, *Narrative* (1796), between pp. 174 and 175. An example of the representation of the West Indies as a hyperbolic transgression of Eden narratives.

Figure 17 William Blake, 'Family of Negro Slaves from Loango': from J.G. Stedman, *Narrative* (1796), between pp. 280 and 281. Blake was concerned to depict Africans' culture and diet in the West Indies, demonstrating that they were not just dehumanised tools.

slaves, including ways of preparing, consuming and representing food, was different from the cultural work that was carried out on Jamaica for outside audiences. The culinary culture of the Caribbean, created by the slaves, drew upon utopian registers such as the idea of soul food, the notion that '"slave food . . . nourished the individual's very essence since it provided a kind of freedom in which he could express himself"'.[40] The *Columbian Magazine* for May 1797 reported a slave work song about food, home and longing:

Guinea corn, I long to see you
Guinea corn, I long to plant you
Guinea corn, I long to mould you
Guinea corn, I long to weed you
Guinea corn, I long to hoe you
Guinea corn, I long to top you
Guinea corn, I long to cut you
Guinea corn, I long to dry you
Guinea corn, I long to beat you
Guinea corn, I long to trash you
Guinea corn, I long to parch you
Guinea corn, I long to grind you
Guinea corn, I long to turn you
Guinea corn, I long to eat you.[41]

'Monk' Lewis, who had an estate on the island, wrote in his journal of 1834 about overhearing a song that thanked Wilberforce but also encouraged its listeners to '*Take force by force! Take force by force!*'[42] Those outside traditions, however, tended to focus narrowly on the fact of slavery and what was practically a sugar monoculture with touches of quaint detail. A description of jerk meat provides an excuse for a picturesque piece of colonial tourism. One writer hunts boar with the Maroons, or 'free negroes'; they 'smoak and dry this animal, from whence the pieces thus smoaked, obtain the appellation of *jirked hog*; and it is, when thus cured, a very savoury and pleasing dish'.[43]

Other contemporary sources on sugar indicate a more Eurocentric attitude. Benjamin Moseley (1742–1819) was a physician who settled in Jamaica in 1768 and became surgeon-general. His *A Treatise on Sugar* (1800), discussed by Richardson for its passages on 'Obi' scorning the fetishism of African religion, is devoted to its own kinds of fetish.[44] He describes the history of the commodity as 'a subject of the first importance in commerce', making much of the spurious idea that sugar cane grew spontaneously in the West Indies and Southern America.[45] Moseley explores sugar's Indo-European past through philology and depicts its medicinal use in India and Arabia. As in Lucretius' famous description of didactic intent as a sweetened medicine, 'Sugar was employed originally to render unpleasant and nauseating medicines grateful to the sick.'[46] Bullein's sixteenth-century medical book describes white sugar as a medicine; and 'Suger Candie is good for the lunges'.[47] Unlike Coleridge and Southey, Moseley does not employ the language of supplementarity in his discussion of sugar's virtues: a unified history that somehow sees the notion of supplementarity as universally modern cannot be written. Instead, he delineates the importance of what was known as the saccharine element in vegetables; the use of sugar as a restorative, a 'salubrious luxury' for African children in the West Indies (a pair of words that Southey would not have put together); and the increase in 'vigour' and sustenance of 'nature' that it imparts in 'tea, milk, and beer'.[48] Europeans are healthier because of the supply of sugar from the East and West Indies:

> The popular diet before was crude, coarse, and unwholesome. A royal English dinner of the twelfth century would be despised by a modern tradesman. Spices, wine, sugar, and culinary chemistry, made no part of the repast.[49]

The historical inaccuracy of the final sentence indicates a cultural register that praises the wonders of modern life, including the availability of sugar. The passage demonstrates a historical shift in class notions of consumption.

Moseley employs vegetarian language, again demonstrating an interest in modernising diet. Animal food is not necessary, and for 'mental pleasure and health' it could even be deleterious; nevertheless in London 'Blood flows in almost every gutter.' His foul picture of Smithfield slaughterhouses is part of the vegetarian rhetoric of dismemberment, or *macellogia*, with its vision of 'poor trembling victims . . . gazing on'.[50] Moseley links this rhetoric with sugar in ways in which the more radical writers of his day would have found bizarre, matching it as they do with the barbarity of treating humans like cattle: 'In the time of PYTHAGORAS, sugar was unknown . . . Otherwise his philosophy would have had more converts.'[51] The odd match is confirmed by Moseley's negative judgement of the rebellion in Santo Domingo (Haiti) as threatening to sugar: 'Of such importance has the agriculture of half a million of Africans, become to the Europeans.'[52]

William Beckford's *A Descriptive Account of the Island of Jamaica* (1790) takes a less optimistic view of the suitability of sugar in the West Indian environment, but having been transplanted there, he hopes that it will stay, along with slavery. Beckford (1744–99), cousin of the author of *Vathek*, was a historian who had lived in Jamaica for thirteen years before writing the book. The Gothic and picturesque figurative language of his period's popular literature permeates the text, from the 'saffron glow' of the sunset to the 'many very pleasing and romantic situations' to be found on the island, like the Gothic caverns worthy of quotations by poets who had never visited, caverns reputedly full of the remains of Arawaks exterminated by the Spanish.[53] Production is prettified: 'There is something particularly picturesque and striking in a gang of negroes, when employed in cutting canes upon the swelling projections of a hill.'[54]

Politics seems threateningly absent from much of the book's two volumes, but in a monoculture not even climatology is politically irrelevant, given the precocious, irritating and unstable qualities that Beckford observes in sugar: 'A sugar plantation is like a little town . . . I have often been surprised . . . how intimately connected is every thing that grows, and every thing that labours, with this very singular, and at one time luxurious, but now very necessary, as it is deemed to be a highly useful and wholesome, plant.' Every word is pulled towards the sugar cane, in the sentence as in life. Beckford almost gives the cane a soul, making it as animate as any fetish: '[It] is perhaps, through all its different stages, the most uncertain production upon the face of the earth; and has . . . the greatest number of foreign and local enemies . . . of any plant that either contributes to the wants, or that administers to the comforts and luxuries of man.' Beckford seems to feel sorrier for it than for the slaves, with whose suffering he sympathises, but only to a certain extent: 'Happy are those, in some instances, who are without property, and are consequently ignorant of law! Such are the *peasantry* in most countries, and such are the *slaves* in all.' This is especially true in Jamaica because 'The negroes are slaves by nature.' Beckford hopes that an integrated, 'consistent' picture of Jamaica might contribute to an aesthetic ideology that could preserve the colonies, the kind of picture against which Coleridge and Southey were working.[55]

A variety of compromising statements about abolition were made in the period. One of the most extreme was James Boswell's anonymously published *No Abolition of Slavery* (1791), a set of highly offensive tetrameters that castigated Wilberforce, Burke and almost everybody else. Especially difficult to read is the passage on the erotics of slavery and the slavery of eros, in which Venus turns the narrator into a slave and drags him off to the island of Paphos:

> You kept me long indeed, my dear,
> Between the decks of hope and fear,
> But this and all the *seasoning* o'er,
> My blessings I enjoy the more.[56]

The eros of slavery is overcoded through sugar: as Mintz has argued, there is a strong association between sugar and 'positive affect' in English terminology.[57] Robert Young has discussed the phenomenon of the Sable Venus, exploring Bryan Edwards's *The History, Civil and Commercial, of the British Colonies in the West Indies* (1793) and Isaac Teale's 'The Sable Venus: an Ode' (1765), a poem that offers to 'portray both "the character of the sable and saffron beauties of the West Indies, and the folly of their paramours"'.[58] As in courtly love discourse, the desire of the lover is mediated through the detour of the Other, in this case embodying the poetics of spice. As Young writes, 'The cultural construction of race has always been fuelled by the corrupt conjunction of hybridised sexual and economic discourses.'[59] The association of blackness with sugar and eros has a long history, featuring such African-American poetry as Langston Hughes's 'Harlem Sweeties' (1942): 'the spill / Of Sugar Hill' (1–2); 'Delicious, *fine* Sugar Hill' (44, the last line).[60] The latter quotation connotes refined sugar, as well as the use of dialect. Spice plays a large part in Hughes's poem: 'Licorice, clove, cinnamon / To a honey-brown dream' (35–6). Hughes admires a racially diverse gradation of skin colours: 'Ginger, wine-gold, / Persimmon, blackberry' (37–8). The colours are also desserts, chiming with the mention of chocolate and cream. To this extent Hughes is revising Porphyro's meal, and the Harlem Sweeties are the embodied literalisation of Keatsian figurative language, which in turn is a literalisation of the Romantic fetishistic imagination.

Returning to Boswell, the eros of slavery is overcoded through sugar.[61] The disturbing reference to 'seasoning' or the breaking-in of slaves illuminates the discourse of supplementarity against which abolitionists struggled. Barbauld's *Epistle to William Wilberforce* (1791) attacks the language of seasoning: 'Where seasoned tools of Avarice prevail, / A Nation's eloquence, combined, must fail'.[62] The planter and his wife occupy an environment from which the possibility of ornamental poetry has been banished:

> Nor, in their palmy walks and spicy groves,
> The form benign of rural Pleasure roves;
> . . .
> But shrieks and yells disturb the balmy air,
> . . .
> Far from the sounding lash the Muses fly. (71–2; 81; 84)

The geography of colonialism, with its spicy ornaments, is severely satirised – in fact, it stinks: 'Nor less from the gay East, on essenc'd wings, / Breathing unnam'd perfumes, Contagion springs' (86–7).[63] We are not prepared for 'Contagion' by the figure of 'essenc'd wings' and the *occupatio* of 'unnam'd perfumes'. The 'Muses fly' from 'the sounding lash' in a reversal of the ambience associated with the poetics of spice. Documents of luxury are read as records of barbarism and as indecorous linguistic aporias, though Barbauld continues to represent that which the Muses flee from in the very moment of flight.[64] Spice is significant to slavery but also to rhetoric and discourse: those who reject the bill are sophists. Anti-slavery poetry is also avowedly anti-rhetorical (as is much early Romantic poetry, such as *Lyrical Ballads*), and hence suspicious about the poetics of spice.

The rhetoric of the commodity fetish predominated in encomia to sugar. After spending four years on the island of St Christopher from 1759, using his scanty physician's income to purchase slaves, James Grainger published *The Sugar-Cane*, a poem praised for its mock-heroic style but denounced by Smollett for not condemning the slave trade. Indeed, far from not condemning the trade, it is a veritable panegyric to the process of sugar production: 'How the hot nectar best to christallize; / And Afric's sable progeny to treat' (1.3). The poem is addressed to the planter:

> But would'st thou see huge casks, in order due,
> Roll'd numerous on the Bay, all fully fraught
> With strong-grained muscovado, silvery-grey,
> Joy of the planter; and if happy Fate
> Permit a choice: avoid the rocky slope . . . (etc.) (1.27)

Grainger follows the history of the West Indies and the sequence of sugar production in a smoothly linear fashion. He praises Columbus, figuratively turning the 'space of flows' into an artificial territory, a place, comparable to 'Grecian Tempe' (I.61), 'purple Enna' (I.64) and so on. A footnote expands more honestly upon the production of this place through capitalist enterprise and competition for possession between the French and English.[65] Grainger's figurative plans for the island are martial, betraying the fact that colonialism is not just innocently economic (if economics was ever innocent). Both land and slave are transformed in a highly disciplined, orderly mode of production, likened to a military campaign: 'So when a monarch rushes to the war, / To drive invasion from his frighted realm' (I.271). Monkeys invading the plantation are equated with the French invading America.[66]

Later on, the real space of flows is allowed to emerge in all its commercial and poetic vastness and emptiness:

> Dear to the Nine, thy [Columbus'] glory shall remain
> While winged Commerce either ocean ploughs;
> While its lov'd pole the magnet coyly shuns;
> While weeps the guaiac, and while joints the Cane. (I.123)

The syntax that links the detail of the cane with the transcendentally global picture denies the contradictions between particular and general in a way that exemplifies the logic of fetishism. Dyer's *The Fleece*, with its juxtaposition of empire and sheep, works in a similar way. It is possible to compare Beckford's animation of the cane with Grainger's equally fetishistic passage:

> as the earth absolves
> Her annual circuit, thy rich ripened Canes
> Shall load thy waggons, mules, and Negroe-train. (I.437)

Another example is Grainger's close observation of the refining process in the third book. If the 'coction' is prolonged too much:

> the viscous waves
> Will in huge flinty masses chrystallize,
> Which forceful fingers scarce can crumble down. (III.435)

Book IV, on the management of slaves, paints a picture of poor helpless and fetish-crazed victims like the Obi-stricken Juba in Maria Edgeworth's *Belinda*, distancing author and audience from a demonised notion of fetishism.[67] The poem closes with a nocturnal prospect of a plantation where labour is *not* occurring, opening with a panegyric to the Thames that, as in Dryden's *Annus Mirabilis*, interconnects the whole watery world of 'Delighted Commerce' (IV.640):

> The moon, in virgin glory, gilds the pole,
> And tips yon tamarinds, tips yon Cane-crown'd vale,
> With fluent silver. (IV.647).

The silver frosting of the landscape is itself rather sugary, as if, to parody Coleridge, the sugar were performing a secret ministry that bathed the land in the spectral glow of monetary value; and, as in the address to Columbus ('Dear to the Nine'), eloquence is allied with capital in the image of the silver's fluency. It advertises a way of life. Abolitionists used the blood sugar topos because disenchantment required a nauseous reaction against such fantastic investment in sugar.

Grainger's sugar-frosted landscape is echoed in Emily Trevenen's poem 'Sugar' in her poem to Coleridge's grandson:

> This sugar so sparkling and shining,
> Which here on the table you see,
> Has gone through all sorts of refining,
> Before it can sweeten our tea.[68]

This fetishistic language is repeated later:

> With other ingredients they [merchants] mix it,
> In furnaces boil it quite clear;
> In moulds, like a cone, then they fix it,
> Where sparkling and white 'twill appear.[69]

Merchants mix the sugar, not workers. On the breakfast table, sugar shines as much as in Grainger's landscape. The black labourers are depicted as defending the cane from damage: protecting bourgeois property after the abolition of the slave trade.[70] Having been the victims of the commodity, commodified themselves, they become its police: the move from id to superego is not that far.

SWEET REVENGE

Arguments have been made that 'By the end of the eighteenth century, Southey, not Coleridge or Wordsworth, was regarded as the leading champion of a new spirit in English poetry.'[71] Even if it were not the case that Southey has been neglected in relation to other poets in his time, it would still be hard to assess the tonal and ideological range of his sonnets on the slave trade. These apparently simple, direct poems challenge a simplistic, unified reading. Several contradictory modes and objects of address are involved. For example, is Southey supporting rebellion by the slaves or reform by the planters and consumers? Are the Africans victims or agents? Like Coleridge's lecture, Southey's reformist text is haunted by the possibility of rebellion, and one has to wonder whether this is meant as a threat and goad to reform, or as a more complex celebration of revolutionary struggle.

Throughout this reading, it should be remembered that the slaves themselves, in addition to the sugar they produce, are *commodities* as well as *subjects*. Some recent poetry had worked through the position of the slave as subject: in Hugh Mulligan's *The Slave, an American Eclogue* (1783), the protagonist, Adala, does all the talking, though he is supplemented with copious notes. Blake's *Visions of the Daughters of Albion* (1793) had also recently discussed slavery through three allegorical characters. But other work, such as Hannah More's *Slavery* (1788), emphasised the slaves as commodities: 'MAN the traffic, SOULS the merchandize!' (145). Southey's sonnets are striking because they figuratively demonstrate the revolutionary potential of people who exist *between* the categories of subject and object.

The anti-slavery sonnets strike hard after Southey's introductory address to Akenside, and the coy first sonnet:

> Lonely my heart and rugged was my way,
> Yet often pluck'd I as I past along
> The wild and simple flowers of Poesy,
> And as beseem'd the wayward Fancy's child
> Entwin'd each random weed that pleas'd mine eye. (5–9)

The preface to the 'Poems on the Slave Trade' summarises a brief history of abolitionism. The Government intended to destroy the trade or to stop using:

> West-Indian productions: a slow but certain method. For a while Government held the language of justice, and individuals with enthusiasm banished sugar from their tables. This enthusiasm soon cooled; the majority of those who had made this *sacrifice*, (I prostitute the word, but they thought it a *sacrifice*) persuaded themselves that Parliament would do all, and that individual efforts were no longer necessary.[72]

Southey is commenting on the woeful sticking power of the so-called enthusiasts, a loaded term in the context of contemporary radical religious movements. Wilberforce is singled out for his 'duplicity'.[73] The main concern is that 'humanity', invoked early on, should not be *supplemented* by revenge. Southey presents the alternatives:

> There are yet two other methods remaining, by which this traffic will probably be abolished. By the introduction of East-Indian or Maple Sugar, or by the just and general rebellion of the Negroes: by the vindictive justice of the Africans, or by the civilized Christians finding it their interest to be humane.[74]

The chiasmic slip between 'just and general rebellion' and 'vindictive justice' is a significant one that is repeated elsewhere in the sequence of poetry itself. Unsure of how he should be addressing his audience, or even of who his audience is precisely, Southey slides between supporting revolution and advocating reform.

The first slave trade sonnet creates a picture of how capitalism and violence are intertwined:

> the pale fiend, cold-hearted Commerce there
> Breathes his gold-gender'd pestilence afar,
> And calls to share the prey his kindred Daemon War. (12–14)

This form of invective was employed by one of the early Southey's greatest admirers, Percy Shelley, in *Queen Mab* v (1813).[75] The anti-slavery passage in the millennial eighth section of Shelley's work incorporates the sense of 'mangling scourge' found in Southey's third sonnet (9; see Shelley, *Queen Mab*, VIII.179); the later passage on vegetarianism in the same section (VIII.211ff.) also uses the language of mangling. The rhetoric of mangling flesh or *macellogia* was a feature of anti-slavery and animal rights rhetoric, often found together in the same work, as Pratt's *Humanity* demonstrates. Southey is describing capitalism as a devourer of bodies. Commerce as a cannibal appears again in the sixth sonnet, in which a slave is hung like Prometheus to be consumed by vultures, 'their living food' (2). In *To the Genius of Africa*, Southey writes: 'The Daemon COMMERCE on your shore / Pours all the horrors of his train' (21), and surveys 'Their [European] blood-fed plains' (49). Consumerism is politicised.

For Pratt, and later for Shelley, the slave trade exemplified a domineering relationship between subject and object, man and nature. Just as the environment and animals can be turned into man's tool, so can other humans: in Aristotle a slave is *organon empsychon*, a tool with a soul.[76] In 1788, Pratt published *Humanity, or the Rights of Nature* (a telling title); the poem is a part of the growing literature about slavery. Near the middle a claim is made for radical humanitarianism that employs vegetarian language:

> 'Tis not enough, our appetites require
> That on their altars hecatombs expire;
> But cruel man, a savage in his power,
> Must heap fresh horrors on life's parting hour:
> Full many a being that bestows its breath,
> Must prove the pang that waits a *ling'ring* death,
> Here, close pent up, must gorge unwholesome food,
> There render drop by drop the smoaking blood;
> The quiv'ring flesh improves as slow it dies,
> And Lux'ry sees th' augmented whiteness rise;
> Some creatures gash'd must feel the torturer's art,
> Writhe in their wounds, tho' sav'd each vital part.
> From the hard bruise the food more tender grows,
> And callous Lux'ry triumphs in the blows:
> Some, yet alive, to raging flames consign'd,
> By piercing shrieks must soothe our taste refin'd![77]

The violent language mimics the action of the butcher by cutting up, reworking, metonymising its contents: it segments the actions into parts that do not bear an organic relationship to the whole. The transformation of the animals in five lines from 'being' to 'flesh', for example, is disjointing. *Macellogia* makes the transformation of 'And Lux'ry sees th' augmented whiteness rise' especially horrible: the art of making veal is shown to be an art both of purity and of torture. The rhetoric invites us to watch, or even to participate in, the slaughter of an animal.

Pratt then praises the 'Bramins [*sic*]'[78] who

> crop the living herbage as it grows,
> And quaff the living water as it flows,
> From the full herds, the milky banquet bear,
> And the kind herds repay with pastures fair.

The use of 'living' opposes the Brahmin diet to flesh eating, construed as the consumption of death. Christians are encouraged by Hindu example to 'prove the *friends* not *tyrants* of the earth'.[79] Pratt attempts to separate luxury from vice. Now that the vegetarian discourse is in place, the slaves travelling over 'Afric's dreadful sand' are compared to oxen; later, a verse paragraph on the slave revolt in Surinam describes them as 'wrought to blood like trooping

Panthers'.[80] Vegetarian rhetoric has ensured that the trading of slaves can be understood as a meat market. Vegetarianism was used in *Humanity* and Shelley's *Queen Mab* VIII to convey an explicit political message, not only about how humans should live with animals, but about how they should live with themselves.

With these thoughts about the power of metonymy in mind, let us return to Southey's third sonnet. The sun's heat, for Southey as for Thomson and Shelley, becomes an emblem of tyranny:

> The scorching Sun,
> As pityless as proud Prosperity,
> Darts on him his full beams; gasping he lies
> Arraigning with his looks the patient skies,
> While that inhuman trader lifts on high
> The mangling scourge. Oh ye who at your ease
> Sip the blood-sweeten'd beverage! thoughts like these
> Haply ye scorn: I thank thee Gracious God!
> That I do feel upon my cheek the glow
> Of indignation, when beneath the rod
> A sable brother writhes in silent woe. (4–14)

Here is the blood sugar topos, spliced between two acts of physical marking and registration of power upon the body: the mangling scourge in the colony, and the blush of indignation in the colonising country. Whereas in the New World those marks are represented in blood on the surface of the body, in the Old World they are represented through the internalised mode of the blush. 'Sip', 'ease' and 'Haply ye scorn' are juxtaposed with language that registers literality and truth, both of colonial power and of sympathetic passion. The language of physical marking relegates the sweetness of the beverage to the status of something useless, a supplement that can be discarded.

Nothing within the figurative scheme falls into that significant ideological category, the 'natural'. In the same volume, Southey's *Inscription* VII, *For a* TABLET *on the Banks of a Stream*, is a proto-ecological *paysage moralisé* that draws upon this discourse of (non-) nature and supplementarity:

> The stream is pure
> In solitude, and many a healthy herb
> Bends o'er its course and drinks the vital wave:
> But passing on amid the haunts of man,
> It finds pollution there. (9–13)

'Pollution' is significantly modern, poised between an older implication of miasma, itself a conflation of physical and moral pollution, and a more literalistic sense of the environmental pollution wreaked by human society. The opposition of nature and society is denatured to some extent, for nature appears to segue into social construction, like the stream finding its way into a dirty town. Though the natural is compromised, however, 'truth' is not. The gradual pollution of the water is as 'truth-heavy' as is supposed to be the sudden pollution of the tea.

What makes the blood sugar passage all the more remarkable is its echo in the fifth sonnet: 'No more on Heaven he [the slave] calls with fruitless breath, / But sweetens with revenge, the draught of death' (13). Here death is figured as a beverage that must be sweetened, and justice is imagined as a wild revenge. 'Wild justice' was a theme in the discourses of anxiety about the justness of the French and American Revolutions and the threat of insurrection in England, where revenge was considered supplementary to law.[81] The figure uses the same image of oppression as the 'blood-sweeten'd beverage', but turns it into an image of revolution.

In Southey's sonnets, sugar is figured both as specious pretence and as deep substance. It is a superficial luxury, but one with a bloody history, a viscerality that belies its sweetness. Southey's rhetoric additionally presents sugar as an emblem for toil, pain, death and slavery: 'Oh ye who at your ease / Sip the blood-sweeten'd beverage! thoughts like these / Haply ye scorn' (III.9–11). Southey forces the sippers to read the barbarism stirred into their luxuries. Sipping is a refined gesture: as sugar is refined, so are bodily movements in the flow from the West Indies to Britain. 'Ease' and 'sweeten'd' chime. It is worth recalling that the luxurious culture of the eighteenth century *was* the culture of ease, so that 'ease' works hard to define forms of conspicuous *sprezzatura*, here materialised in the act of sipping sweetness. The sweet beverage is then a narcotic that blinds the consumer to the means of its production. Southey places the language of sacrifice and cannibalism in the mouths of the bourgeoisie. The sense of waste and cannibalism that the image imparts strikingly deconstructs the bourgeois discourses of prudence, economy and temperance, the discourses that supported the plantations.

How is it possible to counteract the flow of blood into sugar? Three options are presented: revolution, including a slave uprising;

abstaining from the condiment; and redirecting the flow of sugar (looking to the East). The last two arguments fall within normative ideologies very easily. Abstinence as a means of psychic and social control is itself an affordable luxury: there needs to be enough money in one's pocket to be able to *refuse* food. Redirecting the flow is an obvious move within existing trade structures. Sugar is made to seem supplementary in both cases. It is an unnecessary luxury not befitting a moral, social and psychic restricted economy (the abstinence argument). And the West Indies is an unnecessarily barbaric supplement to the East Indies. The West often dreams of the utopian production of supplements, for example in the paradises of medieval orientalism, places that supplemented the duality of earth and Eden, floating spice islands, the oneiric horizon. Despite its imprint of slavery and colonialism, Spaniards and Creoles were drawn to the civic square of the city of Belmiranda in Cuba by the smell of cinnamon.[82]

There are some extraordinary details about this small image of the beverage. Where is the castigating voice coming from in sonnet III? Southey is either trying impossibly to overhear the voice of the Other (the object of colonialism), or mimicking a universal voice that chastises from afar. There is an added complexity in the revision of Old Testament prophetic registers. Unlike the Oriental voices in *Thalaba* or *The Curse of Kehama*, the voices of the slaves seem unavailable, or tantalisingly out of reach. This non-placedness could be positive: after all, the other works construct a sense of the placedness of oriental despotism; a sense of non-location could subvert the fixities of power.[83] There is the question of the sonnets' addressees: were they the guilty or the converted? And forms of radical understanding are presented – reasons why the slaves might have to revolt, not just rationalisations of reform. Southey presents a fantastic series of identifications and divergences, within which various forms of ideological phantasy play, structured around the 'hard kernel' of the viscerally real cup of blood. The beverage is, then, a fantasy object that shows colonial enjoyment to be predicated on cannibalistic consumption.[84]

What stands in a metonymic relation to others along a chain of commodities now becomes metaphorically present in the sugar. The effect is one of removing several mediating links of time and space, collapsing the colonial body from East and West into the teacup. It is as if the flow of blood, of rum and tea, all pooled in the same space, generating recoil and revulsion (and possibly, revolution). Beauty, the sweet, mutates into sublimity, the bloody. What the image does to moral rectitude is quite catastrophic, and in a way similar to Kant's construal of absolute evil as the form of good: the shocking secret in the bloody cup is that sugar and rebellion only *appear* as supplementary to a justice that is already wild, precisely in the fact of the ownership of slaves.

The bloody cup highlights the non-identity of the law and capitalism, whose rage transforms the globe for its own purposes. The bloody cup also implicates a certain form of religion and spirituality as a mode of oppression, for Southey was also horrified about the Trinity and the transubstantiation of blood into wine. He is satirising the religiosity of consumption, the way in which the consumer fetishises the consumed, treating it as 'The Real Thing' (as sugary Coke has been advertised). Anyone who reads the history of capitalism as a process of secularisation has not come to terms with this kind of image.

Which subject position is supplementing the other? 'I', 'you' and 'them' seem to be shifting their places, between rectitude and rebelliousness, bigotry and sympathy, the object of colonial reform and the subject of revolution. Southey's sonnets are ostensibly didactic texts that turn out to be radically unstable and plural in meaning. It is the status of the object, the fetishised sugar and the fetishised cup, which becomes significant as an image of capital itself. Southey's storm in a teacup resembles Marx's two mutually exclusive positions on capital. It is either an alienated substance (the labour of the worker transformed under capitalism), in which case revolution is a mode of disalienation, of getting back/going forward to some essential, non-alienated state; or it is a substantive subject, in which case revolution is to be achieved *through* alienation.[85] (The latter supported Keats's representation of spice.) It is precisely the image of sugar-as-revolution, of rebellion-as-sweet, which holds these two meanings so delicately in (dis)solution together.

One can picture the phrase running on past the ellipsis in a chapter from Deleuze and Guattari's *A Thousand Plateaus*: becoming animal, becoming intense . . . becoming sugar. One can also criticise Southey for the same things that are problematic in the post-structuralists' vicarious enjoyment of the Other's revolt, and, at the other pole of emotional response, the unreconstructed 'victim-speak' that makes of the slaves an object of pity. In one sense, the 'sweet revenge' topos makes a fetish of a truism: if the English fail to help, the slaves will revolt all by themselves. This is an overdetermined position for the slaves, who in European mythologies come from the lands of the fetish.

There thus appear to be two main ways of reading Southey's sonnets: from the 'inside out' and from the 'outside in'. From the 'inside out', they appear to be about interpreting the behaviour of the English consumer, speaking for the Other, goading and advocating reform. But from the 'outside in' the poem is inwardly fractured by the real possibility of revolution. Indeed, this is not only a possibility but a historical event in relation to which the sonnets can only be belated. The second Maroon revolt in Trelawny and St James's parishes in Jamaica (July–March 1795–6) was extremely fresh in the memory, as was the revolution on Santo Domingo (1791). London mercantile companies had invested Santo Domingo to the tune of £300,000. Hence between 1793 and 1798 the British government spent over £4,000,000 to conquer the French colony and bolster slavery.[86] This chance of revolution operates as what Fredric Jameson calls a 'vanishing mediator', pointing to the 'open' situation of the emergence of a new political state, before it has been 'closed'. The logic of the supplement is overturned and surpassed: the 'threat' function of the bloody cup does not entirely sum up that image's power. The bloody cup is a stain on the whitewashed walls of the reformist project, in non-relation to which the liberal Southey articulates nothing less than the positive chance of revolution. The Caribbean has not merely provided threnodic information for Europe.[87] The reality of Caribbean revolution is what gives the poems any bite they might claim to have. In that respect, they demonstrate the anti-colonial infiltration of the 'centre' culture by the culture of the 'periphery'.[88] The supplement emerges as the *most* material (though hardly the most 'natural') element in the sonnets. To a certain extent, reformism has already been surpassed by history, and this gives the blood sugar image its awkward, ambiguous character. The poem's allusion to the cup of bitterness, wished away by Jesus in Gethsemane, is also concerned with a refusal to internalise grief. Here the cup presents the radical outside of the culture of sugar.

Southey was caricatured by Hazlitt for moving from 'Ultra-jacobin' and 'frantic demagogue' to 'Ultra-royalist' and 'senile court-tool'. The former 'maintained second-hand paradoxes' while the latter 'repeats second-hand commonplaces'.[89] My reading of his anti-slavery writing is that he was interestingly less in control of his meanings than Hazlitt asserts. The use of the blood sugar topos is powerful in Southey not only for its evocation of the politics of sympathy, but also for its revolutionary suggestiveness. The stunning feature of the slave trade sonnets is the way in which they materialise the supplement, making it rich and sticky, heavy with history and suffering, while simultaneously seeming arbitrary and artificial and capable of being thrown aside. The sonnets present the possibility of scratching the grooves of the commodity fetish to create unexpected, revolutionary meanings. Whether these meanings are achieved *against* the commodity fetish (boycotting sugar, transcending capitalism), or *through* it, in the revenge of the commodities themselves (an uprising of slaves), is left in the balance.

ZING

There were ambiguities inherent in the eighteenth-century politics of boycotting and abstinence. In the 1760s, the abolitionist Quaker essayist John Woolman (1720–72) advocated not dyeing clothes; but the clothes remained. In the 1780s and 1790s, sugar became the figure for an unnecessary luxury, but what about the luxury drinks into which it was poured? The trade in coffee and tea had eclipsed the spice trade as the main motor of long-distance capitalism. Sugar, as the supplement of a luxury, is perhaps overdetermined in this respect, but it is easy to see the consent involved in boycotting some, but not all, articles of colonialist and imperialist trade. Moreover, amongst the options for changing the situation discussed by Southey, why is there no mention of sugar beet, which had been grown successfully in Germany since the 1740s, whose farming was also being attempted in England? One answer is that Southey is being triumphalist, celebrating the possibility of a revolutionary outcome in the war against the slave trade, while not assuming much responsibility for that war himself.

The study of the literary and cultural representation of consumption and the commodity provides new ways of thinking about orientalism and colonialism, which are often construed through a psychoanalytic discourse of 'Self' and 'Other'. This history of the subject can be expanded with histories of the object in colonial and orientalist texts. On the other hand, the study of the object often presupposes a naive empirical collection of detail as its goal. But the study of consumption raises the question of enjoyment and suffering. The languages of colonialism included fantasies about the sorts of commodity that it was producing.

Cultural analysis often appeals to some kind of metaphysical Real beyond the text, but in the ones studied here, the Real appeared much as it does in Žižek's reading of Lacan, as a hard kernel of desire. This kernel is impossible from a reformist position. A visceral excrescence on the sickly sweet, powerful rhetoric of humanitarianism, it is the real desire for and possibility of (and historical actuality of) revolution in the West Indies. The production of surplus leads to a powerful set of contradictory discourses on supplements which broaches the question of radical social transformation. From the boycotters' point of view, this can be formulated as a question: what do you want after you have what you need? One answer concerns the reality of desire.

Alan Liu's essay on historical work in the Romantic period remarks upon the fetishistic coexistence of transcendence and detail in such studies. It criticises the prose of writers in which culture *is*, not *means*, 'with all the ontological zing of the Real'.[90] 'Zing' is poised between a kind of fetishism of detail and a totalising effect, as of a sudden illumination: 'the ontological zing of the Real' sounds like 'the ring of truth'. 'Zing' chimes punningly with Kant's *das Ding*, but is also onomatopoeic, and resonates with the *jouissance* of a certain glow of a detail on a fetishised object: a glint on the surface of a brand new car, or the sparkle of some advertised clean teeth, or indeed the 'zing' imparted by Coca Cola, that realest of real things. 'Zing' is the *jouissance* of detail, the enjoyment of hallucinated accuracy. In other words, 'zing' is the poetics of spice.

For this queasy Kantian blend of detail and transcendence, Liu substitutes a Barthesian notion of culture as reality effect. This, however, only pushes the problem back a stage further. What is interesting about 'the real' is not merely its reality but its 'zing'. 'Zing' is about enjoyment, not merely modes of realism.

The fascination for 'zing' in historicising prose is illusory given the nature of what Peter Sloterdijk calls cynical reason, the fact that one never actually quite believes in 'reality-effects' anyway. It is true that 'none of us would actually believe' an advertisement, however much 'zing' it had. This is bad news for Grainger's marketing of sugar. It is also true, however, that this would not disqualify advertisements from working. Ideology, never more potent than when one believes one has seen through it, as in the vision of the blood-swilling tea drinkers, does not operate by convincing one of a certain reality-effect. It would be fairer to say, with Žižek, that a certain amount of cynicism is very effective: '"They know that, in their activity, they are following an illusion, but still, they are doing it"' – in this sense, as Eagleton continues, citing Žižek, '"falsity" lies on the side of what we *do*, not necessarily of what we say'.[91]

This reading has refused to be naively economistic. That is precisely the interpretation demanded by the blood sugar topos. It places us in an imaginary relation to a sentimentalised, pain-drenched mode of production, later developed in Marx's notion of the commodity as alienated substance. Lifting the veil of this trite, easily reversible topos is what Southey as a reformist wishes us to do. It is no matter of disillusionment to see that slaves produce sugar: it is crassly obvious. Instead, what is fascinating about Southey's particular use of the topos is that a hole in its symbolic structure, the implication of the sweetness of revenge, outlines the real of revolutionary desire, to be elaborated in Marx's concept of the commodity as substantive subject. It is this hole, in fact, that is more real than the sentimental scene on to which the curtain of the topos rises, since it is formed by the historical chance of revolution in the West Indies.

CHAPTER 5

Sound and scents: further investigations of space

how are we to prevent the voice from sliding into a consuming self-enjoyment that effeminizes the reliable masculine Word?

Slavoj Žižek, 'Re-Visioning "Lacanian" Social Criticism', p. 21

As he gave out this text, his voice 'rose like a steam of rich distilled perfumes'

William Hazlitt on Coleridge, from 'My First Acquaintance with Poets', *Works*, XVII.108

'The Future Will Be Like Perfume'

Brian Eno, installation (Hamburg, 1993)

INTRODUCTION

This concluding chapter is about the ways in which poetry is represented through figures of spice, and specifically about the ways in which these conceptions are constellated with the growth of capitalism. The first two sections, 'Analytical Romanticism' and 'Fantasy Against Itself', explore further the politics of traversing the fantasy with which the previous two chapters closed, through a reading of Leigh Hunt's 'The Panther' (1819). The themes of gender and the debate on luxury are revisited. The chapter maps the changing notions of rhetoric in modernity as they appear in Romantic period poetry. It discusses the way in which spice is taken as an emblem of poetry. The 'spice of poetics', a poetics of ornamentation and sentiment and above all of atmospherics, flourished at precisely the point at which certain poets who reacted against this ornamental poetry wrote works which were later defined as the male Romantic canon. Ironically enough, these anti-ornamental poets came to be defined as too effeminate and sentimental by modernists such as Eliot and Ezra Pound.

This opens into a study of the relationship between the poetics of spice and what Bachelard called the 'poetics of space'. I offer readings of numerous poems already discussed, including those of Darwin, Percy Shelley and Barbauld, Coleridge's 'Kubla Khan' (1797–8, 1816), Jean Adams's 'On the Phoenix' (1734), the works of Sir William Jones (1746–94), Hemans's *Joan of Arc, in Rheims,* (1828), King's *The Art of Cookery*, Leigh Hunt's *A Now, Descriptive of a Hot Day*, Crashaw's *To the Name Above Every Name, the Name of Iesus a Hymn* and Charles Baudelaire's 'Correspondences' (1857). This section, 'Ambience', argues that the poetics of spice is fundamentally 'ambient', and explores the poetic, political and philosophical implications of what this means.

ANALYTICAL ROMANTICISM

Romanticist discourse assumes that it is opposed to capitalism. Is this so, however, in its very nature? If we read Romantic poetry more carefully, it discloses its complicity. *And that is not intrinsically 'bad'*: it is, in fact, what enables a critique to be staged. Fully to grasp this involves a detour through Žižek's interpretation of fantasy.

Hegel's concept of infinite judgement is well explained by Žižek as the use of tautology as the highest form of contradiction. Thus if we take the opposition between centre and supplement, it is not that the supplement undermines the centre (in Derridean fashion) but that it really 'is' the centre. As Žižek puts it: 'instead of the tautology giving form to the radical antagonism between the two appearances of the same term, the very juxtaposition of two terms that seem incompatible renders visible their "speculative identity" – "the Spirit is a bone", for example.' Žižek goes on to elaborate a Lacanian matheme: 'The ultimate Lacanian "infinite judgement", of course, is his formula of fantasy $\$ \diamond a$, positing the co-dependence of the pure void of subjectivity [which Lacan derives from Descartes] and the formless remainder of the Real which, precisely, resists subjectivization: *objet a* is not merely the objectal correlative to the subject, it is the subject itself in its "impossible" objectal existence, a kind of objectal stand-in for the subject'.[1]

A simple way of understanding this is to consider the common idea that 'you are what you eat'. Since as subjects we have no inherent existence, we are constantly engaged in a process of identification with the Other. We postulate 'that' in order to prove the existence of 'this'. Another way to think about this is to consider

Freud's slogan, 'Where Id was there shall Ego be': where it was there shall I be. In one sense this could mean that the ego, after analysis, will replace, fill out or incorporate properly the Id. This is a brief definition of the therapeutic view of Romanticism: that in Romantic art altogether the self is reconciled with the world by internalising it. On the other hand, one should observe that person A does not re-emerge from analysis as person A, but as person A prime: one does not go out of the door cured of the problem one thought one was coming in with. The point of therapy is to identify with the symptom, with *objet petit a*, with that little piece of one that is considered to be extraneous, supplementary, extrinsic or, as Lacan would say, 'extimate' (as opposed to intimate).

$\$ \diamond a$ denotes an orientation of the subject towards enjoyment which is characterised by perversion, but which is much more constitutive of everyday fantasy in capitalism. In *Encore*, Lacan describes three possible relationships with enjoyment (*jouissance* or bliss, rather than pleasure): comicality (noticing the gap between what can and cannot be symbolised); pathos (creating a fantasy image that represents the impossible Thing of enjoyment); or perversion (cathecting 'the partial object which sets in motion the metonymic movement of desire').[2]

A recent British beer commercial (for Castlemaine XXXX) demonstrates amusingly how intersubjective communication depends upon a fantasy object, a thingy, *objet petit a*. Žižek describes the advertisement:

> The first part stages the well-known fairy-tale anecdote: a girl walks along a stream, sees a frog, takes it gently into her lap, kisses it, and, of course, the ugly frog miraculously turns into a beautiful young man. However, the story isn't over yet: the young man casts a covetous glance at the girl, draws her towards him, kisses her – and she turns into a bottle of beer, which the man holds triumphantly in his hand . . . For the woman, the point is that her love and affection (symbolized by the kiss) turn the frog into a beautiful man, a full phallic presence . . . for the man, it is to reduce the woman to a partial object, the cause of his desire (in Lacan's mathemes, the *objet petit a*). Because of this asymmetry, 'there is no sexual relationship': we have either a woman with a frog or a man with a bottle of beer – what we can never obtain is the 'natural' couple of the beautiful woman and the man . . . Why not? Because the phantasmic support of this 'ideal couple' would have been the inconsistent figure of *a frog embracing a bottle of beer.*[3]

Žižek continues by outlining the political implications of his reading of the advertisement: 'This, then, opens up the possibility of undermining the hold a fantasy exerts over us through our very over-identification with it by *embracing simultaneously, within the same space, the multitude of inconsistent phantasmic elements.*' He goes on to say that the appeal of ideology lies in its inconsistency: what appeals about ideology is also what undermines it.[4]

Thus the best strategy for undermining ideology is a traversal of its phantasmic elements rather than a resistance to it or the positing of a non- or anti-ideological presence which ideology cannot assimilate – the strategy of Wordsworthian Romanticism and masculine forms of Romantic ecology, for instance. The best way to subvert ideology is through a form of sincere parody. This is the strategy of what one might call Analytical as opposed to Therapeutic Romanticism, as shown in the work of Keats, Landon and feminine forms of Romantic ecology. (By 'masculine' and 'feminine' I mean subject-positions produced in dialectical relationship to the poetics of spice, not essential biological or poetical categories.) In 'therapy', subjects emerge from the process of engagement with the object, the Other, the world, the analyst, experience and so forth more fully what they already were in the first place. The standard misinterpretation of the Hegelian dialectic is that it is therapeutic in this manner. Thus Wordsworth encounters the traumatic 'spots of time' and grows through them; Romanticism is a cure for the excessive rationality of the Enlightenment. In 'analysis' subjects are interrogated by the object, and so forth, and yield up that extrinsic yet intimate part of themselves, the symptomatic *objet petit a* that sticks out like a sore thumb. In the case of the Romantic writer, this is the relation to the capitalist marketplace. The Romantic poet realises the notion of the privatisation of literature effected by the Copyright Act of 1709.

FANTASY AGAINST ITSELF

The masculine Romantic tradition, consisting of such figures as Wordsworth and Coleridge, took on, resisted and critiqued the ornamental, fanciful (in Coleridge's sense) poetry that the poetics of spice is part of. That tradition provided a way of resisting the commodity form. Their belief is the now familiar story of authenticity versus sell-out. Yet the poetry of Coleridge, Percy Shelley and Seward is subtly dependent upon the poetics of spice which it ostensibly rejects. Shelley's attacks on capitalism are put next to the figurative language of the spice trade in his descriptions of utopia and utopian action. Anticipating the environmental awareness that Wordsworth would popularise in the *Guide to the Lakes*, Seward's attacks on the industrialisation of Colebrook Dale anxiously police the luxurious consumption of tropes and of spice which underpin her larger gestures. These poets do what they do with *objet petit a* – the fantasy-Thing of capitalist enjoyment – as it were surreptitiously. The view of the Lake District as a Terrestrial Paradise is borrowed from the poetics of spice. The 'gentle breeze' that fans Wordsworth's cheek in the first line of *The Prelude* (1805, 1850) seems a once-removed relation of the bountiful effects of providence praised in the spiritual first-person narration of Vaughan.

Other poets, however, explicitly worked with the tradition of writing about spice and the Orient in English literature. Leigh Hunt's 'The Panther' is a complex play around the discourse of the commodity form. The Cockney School, of which Hunt was a member, had a sophisticated relationship with the marketplace, as Jeffrey Cox has recently demonstrated. Here is the complete poem:

> The panther leaped to the front of his lair,
> And stood with a foot up, and snuffed the air;
> He quivered his tongue from his panting mouth,
> And looked with a yearning towards the south;
> For he scented afar in the coming breeze,
> News of the gums and their blossoming trees;
> And out of Armenia that same day,
> He and his race came bounding away.
> Over the mountains and down to the plains
> Like Bacchus's panthers with wine in their veins,
> They came where the woods wept odorous rains;
> And there, with a quivering, every beast
> Fell to his old Pamphylian feast.
>
> The people who lived not far away,
> Heard the roaring on that same day;
> And they said, as they lay in their carpeted rooms,
> 'The panthers are come, and are drinking their gums';
> And some of them going with swords and spears,
> To gather their share of the rich round tears,
> The panther I spoke of followed them back;
> And dumbly they let him tread close in the track,
> And lured him after them into the town;
> And then they let the portcullis down,
> And took the panther, which happened to be

The largest was seen in all Pamphily.

By every one there was the panther admired,
So fine was his shape and so sleekly attired,
And such an air, both princely and swift,
He had, when giving a sudden lift
To his mighty paw, he'd turn at a sound,
And so stand panting and looking around,
As if he attended a monarch crowned.
And truly, they wondered the more to behold
About his neck a collar of gold,
On which was written, in characters broad,
'Arsaces the king to the Nysian God'.
So they tied to the collar a golden chain,
Which made the panther a captive again,
And by degrees he grew fearful and still,
As though he had lost his lordly will.

But now came the spring, when the free-born love
Calls up nature in forest and grove,
And makes each thing leap forth, and be
Loving, and lovely, and blithe as he.
The panther felt the thrill o' the air,
And he gave a leap up, like that at his lair;
He felt the sharp sweetness more strengthen his veins,
Ten times than ever the spicy rains,
And ere they're aware, he has burst his chains:
He has burst his chains, and ah ha! he's gone,
And the links and the gazers are left alone,
And off to the mountains the panther's flown.

Now what made the panther a prisoner be?
Lo! 'twas the spices and luxury.
And what set that lordly panther free?
'Twas Love! – 'twas Love! – 'twas no one but he.[5]

Despite its exotic setting, both in terms of space and time, this poem is situated in relation to contemporary capitalism. This relation is 'antiquing', in which contemporary ideological issues are presented as if frozen in an imaginary past. The more antique the poem seems in form and content, the more explicitly it is acting as *objet petit a* in relation to contemporary discourses of utilitarian capitalism.

Hunt's poem is explicitly about the erotic investment in spice. The flight of the helplessly intoxicated panther down the mountain at the scent of the gums recalls the long literary history of describing transnational trade in terms of the trade winds as they make their way from the Orient. The use of 'luxury' situates the poem in the long eighteenth-century debate on that category, which had emerged out of the surplus economy generated by commercial capitalism. The panther himself becomes commodified, bound in chains and admired pornographically by 'gazers'.

Now it might *appear* that 'luxury' and 'love' are being placed in a binary opposition, of which 'luxury' is the inessential, extrinsic term. This would fit in with one of the discourses on slavery from Behn's *Oroonoko* to the Romantic period, from which the poem definitely borrows: the idea that there is an unalienated core of being within, behind or beyond the commodified subject. This is the sense of the phrase 'free-born love', or the image of the regal animal caught up in the libidinal economy, first of the potlatch sacrifice to the Nysian God and secondly of the crowd of gazers. However, the relationship between luxury and love is not as simple as that. The love that the panther feels is 'Ten times ever the spicy rains'. Love and luxury are not opposed here, but instead they are part of a continuum. One is simply greater than the other. The rather pat 'That's All Folks' ending is quite in keeping with the aesthetic strategies of the Cockney School – a cardboard resolution is more camp, and the Cockneys seemed to play a lot with a parody of consumerism which *traverses* its ideological fantasies rather than opposing them. The cardboard ending should alert us to the other possible reading: that it was not the spices that 'made' the panther a prisoner, it was being bound and gazed at – in other words, fetishised, turned into *objet petit a* in relation to a subject whose only attribute is its gaze ($\$ \diamond a$). As in pornography, enjoyment has to be mediated through an other, the onlooker, in order to complete the structure. The libido itself is still a locus of freedom.

The capitalist imaginary tends to envision spice both as flow – as in the flowing perfume of the gums in the first verse paragraph – and as density or viscosity – as in the 'rich round tears' of the second verse paragraph, an allusion to *Othello* amongst other texts. This kind of viscosity is what Friedrich von Schelling called *geistige Körperlichkeit* – the kind of spectral substantiality associated with the poetics of spice.[6] Significantly the state of frozen enjoyment, embodied in the jewel-like *jouissance* of the rich round tears, is evoked in the context of the human pursuit and capture of the gums with 'swords and spears'. If this poem is an allegory about the form of enjoyment in consumerism, then what it describes are the ways in which consumerism captures, but not entirely, the *jouissance* that sustains it – rather than the subject that might conceivably transcend it. There is an excess flow left over which the end of the poem characterises as the scent of love, in parallel with, rather than in strict opposition to, the spicy breeze which the panther yearns for at the beginning. We have been *extrapellated*, rather than interpellated, in the Althusserian sense, by this traversal of capitalist ideology. The advertisement cannot entirely be bought.

Unlike the gentle breeze at the beginning of *The Prelude*, which one imagines is scented only with the ambient air of the Lakes, and which neutralises the oppressiveness of the commercial city which Wordsworth in the seventh book denigrates with orientalist language, the breeze in 'The Panther' is fully eroticised and orientalised. Hunt does not throw the libidinal baby out with the consumerist bath water. Like Keats in *The Eve of St Agnes*, he is using the *form* of capitalist ideology – the evocation of a non-utilitarian and excessive, non-modern *jouissance* at the very heart of utility – against its *content* – that the world is the object of a neutral capitalist gaze that captures, binds and fetishises everything it sees.

In its engagement with commodity culture, the Cockney School had understood that 'a fantasy constitutes our desire, provides its co-ordinates; that is, it literally "teaches us how to desire"'. As Žižek comments: 'fantasy does not mean that when I desire a strawberry cake and cannot get it in reality, I fantasize about eating it; the problem is, rather: *how do I know that I desire a strawberry cake in the first place? This* is what fantasy tells me.'[7] The camp poetry of Keats and Hunt, by relying on a minimal distance towards fantasy, undermines the fantasy support of capitalism – the myth of the free lunch or the Land of Cockaygne from which the Cockneys got their name. The opposite strategy, more commonly construed to be Romantic, is rejecting $\$ \diamond a$ in favour of the myth of a full subject, and risking the return of *objet petit a* in the guise of the subject – which would ironically repeat the formula – as in Wordsworth's Schellingian attempts to posit himself as the object of his subjective discourse. But to revert to the etymology of 'Romantic', which relies on a play with the idea of figuration itself – Romance, *roman* – the Cockney strategy, which is equally Romantic, but in this second sense, is fully to engage with $\$ \diamond a$. The love of the panther does not escape the libidinal economy of luxury but fulfils it ten times greater than the poetics of spice. *It is more perverse than the perversion itself.* Love is simply the positivised form of lust or luxury.[8] There is no escape from consumerism, because it is the very idea of an escape which reinforces it. The best critique is to reveal the Möbius strip, whose one side is love and whose 'other' (really the same) side is luxury. There is a strong gender implication here, as commercial capitalist ideology inherited the Christian view of luxury as *Luxuria*, feminised libido. The anxiety experienced by critics of the Cockney School hit the mark, in a sense: the Cockneys were playing dangerously with categories of masculinity and femininity, revealing the manly eros that spurns spices and luxury merely to be a version of feminised desire.

AMBIENCE

A common view is that Romantic culture rejects the fantasy of capitalist enjoyment. But the existence of the Cockney School and the very *resistance* of the anti-capitalist Romantics proves that the reverse was the case. Subsequent criticism has tended to reproduce this mistake. Romanticist ecocriticism, for example, assumes that it is recapitulating the resistance of Romantic poetry to the technologies of capitalism. But what if we widened the lens to encompass an expanded view of space, a view that did not take the *oikos* of ecology in the sense of home or dwelling as its centre? We will see that this expanded space is inextricably caught in the poetics of spice.

Three poets already discussed in this book demonstrate this expanded view of space: Darwin, Shelley and Barbauld. Darwin's *The Economy of Vegetation* contains the goddess of nature's address to the trade winds (I.iv.9–24). Darwin establishes the eroticism of the islands and India through the alliterative 'soft susurrant . . . sweep' (19) and the connotations of 'playful' and 'sultry' (17). The susurration associates ambient sound with spice. The Sylphs, featured in *The Rape of the Lock*'s travesty of commodity fetishism, also resemble *The Tempest*'s Ariel, the elemental spirit who invisibly shapes the environment of the island, playing airs to Ferdinand and the clowns on the seashore. 'Earth's green pavilions' (20) is both ornamental and ecological, if ecology is the *logos* of the *oikos* or dwelling-place: again, an ambient interiority is invoked. There are similar implications in 'O'er waving Autumn bend your airy ring' (23).

The beginning of Shelley's *Queen Mab* VIII evokes a utopian ambience deriving in part from Darwin's experiments with ambient poetry (VIII.58–69). There is a gradual modulation from wind to sea to land as the trade winds flow. The figure of wind articulating space, like others in Shelley's early poetry, was to be recapitulated later (in 'Ode to the West Wind'). The 'echoings sweet' (67) that 'murmur through the Heaven-breathing groves' (68) and their metonymic connection with the 'fragrant zephyrs . . . from spicy isles' (64) show how the poetics of spice can invoke ambience: the echoes' sweetness, reciprocally, is almost gustatory. The way in which they 'melodize with man's blest nature' (69) demonstrates how Shelley, even in his early poetry, was thinking about the metaphor of the mind as an Aeolian harp, as found in 'A Defence of Poetry'.[9] The Aeolian harp is the ambient musical instrument *par excellence.*

'Good' ambience is contrasted with 'bad' ambience (like Klein's view of the 'good' and 'bad' partial object). Barbauld's *Epistle to William Wilberforce* describes the planter and his wife occupying an environment from which ornamental poetry has fled. The Muses flee 'the sounding lash' in a reversal of the ambience associated with the poetics of spice, as the 'balmy air' is 'disturbed' rather than harmonised as it is in Shelley's *Queen Mab*. It is disrupted by disembodied voices, the demonic inversion of the poetics of ambient spice, which imagines the disembodied voice as a soft, 'susurrant' (to use Darwin's word) perfumed trace. A whisper is like a tint or a light perfuming of the air.[10]

What, then, are the phenomenological determinants of ambient poetry? In order to understand this, another exploration of the poetics of spice is required. The problem of generalising about the 'spice of poetics' can be solved through work on its specific associations with capitalist ideology. Strictly formalist and essentialist approaches are too solid. If we consider the literature of the so-called Orient, these approaches are soon undermined. Bharata's *Natyashastra* or 'Science of Drama', written about the second century AD, not only established rules governing the creation of drama but also prepared the way for developing the theories of *rasa*, 'meaning' or 'essence'. Feroza Jussawalla's article on Indian literary theory quotes Lee Siegel's explanation:

> Playing on the literal meaning of *rasa*, 'flavor' or 'taste', [Bharata] used the gastronomic metaphor to explain the dynamics of the aesthetic experiences. Just as the basic ingredient in a dish, when seasoned with secondary ingredients and spices, yields a particular flavor which the gourmet can savor with pleasure, so the basic emotion in a play, story, or poem, when

seasoned with secondary emotions, rhetorical spices, verbal herbs, and tropological condiments, yields a sentiment which the connoisseur can appreciate in enjoyment.[11]

There is a tendency here to fit an Aristotelian model of substance and accidence, which is one of the bases of Eurocentric conceptions of spice and flavour. This has a political dimension. To talk about Indian literature in terms of spice, to make exoticisation a core principle of ancient Indian aesthetics, is a kind of overcoding. Conceptions of poetics involving spice appear outside the development of capitalism in the West. The most interesting aspect of Siegel's reading is its ignorance of the apparent contrast, in a Western interpretation at any rate, between *rasa* as 'essence' and as *spice*.

This deconstruction of the difference between essence and supplement is also evident in the poetics of spice in English literature. In his second eclogue (1515), Alexander Barclay associates money with nothingness:

> Thy meate in the court, is neither swanne nor heron,
> Curlewe nor crane, but cours befe and motton,
> Fat porke, or veale, and namely such is bought
> For easier pryce, whan thei be leane and nought.[12]

Barclay stresses the nullity of courtly value, a commonplace repeated by Warton and other writers of eclogues. Criticising the follies of poetry, Mynalcas declares, however, that it can be 'auoyde of honeste / Nothyng seasoned, with spice of grauyte / Auoyde of pleasure, auoyde of eloquence'.[13] The register of supplementarity, of spice as mere surface decoration or accidental embellishment, does not apply. Spiciness applies both to 'grauyte' and to 'eloquence', categories which a more modern, especially a Romantic, poetics would tend to distinguish.

Chronological distinctions are not easy here. A shift towards a dualistic opposition of appearance and reality takes place in the movement from medieval to modern aesthetics. The notion of rhetoric as disguise gains a stronger foothold in drama and poetry. In the Romantic period, this notion was inflated by writers such as Wordsworth and Coleridge into a conception of poetry as an anti-rhetorical rhetoric. This conception implied a weakening of spice's significance as a sign of richness. It is no accident that Keats, the male Romantic period poet who plays most with spice, also adapts medievalism, and with a gender liquidity that was anathema to the masculinising tendency of Coleridge's and Wordsworth's Romanticism.

Percy Shelley condemned the consumption of spice in his vegetarian prose. In 'A Defence of Poetry', he also attacked the bucolic poetry of Theocritus, Bion and Moschus as 'like the odor of the tuberose': 'it overcomes and sickens the spirit with excess of sweetness . . . correlative with that softness in statuary, music, and the kindred arts and even in manners and institutions which distinguished [their] epoch'. He contrasts this supplementarity with the organic, 'harmonizing' scent of a summer 'meadow-gale', perhaps alluding to descriptions of music and wind in Coleridge's *The Rime of the Ancient Mariner* (369–70, 457).[14] However, Shelley's utopian poetry is subtly but decisively influenced by the poetics of spice, and he uses related imagery to describe negative states of being. When Beatrice is raped by her father in the play *The Cenci*, her body-image becomes a miasmatic cloud of nauseating vapour (III.i.6–32).

Similarly, Coleridge's 'Kubla Khan' is an allegory about poetry. The poem's initial evocation of an Oriental paradise of incense trees deconstructs the contrasting naturalised sacred space of the verse paragraph beginning 'But Oh!' (12). The modern poetics, ostensibly opposed to rhetoric-as-disguise, is ironically dependent upon a radically different poetics. (Coleridge's older brother, John, lived in Calcutta since 1771, dying at Tillicherry from malaria in 1787. Richard Holmes speculates that his letters may have inspired Coleridge's interest in travel books such as those of Purchas.)[15]

Adams's 'On the Phoenix', a poem about the role of fantasy in poetry, imagines Arabia as an eroticised, perfumed ambient space:

Our stately trees all kinds of spices bear,
Our fountains gratify the ear,
Each leaf in consort joins to please
With the soft whispers of the evening breeze.
Here doth Phoebus make his bed,
'Tis by him she's thither led. (23–8)

In Tennyson's *Maud*, the fantasy structure equates the perfume-like miasma of Maud's threateningly ambient subjectivity with the shifting middle ground of trade and the abjection of luxury in the figures of orientalised despotism.[16]

What are the characteristics of this different poetics? It is not chronologically prior, though a late-medieval music theorist gave it one of its most concise formulations. There were plenty of theories in the Middle Ages which looked down upon the corporeal, and found dangerous ambiguity in the sense of smell. The Neoplatonic aesthetics of Augustine and Ficino, separated in most histories of ideas by the transition from medieval to Renaissance views, is really not very different in this regard. Two aspects can be ascribed to aesthetic phenomena, one physical, the other rational. In poetry, the bodily aspect consists of sounds and graphics, while the rational aspect consists of the patterns, the meta-structures, which those sounds and graphics evoke. In music, physical sounds are the exterior bodily aspect and musical forms, ideas or structures are the interior, rational, ideal aspect. Thus Milton's *Elegia quinta* (1629, published 1645), on the coming of spring and the onset of poetic inspiration, has a somewhat Dionysian ring in its celebration of inspiration as a spicy air: 'Cinnamea Zephyrus leve plaudit odorifer ala' (69).

But what of a poetics or a music based on smell? Johannes Tinctoris (d. 1511) and other medieval music theorists likened the effects of music to those of a perfume, a cloud of spicy odour diffusing through space to delight both the inward and outward senses.[17] This is remarkably similar to the opinion of the late-twentieth-century composer Brian Eno, who also describes a form of music, 'ambient' music, as a tint or perfume.[18] A phenomenology is being proposed here that is different from the one based on an opposition of appearance and reality (rhetoric-as-disguise). There is no contrast between bodily and rational aspects of aesthetic form, but a deconstructed view of ineffability and diffusion. Like many aspects of postmodern culture, Eno's notion of music as a tint or perfume, a spicing of space, suggests the dissemination of small points of smell or colour.

If there is ambient music, then is there such a phenomenon as ambient poetry? One only has to consider the stanza after the *spice* stanza of Keats's *The Eve of St Agnes*, in which the 'delicates' (271) are depicted heaped in golden dishes and silver baskets:

> sumptuous they stand
> In the retired quiet of the night,
> Filling the chilly room with perfume light. (XXXI.273–5)

Ambience is being evoked: the atmosphere in which the gift is presented (and presentation is really what the non-meal is 'about').

The 'perfume light' could be a delicate touch or tint, or perfumed light, a synaesthetic environment.

Sir William Jones, the major articulator of orientalism in eighteenth-century England, compared poetry with music.[19] He also linked poetry to atmosphere and territory: 'It is observable that *Aden*, in the Eastern dialects, is precisely the same word with *Eden*, which we apply to the garden of paradise: it has two senses, according to a slight difference in its pronunciation; its first meaning is *a settled abode*, its second, *delight, softness*, or *tranquillity*'.[20] Jones extols the intrinsic poetic value of the Orient:

> now it is certain that all poetry receives a very considerable ornament from the beauty of natural images; as the roses of *Sharon*, the verdure of *Carmel*, the vines of *Engaddi*, and the dew of *Hermon*, are the sources of many pleasing metaphors and comparisons in the sacred poetry: thus the odours of *Yemen*, the musk of *Hadramut*, and the pearls of *Omman*, supply the *Arabian* poets with a great variety of allusions; and, if the remark of *Hermogenes* be just, that what is *delightful to the senses* produces the *Beautiful* when it is described, where can we find so much beauty as in the *Eastern* poems, which turn chiefly upon the loveliest objects in nature?[21]

In other words, the fantasy-space of the oneiric horizon itself produces the beauty of poetry. In this light Jones contrasts the nomads with 'the inhabitants of the cities, who traffick with the merchants of Europe in spices, perfumes, and coffee, [and who] must have lost a great deal of their ancient simplicity'.[22]

In Western aesthetics and culture smell is underprivileged. Rindisbacher has demonstrated how it comes to serve as an ironic inversion of Enlightenment representational hierarchies in Patrick Suskind's *Das Parfum*.[23] Psychologists like to describe smell as giving a more direct access than the other senses to the unconscious mind (a Proustian *aperçu*) because of its lack of refined training; and for Freud smell is associated with the primordial experiences of the not-yet-upright human animal, its nose close to the genitals. Smell is associated both with the pungency of the corporeal and with the intangibility of the mental: the sense of *je ne sais quois* or *objet petit a*. Moreover, a smell is *there*, but it is hard to locate it: it can denote both atmosphere and something emerging from an atmosphere, and thus deconstructs the difference between figure and ground. This is clearly seen in the use of *spice* in poetry. The status of perfume as background or foreground, as atmosphere or detail, is radically undecidable.

Furthermore, the notion of perfume creates a sense of space

completely different from the Cartesian notion, and this is where a proper chronology is needed. In Cartesian space, an object can be defined by its position in a fundamentally empty nothingness, like a point on a map. Ironically enough, this view is dependent upon an incompletely mapped space. The Portuguese were able to navigate Africa using perspective geometry, proto-Cartesian space, because nothingness could be conceptualised as the vanishing point on the horizon at which all lines converge. The horizon is thus realised and liquidated at the same time: it is not a point in terrestrial reality but a conceptual tool. This opposition of nothingness and 'somethingness' is in turn dependent upon the phenomenology of zero, introduced into Europe through Arabic and Indian economics. Zero and infinity were developed as part of the history of credit finance by such Hindu and Islamic philosophers and economists as Brahmagupta and Al-Khowârazmi, from whose name 'algorithm' derives. These concepts were crucial in the development of the founding technology of capitalist representation, double-entry bookkeeping. Robert Recorde's *The Whetstone of Witte* (1556) demonstrates crucial mathematical concepts and is dedicated to the Muscovy Company.[24] The Muscovy Company predated the East India Company and employed the older spice routes across Russia and the Middle East.

Zero and infinity appear to be both emptier and fuller than ordinary integers. They have a super-dense quality, like a black hole or a plenitude: they can be divided by themselves, for instance, to obtain either 1 or themselves. They seem to mark an anomalous space in the symbolic system of which they are a part, a space that constitutes that system as such. Being *more* real than reality, that which is in the symbol more than what it symbolises, is the incarnating mark of *spice.*

The calculating principle, as Percy Shelley called it, of absolutist space-time, the modern Cartesian and even postmodern cage, depends upon and is deconstructed by those concepts of infinity and zero which appear to escape, like nuclear radiation, from the cage of space-time, and which are crucial not only to Newtonian calculus but also to the Kantian sublime, whose power forces upon its experiencer the transcendental quality of time and space, with the supposedly un-European despotism of Kubla Khan.[25] Similarly, the culture of luxury, with its modes both of commanding voice and of passive infantilised consumption, is a kind of zero-and-infinity point of ideologies of consumption.

The spice trade is bound up with the phenomenology of zero and its cousin, infinity, during capitalism. Cartesian space also depends upon a related issue, the opposition of a subject (over here) and an object (over there). Early commercial capitalist rhetoric made much of the attempt to literalise the oneiric horizon, and to bring it into view in mappable space. But when all of space has been mapped in a Cartesian way, the subject is part of the space being mapped (a point made at the beginning of Foucault's *The Order of Things*): the subject is no longer an onlooker gazing into a framed perspectivised image. This problem has become clear in recent cosmology and physics. Recent notions of space as enclosed but without a boundary (as proposed by Stephen Hawking) and of time as beginningless but not infinite are a symptom of the Western project coming full circle on itself.

The poetics of spice can create a kind of embodied space, a space that is not zero or nothingness, not caught up in the logic of negative and positive. This embodied space is closer to what is meant by 'environment' or 'ecosystem'. The naturalised ecopoetics of certain Romantic period writers, including Wordsworth, Coleridge, Charlotte Smith (especially in *Beachy Head*) and Landon, ironically creates spaces similar to those perfumed by a cloud of incense in a church or temple. It is an atmosphere, a realm in which events have room to happen. It is a somewhat thick, embodied, clotted kind of atmosphere, neither full nor empty. A good word for it might be 'heightened'. There is a sense of potential: something is 'about' to happen, but there is as yet no label or concept for this. Presence and absence, past and future events, discursive thoughts and memory traces, are contained within this space.

Let us now consider some examples of ambient poetry. Keats is an eminent poet of thick space. The beginning of *Endymion* (1817; published 1818) compares poetry to a variety of thickened, bland, blank or numb atmospheres in which tiny points of detail, like daffodils or musk roses, sparkle: 'the mid-forest brake, / Rich with a sprinkling of fair musk-rose blossoms' (19–20). The brake is the thickest part of a forest. Keatsian space often resembles the syrups and curds in the spicy stanza of *The Eve of St Agnes*. Immediately after the ekphrastic description of the banquet in *Lamia* (1819; published 1820), complete with 'A censer fed with myrrh and spiced wood', the ambient music is described: 'Soft went the music the soft air along' (198). The phobic space of the beginning of the second part of Eliot's *The Waste Land* is also ambient poetics, the tinting of an atmosphere. Landon's *The History of a Child* gives a central role to smell and perfume in the evocation of the child's world, in which the scent of book leather combines with the aromas of the ornamental garden, stories of the spice islands and the scent of musk roses. Landon's relation to consumerism was very similar to Keats's relation to the fantasy of capitalist ideology, and it is not surprising that she was also happy to use the poetics of spice. 'The coming musk-rose, full of dewy wine' (49) also appears in the most ambient stanza of Keats's 'Ode to a Nightingale' (1819; published 1820), in an *occupatio* that describes by not describing: 'I cannot see what flowers are at my feet, / Nor what soft incense hangs upon the boughs' (41–2). The entire poem is ambient: words sound like bells (71), the 'faery lands' (70) seem contiguous to the real, as in the myth of the Terrestrial Paradise, the poet listens 'Darkling' (51) and poetry is figured as the fading of the subject into a Dionysian immersion in nature. Without a sense of how this kind of poetry figures space, a masculine Romantic ecocriticism will remain hostile to the Keatsian poetics which it may easily denigrate as artificial and effeminate.

The poetics of spice, then, is an *ambient* poetics, not a rhetoric of disguise but an *atmospherics*. The resonance of the Song of Songs as a touchstone of ambient poetics has been demonstrated throughout this book in the study of the persistence of the *hortus conclusus*. Paul Napoléon Roinard's *Cantique des Cantiques* was staged by Paul Fort at the Théâtre Moderne in 1891, in front of an audience that included Debussy and the occult poet Joseph Péladan: 'The poetry was augmented by music, colour projections and perfume sprayed rather ineffectually from the theatre boxes and balcony.'[26] Des Esseintes in Huysmans' *Against Nature* creates women, bales of hay and factories out of scents against the hyperreal background of a meadow made of perfumes.[27]

The shift that occurs in this poetics between the medieval and modern periods is a change in the functions of this cloudy, ambient space. Milton suggests this kind of space in his representation of Chaos, itself a hypostatisation of notions of transnational trade. In addition to connoting the mystery of God's presence or the extent of royal space, it was used to suggest the mystery of capitalist value and, emerging precisely from capitalist conditions, the mystery of nature or non-capitalist space. The spectral quality of money and spice, and spice-as-money, is precisely a feature of that poetics that also celebrates the 'hauntological' aspects of God or nature.

Christ is figured as a cloud of perfume in *To the Name Above Every Name, the Name of Iesus a Hymn* by Crashaw (1613?-49). Whether He is a person, an ambience or an object is impossible to tell. Christ is that redemptive flow that overwhelms the narrator with the tumbling generosity of His potlatch, enacted in the snaky, baroque curls of Crashaw's verse:

> O dissipate thy spicy Powres
> (Clowd of condensed sweets) & break vpon vs
> In balmy showrs;
> O fill our senses, And take from vs
> All force of so Prophane a Fallacy
> To think ought sweet but that which smells of Thee.
> Fair, flowry Name; In none but Thee
> And Thy Nectareall Fragrancy,
> Hourly there meetes
> An vniuersall SYNOD of All sweets;
> By whom it is defined Thus
> That no Perfume
> For euer shall presume
> To passe for Odoriferous,
> But such alone whose sacred Pedigree
> Can proue it Self some kin (sweet name) to Thee.
> SWEET NAME, in Thy each Syllable
> A Thousand Blest ARABIAS dwell;
> A Thousand Hills of Frankincense;
> Mountains of myrrh, & Beds of spices,
> And ten Thousand Paradises
> The soul that tasts [*sic*] thee takes from thence.
> How many vnknown WORLDS there are
> Of Comforts, which Thou hast in keeping! (167–90)[28]

The poetics of spice reaches a point of extreme sophistication here. Christ is figured as name, signifier, spice and container of spice. He *is* His name, his metaphorical vehicle, and that which is named by Him. He occupies all semiological positions. The religious ecstatic experience of ambience, figured as an environmental fragrance, is also found in the works of St Teresa and Lorenzo Magalotti's 'abyss of odorous light', which is discussed in the third chapter. Thomas Traherne's *The Odour* imagines the ordinary human body as a Christlike perfume that uplifts itself in self-contemplation: 'My

Members all do yield a sweet Perfume' (5); 'For Use ye permanent remain intire, / Sweet Scents diffus'd do gratify Desire' (11–12); 'Talk with thy self; thy self enjoy and see: / At once the Mirror and the Object be' (53–4); 'What's Cinnamon, compar'd to thee?' (55). Far from being narcissistic, this miasmatic blurring of bodily boundaries is an engagement with the brilliance of the phenomenal world.[29]

In Hemans's poem *Joan of Arc, in Rheims*, the heroine, in her gloriously sublime, Miltonic and republican cloud of incense, ironically resembles the ambient Burkean and reactionary organicism towards which the poem tends:

within, the light
Thro' the rich gloom of pictur'd windows flowing,
Tinged with soft awfulness a stately sight,
The chivalry of France, their proud heads bowing
In martial vassalage! – while midst that ring,
And shadow'd by ancestral tombs, a king
Received his birthright's crown. For this, the hymn
Swell'd out like rushing waters, and the day
With the sweet censer's misty breath grew dim,
As thro' long aisles it floated o'er th' array
Of arms and sweeping stoles. But who, alone
And unapproach'd, beside the altar-stone,
With the white banner, forth like sunshine streaming,
And the gold helm, thro' clouds of fragrance gleaming,
Silent and radiant stood? (7–21)[30]

Sound, light and scent flow together, as Joan of Arc does and does not stand forth in brilliant *enargeia* from the tint or 'tinge' or 'awfulness', the cloud of incense and the 'rushing' voices who echo the approach of the chariot in Ezekiel 1:24.

Sir William Jones, in imitation of Arabic poetry, depicts Solima's *caravanserai* as a perpetual state of ambience:

See yon fair groves that o'er Amana rise,
And with their spicy breath embalm the skies;
Where ev'ry breeze sheds incense o'er the vales,
And ev'ry shrub the scent of musk exhales!
See through yon op'ning glade a glitt'ring scene,
Lawns ever gay, and meadows ever green! ('Solima')[31]

The Palace of Fortune, which inspired Shelley in writing *Queen Mab*, describes how the lady Maia is transported to a magical isle:

Now morning breath'd: the scented air was mild,
Each meadow blossom'd and each valley smil'd;
On ev'ry shrub the pearly dewdrops hung,
On ev'ry branch a feather'd warbler sung;
The cheerful spring her flo'ry chaplets wove,
And incense-breathing gales perfum'd the grove.[32]

An *occupatio* in a vision in *The Seven Fountains* similarly employs ambient poetics, reversing *occupatio* into cornucopia:

Not all the groves, where ancient bards have told
Of vegetable gems, and blooming gold,
Not all the bow'rs which oft in flow'ry lays
And solemn tales Arabian poets praise,
Though streams of honey flow'd through ev'ry mead,
Though balm and amber drop'd from ev'ry reed,
Held half the sweets that nature's ample hand
Had pour'd luxuriant o'er this wondrous land.[33]

At the third door, the protagonist encounters a third fountain. Jones figures Milton's 'wilderness of sweets' as the aura of trade:

His ravish'd sense a scene of pleasure meets,
A maze of joy, a paradise of sweets.
Through jasmine bow'rs, and vi'let-scented vales,
On silken pinions flew the wanton gales,
Arabian odours on the plants they left,
And whisper'd to the woods their spicy theft;
Beneath the shrubs that spread a trembling shade
The musky roses, and fragrant civets play'd.
As when at eve an eastern merchant roves
From Hadramut to Aden's spikenard groves,
Where some rich caravan not long before
Has pass'd, with cassia fraught, and balmy store,
Charm'd with the scent that hills and vales diffuse,
His grateful journey gayly he pursues;
Thus pleas'd the monarch fed his eager soul,
And from each breeze a cloud of fragrance stole.[34]

Ambient poetry can be found in other Romantic period writers. The 'enfolded' sunny spots of 'Kubla Khan' (11) evoke the same kind of ambience as the 'deep romantic chasm' (12) and the charmed space of the vatic poet around whom a circle must be woven (51). Gender identity, dependent upon oppositions of subject and object, figure and ground, or nature and culture, as Hélène Cixous has demonstrated in *The Laugh of the Medusa*, also tends to be placed in a quandary by ambient poetics. Gender boundaries are liquefied as the poem renders equivalent Kubla's despotic command (1–2), the seductive wailing of the woman (16), the prophetic ancestral voices (30), the singing of the maid (37–41) and the narrating voice of the poet with his floating hair (50, floating as it were in a supercharged atmosphere).[35]

Attempts to distinguish poetic language from the poetics of spice, then, have often been preoccupied with binary gender distinctions. This preoccupation is doubly heightened by anxieties about the subject in capitalist space. Rigid distinctions between subject and object, and between substance and space (something and nothing), coincide with the inception of capitalism. Early conceptions of capitalism defined it as a softening art, unrelated to the masculine arts of war and courtesy. The feminised and possibly queer shifts of language, sliding tropologically from one place to another, were exploited and feared in the traffic and translation of the early modern period. The culture of sensibility in the eighteenth century provided aesthetic modes in which softer, less well-defined kinds of gender identity and less tightly bounded experiences of space could be mediated. The opposition to sentimentalism of certain Romantic period writers is an anxious moment in the general slippage of boundaries incurred in the long history of capitalism.

This long history included numerous reactions to ornate rhetoric, which was viewed as oriental. Richard Halpern has shown how Renaissance grammar schools promulgated the copious style, highly ornamented rhetoric, a surplus over the economy of primitive accumulation which formed an aspect of the production of a bourgeoisie whose gender status was questionable, fluid, ambiguous.[36] Although civic humanism excluded or denigrated the role of women, as the work of Richard Mulcaster demonstrates, it did this because of internal anxieties about the feminisation of humane letters, the erotic corrupting influence of vernacular translation and the florid qualities of the copious style. Patricia Parker has remarked on a dangerous Asiatic over-extension of the copious style that could corrupt or be the result of corruption; Jones praised what he saw as the inherently copious style of Arabic.[37] The hesitation here between cause and symptom is itself a symptomatic component of an ambient poetics.[38]

During this period the Phoenix became a myth of a self-grounding, self-inventing masculinity predicated on an anxiety about the fluidity of gender. This myth was associated with the growth of the city, the rise of mercantile culture and the role of the theatre in providing new forms of popular entertainment where authority was freshly at stake.[39] Anxieties proliferated about the new forms of masculinity formed through grammar school education, with its emphasis on the copious style. The Phoenix' pyre of spices is a vanishing mediator, a punctuation mark in the smooth transition from identity to identity associated with the liminal spaces of nest, womb, tomb and crucible. The transitional space is unstable, the space of the pyre of spices and its hint of all-consuming luxury, fecundity and enjoyment, where life and death are inseparable.

The iron cage of the weekday bourgeois world (as Weber puts it) is dependent upon the leisure-time fantasy of infinite exotic consumption imagined as its ideological support, even though such exotic activities appear to escape the rationalised container of absolutist space-time and cause the subject to lose his or her bearings in an infinite sea of desire. During the growth of commercial capitalism, luxury became simultaneously encouraged and policed, as too little of it would cause the inhabitants of the cage to become restive, while too much might undermine the fiction of the cage's rationality.

The dialectic of luxury, written over the body of woman, is evident in Salman Rushdie's advertising copy for the marketing of cream in Britain in the 1980s, where a devil appeared on television to tempt house-bound wives from the weekday world to little indulgences: 'Fresh cream . . . naughty but nice.' It is also evident in the command of Coca-Cola: 'Enjoy' – one of the most difficult commands with which to comply. In this respect the current 'War on [some] Drugs' policies of the USA and other countries is hypocritical. It is not only drugs and drug-like substances, but the militant and militaristic promotion of their enjoyment, which is at stake in the culture of luxury. The poetics of spice fleshes out the fantasy of zero and infinity, evoking the taste of a substance without substance and conjuring up the aroma of lands so far away as to be off the co-ordinates of the Cartesian map. It is no wonder that in a misogynistic, prudish world of objectified bodies, sex should also be imagined as spice, that 'nothing' that nevertheless encapsulates infinite desire.

Sentimentalism is related to the consumption of luxury products, as evidenced in Lewis Carroll's parody of animal rights rhetoric in *Alice's Adventures in Wonderland* (1865), 'The Walrus and the Carpenter'. Feeling intimately for the world is predicated upon a capacity to devour it. In eating the world, boundaries between subject and object are broken down and in another way rigidly maintained. In the poetics of spice, however, a utopian space is imaginable in which boundaries between subject and object evaporate, as they are not predicated on a dialectic of consumer and consumed. Value becomes sacred space.

In the *Spectator* for 19 May 1711, Addison describes the London Stock Exchange as generating a sensory feast:

> [it] gives us a great . . . Variety of what is Useful, and at the same time supplies . . . us with every thing that is Convenient and Ornamental . . . our Eyes are refreshed with the green Fields of Britain, at the same time as our Palates are feasted with Fruits that rise between the Tropicks.[40]

Commercial capitalism is praised for providing an aesthetics of ornamentation. The rise of colonial and imperial Britain instigated an aestheticisation of surplus value.[41] The poetics of spice was employed in the formation of this aesthetic dimension of commercial capitalism. What is *not* seen in this ambient emporium is the labour that produces the surplus value. Thus in writings about sugar which celebrate its production in the West Indies, such as Grainger's, the cane is shown to have mysteriously arisen as if from space.[42] Laura Brown has shown how Pope represents Belinda's perfumes in a similar way in *The Rape of the Lock*, and my reading of Blackmore indicates that religious panegyric could be affected by the very poetics of spice that emanates from it to adorn panegyrics to trade, as in a reinfection.[43]

Such an aesthetics also informs the poetry that deals with domestic consumption, such as King's *The Art of Cookery*. King overdetermines this kind of consumption as itself a form of poetics. It is a poetics in which the rules of decorum operate: 'Let Men and Manners ev'ry Dish adapt, / Who'd force his Pepper where his Guests are clapt?'[44] The mob of common people could never be coerced with 'Ragouts of Peacocks Brains'. Decorum enforces rules of preparation: 'Meat forc'd too much, untouch'd at Table lies.' And different cultures aspire differently to the condition of luxury living. The French are tasteful, the Dutch miserly: 'Where love of Wealth and rusty Coin prevail, / What hopes of sugar'd Cakes or butter'd Ale?'[45] An ornamental aesthetic, determined to create the right sort of atmosphere, is at stake.

King translates Horace's 'Ut pictura, poesis' as 'Tables shou'd be like Pictures to the Sight.'[46] The ekphrastic implications of this line are evident. Less clear but no less significant is the spatial conception of writing that this implies: that poetry, imagined as a meal, establishes an atmosphere that is not simply functional space but vivid space; and conversely, that a picture, imagined as a meal, is a space without a frame in which viewer and viewed exist in the same dimensions.

This frameless space is not discovered in the wilds of nature, but achieved through art. One could contrast this with the primitivism of Xenophon's Socrates, for whom appetite alone is the finest sauce, or 'Our *Cambrian* Fathers', who 'took / Such Salt as issu'd from the native Rock'.[47] A Popean aesthetic of art as nature to advantage dressed informs King's conception of cooking:

> 'Tis a sage Question, if the Art of Cooks
> Is lodg'd by Nature, or attain'd by Books
> . . .
> When Art and Nature join th' Effect will be
> Some nice Ragout, or charming Fricasy.[48]

'Nice' and 'charming' are difficult words for Romanticist discourse. But in context they both suggest accuracy, decorum and an affective interaction of consumer and consumed. The Wordsworthian aesthetics of spontaneity and expression, however, drove a wedge between art and nature, subject and object. It also drove a wedge between consumer and consumed, as the vegetarian Shelley pointed out about the predatory Rousseauvianism of the trout-fishing boys in *The Excursion* (1814).[49]

King imagines poetry as a feast to which a certain kind of invited guest will come: an environment is created, a stage is set. In the Romantic period rhetoric of non-rhetoric, that environment is marked as uncreated, as discovered and explored. The poetry of atmospheres shifts into the poetry of 'natural' environments – marginal, asocial or anti-social spaces. Such a move involves a relegation of the poetics of spice, now labelled as effeminate, artificial sentimentalism. The persistence of spice in the work of Charlotte Smith, Keats and Shelley, however, demonstrates its continuing value as a marker of heightened, utopian or even sacred space. The myth of the Terrestrial Paradise, and the poetics that accompanies it, are not entirely annihilated by Wordsworth's efforts to escape the taint and smell of money ('Getting and Spending').

Wordsworth is remarkable for his poetics of the spot of time, a traumatic, punctuating hole in discursive space which instigates an enveloping, enfolding formation of contemplative verse. He distinguished this pearl-and-oyster poetics as vigorously as possible from the effeminising poetics of fancy, reduced in his eyes to the inorganic (indeed, anti-organic) machinery of the supplement. Wordsworth deprecated the Gothic as a degrading stimulant, using language similar to Burke's attack on the French Revolution.[50] As Mr Flosky, a cipher for Coleridge, declares in Thomas Love Peacock's *Nightmare Abbey* (1818):

> Tea has shattered our nerves; late dinners make us slaves of indigestion; the French Revolution has made us shrink from the name of philosophy . . . That part of the *reading public* which shuns the solid food of reason for the light diet of fiction, requires a perpetual adhibition of *sauce piquante* to the palate of its depraved imagination.[51]

In *Reflections on the Revolution in France* (1790), Burke compares revolutionary sentiments with an over-indulgence in medicine and with the use of 'variety and seasoning' to 'stimulate their cannibal appetites'.[52] In other words, Burke is representing the view that opposes his reactionary organicism as a *pharmakon.*

This view is similar to contemporary anxieties about the Orient. Jones's comparative mythology and jurisprudence stated that Indian myths and the Indian legal system shared the same fundamental truths as Christianity and European reason, but that they had been '"embellished and obscured by the fancy of their poets"' (as Fred Hoerner has pointed out), or marred by a lack of concern for precedent predicated on the fusion of executive and judicial branches of legislature.[53] They could also imply a highly ornamental style, reflecting not Indian but Western anxieties about the Asiatic style and its relationship with the gender and rhetorical issues generated within the discourses of civic humanism: in short, an aspect of the poetics of spice. This is a typical form of orientalism: the construction of a displaced Other that is in fact an unacceptable but unavoidable kernel of European ideology. At stake was not only what Hoerner calls Romantic allegory, then, but also those sentimental traditions that were indeed at the heart of Enlightenment period poetics and forms of luxury consumption ostracised in civic humanism, at the heart of new ideologies of consumption, a kernel of inutility at the heart of utility. This could be understood in terms of the body as an excrescence that is actually intimate: extimate, as Lacan would say. Sentimentalism and ornamental poetics could actually furnish the needs of imperialist ideology, for example in Blackmore; it is not just a case of Enlightenment rationality carving up the world. The radical fact about the spice of poetics is that in its very extimacy, its feminised excrescence, it served the needs of imperialism.[54]

The folded space in 'Kubla Khan', 'Enfolding sunny spots of greenery' (11) is neither quite interior nor exterior: perhaps the best word for it is, again, Lacan's 'extimate', an intimate space that is nevertheless on the 'outside'. It resembles the *hortus conclusus* found in the Song of Songs, the spaces of medieval castles constructed for women and the 'feminine', and Milton's Eden, an ambiguous space of containment and desire. The poetics of this space, with its dependence on the poetry of ornament indicated by the topographical tropes of 'here' and 'there' and the representation of a decorous horticulture marked by the 'sinuous rills', is often read as being in opposition to the sublime poetics of the chasm and the synthetic poetics of the dome, with its caves of ice, and the sublimity of the demonic poet and his taboo consumption of the food of the gods, honey-dew and the milk of paradise. However, although Coleridge makes a mockery of it, there is a direct, though in his imagination asymmetrical, relationship between the caves and the dome, the sublime and the beautiful, the milk of paradise and the incense-bearing tree. The culture of luxury which enables the aestheticisation of the useless fragment in poetry ('A vision in a dream. A fragment') and landscaping has as its fantasy support structure an othered, orientalised despotic pleasure garden (the land of Cockaygne, the paradise garden of Marco Polo's assassins, and so forth) where reason and the self are humbled and stupefied in the act of consuming a potlatch-like flow of precious artificial substance, so sublimely related to the torrent of wild orgasm described in the second stanza of 'Kubla Khan'.

In the culture of the picturesque, the symbolism of ruined fragments of castle depends upon functional dwellings: they symbolise and embody an excess that cannot be used up, utilised, rendered subject to utilitarian 'law'. They symbolise those sumptuary laws that the ideology of the free market has by no means forgotten, the luxury commodities that demarcate the voice of pleasure and power. The power of voice in 'Kubla Khan' is evident, from the despot's decree to 'oh!' and other apostrophes without apposition, to the power of the poet whose spectral power gives him flashing eyes and floating hair. The voice, as Žižek has shown, is that opaque, meaningless excrescence whose very meaninglessness is an aspect of its power: 'Voice is that which, in the signifier, resists meaning; it stands for the opaque inertia which cannot be recuperated by meaning'; and a political problem arises – 'how are we to prevent the voice from sliding into a consuming self-enjoyment that "effeminizes" the reliable masculine Word?'[55] The poetics of the wild sublime in the Romantic period is only a hypostatisation of a certain feature of the arabesqued, ornamental poetics of spice.

Shelley opposes luxury in content and is anti-ornamental in form. While he is weighing the sublime power of a poetry that strips the object of its veil in 'A Defence of Poetry', and condemning barbarous luxury in politics and culture, he is employing that poetics of the sentimental Enlightenment which delights in topos and ornamentation. Keats, on the other hand, by hyperbolically developing the poetics of spice to a bursting point, criticises the culture of luxury through a camp identification with it. One can never quite tell which side of the fence he stands on. Rather than celebrating trade or exotic discovery, an *inner* imperialism, voyaging around the world of interiors created in the culture of luxury, developed a sentimental, ornamental poetry which has been ignored or devalued by a masculinist anti-rhetoric in poetry and literary theory from the preface to the *Lyrical Ballads* to the work of F. R. Leavis and the New Critics. Deconstruction and New Historicism have until recently only either circled around the empty space of this poetics or blown holes in it through which the history that it tries to transcend can be glimpsed. This has meant that we have lost touch with how poetry in the Romantic period worked upon the sensory experience of the commodity form.

Hunt's *A Now, Descriptive of a Hot Day* was published in the first issue of the *Indicator* (1820). It demonstrates how members of the Cockney School were rewriting the rules of poetics, bringing out a latent tendency in ornamental poetry. This latent tendency associated ambience with ornamentation and perfume. The sun is compared with saffron:

Now the rosy- (and lazy-) fingered Aurora, issuing from her saffron house, calls up the moist vapours to surround her, and goes veiled with them as long as she can; until Phoebus, coming forth in his power, looks everything out of the sky, and holds sharp uninterrupted empire from his throne of beams.[56]

Here the sun is not only spice, but space, the 'saffron house' of the feminised dawn. The surrounding of Aurora by 'the moist vapours', the definite article suggesting intimacy or familiarity, blurs boundaries between inside and outside. This semiotic blurring, familiar in Kristevan interpretations of the feminised body, is curtailed by the imperial gesture ('sharp uninterrupted empire') of Apollo, the sun not as space but as solidified subject subjecting everything to a gaze that 'looks everything out of the sky'. The golden age of Titans is contrasted with the imperial regime of 'Now', a subtle comment on emergent British imperialism that reduces the world to an exploitable map, 'looking' all contingency 'out of' it. The soft space, semi-solid and semi-permeable, of the spicy dawn has been replaced by the hard 'beams' that bisect space and turn it into the imperial 'space of flows'. Similarly ornamental poetry, dependent upon the rhetoric of veiling rather than unveiling ('goes veiled with them as long as she can'), conjured up by the epithet doubled upon itself, 'rosy- (and lazy-) fingered Aurora', is replaced by the clarity and sharpness of masculine poetics. The poetics of spice is used to comment upon issues of power and gender.

Spice performs the same poetic work as Žižek's notion of 'voice'. It stands in for the opaque, extimate, grainy, irreducible aspect of the signifier. The spice of poetics is the hypostatisation of voice as ornamentation. This is most obvious in symbolist poetry, where rather than referring to a given cultural referent, symbolic language becomes a symbol of itself, a transumptive symbol. The supposed resistance to commodification of *l'art pour l'art* is art's final collapse into the *ekphanestaton* of the commodity form's sheer appearance. Brian Eno's description of the future as like a perfume chimes with Wicke's analysis of postmodern theory itself as like a perfume in her essay 'Postmodernism: The Perfume of Information'.[57] *Pace* Camporesi, modernity is as subject in its ways to the poetics of spice as earlier ages.

The likening of language and theory to perfume is also a warping of the dichotomies of presence and absence, subject and object, mask and face, essence and supplement, which underpinned the ideologies of colonialism and imperial expansion and the construction of a dualistic modern self. In the crumbling of language before the perfumed space, the thick emptiness of ambience, we get a glimpse of what Žižek would call the Real of desire whose repression warps that modern self into being. Charles Baudelaire's 'Parfum Exotique' evokes the oneiric horizon. But there is an even stronger play with the poetics of spice in 'Correspondences', where the ambience of a forest becomes penetrable and yet mysterious, spacious and yet opaque, gesturing towards and withholding meaningfulness, through the play of sound and scents:

> The pillars of Nature's temple are alive
> and sometimes yield perplexing messages;
> forests of symbols between us and the shrine
> remark our passage with accustomed eyes.
>
> Like long-held echoes, blending somewhere else
> into one deep and shadowy unison
> as limitless as darkness and as day,
> the sounds, the scents, the colors correspond.
>
> There are odors succulent as young flesh,
> sweet as flutes, and green as any grass,
> while others – rich, corrupt and masterful –
> possess the power of such infinite things
> as incense, amber, benjamin and musk,
> to praise the senses' raptures and the mind's.[58]

The 'decadence' of this poem relative to the supposed nature-worship of Romanticism lies precisely in its dovetailing of nature with artifice. Columns become trees; trees become sticks of incense; natural perfume becomes commodified ambience. What this book has shown is that this dovetailing is a feature already latent in Romanticism. It is not only latent, however. The mystical relation to the commodity form that Benjamin noted in Baudelaire's *flâneur* or dandy was enabled by Romantic consumerism. It is Romantic consumerism that makes of the forest a shop window – and allows the ambience of a shop window to be experienced as the temple of nature.

Notes

INTRODUCTION

1 See Majeed, 'Orientalism, Utilitarianism, and British India', p. 8.
2 Campbell, 'Understanding Traditional and Modern Patterns of Consumption in Eighteenth-Century England', in Brewer and Porter, eds., *Consumption and the World of Goods*, pp. 40–57.
3 Campbell, *Romantic Ethic and the Spirit of Modern Consumerism*, p. 29.
4 Kant, *Critique of Judgment*, I.iv.50.
5 Campbell, 'Understanding Traditional and Modern Patterns of Consumption', pp. 52–5, 42, 43.

I THE CONFECTION OF SPICE: HISTORICAL AND THEORETICAL CONSIDERATIONS

1 Žižek, *Plague of Fantasies*, p. 3.
2 Trevenen, *Little Derwent's Breakfast*, pp. 46, 42–5, 33.
3 Ibid., p. 34.
4 I was fortunate to hear this from David Harvey at a paper given on postmodernism, Oxford, 1988.
5 Trevenen, *Little Derwent's Breakfast*, pp. 1–2.
6 Schivelbusch, *Tastes of Paradise*, p. 7.
7 Ibid., p. 12.
8 For a recent study of coffee, tea and chocolate in the early modern period, see Varey, 'Three Necessary Drugs', in Cope, ed., *1650–1850*, IV.3–51.
9 Bullein, *Bulwarke*, fo. 2v.
10 Dyer, 'English Diet in the Later Middle Ages', in Aston, Coss, Dyer and Thirsk, eds., *Social Relations and Ideas*, pp. 191–216. The quotation is from p. 194.
11 Skelton, *Poetical Works*, pp. 1–7.
12 Eagleton, *Literary Theory*, pp. 8–9.
13 Bloom, *Map of Misreading*, pp. 78, 126–43.
14 See Shell, *Money, Language, and Thought*, pp. 150–1.
15 In *Byron*, ed. McGann.

16 *OED*, *spice*, 3.a.
17 Murphy, *Song of Songs*, p. 54.
18 Ibid., pp. 70, 125. See Robotham, *An Exposition on the Whole Booke of Solomons Song*, F3r (37; unreliable pagination).
19 Shell, *Money, Language, and Thought*, p. 175.
20 Mintz, 'Changing Roles of Food in the Study of Consumption', in Porter and Brewer, eds., *Consumption and the World of Goods*, pp. 261–73; the citation is from p. 271.
21 Appadurai, *Social Life of Things*, p. 38.
22 Ibid., p. 38.
23 Murphy, 'William Burroughs Between Indifference and Revalorization', pp. 113–24.
24 See Žižek, *Tarrying with the Negative*, pp. 34–5, 51–2, 244–5.
25 See Schivelbusch, *Tastes of Paradise*, p. 71.
26 Ibid., p. xiv.
27 David Harvey, discussion with Richard Sennett in the Committee on Theory and Culture, New York University, spring 1995.
28 Sahlins, *Culture and Practical Reason*, pp. 126–65.
29 Berry, *Idea of Luxury*, p. 50.
30 Weber, *Protestant Ethic*, p. 171.
31 In *Complete Works*, ed. Alexander.
32 In *Works of Geoffrey Chaucer*, ed. Robinson.
33 Derrida, *Specters of Marx*, p. 162.
34 In *Complete Works*, ed. Bowers.
35 Johnson, *A Dictionary of the English Language*, *spice*.
36 *OED*, *spice*, 7.
37 Keats, *Complete Poems*, ed. Barnard.
38 I am grateful to William Pietz for his remarks on this matter.
39 Adorno, *Negative Dialectics*, pp. 183–94.
40 William Pietz, talk given at Columbia University anthropology department, fall 1994.
41 Smith, *Wealth of Nations*, II.26–7.
42 Krieger, *Ekphrasis*, p. 7.
43 Derrida, *Dissemination*, pp. 54, 104, 205, 208, 222, 253.
44 Žižek, *For They Know Not What They Do*, p. 75.
45 Ibid., pp. 72–80.
46 Derrida, *Dissemination*, pp. 129, 140.
47 Žižek, *For They Know Not What They Do*, p. 124.
48 Ibid., p. 125.
49 Apter, 'Introduction', in Apter and Pietz, eds., *Fetishism as Cultural Discourse*, p. 5.

2 TRADE WINDS

1 Joyce, *A Portrait*, ed. Deane, pp. 221–33.
2 Ibid., p. 112.
3 Marsilio Ficino, commentary on Plato's *Symposium*, in Hofstadter and Kuhns, eds., *Philosophies of Art and Beauty*, pp. 217–19.
4 Joyce, *A Portrait*, p. 164.
5 Ibid., p. 112.
6 Ibid., p. 193.
7 Linschoten, *Discours of Voyages*, book III, pp. 328–9.
8 Joyce, *Dubliners*, pp. 26–32.
9 Derrida, *Dissemination*, pp. 61–171.
10 Ibid., p. 152.
11 See Milton, *Paradise Lost*, ed. Fowler, p. 200. Also, see Diodorus Siculus, *Diodori Siculi bibliothecæ historicæ libri* XV, pp. 85–6. Books I–V were translated by Poggio-Bracciolini.
12 Bullein, *Bulwarke*, fo. 26.
13 Le Guérer, *Scent*, pp. 88–9.
14 Butler, *Hudibras*, ed. Waller, p. 135.
15 In Clough, *Poems*, ed. Norrington.
16 Woolf, *Mrs Dalloway*, pp. 35, 85; Meisel, *The Myth of the Modern*, p. 183.
17 See Schama, *Embarrassment of Riches*, chapter 3, 'Feasting, Fasting and Timely Atonement', pp. 129–220.
18 See Schivelbusch, *Tastes of Paradise*, pp. 3–14 for an example.
19 Quoted in Camporesi, *Exotic Brew*, p. 158.
20 Ibid., p. 112.
21 Pocock, *Virtue, Commerce, and History*, p. 115.
22 Quoted in Camporesi, *Exotic Brew*, pp. 74–5.
23 *Paradise Lost* 'was probably begun as early as 1655': see Smith, *Literature and Revolution in England*, p. 223.
24 Braudel, *Civilization and Capitalism*, II.559.
25 Ibid., I.382. See II.403–8.
26 Ibid., II.456–7.
27 See Appadurai, ed., *Social Life of Things*, p. 22.
28 Braudel, *Civilization and Capitalism*, I.415.
29 Ibid., I.440. See II.436–7.
30 Phillips and Phillips, *Worlds of Christopher Columbus*, p. 28.
31 See Majeed, 'Orientalism, Utilitarianism, and British India', p. 351.
32 Purchas, *Purchas his Pilgrimes*, Part I, book I, pp. 1–2.
33 Ibid., Part I, book I, p. 4.
34 Ibid., Part I, book I, iii (pp. 6–10).
35 Braudel, *Civilization and Capitalism*, II.203–4. For other commodities used as payment in kind (salt, sugar, tobacco, cocoa, bacon, salt meat, wine, oil), see I.442–3, 447.
36 Ibid., I.470.

37 Ibid., III.222.
38 Ibid., I.462. See II.208.
39 Mun, 'A Discourse of Trade from *England* unto the East *Indies*', in Purchas, *Purchas his Pilgrimes*, I.v.17, p. 746.
40 Mandeville, *Fable of the Bees*, pp. 50–2.
41 Poster, 'Postmodern Virtualities', pp. 79–95. The quotation is from pp. 79–80.
42 Braudel, *Civilization and Capitalism*, II.94.
43 Ibid., II.99.
44 Ibid., II.120.
45 Ibid., II.128. Cf. III.76.
46 Steensgaard, 'Growth and Composition of the Long-Distance Trade of England and the Dutch Republic Before 1750', in Tracy, ed., *Rise of Merchant Empires*, pp. 102–52. The citation is from p. 152.
47 Braudel, *Civilization and Capitalism*, II.140ff.
48 Ibid., II.142.
49 Ibid., II.406.
50 Hammond, *Food and Feast in Medieval England*, p. 88.
51 Centlivre, *Works*, III.252.
52 Hofstadter and Kuhns, *Philosophies of Art and Beauty*, p. 174.
53 Ibid., p. 178.
54 Ibid., p. 219.
55 Ricardo, *Political Economy*, p. 379.
56 Ibid., p. 389.
57 Ibid., pp. 380–1.
58 Camões, *The Lusiads*, pp. 219–20.
59 Bullein, *Bulwarke*, fo. 12.
60 Ibid., fo. 57.
61 Caxton, *The Mirrour of the World*, fos. E5–E6v.
62 Deleuze and Guattari, *Anti-Oedipus*, p. 153.
63 Maximilianus, *De Moluccis insulis*, fo. B7v.
64 Purchas, *Purchas his Pilgrimes*, Part I, book I, pp. 1–2; Eden, *History of Trauayle in the West and East Indies* fo. II.
65 Purchas, *Purchas his Pilgrimes*, Part I, book I, v.55.
66 Camões, *The Lusiads*, p. 214.
67 Polo, *Travels*, pp. 70–3.
68 Rawson, 'A Primitive Purity', pp. 3–4; the citation is from p. 3.
69 I am grateful to Robert Markley for a discussion of this.
70 Crosthwaite, 'An Accurate Map of the beautiful Lake of Ullswater, situate in Cumberland and Westmorland', reprinted as *A Series of Accurate Maps of the Principal Lakes of Cumberland, Westmorland & Lancashire*, ed. William Rollinson, epigraph, my emphasis. I am grateful to Michael Wiley for helping me with this citation.
71 Montanari, *Culture of Food*, tr. Carl Ipsen, p. 63.
72 Phillips and Phillips, *The Worlds of Christopher Columbus*, pp. 183–5.

73 Purchas, *Purchas his Pilgrimes*, III.iv.v.
74 Trevenen, *Little Derwent's Breakfast*, pp. 38, 39, 41.
75 Landon, *Complete Works*, I.467, 465.
76 See Fulford, 'Romanticism, Breadfruit and Slavery'.
77 Deleuze and Guattari, '1440: The Smooth and the Striated', *A Thousand Plateaus*, pp. 474–500.
78 Smith, *Wealth of Nations*, II.249–50.
79 For a discussion of the oneiric horizon of spicy lands, see Le Goff, 'L'Occident médiévale et l'océan Indien', in *Pour un autre Moyen Age*, pp. 230–98; the citation about the Brahmins in the Alexander cycle is from pp. 198–9. (Translated as *Time, Work and Culture in the Middle Ages*, tr. Goldhammer, pp. 189–200.)
80 See Evans, *Milton's Imperial Epic*.
81 In *John Milton: Complete Shorter Poems*, ed. Carey.
82 John Carey, private communication.
83 Evans, *Milton's Imperial Epic*, pp. 43–52.
84 Baudrillard, *Selected Writings*, pp. 6, 7 (Poster's introduction). See Deleuze, *Différence et Répétition*, p. 92.
85 For further discussion of the figure of the *hortus conclusus*, see Stewart, *Enclosed Garden*.
86 See Hammond, *Food and Feast in Medieval England*, p. 150; Montanari, *Culture of Food*, pp. 61, 120.
87 *OED*, *void*, A. adj. 4, 6.c, v.III.17.
88 Milton, *Paradise Lost*, p. 208.
89 Compare the non-alcoholic meal of Middle-Eastern fruit and grapes celebrated in canto V of Percy Shelley's *Laon and Cythna* (1817).
90 Le Guérer, *Scent*, p. 72.
91 Monardes, *Ioyfull Newes out of the New-found Worlde*, fo. 122 (Hh2).
92 Ibid., p. 120.
93 Siculus, *Diodori Siculi bibliothecæ historicæ libri* XV, p. 85. The typographical use of 'u' instead of 'v' has been retained. Some textual abbreviations have been expanded.
94 The subtitle of chapter 2 of *The Honourable Company*.
95 Braudel, *Civilization and Capitalism*, III.139.
96 Gilman, 'Madagascar on My Mind'.
97 For further discussion of Camões, see Helgerson, *Forms of Nationhood*, pp. 155–63. For a discussion both of *Paradise Lost* and *The Lusiads*, see Smith, *Literature and Revolution in England*, pp. 223–33.
98 Braudel, *Civilization and Capitalism*, III.215.
99 See Smith, *Literature and Revolution in England*, p. 227.
100 Markley, '"The Destin'd Walls /Of *Cambalu*"', in Rajan and Sauer, eds., *Milton and the Imperial Vision*, pp. 205–7.
101 Appleby, *Economic Thought*, p. 73. Also, see Dodge, *Islands and Empires*, pp. 238–40.
102 I am grateful to David Norbrook for pointing this out.

103 Shakespeare, *Othello* II.i.72–3, 83, Shell, *Money, Language and Thought*, p. 24.
104 Armitage, 'John Milton: Poet Against Empire', in Armitage, Himy and Skinner, eds., *Milton and Republicanism* pp. 206–25. The quotation is from p. 225.
105 Langland, *Piers Plowman: The Three Versions*, ed. Donaldson and Kane.
106 Vaughan, *Silex Scintillans*.
107 Milton, *Paradise Lost*, p. 274, note on V.292–4.
108 Rajan, 'The Imperial Temptation', p. 313 and Bhabha, 'Afterword', pp. 315–22, both in Rajan and Sauer, eds., *Milton and the Imperial Vision*.
109 Braudel, *Civilization and Capitalism*, I.220.
110 Ibid., I.222.
111 See Dodge, *Islands and Empires*, p. 243.
112 See McKeon, *Politics and Poetry in Restoration England*, chapter 5, for a discussion of *Annus Mirabilis*.
113 *Dryden: The Critical Heritage*, ed. Kinsley and Kinsley, pp. 295, 389–91.
114 Ibid., pp. 62–3.
115 Dryden, *Works*, ed. Hooker and Swedenberg, I.285, note.
116 Ibid.
117 See Martindale, 'John Dryden and the Mercantile Ideal', pp. 62–3. Martindale's chapter on *Annus Mirabilis* was useful to my work in this section. For further discussion of mercantilism, see Heckscher, *Mercantilism*.
118 Petty, *Economic Writings*, p. 256.
119 Appleby, *Economic Thought*, pp. 25, 175.
120 For further discussion, see Kuchta, 'Moral Economy of English Mercantilism', and Berry, *Idea of Luxury*, Part III.
121 Grotius, *The Freedom of the Seas*, pp. 7–8.
122 Martindale, *John Dryden and the Mercantile Ideal*, p. 86.
123 See stanzas 3, 5, 11, 304 and especially 293, 298, 302.
124 Blake, *Blake's Poetry and Designs*, p. 53. See Erdman, *Blake*, p. 81.
125 Grotius, *Freedom of the Seas*, pp. 5, 8, 63. Also, see Weinbrot, *Britannia's Issue*, pp. 237ff.
126 Thompson, *Customs in Common*, p. 273.
127 Trevenen, *Little Derwent's Breakfast*, p. 32.
128 Blackmore, *Creation*, I.3–4.
129 Ibid., I.293–94.
130 Žižek, *For They Know Not What They Do*, p. 64. The citation is from Hegel, *Phenomenology of Spirit*, pp. 331–2.
131 Blackmore, *Creation*, IV.207.
132 Ibid., I.32–4.
133 Ibid., IV.186.
134 Ibid., II.99.
135 It is uncertain whether the Peruvian drugs to which Blackmore refers include cocaine, but that is certainly a likely referent.

136 Blackmore, *Creation*, II.98.
137 Ibid., II.65–7. Cf. II.60, a description of the heat of the tropics of Borneo, Sumatra, the 'Indian Isles', Guinea, Libya and Morocco.
138 Ibid., I.41–2.
139 Ibid., I.42.
140 Ibid., xlix.
141 Ibid., VII.313.
142 Ibid., VII.131.
143 Ibid., VII.132.
144 Ibid., VII.358.
145 Thomson, *The Seasons*, ed. Sambrook.
146 Kowaleski-Wallace, 'Women, China, and Consumer Culture', pp. 155, 158.
147 Wordsworth, *Poems*, ed. Hutchinson, revised Selincourt.
148 I am indebted to a paper given by Timothy Fulford at the British Association of Romantic Studies, University of Wales, Bangor, 15–18 July, 1995, entitled 'A Late Poem of Wordsworth's'.
149 Hakluyt, *Voyages and Discoveries*, pp. 252–65.
150 Elliott, *Poetical Works of Ebenezer Elliott, the Corn-Law Rhymer.*
151 Shelley, *Prose*, pp. 82, 85, 94. All references to Shelley's poetry are from *Poetical Works*, ed. Hutchinson, and references to Shelley's prose are from *Prose*, ed. Clark. For further discussion of the poison tree image, see Morton, *Shelley and the Revolution in Taste*, pp. 178–9, 218–19.
152 *Prose*, p. 85.
153 Acton, *Poems*, p. 69.
154 Shelley, 'A Refutation of Deism', *Prose*, p. 128.
155 Shelley, 'A Defence of Poetry', *Prose*, p. 291.
156 In Cowper, *Poems*, ed. Baird and Ryskamp.
157 Bewell, *Romanticism and Colonial Disease*, pp. 227–40.
158 Plutarch, *Plutarch's Moralia*, XII.553–55; *Moralia*, 995C.
159 Shelley, *A Vindication*, *Shelley's Prose*, pp. 87–8.
160 Plutarch, *Plutarch's Moralia*, XII.573, 998B–C.
161 Mun, 'A Discourse of Trade from *England* unto the East *Indies*', in Purchas, *Purchas his Pilgrimes*, I.v.17, p. 732.
162 Ibid., I.v.17, p. 733.
163 Braudel, *Civilization and Capitalism*, II.418. It is strange that Braudel should puzzle over the oddity of this protest, since it underscores the efficacy of spice as capital and object of luxury consumption.
164 See Drummond and Wilbraham, *Englishman's Food*, pp. 214–15, 252–4.
165 Shelley, *A Vindication*, in *Prose*, p. 87.
166 Colwell, 'Shelley's *The Witch of Atlas*', p. 81.
167 In Smith, *Poems*, ed. Curran.
168 I am grateful to Bradley Johnson for a discussion of this.
169 Pratt, *Imperial Eyes*, p. 204. I have been influenced by Ang Jordan's paper, '"Imperial Mistress of the Obedient sea"'.

170 Shell, *Money, Language and Thought*, p. 24.
171 Shelley, *The Last Man*, ed. Paley, pp. 233–4.
172 Appadurai, *Social Life of Things*, p. 22.
173 Žižek, *Sublime Object of Ideology*, pp. 23–6.
174 Hakluyt, *Voyages and Discoveries*, pp. 34–5.
175 Purchas, *Purchas his Pilgrimes*, Part I, book III, 3.154.
176 Ibid., Part I, book I, p. 5.
177 Lillo, *The London Merchant*, ed. McBurney, p. 40.
178 Tavernier, *The Six Voyages*, II.106.
179 Pennant, *Outlines of the Globe*, IV.149.
180 Ibid., IV.170–1.
181 Ibid., II.5.
182 Wicke, *Advertising Fictions*, p. 16.
183 I am grateful to Jennifer Wicke for a discussion of these issues.
184 Wicke, *Advertising Fictions*, pp. 174–5.
185 See Rzepka, *Sacramental Commodities*, pp. 42, 67.
186 Derrida, *Given Time*, pp. 12–13, 24–5, 138–9, 142.
187 Pearson, 'The Economy has No Surplus', in Polanyi, Arensberg and Pearson, eds., *Trade and Market in the Early Empires*, pp. 320–41. The citation is from p. 338.
188 Deleuze and Guattari, *Anti-Oedipus*, pp. 235–7.

3 PLACE SETTINGS

1 Montanari, *Culture of Food*, p. 119.
2 Elias, *History of Manners*, p. 118.
3 See Montanari, *Culture of Food*, p. 62.
4 Lauriaux, 'Spices in the Medieval Diet', pp. 43–75.
5 Godwin, *Political Justice*, II.806.
6 See Murray, *An Elegant Madness*, pp. 176–200.
7 See Cocchi, *The Pythagorean Diet, of Vegetables Only, Conducive to the Preservation of Health, and the Cure of Diseases.*
8 Pocock, *Virtue, Commerce, and History*, p. 69.
9 Markley, '"So Inexhaustible a Treasure of Gold"', p. 164.
10 See Mackie, *Market à la Mode*, pp. 144–202.
11 See Simpson, *Academic Postmodern*, pp. 79–80.
12 Drummond and Wilbraham, *Englishman's Food*, pp. 214–15, 252–3.
13 Steele, *The Tatler*, ed. Bond, II. 335–9.
14 Anon., *Adam's Luxury, and Eve's Cookery*, title page.
15 Ibid., recipes for asparagus preserve, bean tart, pickled kidney beans, pear pudding, spinach tart (all containing nutmeg, cloves and mace).
16 Bullein, *Bulwarke*, fo. 83v.
17 Ibid., fos. 29, 14.
18 Montanari, *Culture of Food*, p. 59.
19 Hamond, *A Paradox*, fo. F.

20 Ibid., fo. F2.
21 Linschoten, *Discours of Voyages*, book I, p. 61.
22 Simpson, *Academic Postmodern*, pp. 100–2.
23 Mandeville, *The Fable of the Bees*, pp. 117, 123–4.
24 Leonardo y Argensola, *The Discovery and Conquest of the Molucco and Philippine Islands*, p. 14.
25 Ibid., pp. 28–9.
26 Landon, *Complete Works*, III.186.
27 For an extended discussion of this and related issues, see Leask, 'Murdering One's Double', in *British Romantic Writers and the East*, pp. 170–228.
28 Ogilby, *Asia*, p. 52.
29 Tavernier, *The Six Voyages*, I.241–3.
30 *Dictionary of National Biography*.
31 Simpson, *Academic Postmodern*, pp. 100–2.
32 Ibid., p. 101.
33 Sedgwick, *Between Men*, p. 14.
34 See Eagleton, *Ideology*, p. 37.
35 Guillory, *Cultural Capital*, chapter 2.
36 Mukařovský, *Aesthetic Function, Norm and Value as Social Facts*, pp. 21–3; the quotation is from p. 22. For further discussion of the notion of the antique, see Stewart, 'Notes on Distressed Genres', in *Crimes of Writing*, pp. 66–101.
37 Eagleton, *Ideology of the Aesthetic*, chapters 1 and 2.
38 McGann, *Beauty of Inflections*, pp. 135–72.
39 *Dictionary of National Biography*.
40 Warner, *Antiquitates Culinariæ*, p. i.
41 Bacon, *Sylva Sylvarum*, I.18.56.
42 Cheyne, *Philosophical Principles of Natural Religion*, p. 91.
43 Cheyne, *Essay on Regimen*, pp. xxvii, xlv.
44 Ibid., p. 75.
45 Ibid., p. 76.
46 Joris-Karl Huysmans, *Against Nature*, p. 199.
47 Ibid., p. 52, 120–1.
48 Quoted in Bate, *John Keats*, p. 463, from *The Autobiography and Memoirs of Benjamin Robert Haydon, 1786–1846*, compiled from his 'Autobiography and Journals' and 'Correspondence and Table-Talk', ed. Alexander Penrose (London; G. Bell and Sons, 1927), p. 259.
49 For example, by Charles Cowden Clarke when Haydon's autobiography was published in 1853. Clarke said that Keats did not drink as much as Haydon implied and probably did not take the cayenne. His statement is in the *Keats Circle*, II.319–21.
50 Haydon, *Autobiography*, ed. Taylor, I.253.
51 Peacock, *Works*, VIII.80.
52 Motion speculates that this is an allusion to *Hamlet* II.ii.428–43 (*Keats*,

p. 515; the citation has been corrected to accord with the Alexander text). See Levinson, *Keats's Life of Allegory*, pp. 52–3.
53 See Anon., *A Short Abstract*; Anon., *The Profit and Loss of the East-India-Trade*.
54 For details see Flower and Rosenbaum, *The Roman Cookery Book*.
55 King, *The Art of Cookery*, inscription, introductory letter.
56 Ibid., pp. 2–3, 3, 79, 97, 105.
57 Campbell, *Romantic Ethic*, p. 25; Campbell is citing Joan Thirsk, *Economic Policy and Projects*, p. 14.
58 King, *The Art of Cookery*, pp. 9, 10, 12.
59 Ibid., pp. 18, 29, 30–3.
60 Ibid., p. 55.
61 Ibid., pp. 75, 76, 79.
62 Ibid., p. 142.
63 Krieger, *Ekphrasis*, p. 68.
64 See Lacoue-Labarthe, 'Sublime Truth', in Librett, ed., *On the Sublime*, pp. 71–109, especially pp. 76, 105–8.
65 Carey in Milton, *Complete Shorter Poems*, p. 282.
66 Ibid., p. 277.
67 Butler, *Hudibras*, p. 120.
68 Ortelius, *Theatrum orbis terrarum*, fo. A3.
69 St Teresa, *Works*, II.243.
70 Ibid., I.100, 109.
71 Camporesi, *Incorruptible Flesh*, pp. 184–6.
72 *Ancrene Wisse*, pp. 41–2.
73 Ibid., p. 129.
74 Ibid., pp. 44, 170–1, 172.
75 Warner, *Alone of All Her Sex*, p. 99.
76 Warner, *From the Beast to the Blonde*, p. 106.
77 Levinson, *Keats's Life of Allegory*, p. 105.
78 See Camporesi, 'The Consecrated Host', p. 223.
79 Camporesi, *Incorruptible Flesh*, pp. 181–2.
80 'Coffined thoughts around me, in mummycases, embalmed in spice of words. Thoth, god of libraries, a birdgod, moonycrowned. And I heard the voice of that Egyptian highpriest.' Stephen Dedalus, in 'Scylla and Charybdis', Joyce, *Ulysses*, p. 159; Pope's *Dunciad* (1729, 1742) describes the texts of Caxton and Wynkyn de Worde as 'sauc'd by spice' or 'saved by spice, like mummies' (I.151); Pope, *Poems*, ed. Butt.
81 Printed in Hemans, *The Siege of Valencia*, pp. 288–93.
82 Brown, *Ada, and Other Poems*.
83 'Z' (John Gibson Lockhart and John Wilson), 'Cockney School of Poetry', pp. 519–24; the quotation is from p. 520.
84 Ibid., p. 524.
85 Bewell, 'Keats's "Realm of Flora"', p. 78.

86 Moore, *Poetical Works.*
87 De Quincey, *Confessions*, pp. 47–53.
88 Trevenen, *Little Derwent's Breakfast*, pp. 30ff.
89 Leask, *British Romantic Writers and the East*, pp. 211–15.
90 Trevenen, *Little Derwent's Breakfast*, p. 30.
91 Eliot, *Collected Poems 1909–1962.*
92 Coleridge, *Samuel Taylor Coleridge*, ed. Jackson.
93 Shuger, '"Gums of Glutinous Heat"', pp. 1–21.
94 Hunt, *Autobiography*, II.209.
95 Roe, *John Keats and the Culture of Dissent*, chapters 6 and 7; the citation is from p. 162.
96 Rajan, *Dark Interpreter*, pp. 106–15.
97 Trilling, *Opposing Self*, pp. 17–18. I am grateful to Denise Gigante for discussing this with me.
98 Montanari, *Culture of Food*, p. 65.
99 Warner, *Antiquitates Culinariæ*, pp. 10, 34.
100 Mintz, 'Color, Taste and Purity', pp. 103–8; the quotation is from p. 106.
101 Ibid., p. 104.
102 Levinson, *Keats's Life of Allegory*, p. 121.
103 Ibid., pp. 120–1, 264–70.
104 Ibid., pp. 264–70, 120–1.
105 Ibid., p. 121.
106 Ibid., pp. 121–2.
107 Ibid., pp. 122, 123.
108 I am grateful to Denise Gigante for bringing this to my attention.
109 Levinson, *Keats's Life of Allegory*, p. 124.
110 Leigh Hunt, review of Keats, *Lamia* (etc.), pp. 337–44; the quotation is from p. 343.
111 King, *The Art of Cookery*, p. 59.
112 Mintz, *Sweetness and Power*, p. 93.
113 Warner, *Antiquitates Culinariæ*, p. 136.
114 Quoted in Warton, *The History of English Poetry*, III.147.
115 Ibid., III.147; Warner, *Antiquitates Culinariæ*, p. 136.
116 Mintz, *Sweetness and Power*, p. 89.
117 Warner, *Antiquitates Culinariæ*, p. 136.
118 Rabisha, *The Whole Body of Cookery Dissected*, p. 35.
119 *OED*, *curious*, a.
120 Warner, *Antiquitates Culinariæ*, p. 1.
121 Ibid., p. xxxiii.
122 Ibid., pp. 136–7.
123 Radcliffe, *Posthumous Work.*
124 King, *The Art of Cookery*, pp. 88–9.
125 Kowaleski-Wallace, 'Women, China, and Consumer Culture in Eighteenth-Century England', pp. 153–67.

126 King, *The Art of Cookery*, p. 91.
127 In Ashfield, ed., *Romantic Women Poets 1770–1838*.
128 Winnicott, *Playing and Reality*, p. 12.
129 *OED*, *argosy*, n. 1.
130 Printed in Hemans, *The Siege of Valencia*, pp. 269–76.
131 More, *Works*, VI.162.
132 Martyr, *Decades of the Newe Worlde*, fo. 228v.
133 Keats, *Letters*, ed. Buxton Forman, p. 337.
134 Bennett, *Keats, Narrative and Audience*, p. 102.
135 Bewell, 'Keats's "Realm of Flora"', p. 93.
136 Lau, *Keats's* Paradise Lost, pp. 39–41.
137 Garnett, *The Wanderer's Legacy*.
138 See Keats, *Letters*, p. 71.
139 My thanks to Joel Simon for pointing this out.
140 Leigh Hunt, review of Keats, *Poems*, p. 345.
141 *Tait's Edinburgh Magazine*, 9 (1842), p. 239.
142 *OED*, 'Cockaigne, Cockayne', 2.
143 'Z' (John Gibson Lockhart and John Wilson), 'On the Cockney School of Poetry', pp. 70–6; the quotation is from p. 76; cf. George Croly, 'Remarks on Shelley's *Adonais*', p. 697.
144 See Jameson, *The Political Unconscious*, p. 86.
145 Franklin, 'Information to Those Who Would Remove to America', *Works*, p. 283.
146 Lyotard, *Postmodern Condition*, pp. 71–82.
147 Žižek, *Metastases of Enjoyment*, p. 72.
148 Žižek, *Tarrying with the Negative*, p. 239.
149 Bewell, 'Keats's "Realm of Flora"', pp. 79–83.
150 See Morton, '*Queen Mab* as Topological Repertoire', in Fraistat, ed., *Early Shelley*.
151 Krieger, *Ekphrasis*, p. 10.
152 Levinson, *Keats's Life of Allegory*, p. 105.
153 Ibid., p. 125.
154 Camporesi, *Incorruptible Flesh*, p. 25.
155 Obsession advertisement, Calvin Klein, 1992.

4 BLOOD SUGAR

1 Mintz, *Sweetness and Power*, p. 180.
2 Hammond, *Food and Feast in Medieval England*, p. 11.
3 Ibid., pp. 71, 130.
4 See Sussman, 'Women and the Politics of Sugar, 1792', pp. 1–22.
5 Franklin, 'Precautions to be Used by Those Who Are about to Undertake a Sea Voyage', *Works*, p. 229.
6 Sussman, 'Women and the Politics of Sugar, 1792', p. 7.
7 Rogin, 'Unmistakable', pp. 14–15.

8 Stedman, *Narrative of a Five Years' Expedition*, pp. 315–16.
9 Gilroy, 'Urban Social Movements, "Race" and Community', in Williams and Chrisman, eds., *Colonial Discourse*, p. 407.
10 See Kitson, 'Coleridge, Southey, and Richard Brothers', pp. 405–7.
11 For a discussion of the lecture, see Baum, *Mind-Forg'd Manacles*, chapter 1.
12 Coleridge, *Collected Works*, I.xxxix.
13 Ibid., I.xxxviii.
14 Ibid., I.235.
15 Ibid., I.236–7.
16 For further discussion, see Appleby, *Economic Thought and Ideology in Seventeenth-Century England.*
17 For a full discussion, see Mintz, *Sweetness and Power*, especially p. 214.
18 Mintz, 'Tropical Production and Mass Consumption', p. 8.
19 Coleridge, *Collected Works*, I.240.
20 I am grateful to Lauren Henry for discussing this with me.
21 Coleridge, *Collected Works*, I.246.
22 Sussman, 'Women and the Politics of Sugar, 1792', p. 8.
23 Coleridge, *Collected Works*, I.248.
24 The student-led 'Boycott Barclays' campaign in Britain in the mid 1980s (for complicity with the South African regime) worked in similar ways.
25 Coleridge, *Collected Works*, I.248.
26 See Shell, *Money, Language, and Thought*, pp. 41–3 for a discussion of the Holy Grail, another kind of blood container.
27 McKusick, *Coleridge's Philosophy of Language*, p. 26; pp. 18–26 discuss the lectures.
28 Kitson, 'Whore of Babylon and the Woman in White', p. 6.
29 Somerville, *A Discourse*, pp. 48–9, 17.
30 Coleridge, *Collected Works*, I.248.
31 Ibid., I.250–1.
32 Coleman, 'Conspicuous Consumption', p. 349; the discussion of the Eucharist is on pp. 348–9.
33 Braudel, *Civilization and Capitalism*, I.227.
34 Ibid., II.275, 279.
35 Castells, *Informational City*, pp. 169–71; this discussion of the consequences for spatial organisation of electronic information networks may be applied in a broader sense.
36 Sennett, *Flesh and Stone*, pp. 212–51; see Poster, 'Postmodern Virtualities' and Agnew, *Worlds Apart.*
37 For example, see Beckford, *Jamaica*, I.44.
38 A recent conference highlighted problems of unity and diversity in Caribbean literary culture: 'Sisyphus and Eldorado: Literary Culture in Two Caribbeans?', 31st Annual Eastern Comparative Literature Conference, 7 May 1994, New York University.

39 See Benghiat, *Traditional Jamaican Cookery*, pp. 17–20.
40 Mintz, 'Tasting Food, Tasting Freedom', p. 269.
41 *Columbian Magazine* (May 1797), II.766; see Brathwaite, *Folk Culture*, p. 18.
42 Quoted in Brathwaite, *Folk Culture*, p. 19.
43 Beckford, *Jamaica*, I.330.
44 See Richardson, 'Romantic Voodoo', p. 9.
45 Moseley, *A Treatise on Sugar*, pp. 5–74.
46 Ibid., pp. 53, 75.
47 Bullein, *Bulwarke*, fos. 62, 72.
48 Moseley, *A Treatise on Sugar*, pp. 139, 144, 157. Moseley also discusses the importance of spices in the Old Testament (pp. 128–33).
49 Ibid., pp. 168–9.
50 Ibid., pp. 159–60; see Morton, *Shelley and the Revolution in Taste*, chapter 1.
51 Moseley, *A Treatise on Sugar*, p. 160; the vegetarian passage extends to p. 161. Beckford also makes a vegetarian reference about killing turtles: 'What would the simple and unlettered Bramin [*sic*] or what would the Pythagorean philosophy say to this cruel instance of refinement and gluttony?' (*Jamaica*, I.374–5).
52 Moseley, *A Treatise on Sugar*, p. 164.
53 Beckford, *Jamaica*, I.84, 233–48.
54 Ibid., II.48.
55 Ibid., I.141, II.11, II.132, II.382, II.399.
56 Boswell, *No Abolition of Slavery*, p. 23.
57 Mintz, 'Sweet, Salt, and the Language of Love', p. 858.
58 Young, *Colonial Desire*, pp. 152–8.
59 Ibid., p. 154.
60 Hughes, *Collected Poems*, ed. Rampersad and Roessel.
61 See Mintz, 'Sweet, Salt, and the Language of Love', p. 858.
62 Barbauld, *Epistle to William Wilberforce*, p. 7.
63 Ibid., pp. 10–11.
64 See Benjamin, *One-Way Street*, p. 359.
65 Grainger, *The Sugar-Cane*, pp. 9–10.
66 Ibid., p. 56.
67 Edgeworth, *Belinda*, II.138–47. See Richardson, 'Romantic Voodoo', pp. 19–20. A more accurate picture of Jamaican religion can be found in Brathwaite, *Folk Culture*, pp. 12–16.
68 Trevenen, *Little Derwent's Breakfast*, p. 35.
69 Ibid., p. 37.
70 Ibid., p. 36.
71 Raimond, 'Southey's Early Writings and the Revolution', pp. 181–96.
72 Southey, *Poems*, p. 31.
73 Ibid.
74 Ibid., p. 32.
75 Shelley's debts in *Queen Mab* to Southey's *Joan of Arc* have already been noted: see Raimond, 'Southey's Early Writings', p. 194.

76 Aristotle, *Politics*, pp. 16–17 (I.ii.4, 1253b).
77 Pratt, *Humanity*, p. 39.
78 Ibid., p. 40.
79 Ibid., p. 41.
80 Ibid., pp. 85–6, 103.
81 See Magnuson, 'Wild Justice', pp. 88–91.
82 Kutzinski, *Sugar's Secrets*, p. 108.
83 See Butler, 'Plotting the Revolution', pp. 144–9.
84 For further exploration of some of these points, see Žižek, *Tarrying with the Negative*, pp. 116–17.
85 I am here following the arguments of Žižek in *Tarrying with the Negative*, p. 27.
86 Erdman, *Blake*, p. 237.
87 See Torres-Saillant, 'Problem of Unity'.
88 See Williams and Chrisman, eds., *Colonial Discourse*, pp. 16–17.
89 Hazlitt, 'Wat Tyler and the Quarterly Review', in *Works*, VII.169.
90 Liu, 'Local Transcendence', p. 86.
91 Eagleton, *Ideology*, p. 40; Žižek, *Sublime Object of Ideology*, p. 33.

5 SOUND AND SCENTS: FURTHER INVESTIGATIONS OF SPACE

1 Žižek, *Indivisible Remainder*, pp. 101–2.
2 Žižek, *Plague of Fantasies*, pp. 175–6.
3 Ibid., p. 74.
4 Ibid., pp. 74, 75.
5 Hunt, *Poetical Works of*, ed. Milford.
6 Žižek, *Indivisible Remainder*, p. 32.
7 Žižek, *Plague of Fantasies*, p. 7.
8 Ibid., p. 76.
9 Shelley, 'A Defence of Poetry', in *Shelley's Prose*, p. 277.
10 Barbauld, *Epistle to William Wilberforce*, pp. 10–11.
11 From Jussawalla, 'Indian Theory and Criticism', in Groden and Kreiswirth, eds., *The Johns Hopkins Guide to Literary Theory and Criticism*, p. 401.
12 Barclay, *Egloges*, I3r.
13 Ibid., (1515), IV.Ciii.
14 Shelley, 'A Defence of Poetry', in *Shelley's Prose*, p. 286.
15 Holmes, *Coleridge*, p. 10.
16 Braddock, '*Maud* as Symptom of the Crimean War'.
17 See Page, 'Reading and Reminiscence', pp. 1–31.
18 See Toop, *Ocean of Sound*, pp. 8–11.
19 Jones, 'On the Arts, Commonly Called Imitative', in *Poems*, p. 207.
20 Ibid., p. 175.
21 Ibid., p. 176.
22 Ibid., p. 179.

23 Rindisbacher, *Smell of Books*, pp. 13, 103.
24 Shell, *Money, Language and Thought*, p. 151.
25 Shelley, 'A Defence of Poetry', in *Shelley's Prose*, p. 293.
26 Toop, *Ocean of Sound*, p. 7.
27 Huysmans, *Against Nature*, pp. 124–5.
28 Crashaw, *Poems English, Latin and Greek*, ed. Martin.
29 Traherne, *Poems, Centuries and Three Thanksgivings.* For a criticism of readings of Traherne as narcissistic, see Clements, *Mystical Poetry*, pp. 8–9.
30 Hemans, *Works*, v.
31 Jones, *Poems*, p. 2.
32 Ibid., p. 32.
33 Ibid., pp. 50–1.
34 Ibid., p. 54.
35 I have been inspired in this reading of the poem's collapse of gender boundaries by James Holt McGavran, 'DisLocations of Culture and Gender in "Kubla Khan"', paper presented at the NASSR conference, Boston, 14–16 November, 1996.
36 Halpern, 'A Mint of Phrases', in *Poetics of Primitive Accumulation*, pp. 19–60.
37 Jones, *Poems*, p. 182. See Parker, 'On the Tongue', pp. 445–50.
38 See Ferguson, 'Redefining Femininity'.
39 Thanks to Joel Simon for discussing this with me.
40 Addison, *Spectator* 69:1 (19 May 1711), p. 395.
41 Bohls, 'Aesthetics of Colonialism', pp. 363–90.
42 See ibid., p. 370.
43 Brown, *Ends of Empire*, chapter 2, 'The Romance of Empire'.
44 King, *The Art of Cookery*, p. 107.
45 Ibid., pp. 107, 109.
46 Ibid., p. 113.
47 Ibid., p. 119.
48 Ibid., p. 123.
49 See Morton, *Shelley and the Revolution in Taste*, pp. 102–5.
50 See Voller, *Supernatural Sublime*, pp. 130, 132–3, and Bruhm, *Gothic Bodies*, pp. 64–9.
51 Peacock, *Nightmare Abbey*, p. 68.
52 Burke, *Reflections*, pp. 159, 249.
53 Hoerner, 'Paring Away Excrescences'.
54 Ibid.
55 Žižek, 'Re-Visioning "Lacanian" Social Criticism', p. 21.
56 Hunt, 'A Now, Descriptive of a Hot Day', *Indicator* 1 (1820), pp. 300–2; the quotation is from p. 300.
57 Wicke, 'Postmodernism', pp. 145–60.
58 Baudelaire, 'Correspondences', *Les Fleurs du Mal*, tr. Howard.

Bibliography

Accum, Friedrich, *A Treatise on Adulterations of Food, and Culinary Poisons, Exhibiting the Fraudulent Sophistications of Bread, Beer, Wine, Spiritous Liquors, Tea, Coffee, Cream, Confectionery, Vinegar, Mustard, Pepper, Cheese, Olive Oil, Pickles, and Other Articles Employed in Domestic Economy. And Methods of Detecting Them* (London: Longman, Hurst, Rees, Orme and Brown, 1820).

Acton, Eliza, *Poems* (Ipswich: R. Deck, 1826).

Adorno, Theodor W., *Negative Dialectics*, tr. E. B. Ashton (New York: Seabury Press, 1973).

Agnew, Jean-Christophe, *Worlds Apart: The Market and the Theatre in Anglo-American Thought, 1550–1750* (Cambridge and New York: Cambridge University Press, 1986).

Ancrene Wisse: Guide for Anchoresses, tr. Hugh White (Harmondsworth: Penguin, 1993).

Anon., *Adam's Luxury, and Eve's Cookery; Or, the Kitchen-Garden Display'd. In Two Parts* (London: printed for R. Dodsley, 1744).

Anon., *A Letter to a Friend, Concerning a Late Pamphlet, Entituled, Angliae Tutamen, or The Safety of England; Being an Account of the Banks, Lotteries, Mines, Divings, Drawings, Liftings, and other Engines; and many Pernicious Projects now on Foot, Tending to the Destruction of Trade and Commerce, and the Impoverishing of this Realm. With Reflections thereupon, of Great Import to all Sorts of People* (London: n.p., 1696).

Anon., *A Short Abstract of a Case which was Last Session Presented to the Parliament: Being a True Relation of the Rise and Progress of the East-India Company, Shewing how their Manufactures have been, are, and will be Prejudicial to the Manufactures of England, and what Endeavours have been Used for and against any Restrictions. Together with some Remarks and Query's thereon* (London: *c.* 1700).

Anon., *The Profit and Loss of the East-India-Trade, Stated, and Humbly Offer'd to the Consideration of the Present Parliament* (London: n.p., 1700).

Appadurai, Arjun, ed., *The Social Life of Things: Commodities in Cultural Perspective* (Cambridge: Cambridge University Press, 1986).

'Disjuncture and Difference in the Global Cultural Economy', *Public Culture* 2:2 (spring 1990), pp. 1–24.

Appleby, Joyce Oldham, *Economic Thought and Ideology in Seventeenth-Century England* (Princeton: Princeton University Press, 1976).

Apter, Emily and Pietz, William, *Fetishism as Cultural Discourse* (Ithaca and London: Cornell University Press, 1993).

Aristotle, *The Politics*, tr. H. Rackham (Cambridge, Mass.: Harvard University Press, 1944).

Armitage, David, Himy, Armand and Skinner, Quentin, eds., *Milton and Republicanism* (Cambridge and New York: Cambridge University Press, 1995).

Ashfield, Andrew, ed., *Romantic Women Poets 1770–1838: An Anthology* (Manchester: Manchester University Press, 1995).

Aston, T. H., Coss, P. R., Dyer, C. and Thirsk, J., eds., *Social Relations and Ideas: Essays in Honour of R. H. Hilton* (Cambridge and New York: Cambridge University Press, 1983).

Austen, Jane, *Mansfield Park*, ed. Tony Tanner (Harmondsworth: Penguin, 1966; 1983).

Bachelard, Gaston, *The Poetics of Space*, tr. Maria Jolas (Boston: Beacon Press, 1969, 1994).

Bacon, Francis, *Sylva Sylvarum: Or a Naturall Historie. In Ten Centuries* (London: printed for William Lee, 1626).

Barbauld, Anna Letitia, *Epistle to William Wilberforce, Esq. on the Rejection of the Bill for Abolishing the Slave Trade* (London: printed for J. Johnson, 1791).

Barbon, Nicholas, *A Discourse of Trade* (London: Thomas Milboun, 1690).

Barclay, Alexander, *Egloges* (London: Wynkyn de Worde, 1515).

Egloges (London: Humfrey Powell, 1548?).

Bate, Walter Jackson, *John Keats* (Cambridge, Mass.: Harvard University Press, 1963).

Baudelaire, Charles, *Les Fleurs du Mal*, tr. Richard Howard (Brighton: Harvester, 1982).

Baudrillard, Jean, *Selected Writings*, ed. Mark Poster (Stanford: Stanford University Press, 1988).

Baum, Joan, *Mind-Forg'd Manacles: Slavery and the English Romantic Poets* (North Haven, Conn.: Archon, 1994).

Beckford, William, *A Descriptive Account of the Island of Jamaica: With Remarks upon the Cultivation of the Sugar-Cane, throughout the Different Seasons of the Year, and Chiefly Considered in a Picturesque Point of View; also Observations and Reflections upon what would probably be the Consequences of an Abolition of the Slave-Trade, and of the Emancipation of the Slaves*, 2 vols. (London: printed for T. and J. Edgerton, 1790).

Belleforest, François, *L'Histoire universelle du monde, contenant l'entiere description & situation des quatre parties de la terre, la diuision & estendue d'une chacune Region & Prouince d'icelles* (Paris: Gervais Mallot, 1577).

Benghiat, Norma, *Traditional Jamaican Cookery* (Harmondsworth: Penguin, 1985).

Benjamin, Walter, *One-Way Street and Other Writings*, tr. E. Jephcott and K. Shorter (London: Verso, 1979, paperback 1985).

Bennett, Andrew, *Keats, Narrative and Audience* (Cambridge and New York: Cambridge University Press, 1994).

Bennett, J. A. W. and Smithers, G. V., eds., *Early Middle English Verse and Prose*, glossary by Norman Davis, 2nd edn (Oxford: Clarendon Press, 1968, 1987).

Berry, Christopher, *The Idea of Luxury: A Conceptual and Historical Investigation* (Cambridge and New York: Cambridge University Press, 1994).

Bewell, Alan, *Romanticism and Colonial Disease* (Baltimore: Johns Hopkins University Press, 1999).

'Keats's "Realm of Flora" ', *Studies in Romanticism* 31:1 (1992), pp. 71–98.

Bhabha, Homi K., 'Afterword: An Ironic Act of Courage', in Rajan and Sauer, eds., *Milton and the Imperial Vision*, pp. 315–22.

Binder, Wolfgang, ed., *Slavery in the Americas*, (Würzburg: Königshausen and Neumann, 1993).

Blackmore, Richard, *Creation. A Philosophical Poem. Demonstrating the Existence and Providence of a God. In Seven Books*, 2nd edn (London: printed for S. Buckley and J. Tonson, 1712).

Blake, William, *Blake's Poetry and Designs*, ed. Mary Lynn Johnson and John E. Grant (London and New York: Norton, 1979).

Blanchard, Laman, *Life and Literary Remains of L.E.L* (London: Henry Colburn, 1841).

Bloom, Harold, *A Map of Misreading* (Oxford and New York: Oxford University Press, 1975).

Blundeville, Thomas, *The Fower Chiefyst Offices Belongyng to Horsemanshippe. The Order of Breding. The Arte of Ridynge Newly Corrected. Howe to Dyet Them. To What Diseases They be Subiecte, and Howe to Cure the Same*, 4 vols. (London: W. Seres, 1565, 1566).

Bohls, Elizabeth, 'The Aesthetics of Colonialism: Janet Schaw in the West Indies, 1774–75', *Eighteenth-Century Studies* 27 (1994), pp. 363–90.

Bondanella, Peter and Bondanella, Julia Conway, eds., *Dictionary of Italian Literature* (Westport, Conn.: Greenwood Press, 1979).

Boswell, James, *No Abolition of Slavery; Or the Universal Empire of Love: A Poem* (London: printed for R. Faulder, 1791).

Braddock, Jeremy, 'Maud as Symptom of the Crimean War', unpublished article, 1996.

Brathwaite, Edward Kamau, *Folk Culture of the Slaves in Jamaica* (London and Port of Spain: New Beacon Books, 1970, revised 1981).

Braudel, Fernand, *Civilization and Capitalism, 15th–18th Century*, tr. S. Reynolds, 3 vols. (Berkeley and Los Angeles: University of California Press, 1982–4).

Brewer, John, and Porter, Roy, eds., *Consumption and the World of Goods* (London and New York: Routledge, 1993).

British Museum, MS. Harl. 913 (*The Land of Cockaygne*).

Brown, Laura, *Ends of Empire: Women and Ideology in Early Eighteenth-Century English Literature* (Ithaca, N.Y.: Cornell University Press, 1993).

Brown, Mary Ann, *Ada, and Other Poems* (London: Longman, Hatchard, and W. Benning, 1828).

Bruhm, Steven, *Gothic Bodies: The Politics of Pain in Romantic Fiction* (Philadelphia: University of Pennsylvania Press, 1994).

Bullein, William, *A Dialogue both Pleasaunte and Pietiefull, wherein there is a Goodly Regiment Against the Fever Pestilence with a Consolation and Comfort against Death* (London: printed by I. Kingston, 1564).

A Newe Booke Entituled the Gouernement of Healthe (London: printed by John Day, 1558).

Bulleins Bulwarke of Defence Against all Sicknes, Sornes, and Woundes, that doo Daily Assaulte Mankinde, which Balwarke is Kepte with Hillarius the Gardiner, Health and Phisician, with their Chyrurgian, to Helpe the Wounded Soldiors. Gathered and Practised from the Most Worthie Learned, bothe Old and Newe; to the Great Comforte of Mankinde (London: printed by I. Kingston, 1562).

Burke, Edmund, *Reflections on the Revolution in France*, ed. Conor Cruise O'Brien (Harmondsworth: Penguin, 1986).

Butler, Marilyn, ed., *Burke, Paine, Godwin, and the Revolution Controversy* (Cambridge and New York: Cambridge University Press, 1984).

'Plotting the Revolution: The Political Narratives of Romantic Poetry and Criticism', in K. R. Johnston, K. H. Chaitin and H. Marks, eds., *Romantic Revolutions: Criticism and Theory* (Bloomington and Indianapolis: Indiana University Press, 1990), pp. 133–57.

Butler, Samuel, *Hudibras: Written in the Time of the Late Wars*, ed. A. R. Waller (Cambridge: Cambridge University Press, 1905).

Satires and Miscellaneous Poetry and Prose, ed. René Lamar (Cambridge: Cambridge University Press, 1928).

Byron, Lord George Gordon, *Byron*, ed. Jerome McGann (Oxford and New York: Oxford University Press, 1986).

Camões, Luis de, *The Lusiad, or, Portugals Historicall Poem Written in the Portingall Language by Luis de Camoens, and Now Newly Put into English by Richard Fanshaw Esq.* (London: printed for Humphrey Moseley, 1655).

Campbell, Colin, *The Romantic Ethic and the Spirit of Modern Consumerism* (Oxford and New York: Basil Blackwell, 1987).

Camporesi, Piero, *Exotic Brew: The Art of Living in the Age of Enlightenment*, tr. Christopher Woodall (Oxford, Cambridge and Cambridge, Mass.: Polity Press, 1994).

The Incorruptible Flesh: Bodily Mutilation and Mortification in Religion and Folklore, tr. Tania Croft-Murray, Latin tr. Helen Elsom (Cambridge: Cambridge University Press, 1988).

'The Consecrated Host', *Zone*, vol. 1 of M. Feher, R. Nadaff and N. Tazi, eds., *Fragments for a History of the Human Body*, 3 vols. (New York: Urzone, 1989), pp. 220–37.

Castells, Manuel, *The Informational City: Information Technology, Economic*

Restructuring, and the Urban-Regional Process (Oxford: Basil Blackwell, 1989).

Caxton, William, *The Mirrour of the World* (Westminster: William Caxton, 1481).

Centlivre, Susanna, *The Busie Body: A Comedy* (London: printed for Bernard Lintott, [709].

The Works of the Celebrated Mrs Centlivre, 3 vols. (London: printed for J. Knapton, C. Hitch, L. Hawes, J. and R. Tonson, S. Crowder, W. Bathoe, T. Lownds, T. Caston, H. Woodgate, S. Brooks, G. Kearly, 1760).

Chaucer, Geoffrey, *The Works of Geoffrey Chaucer,* ed. F. N. Robinson, 2nd edn (Oxford and London: Oxford University Press, 1957).

Cheyne, George, *An Essay on Regimen. Together with Five Discourses, Medical, Moral, and Philosophical: Serving to Illustrate the Principles and Theory of Philosophical Medicin* [sic] *, and Point out Some of its Moral Consequences* (London: C. Rivington, and Bath: J. Leake, 1740).

Philosophical Principles of Natural Religion, 2 parts, 2nd edn (London: printed for G. Strahan, 1716).

Classen, Constance, Howes, David and Synnott, Anthony, *Aroma: The Cultural History of Smell* (London and New York: Routledge, 1994).

Clements, A. L., *The Mystical Poetry of Thomas Traherne* (Cambridge, Mass.: Harvard University Press, 1969).

Clough, Arthur Hugh, *The Poems of Arthur Hugh Clough,* ed. A. L. P. Norrington (London and New York: Oxford University Press, 1968).

Cocchi, Antonio, *The Pythagorean Diet, of Vegetables Only, Conducive to the Preservation of Health, and the Cure of Diseases. A Discourse Delivered at Florence, in the Month of August, 1743,* tr. anon. (London: printed for R. Dodsley, 1745).

Coleman, Deirdre, 'Conspicuous Consumption: White Abolitionism and English Women's Protest Writing in the 1790s', *English Literary History* 61:2 (summer 1994), pp. 341–62.

Coleridge, Samuel Taylor, *The Collected Works of Samuel Taylor Coleridge,* vol. 1, *Lectures 1795, on Politics and Religion,* ed. L. Patton and P. Mann (London: Routledge and Kegan Paul, and Princeton: Princeton University Press, 1971).

Samuel Taylor Coleridge, ed. H. J. Jackson, Oxford Authors series (Oxford and New York: Oxford University Press, 1985).

Colwell, Frederic, 'Shelley's *The Witch of Atlas* and the Mythic Geography of the Nile', *English Literary History* 45 (1978), pp. 69–92.

Cooper, Robert M., *A Concordance to the English Poetry of Richard Crashaw* (Troy, N.Y.: Whitson, 1981).

Cornwall, Barry (Bryan Waller Procter), *The Poetical Works of Barry Cornwall* (London: H. Colburn, 1822).

Cowper, William, *The Poems of William Cowper,* ed. John D. Baird and Charles Ryskamp, 3 vols. (Oxford: Clarendon Press, 1995).

Cox, Jeffrey, *Poetry and Politics in the Cockney School: Keats, Shelley, Hunt and their Circle* (Cambridge and New York: Cambridge University Press, 1998).

Crashaw, Richard, *The Poems English, Latin and Greek of Richard Crashaw*, ed. L. C. Martin (Oxford: Clarendon Press, 1927).

Croly, George, 'Remarks on Shelley's *Adonais*', *Blackwood's Edinburgh Magazine* 10 (December 1821), pp. 696–700.

Crosthwaite, Peter, *A Series of Accurate Maps of the Principal Lakes of Cumberland, Westmorland & Lancashire . . . First Surveyed and Planned Between 1783 and 1794 by Peter Crosthwaite*, ed. William Rollinson (Newcastle-on-Tyne: Frank Graham, 1968).

Curtin, D. W. and Heldke, L. M., eds., *Cooking, Eating, Thinking: Transformative Philosophies of Food* (Bloomington: Indiana University Press, 1992).

Darwin, Erasmus, *The Botanic Garden; A Poem, in Two Parts* (London: printed for J. Johnson, 1790–1).

The Loves of the Plants, vol. II, *The Botanic Garden*, (London: printed for J. Johnson, 1789).

Defoe, Daniel, *A New Voyage Round the World, by a Course Never Sailed Before*, in George A. Aitken, ed., *Romances and Narratives by Daniel Defoe*, 16 vols. (New York: AMS Press, 1974), vol. XIV.

Deleuze, Gilles, *Différence et Répétition* (Paris: PUF, 1968).

Deleuze, Gilles and Guattari, Félix, *Anti-Oedipus: Capitalism and Schizophrenia*, tr. Robert Hurley, Mark Seem and Helen R. Lane (Minneapolis: University of Minnesota Press, 1983).

A Thousand Plateaus: Capitalism and Schizophrenia, tr. Brian Massumi (Minneapolis: University of Minnesota Press, 1987).

De Quincey, Thomas, *Confessions of an English Opium-Eater*, ed. Grevel Lindop (Oxford and New York: Oxford University Press, 1985).

Derrida, Jacques, *Dissemination*, tr. Barbara Johnson (Chicago: University of Chicago Press, 1981).

Given Time: 1. Counterfeit Money, tr. Peggy Kamuf (Chicago and London: University of Chicago Press, 1992).

Specters of Marx: The State of the Debt, the Work of Mourning, and the New International, tr. Peggy Kamuf (London and New York: Routledge, 1994).

The Truth in Painting, tr. Geoff Bennington and Ian McLeod (Chicago and London: University of Chicago Press, 1987).

Diodorus Siculus, *Diodori Siculi bibliothecæ historicæ libri* XV. *hoc est, quotquot Græce extant, de quadraginta. quorum quinque nunc primum Latine eduntur, de quibus in præstione edoceberis. Adiecta his sunt ex iis libris qui non extant, fragmenta quaedam. Sebastiano Castalione totius operis correctore, partim interprete. Præterea interiecta est Dictys Cretensis & Daretis Phrygii de bello Troiano historia, ad supplendam lacunam quinque librorum, qui inter quintum & undecimum desiderantur* (Basileæ: per H. Petri, 1559).

Dizionario enciclopedico della letteratura Italiana, 6 vols. (Rome: Unione Editoriale, 1967).

Dodge, Ernest S., *Islands and Empires: Western Impact on the Pacific and East Asia* (Minneapolis: University of Minnesota Press, 1976).

Drummond, J. C. and Wilbraham, Anne, *The Englishman's Food: A History of Five Centuries of English Diet* (London: Jonathan Cape, 1939, reprinted London: Pimlico, 1991).

Dryden, John, *Dryden: The Critical Heritage*, ed. James Kinsley and Helen Kinsley (New York: Barnes and Noble, 1971).

The Poems of John Dryden, ed. James Kinsley, 4 vols. (Oxford: Clarendon Press, 1958).

The Works of John Dryden, ed. Edward Niles Hooker and H. T. Swedenberg, 20 vols. (Berkeley and Los Angeles: University of California Press, 1956–).

Dyer, John, *The Fleece: A Poem. In Four Books* (London: printed for R. and J. Dodsley, 1757).

Eagleton, Terry, *Ideology: An Introduction* (London and New York: Verso, 1991).

Literary Theory: An Introduction (Oxford: Basil Blackwell, 1983; 1993).

The Ideology of the Aesthetic (Oxford and Cambridge, Mass.: Basil Blackwell, 1990).

Eden, Richard, *The History of Trauayle in the West and East Indies, and Other Countreys Lying eyther Way, towardes the Fruitfull and Ryche Moluccaes. As Moscouia, Persia, Arabia, Syria, Ægypte, Ethiopia, Guinea, China in Cathayo, and Giapan: With a Discourse of the Northwest Passage* (London: printed by Richard Jugge, 1577).

Edgeworth, Maria, *Belinda*, 3 vols. (London: printed for J. Johnson, 1801).

Elias, Norbert, *The History of Manners*, vol. 1, *The Civilizing Process*, tr. Edmund Jephcott (New York: Pantheon, 1978).

Eliot, T. S., *Collected Poems 1909–1962* (London: Faber and Faber, 1963, 1983).

Elliott, Ebenezer, *The Poetical Works of Ebenezer Elliott, the Corn-Law Rhymer*, 2nd edn (Edinburgh: W. Tait, and London: Simpkin, Marshall and Co., 1840).

Entry into the Realm of Reality (the *Gandayyuha*), tr. Thomas Cleary (Boston and Shaftesbury: Shambhala, 1989).

Erdman, David V., *A Concordance to the Writings of William Blake* (Ithaca, N.Y.: Cornell University Press, 1967).

Blake: Prophet Against Empire, 3rd edn (New York: Dover, 1991).

Evans, J. Martin, *Milton's Imperial Epic:* Paradise Lost *and the Discourse of Colonialism* (Ithaca, N.Y. and London: Cornell University Press, 1996).

Ferguson, Margaret, 'Redefining Femininity: Female Literacies in Early Modern England', paper presented at the Program for the Western Humanities Conference Meeting, the University of Colorado at Boulder, 3–5 October 1996.

Flower, B. and Rosenbaum, E., *The Roman Cookery Book: A Critical Translation of The Art of Cooking by Apicius for Use in the Study and the Kitchen* (London: Harrap, 1958).

Foucault, Michel, *Discipline and Punish: The Birth of the Prison* (New York: Pantheon, 1977).

Franklin, Benjamin, *Works of the Late Doctor Benjamin Franklin: Consisting of His Life, Written by Himself, together with Essays, Humorous, Moral & Literary, Chiefly in the Manner of The Spectator* (Dublin: printed for P. Wogan, P. Byrne, J. Moore and W. Jones, 1793).

Fulford, Timothy, 'A Late Poem of Wordsworth's: The Iconography of Place and the Sexual Politics of the Regency', paper presented at the British Association of Romantic Studies, the University of Wales, Bangor, 15–18 July 1995.

'Romanticism, Breadfruit and Slavery', paper presented at the NASSR conference, Halifax, Nova Scotia, 12–15 August 1999.

Garnett, Catherine Grace, *The Wanderer's Legacy* (London: Samuel Maunder, 1829).

Garrod, Alfred Baring, *The Essentials of Materia Medica and Therapeutics* (London: Walton and Maberly, 1855).

Gilman, Ernest B., 'Madagascar on My Mind: Van Dyck, Arundel, Junius and the Arts of Colonization', paper given at the New York University Seminar on the Renaissance, 28 March 1995.

Godwin, William, *An Enquiry Concerning Political Justice, and its Influence on General Virtue and Happiness* (London: printed for G. G. and J. Robinson, 1793).

Gowers, Emily, *The Loaded Table: Representations of Food in Roman Literature* (Oxford and New York: Oxford University Press, 1993).

Grainger, James, *The Sugar-Cane: A Poem. In Four Books. With Notes* (London: printed for R. and J. Dodsley, 1764).

Groden, Michael, and Kreiswirth, Martin, eds., *The Johns Hopkins Guide to Literary Theory and Criticism* (Baltimore: Johns Hopkins University Press, 1994).

Grotius, Hugo, *The Freedom of the Seas; Or, the Right Which Belongs to Dutch to Take Part in the East Indian Trade; A Dissertation by Hugo Grotius*, tr. with a revision of the Latin text of 1633 by Ralph Van Deman Magoffin, ed. James Brown Scott (New York: Oxford University Press, 1916).

Guillory, John, *Cultural Capital: The Problem of Literary Canon Formation* (Chicago and London: University of Chicago Press, 1993).

Hakluyt, Richard, *Voyages and Discoveries: The Principal Navigations, Voyages, Traffiques and Discoveries of the English Nation*, ed. Jack Beeching (Harmondsworth: Penguin, 1972, 1985).

Halpern, Richard, *The Poetics of Primitive Accumulation: English Renaissance Culture and the Genealogy of Capital* (Ithaca, N.Y. and London: Cornell University Press, 1991).

Hammond, P. W., *Food and Feast in Medieval England* (Stroud and Dover, N.H.: Alan Sutton, 1993).

Hamond, Walter, *A Paradox, Prooving, that the Inhabitants of the Isle Called Madagascar or St Laurence, (in Temporall Things) are the Happiest People in the World. Whereunto is Prefixed, a Briefe and True Description of that Island: The Nataure of the Climate, and Condition of the Inhabitants, and their Speciall Affection to the English Above Other Nations. With Most Probable Arguments of a Hopefull and Fit Plantation of a Colony There, in Respect of the Fruitfulnesse of the Soyle, the Benignity of the Ayre, and the Relieving of our English Ships, both to and from the East Indies* (London: printed for Nathaniel Butter, 1640).

Harvey, David, discussion with Richard Sennett in the Committee on Theory and Culture, New York University, spring 1995.

Haydon, Benjamin Robert, *The Autobiography and Memoirs of Benjamin Robert Haydon, 1786–1846*, ed. T. Taylor, 2 vols. (London: Peter Davies, 1926).

Hazlitt, William, *The Complete Works of William Hazlitt*, ed. P. P. Howe, 21 vols. (London and Toronto: J. M. Dent and Sons, 1930–4).

Heckscher, Eli Filip, *Mercantilism*, tr. Mendel Shapiro, ed. E. F. Soderlund, 2 vols. (London: George Allen and Unwin, 1935; revised 1955).

Hegel, Georg Wilhelm Friedrich, *Hegel's Phenomenology of Spirit*, tr. A. V. Miller, analysis and foreword by J. N. Findlay, (Oxford: Oxford University Press, 1977).

Helgerson, Richard, *Forms of Nationhood: The Elizabethan Writing of England* (Chicago and London: University of Chicago Press, 1992; paperback 1994).

Hemans, Felicia, *The Siege of Valencia; A Dramatic Poem. The Last Constantine: with Other Poems* (London: John Murray, 1823).

The Works of Mrs Hemans, 7 vols. (London: Thomas Cadell, and Edinburgh: William Blackwood and Sons, 1839).

Herbert, Frank, *Dune* (New York: Ace Books, 1965).

Hobhouse, Henry, *Seeds of Change: Five Plants that Transformed Mankind* (New York: Harper and Row, 1986).

Hoerner, Fred, 'Paring Away Excrescences: The East India Company and Sir William Jones as Political Context for Romantic Allegory', paper presented at the NASSR conference, Boston, 14–16 November 1996.

Hofstadter, Albert and Kuhns, Richard, *Philosophies of Art and Beauty: Selected Readings in Aesthetics from Plato to Heidegger* (Chicago: University of Chicago Press, 1976).

Holmes, Richard, *Coleridge: Early Visions* (London and New York: Viking, 1989, 1990).

Horkheimer, Max and Adorno, Theodor, *Dialectic of Enlightenment*, tr. John Cumming (New York: Continuum, 1993).

Hughes, Langston, *The Collected Poems of Langston Hughes*, ed. Arnold Rampersad and David Roessel (New York: Knopf, 1994).

Hunt, James Henry Leigh, *The Autobiography of Leigh Hunt*, 3 vols. (London: Smith and Elder, 1850).

The Poetical Works of Leigh Hunt, ed. H. S. Milford (Oxford: Oxford University Press, 1923).

'A Now, Descriptive of a Hot Day', *Indicator* 1 (1820), pp. 300–2.
Review of Keats, *Lamia* (etc.), *Indicator* 43 (2 August 1820), pp. 337–44.
Huysmans, Karl-Joris, *Against Nature: A New Translation of A Rebours*, tr. Robert Baldick (Harmondsworth: Penguin, 1959; 1982).
Jameson, Fredric, *The Political Unconscious: Narrative as a Socially Symbolic Act* (Ithaca, N.Y.: Cornell University Press, 1981).
Jardine, Lisa, *Worldly Goods: A New History of the Renaissance* (London and New York: Macmillan, 1996).
Jeanneret, Michel, *A Feast of Words: Banquets and Table Talk in the Renaissance* (Chicago: University of Chicago Press, 1991).
John, Abbot of Ford, *Sermons on the Final Verses of the Song of Songs*, tr. Mary Beckett, 2 vols. (Kalamazoo, Michigan: Cistercian Publications, 1982–4).
Johnson, Samuel, *A Dictionary of the English Language; In which the Words are Deduced from their Originals, Explained in their Different Meanings, and Authorized by the Names of the Writers in Whose Works they are Found* (London: printed for Thomas Tegg, 1822).
Jones, Sir William, *Poems Consisting Chiefly of Translations from the Asiatick Languages. To which are Added Two Essays, I. On the Poetry of the Eastern Nations. II. On the Arts, Commonly Called Imitative* (Oxford: Clarendon Press, 1772).
Jordan, Ang, '"Imperial Mistress of the Obedient Sea": The Spatiality of Imperialism in Charlotte Smith's *Beachy Head*', paper presented at the NASSR conference, Boston, 14–16 November 1996.
Joyce, James, *Dubliners*, ed. John W. Jackson and Bernard McGinley (New York: St Martin's Press, 1993).
A Portrait of the Artist as a Young Man, ed. Seamus Deane (Harmondsworth: Penguin, 1993).
Ulysses, ed. Wolfhaard Steppe, Hans Walter Gabler and Claus Melchior (New York: Random House, 1986).
Kæmpfer, Engelbert, *Amœnitarum exoticarum politico-physico-medicarum fasciculi v, quibus continentur variæ relationes, observationes, & descriptiones rerum Persicarum & ulterioris Asiæ, multa attentione, in peregrinationibus per universum Orientem, collectæ* (Lemgovæ: H. W. Meyer, 1712).
Kant, Immanuel, *Critique of Judgment*, tr. Werner S. Pluhar (Indianapolis: Hacket, 1987).
Keats, John, *The Complete Poems*, ed. John Barnard, 2nd edn (Harmondsworth: Penguin, 1977, 1987).
The Letters of John Keats, ed. Maurice Buxton Forman (London and New York: Oxford University Press, 1952).
Keay, John, *The Honourable Company: A History of the East India Company* (London, New York and Toronto: Macmillan, 1991).
Kilgour, Maggie, *From Communion to Cannibalism: An Anatomy of Metaphors of Incorporation* (Princeton: Princeton University Press, 1990).
King, William, *The Art of Cookery, in Imitation of Horace's Art of Poetry. With*

Some Letters to Dr Lister, and Others: Occasion'd Principally by the Title of a Book Publish'd by the Doctor, Being the Works of Apicius Coelius, Concerning the Soups and Sauces of the Antients. With an Extract of the Greatest Curiosities Contain'd in that Book. To which is Added, Horace's Art of Poetry, in Latin (London: printed for B. Lintott, 1709).

Kitson, Peter, 'Coleridge, Southey, and Richard Brothers: An Incident from Charles Lloyd's *Edmund Oliver*', *Notes & Queries* 235 (37):4 (December 1990), pp. 405–7.

'The Whore of Babylon and the Woman in White: Coleridge's Radical Unitarian Language', in Timothy Fulford and Morton D. Paley eds., *Coleridge's Visionary Languages: Essays in Honour of J. B. Beer* (Cambridge: D. S. Brewer, 1993), pp. 1–14.

Kolb, Jocelyne, *The Ambiguity of Taste: Freedom and Food in European Romanticism* (Ann Arbor: University of Michigan Press, 1995).

Kowaleski-Wallace, Beth, 'Women, China, and Consumer Culture in Eighteenth-Century England', *Eighteenth-Century Studies* 29:2 (1995/6), pp. 153–67.

Krieger, Murray, *Ekphrasis: The Illusion of the Natural Sign* (Baltimore and London: Johns Hopkins University Press, 1992).

Kristeva, Julia, *Powers of Horror: An Essay on Abjection*, tr. L. S. Roudiez (New York: Columbia University Press, 1982).

Kuchta, David, 'The Moral Economy of English Mercantilism, 1660–1760', paper given at the conference 'New Economic Criticism' presented by the Society for Critical Exchange, Case Western Reserve University, Ohio, 20–3 October 1994.

Kutzinski, Vera M., *Sugar's Secrets: Race and the Erotics of Cuban Nationalism* (Charlottesville: University of Virginia Press, 1993).

Landon, Letitia Elizabeth, *The Complete Works of L. E. Landon*, 3 vols. (Boston: Phillips, Sampson and Co., 1854).

Langland, William, *Piers Plowman: The Three Versions*, ed. E. Talbot Donaldson, and George Kane, 3 vols. (Berkeley: University of California Press, 1960, revised 1988).

Lau, Beth, *Keats's* Paradise Lost (Gainesville: University of Florida Press, 1998).

Lauriaux, Bruno, 'Spices in the Medieval Diet: A New Approach', *Food and Foodways*, 1:1 (1985), pp. 43–75.

Leask, Nigel, *British Romantic Writers and the East: Anxieties of Empire* (Cambridge: Cambridge University Press, 1992).

Le Goff, Jacques, *Pour un autre Moyen Age: temps, travail et culture en Occident* (Paris: Editions Gallimard, 1977).

Time, Work, and Culture in the Middle Ages, tr. Arthur Goldhammer (Chicago: University of Chicago Press, 1980).

Le Guérer, Annick, *Scent: The Mysterious and Essential Powers of Smell*, tr. Richard Miller, (New York: Turtle Bay Books, 1992).

Leonardo y Argensola, Bartolomé Juan, *The Discovery and Conquest of the*

Molucco and Philippine Islands Containing, Their History, Ancient and Modern, Natural and Political: Their Description, Product, Religion, Government, Laws, Languages, Customs, Manners, Habits, Shape, and Inclinations of the Natives. With an Account of Many Other Adjacent Islands, and Several Remarkable Voyages through the Streights of Magellan, and in Other Parts, tr. John Stevens (London, 1708).

Levinson, Marjorie, *Keats's Life of Allegory: The Origins of a Style* (Oxford and New York: Basil Blackwell, 1988).

Librett, Jeffrey S., ed., *On the Sublime: Presence in Question* (Albany: State University of New York Press, 1993).

Lillo, George, *The London Merchant* (1731), ed. William H. McBurney (Lincoln and London: University of Nebraska Press, 1965).

Linschoten, Jan Huigen van, *John Huigen van Linschoten His Discours of Voyages into the Easte and West Indies. Deuided into Foure Bookes* (London: printed by John Wolfe, 1598).

Liu, Alan, 'Local Transcendence: Cultural Criticism, Postmodernism, and the Romanticism of Detail', *Representations* 32 (fall 1990), pp. 75–113.

Lockyer, Charles, *An Account of the Trade in India: Containing Rules for Good Government in Trade, Price Courants, and Tables: With Descriptions of Fort St George, Acheen, Malacca, Condore, Canton, Anjengo, Muskat, Gombroon, Surat, Goa, Carwar, Telichery, Panola, Calicut, the Cape of Good-Hope, and St Helena. Their Inhabitants, Customs, Religion, Governement, Animals, Fruits, &c. To which is Added, an Account of the Management of the Dutch in their Affairs in India* (London: printed for the author, 1711).

Lonsdale, Roger, ed., *Eighteenth-Century Women Poets: An Oxford Anthology* (Oxford and New York: Oxford University Press, 1989).

Lyotard, Jean-François, *The Postmodern Condition: A Report on Knowledge*, tr. Geoff Bennington and Brian Massumi (Minneapolis: University of Minnesota Press, 1984).

Mackie, Erin, *Market à la Mode: Fashion, Commodity, and Gender in the* Tatler *and the* Spectator (Baltimore and London: Johns Hopkins University Press, 1997).

Magnuson, Paul, 'Wild Justice', *Wordsworth Circle* 19:2 (spring, 1988), pp. 88–91.

Majeed, Javed, 'Orientalism, Utilitarianism, and British India: James Mill's *The History of British India* and the Romantic Orient', D. Phil. dissertation, University of Oxford, 1988.

Mandeville, Bernard de, *The Fable of the Bees: Or, Private Vices, Publick Benefits. The Second Edition, Enlarged with many Additions. As also an Essay on Charity and Charity-Schools. And a Search into the Nature of Society* (London: printed for Edmund Parker, 1723).

Markley, Robert, '"The Destin'd Walls /Of *Cambalu*": Milton, China, and the Ambiguities of the East', in Rajan and Sauer, eds., *Milton and the Imperial Vision*. pp. 191–213.

'"So Inexhaustible a Treasure of Gold": Defoe, Capitalism, and the Romance of the South Seas', *Eighteenth-Century Life* 18 (November 1994), pp. 148–67.

Marlowe, Christopher, *The Complete Works of Christopher Marlowe*, ed. Fredson Bowers, 2 vols. (Cambridge and New York: Cambridge University Press, 1973, 1981).

Martindale, Wight, 'John Dryden and the Mercantile Ideal', Doctoral dissertation, New York University, 1995.

Martyr, Peter, *The Decades of the Newe Worlde or West India, Conteynyng the Nauigations and Conquestes of the Spanyardes, with the Particular Description of the Moste Ryche and Large Landes and Islandes lately Founde in the West Ocean Perteynyng to the Inheritaunce of the Kinges of Spayne. In the which the Diligent Reader may not only Consider what Commoditie may hereby Chaunce to the Hole Christian World in Tyme to Come, but also Learne Many Secreates Touchynge the Lande, the Sea, and the Starres, very Necessarie to be Knowen to al such as shall Attempte any Nauigations, or otherwise Haue Delite to Beholde the Strange and Woonderfull Woorkes of God and Nature*, tr. Richard Eden (London: printed by William Powell, 1555).

Mauss, Marcel, *The Gift: The Form and Reason for Exchange in Archaic Societies*, tr. W. D. Halls (New York and London: Norton, 1990, first published 1950 as *Essai sur le don*).

Maximilianus, Transylvanus, *De Moluccis insulis, itemque; alijs pluribus mirandis, quae nouissima Castellanorum nauigatio Serenissimi Imperatoris Caraoli .v. auspicio suscepta, nuper inuenit: Maximilliani Transyluani ad Reuerendissimum Cardinalem Satlzburgensem epistola lectu perquam iucunda* (Cologne: E. Cervicornus, 1523).

McGann, Jerome, *The Beauty of Inflections: Literary Investigations in Historical Method and Theory* (Oxford: Clarendon Press, 1985).

McGavran, James Holt, 'DisLocations of Culture and Gender in "Kubla Khan"', paper presented at the NASSR conference, Boston, 14–16 November 1996.

McKendrick, Neil, Brewer, John, and Plumb, J. H., *The Birth of a Consumer Society: The Commercialization of Eighteenth-Century England* (Bloomington: Indiana University Press, 1982).

McKeon, Michael, *Politics and Poetry in Restoration England: The Case of Dryden's Annus Mirabilis* (Cambridge, Mass.: Harvard University Press, 1975).

McKusick, James, *Coleridge's Philosophy of Language* (New Haven and London: Yale University Press, 1986).

Meisel, Perry, *The Myth of the Modern: A Study in British Literature and Criticism after 1850* (New Haven and London: Yale University Press, 1987).

Milton, John, *John Milton: Complete Shorter Poems*, ed. John Carey (London and New York: Longman, 1968, 1971).

Paradise Lost, ed. Alastair Fowler (London and New York: Longman, 1968, 1971).

Mintz, Sidney, *Sweetness and Power: The Place of Sugar in Modern History* (New York: Viking, 1985).

'Color, Taste and Purity: Some Speculations on the Meanings of Marzipan', *ETNOFOOR* 4:1 (1991), pp. 103–8.

'Sweet, Salt, and the Language of Love', *Modern Language Notes* 106:4 (September 1991), pp. 852–60.

'Tasting Food, Tasting Freedom', in Binder, ed., *Slavery in the Americas*, pp. 257–75.

'Tropical Production and Mass Consumption: A Historical Comment', *Bulletin of the Institute of Ethnology*, Academica Sinica, 70 (autumn 1990), pp. 1–12.

Monardes, Nicolás, *Ioyfull Newes out of the New-found Worlde. Wherein are Declared, the Rare and Singular Vertues of Diuers Herbs, Trees, Plantes, Oyles & Stones, with their Applications, as well to the Use of Phisicke, as of Chirurgery: which being well Applyed, Bring such Present Remedie for all Diseases, as May Seem altogether Incredible: notwithstanding by Practice found out to be True*, tr. John Frampton (London: printed by E. Allde, 1596).

Montague, Charles, Earl of Halifax, *The British Merchant; Or, Commerce Preserv'd: In Answer to the Mercator, or Commerce Retriev'd* (London: printed for A. Baldwin and Ferdinand Burleigh, 1713–14).

Montanari, Massimo, *The Culture of Food*, tr. Carl Ipsen (Oxford and Cambridge, Mass.: Basil Blackwell, 1994).

Moore, Thomas, *Lalla Rookh, an Oriental Romance*, 2nd edn (London: printed for Longman, Hurst, Rees, Orme and Brown, 1817).

The Epicurean, a Tale (London: printed for Longman, Rees, Orme, Brown and Green, 1827).

The Poetical Works of Thomas Moore, Collected by Himself, 10 vols. (London: Longman, Orme, Brown, Green and Longmans, 1840–1).

More, Hannah, *Slavery, a Poem* (London: printed for T. Cadell, 1788).

The Works of Hannah More, vol. VI (London: Fisher, Fisher and Jackson, 1835).

Morrison, Toni, *Song of Solomon* (New York: Knopf, 1977).

Morton, Timothy, *Shelley and the Revolution in Taste: The Body and the Natural World* (Cambridge and New York: Cambridge University Press, 1994).

'*Queen Mab* as Topological Repertoire', in Neil Fraistat, ed., *Early Shelley: Vulgarisms, Politics and Fractals* (Romantic Praxis Website, 1997: http:/ www.otal.umd.edu/c/praxis/praxis-shelley/morton.html).

Moseley, Benjamin, *A Treatise on Sugar. With Miscellaneous Medical Observations* (London: printed by John Nichols for G. G. and J. Robinson, 1800).

Motion, Andrew, *Keats* (New York: Farrar, Straus and Giroux, 1997).

Mukařovský, Jan, *Aesthetic Function, Norm and Value as Social Facts*, tr. Mark E. Suino (Ann Arbor: University of Michigan Press, 1970).

Mulligan, Hugh, *Poems Chiefly on Slavery and Oppression, with Notes and Illustrations* (London: printed for W. Lowndes, 1788).

Murphy, Roland E., *The Song of Songs: A Commentary on the Book of Canticles or the Song of Songs*, ed. S. Dean McBride, Jr. (Minneapolis: Fortress Books, 1990).

Murphy, Timothy, 'William Burroughs Between Indifference and Revalorization: Notes Towards a Political Reading', *Angelaki* 1:1 (1993), pp. 113–24.

Murray, Venetia, *An Elegant Madness: High Society in Regency England* (New York: Viking, 1999).

High Society: A Social History of the Regency Period, 1788–1830 (London and New York: Viking Penguin, 1998).

Ogilby, John, *Asia, the First Part. Being an Accurate Description of Persia, and the Several Provinces thereof. The Vast Empire of the Great Mogol, and other Parts of India: And their Several Kingdoms and Regions: with the Denominations and Descriptions of the Cities, Towns, and Places of Remark therein Contain'd. The Various Customs, Habits, Religion, and Languages of the Inhabitants. Their Political Governments, and Way of Commerce. Also the Plants and Animals Peculiar to Each Country* (London: printed by the author, 1673).

Ortelius, Abraham, *Theatrum orbis terrarum* (Antwerp: E. C. Diesth, 1570).

Ovid, *Ovid in Six Volumes*, tr. F. J. Miller, 6 vols. (Cambridge, Mass.: Harvard University Press, and London: Heinemann, 1984).

Page, Christopher, 'Reading and Reminiscence: Tinctoris on the Beauty of Music', *Journal of the American Musicological Society* 49:1 (spring 1996), pp. 1–31.

Paley, William, *The Principles of Moral and Political Philosophy* (London: printed for R. Faulder, 1785).

Parker, Patricia, 'On the Tongue: Cross Gendering, Effeminacy, and the Art of Words', *Style* 23:3 (fall 1989), pp. 445–50.

Peacock, Thomas Love, *Nightmare Abbey/Crotchet Castle*, ed. Raymond Wright (Harmondsworth: Penguin, 1969, 1986).

The Works of Thomas Love Peacock, ed. H. F. B. Brett-Smith and C. E. Jones, 10 vols. (London: Constable and Co., and New York: Gabriel Wells, 1924–34).

Pearson, Harry W., 'The Economy has No Surplus: Critique of a Theory of Development', in Polanyi, Arensberg and Pearson, eds., *Trade and Market in the Early Empires*, pp. 320–41.

Pennant, Thomas, *Outlines of the Globe*, 4 vols. (London: Henry Hughes and Luke Hansard, 1798–1800).

Petty, Sir William, *A Treatise of Taxes and Contributions Shewing the Nature and Measures of [Brace] Crown-Lands, Assessments, Customs, Poll-Moneys, Lotteries, Benevolence, Penalties, Monopolies, Offices, Tythes, Raising of Coins, Harth-Money, Excize, &c.: [Brace] Warres, the Church, Universities, Rents and Purchases, Usury and Exchange, Banks and Lombards, Registries for Conveyances, Beggars, Ensurance, Exportation of Money/Wool, Free-Ports, Coins, Housing, Liberty of Conscience, &c.: The Same Being Frequently Applied to the Present State and Affairs of Ireland* (London: printed for N. Brooke, 1662).

The Economic Writings of Sir William Petty, together with the Observations upon the Bills of Mortality, more Probably by Captain John Graunt, ed. Charles Henry Hull, 2 vols. (Cambridge: Cambridge University Press, 1899).

Phillips, William D., Jr. and Phillips, Carla Rahn, *The Worlds of Christopher Columbus* (Cambridge and New York: Cambridge University Press, 1992).

Plutarch, *Plutarch's Moralia*, tr. H. Cherniss and W. C. Helbold, vol. XII (London: William Heinemann, and Cambridge, Mass.: Harvard University Press, 1957).

Pocock, J. G. A., *The Machiavellian Moment: Florentine Political Thought and the Atlantic Republican Tradition* (Princeton: Princeton University Press, 1975).

Virtue, Commerce, and History: Essays on Political Thought and History, Chiefly in the Eighteenth Century (Cambridge: Cambridge University Press, 1985).

Poe, Edgar Allan, *Edgar Allen Poe*, ed. Philip Van Doren Stern (New York: Viking, 1945, 1968).

Polanyi, Karl, Arensberg, Conrad M. and Pearson, Harry W., eds., *Trade and Market in the Early Empires: Economies in History and Theory* (Glencoe, Ill.: Free Press, 1957).

Polo, Marco, *The Travels of Marco Polo*, tr. Ronald Latham (Harmondsworth: Penguin, 1958).

Pope, Alexander, *The Poems of Alexander Pope: A One-Volume Edition of the Twickenham Text, with Selected Annotations*, ed. J. Butt (London and New York: Routledge, 1963, 1989).

Porcacchi, Thomaso, *L'isole piu famose del mondo descritte da Thomaso Porcacchi da Castiglione Arretino e intagliate da Girolamo Porro* (Venice: printed by Simon Galignani and Girolamo Porro, 1576).

Poster, Mark, 'Postmodern Virtualities', *Body and Society*, 1:3–4 (November 1995), pp. 79–95.

Pratt, Mary Louise, *Imperial Eyes: Travel Writing and Transculturation* (London and New York: Routledge, 1992).

Pratt, Samuel Jackson, *Humanity, or the Rights of Nature, a Poem; in Two Books* (London: T. Cadell, 1788).

Purchas, Samuel, *Purchas his Pilgrimes. In Five Bookes*, 4 vols. (London: printed for Henry Fetherstone, 1625).

Rabisha, William, *The Whole Body of Cookery Dissected: Taught, and Fully Manifested, Methodically, Artistically, and According to the Best Tradition of the English, French, Italian, Dutch, &c. Or, A Sympathy of All Varieties in Natural Compounds in that Mystery. Wherein is Contained Certain Bills of Fare for the Seasons of the Year, for Feasts and Common Diets*, 2nd edn (London: printed for E. C., 1675).

Radcliffe, Ann, *The Posthumous Works of Anne Radcliffe . . . : To which is Prefixed a Memoir of the Authoress, with Extracts from Her Private Journals* (London: H. Colburn, 1833).

Raimond, Jean, 'Southey's Early Writings and the Revolution', *Yearbook of English Studies* vol. 19 (1989), pp. 181–96.

Rajan, Balachandra and Sauer, Elizabeth, eds., *Milton and the Imperial Vision* (Pittsburgh: Duquesne University Press, 1999).

'The Imperial Temptation', in Rajan and Sauer, eds., *Milton and the Imperial Vision*, pp. 294–314.

Rajan, Tillotama, *Dark Interpreter: The Discourse of Romanticism* (Ithaca, N.Y. and London: Cornell University Press, 1980).

Rawson, Claude, 'A Primitive Purity: Cannibalism, Utopias and the Invitation to Disbelief in Early Travel Narratives', review, *Times Literary Supplement*, 26 July 1996, pp. 3–4.

Ricardo, David, *On the Principles of Political Economy and Taxation* (London: John Murray, 1817).

Richardson, Alan, 'Romantic Voodoo: Obeah and British Culture, 1797–1807', *Studies in Romanticism* 32 (spring 1993), pp. 3–28.

Ricks, Christopher, *Keats and Embarrassment* (Oxford: Clarendon Press, 1974).

Rindisbacher, Hans J., *The Smell of Books: A Cultural-Historical Study of Olfactory Perception in Literature* (Ann Arbor: University of Michigan Press, 1992).

Roberts, Lewes, *The Merchants Mappe of Commerce: Wherein, the Universall Manner and Matter of Trade, is Compendiously Handled. The Standard and Currant Coines of Sundry Princes, Observed. The Reall and Imaginary Coines of Accompts and Exchanges, ExPressed. The Naturall and Artificiall Commodities of all Countries for Transportation Declared. The Weights and Measures of all Eminent Cities and Townes of Traffique, Collected and Reduced one into Another; and all to the Meridian of Commerce Practised in the Famous Citie of London. Necessary for all Such as shall be imployed in the publique Affairs of Princes in Forreigne Parts. For all Gentlemen and Others that Travell Abroad for Delight or Pleasure. And for all Merchants or their Factors that Exercise the Art of Merchandizing in any Part of the Habitable World* (London: printed for Ralph Mabb, 1638).

Robotham, John, *An Exposition on the Whole Booke of Solomons Song, Commonly Called the Canticle. Wherein the Text is Explained and Usefull Observations Raised Thereupon* (London: printed by Matthew Simmons, 1651).

Roe, Nicholas, *John Keats and the Culture of Dissent* (Oxford and New York: Oxford University Press, 1997).

Rogin, Michael, 'Unmistakable', review of Wendy Wick Reaves, *Celebrity Caricature in America* and David Alexander, *Richard Newton and English Caricature in the 1790s*, *London Review of Books*, 20:16 (20 August 1998), pp. 14–15.

Rollins, Hyder Edward, *The Keats Circle: Letters and Papers, 1816–1878*, 2 vols. (Cambridge, Mass.: Harvard University Press, 1948).

Rushdie, Salman, *The Moor's Last Sigh* (New York: Pantheon Books, 1995).

Rzepka, Charles J., *Sacramental Commodities: Gift, Text, and the Sublime in De Quincey* (Amherst: University of Massachusetts Press, 1995).

Sahlins, Marshall, *Culture and Practical Reason* (Chicago and London: University of Chicago Press, 1976).

Said, Edward, *Orientalism* (New York: Vintage, 1979).

St Teresa, *The Collected Works of Saint Teresa of Avila*, tr. Kieran Kavanaugh and Otilio Rodriguez, 3 vols. (Washington, D.C.: Institute of Carmelite Studies, 1980).

Sandys, George, *A Relation of a Iourney Begun An: Dom: 1610. Four Bookes. Containing a Description of the Turkish Empire, of Ægypt, of the Holy Land, of the Remote Parts of Italy, and Islands Adioyning* (London: printed for W. Barrett, 1615).

Schama, Simon, *The Embarrassment of Riches: An Interpretation of Dutch Culture in the Golden Age* (Berkeley and London: University of California Press, 1988; first published New York: Knopf, 1987).

Schivelbusch, Wolfgang, *Tastes of Paradise: A Social History of Spices, Stimulants, and Intoxicants* (New York: Pantheon, 1992).

Sedgwick, Eve Kosovsky, *Between Men: English Literature and Homosocial Desire* (New York: Columbia University Press, 1985).

Sennett, Richard, *Flesh and Stone: The Body and the City in Western Civilization* (New York and London: Norton, 1994).

Shakespeare, William, *The Complete Works*, ed. Peter Alexander (London and Glasgow: Collins, 1951).

Shell, Marc, *Money, Language, and Thought: Literary and Philosophical Economies from the Medieval to the Modern Era* (Berkeley and London: University of California Press, 1982).

Shelley, Mary, *The Last Man*, ed. Morton D. Paley (Oxford and New York: Oxford University Press, 1994, 1998).

Shelley, Percy Bysshe, *Shelley: Poetical Works*, ed. Thomas Hutchinson (London and New York: Oxford University Press, 1970).

Shelley's Prose: Or The Trumpet of a Prophecy, ed. David Lee Clark (London: Fourth Estate, 1988).

Shuger, Debora, '"Gums of Glutinous Heat" and the Stream of Consciousness: The Theology of Milton's *Maske*', *Representations* 60 (fall 1997), pp. 1–21.

Simpson, David, *The Academic Postmodern and the Rule of Literature: A Report on Half-Knowledge* (Chicago and London: University of Chicago Press, 1995).

Skelton, John, *The Poetical Works of John Skelton: With Notes, and Some Account of the Author and His Writings*, ed. Alexander Dyce (New York: AMS Press, 1965).

Smith, Adam, *An Inquiry into the Nature and Causes of the Wealth of Nations*, 2 vols. (London: printed for W. Strahan and T. Cadell, 1776).

Smith, Charlotte Turner, *The Poems of Charlotte Smith*, ed. Stuart Curran (Oxford and New York: Oxford University Press, 1993).

Smith, Nigel, *Literature and Revolution in England, 1640–1660* (New Haven and London: Yale University Press, 1994).

Somerville, Thomas, *A Discourse on Our Obligation to Thanksgiving, for the Prospect of the Abolition of the African Slave-Trade. With a Prayer* (Kelso: printed by J. Palmer, 1792).

Southey, Robert, *Poems* (Bristol: printed for Joseph Cottle, and London: printed for G. G. and J. Robinson, 1797).

Stedman, John G., *Narrative of a Five Years' Expedition, Against the Revolted Negroes of Surinam, in Guiana, on the Wild Coast of South America; from the Year 1772, to 1777: Elucidating the History of that Country, and Describing its Productions, Viz. Quadrupedes, Birds, Fishes, Reptiles, Trees, Shrubs, Fruits, & Roots; with an Account of the Indians of Guiana, & Negroes of Guinea* (London: printed for J. Johnson, 1796).

Steele, Richard, *The Tatler*, ed. Donald, Bond, 3 vols. (Oxford: Clarendon Press, 1987).

Steensgaard, Niels, 'The Growth and Composition of the Long-Distance Trade of England and the Dutch Republic before 1750', in Tracy, ed., *Rise of Merchant Empires*, pp. 102–52.

Stewart, Stanley, *The Enclosed Garden: The Tradition and the Image in Seventeenth-Century Poetry* (Madison, and London: University of Wisconsin Press, 1966).

The Expanded Voice: The Art of Thomas Traherne (San Marino, Calif.: Huntington Library, 1970).

Stewart, Susan, *Crimes of Writing: Problems in the Containment of Representation* (Oxford and New York: Oxford University Press, 1991).

Sussman, Charlotte, 'Women and the Politics of Sugar, 1792', *Representations* 48 (fall 1994), pp. 1–22.

Tavernier, Jean Baptiste, *The Six Voyages of John Baptista Tavernier, a Noble Man of France now Living, through Turky [sic] into Persia, and the East-Indies, Finished in the Year 1670, Giving an Account of the State of those Countries. Together with a New Relation of the Present Grand Seignor's Seraglio, by the Same Author. To Which is Added a Description of all the Kingdoms which Encompass the Euxine and Caspian Seas. By an English Traveller, Never Before Printed*, tr. John Phillips (London: printed for 'R. L.' and 'M. P.', 1678).

Tennyson, Alfred Lord, *The Poems of Tennyson in Three Volumes*, ed. Christopher Ricks, 3 vols., 2nd edn (Harlow: Longman, 1987).

Thirsk, Joan, *Economic Policy and Projects: The Development of a Consumer Society in Early Modern England* (Oxford: Clarendon Press, 1978).

Thomas, Keith, *Man and the Natural World: Changing Attitudes in England, 1500–1800* (London: Allen Lane, 1983, reprinted Harmondsworth: Penguin, 1984).

Thompson, E. P., *Customs in Common*, (New York: New Press, 1991).

Thomson, James, *The Seasons*, ed. James Sambrook (Oxford: Clarendon Press, 1981).

Tonge, Eliza, *Poetical Trifles* (Cheltenham: J. J. Hadley, 1832).

Toop, David, *Ocean of Sound: Aether Talk, Ambient Sound and Imaginary Worlds* (London and New York: Serpent's Tail, 1995).

Torres-Saillant, Sylvio A., 'The Problem of Unity in Caribbean Literature', paper given at the conference 'Sisyphus and Eldorado: Literary Culture in Two Caribbeans?', 31st Annual Eastern Comparative Literature Conference, New York University, 7 May 1994.

Tracy, James D., ed., *The Rise of Merchant Empires: Long-Distance Trade in the Early Modern World, 1350–1750* (Cambridge and New York: Cambridge University Press, 1990).

Traherne, Thomas, *Poems, Centuries and Three Thanksgivings*, ed. Anne Ridler (London and New York: Oxford University Press, 1966).

Trevenen, Emily, *Little Derwent's Breakfast. By a Lady. With Engravings* (London: Smith, Elder and Co., 1839).

Trilling, Lionel, *The Opposing Self: Nine Essays in Criticism* (New York: Viking, 1955).

Tuttle, Imilda, *Concordance to Vaughan's* Silex Scintillans (University Park: Pennsylvania State University Press, 1969).

Varey, Simon, 'Three Necessary Drugs', in Kevin Cope, ed., *1650–1850: Ideas, Aesthetics, and Inquiries in the Early Modern Era*, (New York: AMS Press, 1998) vol. IV, pp. 3–51.

Vaughan, Henry, *Silex Scintillans: Or Sacred Poems and Priuate Eiaculations by Henry Vaughan Silurist* (London: printed for H. Blunden, 1650).

Voller, Jack G., *The Supernatural Sublime: The Metaphysics of Terror in Anglo-American Romanticism* (DeKalb: Northern Illinois University Press, 1994).

Warner, Marina, *Alone of All Her Sex: The Myth and Cult of the Virgin Mary* (London: Pan, 1985, first published London: Wiedenfeld and Nicholson, 1976).

From the Beast to the Blonde: On Fairytales and Their Tellers (London: Chatto and Windus, 1994).

Warner, Richard, *Antiquitates Culinariæ; Or Curious Tracts Relating to the Culinary Affairs of the Old English, with a Preliminary Discourse, Notes, and Illustrations* (London: printed for R. Blamire, 1791).

Warton, Thomas, *The History of English Poetry. From the Close of the Eleventh to the Commencement of the Eighteenth Century. To Which are Prefixed, Two Dissertations* (London: printed for J. Dodsley, J. Walter, T. Becket, J. Robson, G. Robinson, and J. Bew, and Messrs Fletcher, 1774–81).

The Pleasures of Melancholy: A Poem (London: printed for R. Dodsley, 1747).

Weber, Max, *The Protestant Ethic and the Spirit of Capitalism*, tr. Talcott Parsons (London and New York: Routledge, 1992).

Weinbrot, Howard D., *Britannia's Issue: The Rise of British Literature from Dryden to Ossian* (Cambridge and New York: Cambridge University Press, 1993).

Wicke, Jennifer, *Advertising Fictions: Literature, Advertisement, and Social Reading* (New York: Columbia University Press, 1988).

'Postmodernism: The Perfume of Information', *Yale Journal of Criticism* 1:2 (spring 1988), pp. 145–60.

Williams, Patrick and Chrisman, Laura, eds., *Colonial Discourse and Post-Colonial Theory: A Reader* (New York: Columbia University Press, 1994).

Winnicott, D. W., *Playing and Reality* (New York: Basic Books, 1971).

Woolf, Virginia, *Mrs Dalloway* (London: Grafton, 1976, 1987).

Wordsworth, William, *The Poems of Wordsworth*, ed. Thomas Hutchinson, revised E. de Selincourt (London: Oxford University Press, 1936).

'Z' (John Gibson Lockhart and John Wilson), 'Cockney School of Poetry: No. IV', *Blackwood's Edinburgh Magazine* 3 (August 1818), pp. 519–24.

'On the Cockney School of Poetry: No. VI', *Blackwood's Edinburgh Magazine* 6 (October 1819), pp. 70–6.

Žižek, Slavoj, *For They Know Not What They Do: Enjoyment as a Political Factor* (London and New York: Verso, 1991).

The Indivisible Remainder: An Essay on Schelling and Related Matters (London and New York: Verso, 1996).

The Metastases of Enjoyment: Six Essays on Woman and Causality (London and New York: Verso, 1994).

The Plague of Fantasies (London and New York: Verso, 1997).

The Sublime Object of Ideology (London and New York: Verso, 1989, 1991).

Tarrying with the Negative: Kant, Hegel, and the Critique of Ideology (Durham: Duke University Press, 1993).

'Re-Visioning "Lacanian" Social Criticism: The Law and its Obscene Double', *Journal for the Psychoanalysis of Culture and Society* 1:1 (spring 1996), pp. 15–25.

NON-LITERARY WORKS

Carpenter, John (director), *The Thing* (Universal Studios, 1982).

Eno, Brian, 'The Future Will Be Like Perfume', installation, Hamburg, 1993.

Public Enemy, *It Takes a Nation of Millions to Hold Us Back* (Def Jam Recordings, 1987).

Index

CAMBRIDGE STUDIES IN ROMANTICISM

GENERAL EDITORS

MARILYN BUTLER, *University of Oxford*

JAMES CHANDLER, *University of Chicago*

1. *Romantic Correspondence: Women, Politics and the Fiction of Letters*
MARY A. FAVRET

2. *British Romantic Writers and the East: Anxieties of Empire*
NIGEL LEASK

3. *Edmund Burke's Aesthetic Ideology*
Language, Gender and Political Economy in Revolution
TOM FURNISS

4. *Poetry as an Occupation and an Art in Britain, 1760–1830*
PETER MURPHY

5. *In the Theatre of Romanticism: Coleridge, Nationalism, Women*
JULIA A. CARLSON

6. *Keats, Narrative and Audience*
ANDREW BENNETT

7. *Romance and Revolution: Shelley and the Politics of a Genre*
DAVID DUFF

8. *Literature, Education, and Romanticism*
Reading as Social Practice, 1780–1832
ALAN RICHARDSON

9. *Women Writing about Money: Women's Fiction in England, 1790–1820*
EDWARD COPELAND

10. *Shelley and the Revolution in Taste: The Body and the Natural World*
TIMOTHY MORTON

11. *William Cobbett: The Politics of Style*
LEONORA NATTRASS

12. *The Rise of Supernatural Fiction, 1762–1800*
E. J. CLERY

13. *Women Travel Writers and the Language of Aesthetics, 1716–1818*
ELIZABETH A. BOHLS

14. *Napoleon and English Romanticism*
SIMON BAINBRIDGE

15. *Romantic Vagrancy: Wordsworth and the Simulation of Freedom*
CELESTE LANGAN

16. *Wordsworth and the Geologists*
JOHN WYATT

17. *Wordsworth's Pope: A Study in Literary Historiography*
ROBERT J. GRIFFIN

18. *The Politics of Sentimentalism*
Race, Gender and Commerce in the Novel of Sensibility
MARKMAN ELLIS

19. *Reading Daughters' Fictions 1709–1834*
From Delarivier Manley to Maria Edgeworth
CAROLINE GONDA

20. *Romantic Identities: Varieties of Subjectivity, 1774–1830*
ANDREA K. HENDERSON

21. *Print Politics: The Press and Radical Opposition*
in Early Nineteenth-Century England
KEVIN GILMARTIN

22. *Reinventing Allegory*
THERESA M. KELLEY

23. *British Satire and the Politics of Style, 1789–1832*
GARY DYER

24. *The Romantic Reformation*
Religious Politics in English Literature, 1789–1824
ROBERT M. RYAN

25. *De Quincey's Romanticism*
Canonical Minority and the Forms of Transmission
MARGARET RUSSETT

26. *Coleridge on Dreaming: Romanticism, Dreams and the Medical Imagination*
JENNIFER FORD

27. *Romantic Imperialism: Universal Empire and the Culture of Modernity*
SAREE MAKDISI

28. *Ideology and Utopia in the Poetry of William Blake*
NICHOLAS M. WILLIAMS

29. *Sexual Politics and the Romantic Author*
SONIA HOFKOSH

30. *Lyric and Labour in the Romantic Tradition*
ANNE JANOWITZ

31. *Poetry and Politics in the Cockney School: Keats, Shelley, Hunt and their Circle*
JEFFREY N. COX

32. *Rousseau, Robespierre and English Romanticsm*
GREGORY DART

33. *Contesting the Gothic: Fiction, Genre and Cultural Conflict, 1764–1832*
JAMES WATT

34. *Romanticism, Aesthetics, and Nationalism*
DAVID ARAM KAISER

35. *Romantic Poets and the Culture of Posterity*
ANDREW BENNETT

36. *The Crisis of Literature in the 1790s: Print Culture and the Public Sphere*
PAUL KEEN

37. *Romantic Atheism: Poetry and Freethought, 1780–1830*
MARTIN PRIESTMAN

38. *Romanticism and Slave Narratives: Transatlantic Testimonies*
HELEN THOMAS

39. *Imagination Under Pressure, 1789–1832: Aesthetics, Politics, and Utility*
JOHN WHALE

40. *Romanticism and the Gothic*
Genre, Reception, and Canon Formation, 1790–1820
MICHAEL GAMER

41. *Romanticism and the Human Sciences*
Poetry, Population, and the Discourse of the Species
MAUREEN N. MCLANE

42. *The Poetics of Spice: Romantic Consumerism and the Exotic*
TIMOTHY MORTON

For EU product safety concerns, contact us at Calle de José Abascal, 56–1°, 28003 Madrid, Spain or eugpsr@cambridge.org.

www.ingramcontent.com/pod-product-compliance
Ingram Content Group UK Ltd.
Pitfield, Milton Keynes, MK11 3LW, UK
UKHW010033140625
459647UK00012BA/1353